Theories of Comparative Economic Growth

THEORIES OF COMPARATIVE ECONOMIC GROWTH

KWANG CHOI
Senior Fellow
Korea Developmental Institute
Seoul

The Iowa State University Press / *Ames*

To my father,

Yeup Jong Choi

on his sixtieth birthday

Printed by The Iowa State University Press, Ames, Iowa 50010

First edition, 1983

Library of Congress Cataloging in Publication Data

Choi, Kwang, 1947–
    Theories of comparative economic growth.

    1. Economic development.   2.   Comparative economics.
I. Title.
HD82.C522   1983   338.9′001   83–284
ISBN 0–8138–1771–4

Contents

Preface

In spite of the persistent interest in the question of why some countries or regions in a country are growing faster than others, there is no single source to which one can turn for a survey of existing theories of comparative economic growth. The present volume is intended to correct this shortcoming.

The aim of this book is twofold: to provide comprehensive summaries of the major contemporary theories and hypotheses of comparative economic growth and to assess the empirical validity of each hypothesis considered, not only by reviewing existing empirical evidences but also by examining each hypothesis against new comprehensive sets of data. It should be conceded at the outset that although some partial explanations are offered, no firm conclusion is reached as to why some countries or regions have experienced more rapid growth than others.

In the preparation of this book, I received assistance and encouragement from many people, and to all of them I express my sincere thanks. My main debt of gratitude must be to Professor Mancur Olson, University of Maryland. Throughout the preparation and while working on the last three chapters, his guidance, helpful suggestions, and continual encouragement were invaluable. Furthermore, my initial interest in the subject and motivation to embark on this project were the product of Professor Olson's influence.

I also wish to acknowledge my indebtedness to the following individuals, each of whom read and improved, by their suggestions, one or more chapters of the manuscript: William Morgan, John Mutti, and Todd Sandler, my former colleagues at the University of Wyoming; James Fry, Peter Murrell, Arvind Panagariya, and Steve Silver at the University of Maryland. I am indebted to Betty McClurkin, manuscript editor at the Iowa State University Press, for offering a number of valuable suggestions and for providing patient help with the publication. During the volume's gestation period I was assisted by Steve Pince and John Castleberry at the

University of Wyoming. To Sheila Donohue and Debbie Feaver I am grateful for their typing of the manuscript.

And finally, I wish to express my gratitude to the National Science Foundation for their postdoctoral research grant that allowed me to finalize the manuscript during the summer of 1981 and to the Ford Foundation for their fellowship that financed the first two and one-half years of graduate study at the University of Wisconsin and the University of Maryland

Theories of Comparative Economic Growth

1

Introduction

SUBJECT OF THE STUDY

   The primary question that is going to be examined in this study is, What causes the differences in "area" growth rates, whether the term is applied to different countries or different regions within the same country?

   The postwar period saw development with remarkable variations in the rates at which different economies grew. (Unless otherwise stated, "postwar" will refer to the period after World War II.) Table 1.1 summarizes the story concerning comparative growth rates among the democratic industrial countries over the last 100 years.

   Although there is a margin of error in computed growth rates due to differences in national accounting procedures, the most striking feature of the table is the very great spread of the observed growth rates between countries since 1950 and the unprecedented acceleration of productivity growth during the postwar period.

   Differences in growth rates, measured in terms of the increase in per capita gross domestic product, span 5 whole percentage points since 1950, while growth rates differ by at most 2 percent in the previous 80 years. Productivity levels have been highest in the United States since the turn of the century. However, the gap in productivity levels between the United States and other nations has narrowed considerably because of the rapid economic growth of other countries. The spread in the productivity level between the countries in Table 1.1 is less than 2 to 1 now, whereas it was 4 or 5 to 1 before.

   The growth experiences of the advanced developed countries during the postwar period are, in many respects, quite perplexing. In describing them, references have been made to miracles. We have been told about "the Japanese miracle," "the German miracle," "the

3

Table 1.1. Comparative statistics on productivity growth and productivity level

Country	Growth of per capita GDP			Level of productivity (U.S. = 100)			
	1870-1913	1913-1950	1950-1978	1901	1925	1950	1978
Australia	0.9	0.5	2.3	95	90	73	77
Austria	1.8	0.2	4.5	na	48	35	68
Belgium	1.0	0.7	3.4	85	75	59	83
Canada	2.0	1.3	2.8	75	63	74	90
Denmark	1.6	1.5	2.8	58	58	60	72
Finland	1.5	1.7	3.7	na	39	43	66
France	1.5	1.0	3.8	61	61	53	83
Germany	1.6	0.7	4.5	55	50	43	81
Italy	0.8	0.7	4.1	41	40	32	54
Japan	1.5	0.5	7.3	27	30	18	70
Netherlands	0.9	1.1	3.3	69	67	55	76
Norway	1.3	2.1	3.5	44	47	58	84
Sweden	2.1	2.2	2.6	45	56	69	80
Switzerland	1.2	1.5	2.5	na	77	70	77
United Kingdom	1.0	0.9	2.1	88	70	65	65
United States	2.0	1.6	2.2	100	100	100	100

Source: Maddison 1979.

Italian miracle," and "the French miracle." The growth performance
by these countries since World War II is exceptional by historical
standards and as compared with other countries in the group.

Growth rates of income have also varied substantially among
regions within the United States. Growth rates of total and per
capita income levels by state for the last two decades are shown in
Table 1.2. Regional differences in the growth performance of income among states in the United States span 5 percent for the total
income measure and 2 percent for the per capita income measure.
There has been a considerable convergence in per capita income levels, especially between states in the Northeast and those in the
South because of slow growth in the former and rapid growth in the
latter.

The regional differences in growth performance within the
United States are remarkable, particularly in view of the fact that
differences in political and economic institutions and in the tim-
ing and amplitude of business fluctuations are much smaller among
the U.S. regions. The rapid growth of the so-called Sunbelt states
coupled with the economic stagnation prevalent throughout much of
the Northeast have led to charges of regional favoritism in federal
spending and declarations of a "second war between the states"
(*Business Week* 1976; *National Journal* 1976).

The implication of sustained substantial differences in growth
rates among countries and regions can be strikingly illustrated by
simple arithmetic. If current growth rates are permanently maintained for the next three and a half decades (approximately the
length of the postwar period), the low growth rate of the United
Kingdom will lead to a doubling of per capita national product,
whereas the high growth rate of Japan will result in a fourfold increase in per capita national income.

Why have some countries or regions grown much faster than others? Is the disparity in growth rates temporary, or are there
causal factors that could reproduce or perpetuate the trend? Economic theorists since Adam Smith have been intensely involved in
developing models of economic growth. The theory of economic

Table 1.2. Growth rate of income and per capita income level by state in the United States

State	Growth rate, 1958–1978 Total labor and proprietors' income	Population	Per capita labor and proprietors' income, 1978	Per capita labor and proprietors' income as percentage of U.S. average 1958	1978
New England					
Connecticut	6.96	1.18	6,499	121	108
Maine	6.70	0.72	4,652	83	77
Massachusetts	6.63	0.71	5,966	108	99
New Hampshire	8.22	2.02	5,163	88	85
Rhode Island	6.52	0.43	5,418	95	90
Vermont	7.64	1.24	4,984	82	82
Mideast					
Delaware	7.29	1.49	6,825	126	113
Maryland	7.90	1.64	5,759	97	95
New Jersey	7.01	1.17	6,169	113	102
New York	5.81	0.33	6,253	123	103
Pennsylvania	6.42	0.30	5,923	102	98
Great Lakes					
Illinois	6.78	0.64	6,970	120	115
Indiana	7.33	0.80	6,169	99	102
Michigan	7.61	0.91	6,837	106	113
Ohio	6.89	0.57	6,264	104	104
Wisconsin	7.36	0.98	5,886	97	97
Plains					
Iowa	7.13	0.34	6,055	91	100
Kansas	6.91	0.46	5,742	93	95
Minnesota	7.87	0.95	6,341	94	105
Missouri	7.02	0.75	5,932	100	98
Nebraska	7.01	0.62	5,747	94	95
North Dakota	6.98	0.37	5,427	85	90
South Dakota	6.94	0.25	5,211	81	86
Southeast					
Alabama	7.83	0.84	4,871	71	81
Arkansas	8.36	1.18	4,414	62	73
Florida	9.49	3.09	5,082	83	84
Georgia	8.52	1.45	5,379	77	89
Kentucky	8.04	0.83	5,072	71	84
Louisiana	8.12	1.14	5,282	77	87
Mississippi	8.24	0.71	4,210	55	70
North Carolina	8.44	1.21	5,275	73	87
South Carolina	8.76	1.18	4,958	64	82
Tennessee	8.35	1.22	5,266	74	87
Virginia	8.40	1.37	5,657	82	94
West Virginia	6.89	0.04	5,081	76	84
Southwest					
Arizona	9.87	3.40	5,550	90	92
New Mexico	7.49	1.57	5,065	91	84
Oklahoma	7.71	1.20	5,168	83	86
Texas	8.62	1.66	6,059	89	100
Rocky Mountain					
Colorado	9.02	2.36	6,376	99	106
Idaho	8.08	1.53	5,419	86	90
Montana	6.47	0.82	5,035	96	83
Utah	8.40	2.18	5,332	91	88
Wyoming	8.45	1.49	6,936	101	114
Far West					
California	8.09	2.02	6,879	120	113
Nevada	10.87	4.31	8,055	128	133
Oregon	8.45	1.76	6,303	98	104
Washington	8.00	1.50	6,581	106	109
U.S. average	7.48	1.12	6,043	100	100

Source: U.S. Department of Commerce 1979.
Note: The calculation of growth rates of U.S. states is based on the current price level, with no allowance being made for the change in price level, while that for nations in Table 1.1 is based on constant price level.

growth has attracted a good deal of attention from economists in
the postwar period. To a large extent, this attention was engen-
dered by the importance attached to high rates of growth of national income by policymakers. Economic growth is now firmly established as one of the policy objectives of modern governments. In
the 1970s almost all countries experienced sluggish real economic
growth. It is not surprising that the greatest interest in economic growth comes at two different stages: the initial stages of industrial development and the initial stages of industrial maturity
or stagnation. For while an economy is growing, there may be no
need to wonder about the cause, but when it is not, there is a
pressing necessity to find out why not.

     Though growth models abound, understanding of the growth proc-
ess still remains limited. Given the significance of disparities
in growth rates among countries and regions and no lack of theories
offered to explain the disparities, no systematic examination of
theories of comparative economic growth has been conducted. The
primary objective of this study is to advance our understanding of
why growth rates differ so greatly in one country or region as compared with another. The study examines and tests major hypotheses
offered in the literature--as explanations of different growth performances among countries and regions and as a means of investigating the theoretical validity and explanatory power of the leading
hypotheses. Some of the hypotheses we will examine have already
undergone some systematic investigation, but most of them have been
misunderstood or inadequately tested. A couple of hypotheses are
receiving their first thorough systematic treatment in this book.

DEFINING ECONOMIC GROWTH
     The first part of the analysis of economic growth consists of
deriving concepts of it and devising a means for measuring it. It
might be well to define rather specifically what is meant by economic growth. Although historians and economists seem to know well
enough what they mean by economic growth or contraction, this is so
only because in most cases it is not necessary to be very precise
about it. If we wish to be precise, especially numerically precise, we run at once into a series of difficulties. However, this
should not lead to a skeptical view of the value of such a study.
It is quite possible to do useful and significant work relating to
the causes and consequences of economic growth without ever having
defined and measured the concept of growth precisely.

     Since there is no general consensus on exactly how to define
and measure economic growth, it is convenient to adhere to the con-
vention. Two related definitions are commonly offered. The first
defines economic growth as an increase in the real gross national
product of the economy. An expanding real output means that the
economy is growing. The second and somewhat more refined definition links economic growth to increases in real per capita output.
This definition correctly recognizes that the standard of living of
any economy is best measured in terms of real output per person.

The two definitions are in line with the distinction made by Raymond W. Goldsmith (1959, p. 115) between "intensive economic growth," defined as an increase in real income per head, and "extensive growth," which represents simply "the multiplication of economic units without increase in real income per head and without the operation of external economies."

Simon Kuznets (1973, p. 247), a pioneer in the measurement and analysis of historical growth of national income in developed nations, has defined a country's economic growth as "a long-term rise in capacity to supply increasingly diverse economic goods to its population, this growing capacity based on advancing technology and the institutional and ideological adjustments that it demands." Notice that Kuznets's definition emphasizes production possibilities rather than actual production. There is a good reason for this: an economy recovering from a business cycle through a recession may greatly increase its output of goods and services, but this is not evidence of economic growth.

While Kuznets does not make a clear distinction between intensive and extensive economic growth in his definition, W. Arthur Lewis (1963, p. 1), in his well-known book, *Theory of Economic Growth,* makes clear his opinion about the object of growth theory: "The subject matter of this book is the growth of output per head of population." The conception of growth by R. A. Shearer (1961, p. 524) is a bit different. He contends that "the economic system can be said to grow if its normal aggregate physical capacity to produce goods and services expands."

Definitions are necessary to establish the ground rules for discussion. In this book we shall define economic growth as a sustained increase either in real per capita income or in real total income, depending on the specific question under review. We are relaxing the general insistence that economic growth be defined as growth of output per head and are considering the growth of total real income, not only because there are points of view from which this is an object of interest in its own right but because there are circumstances in which the rate of growth of per capita product might be regarded (in part) as a passive outcome of an economically determined rate of increase of aggregate real product and an exogenously determined rate of population increase. Our definition of economic growth is not meant to deny that in the discussion it is important to know what outputs are increasing and how that increase is distributed. But inclusion of these things into a definition of economic growth is confusing, as our distinction between economic growth and economic development in the next section indicates.

DISTINCTION BETWEEN ECONOMIC GROWTH AND ECONOMIC DEVELOPMENT

Economic growth and economic development are quite often used synonymously in the discussion of economics, but the two terms represent different concepts. Economic growth refers to the sustained increase in per capita or total income (as defined above), while the term economic development implies sustained structural change, including all the complex effects of economic growth. Such a linguistic usage would not, of course, imply any denial that the two processes are usually intimately linked. However, the English language has been impoverished by indiscriminate use of these two different concepts. By using the terms as synonyms, economists have not followed the example of Schumpeter (1934, pp. 57-64), who drew a sharp distinction between development and growth.

Even though developmental and growth processes are interrelated, there should be a distinction between them. Sir John Hicks made it clear that "growth economics" has nothing to do with the problem of developing the underdeveloped. According to Hicks (1965, pp. 3-4), "Underdevelopment economics is a vastly important subject, but it is not a formal or theoretical subject." He doubted the connection between growth economics and development economics by observing that "the appearance of a branch of theory called Growth Theory, at a time when the economics of underdevelopment has been a major preoccupation of economists, has made it look as if there must be a real connection."

The same distinction receives the approval of Hahn and Matthews (1964, p. 804) in their survey, where it was maintained that, in the case of dualistic economies, the "Growth Theory is applicable only to the advanced sector whereas the problems of the backward sector must be regarded as part of the theory of development rather than the theory of growth." If the linguistic usage is to be precise, Walter Rostow's well-known *The Stages of Economic Growth* certainly ought to be titled *The Stages of Economic Development*.

There is one important facet of economic growth that may be seriously affected by limiting the subject to measurable phenomena. Whether the difference between economic growth, as measured by the national income or product accounts, and economic growth, as measured by a welfare-oriented and fully comprehensive set of economic accounts or social indicators, is large or small has received a great deal of public and professional attention of late. The welfare aspect of economic growth has been brought to the fore since Pigou's basic treatment. Despite great effort on the part of economic theorists, it has not been possible to give a quantitative, measurable meaning to the concept of economic welfare, a concept as important for economic policy and analysis in the field of economic growth as elsewhere. One of the few exceptions is a work by Dan Usher (1980), who has made a comprehensive study of the concept and measurement of economic growth with emphasis on quality change in the growth of real consumption. Though the welfare implication of economic growth is very important, this study will consider only production- or activity-oriented economic growth.

COMPARATIVE STUDY OF ECONOMIC GROWTH

Our main concern in this work is the study of economic growth on a comparative basis. Comparative analysis occupies a distinguished place in most scientific inquiries. Comparison is an inte-

gral part of explanation. All meaningful description is comparative. Comparison is basic to perception, conceptualization, explanation, thought, and expression. Roy Macridis (1951, p. 2) explains that comparative study "entails the comparison of variables
against a background of uniformity either actual or analytical for
the purpose of discovering causal factors that account for variations."

In most research on economic growth, nations form the units of
measurement and analysis. For most aspects of economic growth, the
national state is the logical unit of study by virtue of the decisive importance of economic and noneconomic factors, e.g., the monetary regime, the credit system, tariffs, commercial law, taxation,
and political stability, that are tied to national boundaries.

Each country is something special and each situation unique.
A study of comparative economic growth would have to cover every
country in the world and extend over all the recorded history of
each. This is neither feasible nor necessary for an adequate analysis. Our aim in the comparative study of economic growth, as in
any scientific investigation, is to discover common basic traits.
The discovery and distinction of those traits may be aided by enlarging the number of cases (countries and periods) studied, but
the law of diminishing returns operates here as elsewhere.

It must be stressed that our study of comparative growth employs data from advanced industrial countries, primarily from Organization for Economic Cooperation and Development (OECD) member
countries, excluding less developed countries from our sample.
Even some of the advanced industrial countries are not included in
our cross-country study. Greece, Portugal, Spain, and Turkey are
excluded because these countries differ from other countries in the
OECD group in their political system and because one of the theories to be discussed, Olson's theory of political economy of comparative economic growth, is more or less limited in its application to those countries that have enjoyed democratic freedom of organization. Furthermore, two advanced economies, Ireland and Luxembourg, are excluded from the sample because the available data
are not sufficient to test all hypotheses examined below.

Our analysis of factors that exert a predominant influence on
economic growth employs not only cross-country data but also cross-
regional data for the United States, which is a large and diverse
federation composed of different regions with very different histories as well as growth rates. The major regions, and even several
states, of the United States are larger in size and population than
many of the individual nations of Western Europe. So far, there
has been no systematic study of economic growth among regions in
the United States. Furthermore, many theories developed originally
for cross-national comparison have not been applied to the growth
performance among regions in the United States or in other countries. Fortunately, the very fact that the United States is a
large federation composed of separate states with different histories and policies provides more data points than can be obtained
from the developed industrial countries. Also, data on relevant

variables are prepared on a more comparable basis for regions in the United States than for countries. More data points and more nearly comparable data will make our formal tests of hypotheses more useful. In this investigation, the 48 contiguous states will constitute our sample.

SCOPE AND ORGANIZATION OF THE STUDY

The different rates of economic growth of the industrial countries since World War II have provided a rich supply of surprises and paradoxes and a simultaneous and corresponding stimulus to research. Hypotheses have been advanced to explain differing growth rates of productivity or total output, stressing different strategic factors. Quantitative research has tested the explanatory power of some of these hypotheses with varying degrees of thoroughness.

This book represents an attempt to bring together and survey the various theories and hypotheses offered to explain comparative economic growth. It is not its objective to formulate a new theory; the book will serve its purpose if it helps the reader ascertain what the available theoretical and empirical literature offers for a better understanding and interpretation of the economic growth problem in the future as well as in the past. Any merit, therefore, must rest in the clarification of issues involved and in the tests of competing theories.

The very fact that there are many hypotheses offered to explain a single reality--economic growth--is evidence of the disagreement among researchers. One disagreement worth emphasizing evolves into two different schools: the "one-sword" school and the "literary" school, as dubbed by Martin Bronfenbrenner (1979). The one-sword school, or monotheistic view, emphasizes a particular factor to explain growth, while the literary school, or polytheistic view, lists a number of factors responsible for economic growth. Even though we treat each hypothesis as if it alone explains sufficiently the complex economic growth process, perhaps it is more true to the case that all the factors behind each hypothesis are working together to produce the different growth rates we observe among countries or regions. At the moment we do not have a general theory incorporating all the factors suggested by different hypotheses in a consistent way.

Many explanations are offered to account for different growth performance other than those we will examine, but most of them are not of a type economists are eager to embrace. Many of those that examine the slow economic growth of the United Kingdom relative to its European neighbors result in an abundance of "amateur sociology" (Solow 1970), suggesting that various British sociocultural characteristics are responsible for the poor performance of the British economy. However, the mere identification of these characteristics does not constitute a theory of economic growth. Moreover, a formal empirical testing of these ad hoc explanations is usually impossible.

In the following chapters, we not only examine the theoretical construct of the major hypotheses of comparative economic growth but also their empirical validity. Empirical testing is a necessary complement to the construction of theories, and it sobers the excess of pure speculation. With regard to the empirical testing of the hypotheses examined, two points should be borne in mind. First, empirical analysis can never prove the general validity of an economic theory, since subsequent observations may contradict the conclusions of the theory or the observed data may better be explained by an alternative theory. In principle, empirical tests tell us the extent to which the theory conflicts with reality; they generally do not lead to a final and definitive assessment of existing economic theories, but to the recognition of new problems and the subsequent formulation of new theories.

In addition, it should be pointed out that data availability and proper quantification of relevant variables are problems of long standing in economics in general and in our research in particular. Quite often, it is extremely difficult to measure a phenomenon or obtain data on it from a published source. Specifications employed to test some hypotheses are constrained by the availability of an acceptable set of data. Not infrequently, the underlying set of relations is not amenable to direct testing and identification. Although the author has cast the book in relatively objective terms, it is possible that he may not have attained a truly objective perspective on the controversy.

At present, those interested in the question of why one economy is growing faster than others are confronted with numerous fragmented theories that are presented as complete theories. In this book we present a selection of different hypotheses and attempt to delineate their skeletal structure. The hypotheses we will examine have been selected because they are representative of certain approaches and/or are widely used as points of reference.

To provide the reader with a sense of overall unity, we present a brief summary of the argument and a short note on the main purpose of each chapter.

Chapter 2 provides an outline of various approaches to the theory of economic growth in general. Though not exhaustive, the chapter discusses the major theoretical contributions in growth theory from a historical perspective and along different lines of thought. Included in this critical examination are the classical theory of Adam Smith and David Ricardo, the growth models of Harrod and Domar, the neoclassical and neo-Keynesian theories of growth, and the sources-of-growth analysis. Since some of the hypotheses discussed in the remaining chapters are direct offsprings of the theories of economic growth to be reviewed, the chapter will serve as a function of reference for later chapters.

In Chapter 3 we examine the theoretical construct and empirical evidence of the catch-up hypothesis, which maintains that some countries have experienced rapid growth during the postwar period largely because their economies grew so slowly before or because they had the opportunity to absorb a considerable amount of ad-

vanced technology from the technological leader. The chapter begins with an investigation of the relationship between technological change and economic growth and establishes the quantitative importance of technology in economic growth. Subsequently, we investigate the sources and processes of the international transfer
of technology on both theoretical and empirical grounds.

Chapter 4 focuses on the logical and empirical relationship
between capital formation and economic growth. The chapter discusses theoretical models that alternately show that changes in
capital or investment can and cannot affect the long-term growth
rate of an economy. International and interregional comparisons
suggest that while slow economic growth may not always be attributable to a low rate of net capital formation, there are no developed
countries or regions appearing to combine high rates of economic
growth with low rates of capital investment. The roles of saving
in economic growth and of investment as a carrier of technical
change are also discussed.

The hypothesis that economic growth is export led is the topic
of Chapter 5. A large body of theoretical literature emphasizing
the role of exports in leading an economy is analyzed along with a
substantial number of corresponding empirical investigations. The
export-led growth hypothesis is different from other hypotheses examined in the book in that it emphasizes the demand factor in economic growth, while others largely concentrate on the supply factors.

Chapter 6 examines Kaldor's macrodynamic model of why growth
rates differ. The theoretical foundation and empirical validity of
Verdoorn's Law, which says that the growth of productivity in manufacturing depends largely on the growth of manufacturing output,
are critically examined, since the law itself is a key element in
the overall framework of Kaldor's two-sector model of macrodynamics, which depicts manufacturing as an engine of growth, and in
subsequent controversies between Kaldor and others. The affinity
between the model of manufacturing as an engine of growth and the
model of the dual economy as applied to developed economies leads
us to review and analyze some recent works on the latter.

Because of the considerable broadening of the impact of the
public sector upon the economy and the continuing poor growth performance, some interest has been directed toward studying the behavior of government activities, with the aim of discovering whether any relationship between low economic growth and a growing public sector exists. Chapter 7 focuses on hypotheses that advance a
large public sector as an explanation for the poor growth performance of industrialized countries. To examine their empirical validity, an extensive set of data on the size of public sector is
collected and analyzed.

Chapters 8 to 10 discuss and test a new hypothesis by Mancur
Olson--the political economy of comparative growth rates. The essence of the hypothesis is that democratic societies have an inherent tendency to develop growth-retarding common interest groups if
they enjoy long-term stability and freedom of organization. The

overall rate of growth slows down as a result of the continuing accumulation of common-interest groups. Olson hypothesizes that the
increasing power of interest groups has a negative effect on the
economic growth of the community. Different growth performances
among countries or regions are due, therefore, to the different degrees of institutional sclerosis, which in turn are due to the accumulation of common-interest groups. Chapter 8 summarizes and extends Olson's theory of comparative economic growth, while Chapters
9 and 10 examine whether the hypotheses derived from Olson's model
are consistent with the cross-national evidence of 18 countries and
the cross-regional evidence of the contiguous 48 states respectively.

REFERENCES

Bronfenbrenner, M. 1979. On Japanese economic growth. *Fed. Reserve Bank San Francisco Econ. Rev.* Summer:7-17.
Business Week. 1976. The second war between the states. May 17:
92-114.
Goldsmith, R. W. 1955. Financial structure and economic growth in
advanced countries: An experiment in comparative financial
morphology. In *Capital Formation and Economic Growth.*
Princeton: National Bureau of Economic Research.
————. 1959. Financial structure and development as a subject
for international comparative study. In *The Comparative Study
of Economic Growth and Structure.* New York: National Bureau
of Economic Research.
Hahn, F. H., and R. C. O. Matthews. 1964. The theory of economic
growth: A survey. *Econ. J.* 74:779-902.
Hicks, J. R. 1965. *Capital and Growth.* London: Oxford Universi-
ty Press.
Kuznets, S. 1956. Levels and variability of rates of growth.
Econ. Dev. Cult. Change 5:5-94.
————. 1973. Modern economic growth: Findings and reflections.
Am. Econ. Rev. 63:247-58.
Lewis, W. A. 1963. *Theory of Economic Growth.* London: Macmil-
lan.
Macridis, R. C. 1951. *The Study of Comparative Government.* New
York: Doubleday.
Maddison, A. 1979. Per capita output in the long run. *Kyklos* 32
(Fasc. 1/2):412-29.
National Bureau of Economic Research. 1959. *The Comparative Study
of Economic Growth and Structure.* New York: National Bureau
of Economic Research.
National Journal. 1976. Federal spending: The North's loss is
the Sunbelt's gain. June 26:878-91.
Pesek, B. P. 1961. Economic growth and its measurement. *Econ.
Dev. Cult. Change* 9:295-315.
Schumpeter, J. A. 1934. *The Theory of Economic Development.* Cam-
bridge, Mass.: Harvard University Press.

————. 1947. Theoretical problems of economic growth. *J. Econ. Hist.* [Suppl. 7]:1-9.

Shearer, R. A. 1961. The concept of economic growth. *Kyklos* 14 (Fasc. 4):497-532.

Solow, R. M. 1970. Science and ideology in economics. *Public Interest* 21:94-107.

U.S. Department of Commerce. 1979. Computer printout. Regional Economic Information System, Bureau of Economic Analysis.

Usher, D. 1980. *The Measurement of Economic Growth.* New York: Columbia University Press.

2
Review of Theories
of Economic Growth

Few areas of economics can claim to be more controversial than the subject of economic growth. The search for a satisfactory explanation of growth has engaged the minds and energies of those who made significant contributions in economics. This was, in fact, the main focus of the work of Adam Smith and the classicists endeavoring to explain industrialization in eighteenth- and nineteenth-century England, of Karl Marx and Joseph Schumpeter in the long neoclassical eclipse of interest, and, most recently, of the post-World War II revival by those concerned with growth, both in the mature and in the less developed societies.

As a result of a great deal of work, various theories and models have been produced. They have encompassed descriptive studies as well as studies concerned mainly with uncovering the causal chain of events, empirical research as well as the construction of abstract theoretical models, quantitative as well as qualitative analysis, studies of detail as well as studies focused on broad aggregates. Investigations of national growth have been made along with international comparisons of economic structures. Sometimes the emphasis has been on the past and sometimes on prediction. Analysis as well as policy formulation has been stressed. Each theory and model has its own adherents, and they often appear unable or unwilling to attribute any merit to any alternative approach. It is not possible to speak of the theory of economic growth, only of various competing theories and models.

The very possibility of a general theory of economic growth has been disputed. Simon Kuznets (1952) observes that there is enormous variety in the different growth processes in the world, for which reason, whether formulating or evaluating theoretical assumptions as to economic growth, any attempt to go beyond mere lists of factors would have to be made, bearing in mind the characteristics of countries and of the periods relating to the growth process it is intended to explain.

Äkerman holds that a general theory of economic growth is not

15

even conceivable since there must be growth analysis strictly
linked to the institutional and structural environment of the countries under consideration, in order to pinpoint the individual factors that promote structural changes, within the limits set in each
country by the existing institutional system (see Vaciago 1970).

    We do not have a theory of economic growth general enough to
serve as a basis for a policy at all stages of economic advance and
with all types of economic systems. Most theories of economic
growth vary mainly because they place different emphasis on the
relative importance among the various factors and the interrelationships among the identified factors.

    Despite the inevitable risk of arbitrariness, broad approaches
to theorizing about economic growth that have been advanced in the
literature can be divided into two approaches: "classical theory"
and "modern theory." Hywel G. Jones (1976, p. 4) distinguishes between three broad approaches: "grand theory," "development theory," and "modern theory." The classical (or grand) theory refers
to "the type of theory which is intended to capture the essence of
the process for all societies at every point of time." Theories on
this line are never purely economic and seldom precise--a large variety of political, sociological, and even psychological factors
are intermixed so as to produce an all-encompassing vision of the
long-run process not only of economic growth but of the development
of society. The great names of the eighteenth and nineteenth cen-
turies--A. Smith, D. Ricardo, R. Malthus, and J. S. Mill--are all
classical theorists.

    The description "modern" is simply intended to mean that these
theories have been developed relatively recently, in particular in
the years since the publication of Keynes's *General Theory*. The
principal characteristic of the modern theories of economic growth
is that they use "a relatively small number of precisely defined
economic variables in the construction of a formal model of an aspect of the process of economic growth" (Jones 1976, p. 5). Distinctive approaches in modern growth theories discussed include
Harrod and Domar models of economic growth, neoclassical theory of
economic growth, neo-Keynesian growth theory, and sources-of-growth
analysis. Our task in this survey is to concentrate on some important theoretical contributions in growth theory. No effort is made
to be exhaustive; limitations of time and space have made it necessary to confine the discussion to major contributions in historical
perspective and along different lines of thought.

CLASSICAL THEORY OF ECONOMIC GROWTH
    The classical economists approach the study of economics with
a bold and expansive outlook. They wish primarily to discover the
causes of long-term growth in national income and wealth and the
process by which this growth occurs. The classical thinkers, unlike most of their present-day counterparts, construct theories of
economic growth that incorporate both purely economic and metaeco-
nomic variables comprising nature and society. Even though the

handling of these variables is not always consistent, the classicists do manage to formulate logical models so that a grand set of
schemes emerges, and a rather lofty view of the growth process becomes discernible.

There is considerable variation among the members of the
classical school. The differences arise either from the different
assumptions made regarding the "set of natural, psychological, and
institutional constraints" (Lowe 1954, p. 140) or from the different circular mechanisms that link the changes in the variables involved with the course of economic advancement. It is not our in-
tention to present a systematic survey of all the variants of the
classical theory of economic growth. The classical analysis of
growth may be best understood by studying the thoughts of two gi-
ants, Adam Smith and David Ricardo.

Adam Smith was a writer centrally concerned with the problem
of economic growth. He offers the earliest and most comprehensive
treatise on economic growth in his *Wealth of Nations*. He sees
growth as the outcome of an increased productivity, of which a major source is the division of labor that arises out of the propensity to exchange. Division of labor, in turn, is dependent on a
widening of the market and the accumulation of capital and thus dependent on saving. Smith (1937, pp. 261-62) writes:

> In that rude state of society in which there is no division of
> labor, in which exchanges are seldom made, and in which every
> man provides everything for himself, it is not necessary that
> any stock should be accumulated or stored up beforehand, in
> order to carry on the business of the society. . . . As the
> accumulation of stock must, in the nature of things, be previ-
> ous to the division of labor, so labor can be more and more
> subdivided in proportion only as stock is previously more and
> more accumulated.

Although he mentions the widening of the market as a factor in increasing productivity, his emphasis is on increased supply as a
cause of growth rather than increased demand. He seems to count on
international trade as a chief source of increased demand and the
widening market since he puts considerable stress on the advantages
of international trade.

Accumulation of capital is the keystone of Smith's theory of
growth. His emphasis on the importance of capital accumulation in
the growth process is a fundamental element in later growth theories. Capital accumulation would take place only if there were
profits, for workers had no capacity to save. Only through capital
accumulation could the level of technique improve, and in turn this
increased profits. To Smith (1937, pp. 263-69), capital is divided
into three parts: that portion reserved for immediate consumption
(food, clothes, furniture), circulating capital (money, stocks of
provisions, raw materials, stocks of finished goods), and fixed
capital (machines, profitable buildings, land improvements, acquired and useful abilities). Smith (1937, pp. 341-56) also dis-

cusses four different ways of employing the accumulated capital:
producing rude produce (agriculture), manufacturing, transportation, and distribution.

For a given institutional setting, an upward spiral of growth
in Smith's analysis is produced by the existence of basic economic
phenomena, the relationship between which is well summarized by D.
P. O'Brien (1975, p. 207):

> They [narrow economic relationships] involved the accumulation
> of capital, which supported the division of labor, which in
> turn increased the size of the total product through increas-
> ing productivity. This increased the scope for further capi-
> tal accumulation. As capital was accumulated, wages were bid
> up. Population increase ensued, ensuring increased demand for
> the final product. This in turn stimulated further division
> of labor.

Thus, once started, growth tends to be cumulative, and Smith might
well have said that only growth permits growth.

Although Smith does not deny the important role of agriculture
in feeding the urban population with an agricultural surplus and in
forming the basis for a demand for manufactured goods, he emphasizes the crucial importance of the nonagricultural sector in economic growth because he believes that division of labor and the accumulation of capital by savings out of profits, his two major
sources of growth, are considered better suited to trading and manufacturing activities than to agricultural activities.

The following succinct summary provided by Phyllis Deane
(1978, p. 37) recapitulates our discussion so far:

> The distinctive features of Adam Smith's theory of economic
> growth were: (i) his emphasis on the role of labour speciali-
> zation and its relation to the size of the market; (ii) the
> importance he attached to the role of the manufacturing sector
> in accelerating the pace of productivity growth for three rea-
> sons--(a) because there was more scope for division of labour
> in manufacturing, (b) because the commercial and manufacturing
> sectors tended to save a relatively high proportion of income,
> and (c) because the demand for their products was less readily
> satiated than the demand for, e.g., foodstuffs; and (iii) the
> way he made the growth of population, output and productivity
> all hinge on the rate of growth of capital accumulation.

To Smith, the growth process generated as discussed above is
likely to continue so long as produce per head grew faster than
consumption per head, for this would ensure a continuing surplus, a
rising demand for labor, and hence a growing population. Smith's
optimistic view on the prospects for growth was not shared by many
of his immediate followers.

It must be emphasized that putting Smith's theory in this
purely economic format does not capture the whole spirit or the en-

tire novelty of his approach to an explanation of growth. A greatly simplified, but still in purely economic format, interpretation of the Smithian theory of growth is provided by Sir John Hicks (1965, pp. 36-42), based on the third chapter of the second book of the *Wealth of Nations* titled "Of the Accumulation of Capital or of Productive and Unproductive Labor," in the following simple equation

$$Y_t = (p/w)Y_{t-1} = (p/w)K_t = k(p/w)Y_{t-1}$$

where Y_t and Y_{t-1} are output (in terms of corn) of this year and last year respectively, p is the productivity of the average laborer, w is wage, K_t is capital available for the production, and k is the fraction of output available as capital after all "nonproductive leaks" are accounted for, i.e., $k = K_t/Y_{t-1}$. Under this formulation the growth rate of the economy is $(p/w) - 1$ or $k(p/w) - 1$, depending on whether the economy devoted capital only to the productive sector or diverts to the unproductive sector. We obtain a positive growth rate when productivity rises faster than the wage rate and the level of unproductive consumption. A. Lowe (1975) and W. A. Eltis (1975) also present different schemes of Smith's growth theory.

Smith views the proper motivation of individuals as of utmost importance in starting and maintaining the process of growth and sees growth encouraged by letting individuals follow their own self-interest. He also emphasizes programs of reform. Monopoly and efforts to restrain trade are considered harmful to growth and are to be eliminated. Smith is not against government intervention per se, but against bad government interference. If the right institutions--free enterprise, private profits, freedom of exchange, and private property--prevailed, it would not be necessary to bother about growth because individuals would work, accumulate knowledge, and accumulate capital under the incentive of self-interest.

Smith's model has remained the formal pattern for major strands of classical economics, though the later models differ substantially from it and also from one another. The differences come from a change in the institutional setting or from the introduction of new variables in the circular mechanism. The outstanding example in both respects is David Ricardo, who weaves classical doctrine into a consistent body of economic analysis. Ricardo accepts as axiomatic Smith's emphasis on capital accumulation but develops the argument along a narrower line to a more pessimistic conclusion.

Ricardo, the most theoretical of the classical economists, demonstrated that the ultimate outcome of the growth process rested upon three basic propositions: (1) the Malthusian law of population, which held that population, unless checked by disease, famine, or war, tends to expand at an exponential rate; (2) the fundamental economic principle of diminishing returns, especially as applied to the scarce resource of agricultural land; and (3) a theory of capital accumulation in which profit is a key variable.

The process that Ricardo and other classical economists envis-
aged begins at an early stage of development when population is
small as compared to available arable land and, consequently, profits and the opportunity for capital accumulation are high.   The
high level of profits stimulates investment-capital accumulation,
which in turn increases the demand for labor, thereby driving market wage rates above the subsistence level.   This sets in motion
the forces that induce an expansion in population.   Two developments take place.   First, as market wage rates rise above the subsistence level, profits will be squeezed and thus the rate of capital accumulation slows down.   Second, more land must be brought
into use to accommodate the food requirements of a growing population.   The employment of more and more labor on a fixed quantity of
land brings diminishing returns into play.   Market wages will tend
to fall back toward the subsistence level.   When this happens, capital accumulation will cease, population will stabilize, and the
economy will enter into the stationary state.
    We may now readily see the "magnificent dynamics," so dubbed
by W. J. Baumol (1970) to describe the development of the economy
from a progressive into a stationary state, with the aid of a diagram (Fig. 2.1).
    The vertical axis measures total production and total wage af-
ter the payment of rent and the horizontal axis measures the size
of working population.   The line OS indicates the subsistence wage
line.   The slope of OS (total subsistence wage payment divided by
the size of working population) is the wage necessary to keep one
person at the minimum standard. OP is the curve showing the total
product after deduction of rent payments, i.e., the sum of wages
and profits.   Because of the law of diminishing returns and the increasing rent payment with growing population, OP must be convex
upward.   With ON_1 population, production is P_1N_1, wage per unit is
S_1N_1 and surplus or profit is P_1S_1.   The emergence of a surplus en-
genders accumulation, which leads to an increase in demand for labor.   Wages rise to P_1N_1 since the demand for labor rises with accumulation, but population and labor supply remain constant at ON_1.
But once wages are above the subsistence level, population will increase until wages are again driven down to subsistence level,
i.e., population will rise to ON_2.   Once the population is ON_2,
there will again be surplus, given by P_2S_2, so accumulation begins
again.   The whole process is repeated until the economy reaches a

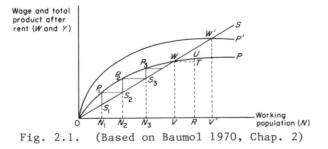

Fig. 2.1.   (Based on Baumol 1970, Chap. 2)

point like W, where the curve OP and the line OS meet. Once W is reached, there will be no surplus with even wages at subsistence level because wages are equal to production. With no surplus, there will be no further accumulation, and population will remain stationary at OV. The stationary state (day of doom) is reached. If an increase in productivity is brought about by inventions or discovery, as shown by a shift of OP to OP', the day of judgment can be postponed but not eliminated. The shift of the total product curve from OP to OP' moves the point of stationary equilibrium along OS from W to W' and the upper limit of population from OV to OV'.

     Given acceptance of the necessary simplifying assumptions, Ricardo's theory is simple, consistent, and complete. However, this very virtue of his theory, and its abstraction, limits its applicability to a fairly narrowly defined analytical purpose. What is missing from the classical economists' thinking about the process of economic growth is any notion of technological progress. Their model is dominated by the ironclad working of the law of diminishing returns, and since they do not envision technological progress, they see the process of growth as a race between population growth and exhaustion of resources on one hand and capital accumulation and expansion of the market on the other. So the stationary state is considered inevitable. According to Joseph A. Schumpeter (1954, p. 562), John Stuart Mill was the first to recognize explicitly the importance of the stationary state as a "conceptual construct or tool of analysis" that serves to isolate economic phenomena in an unchanging economic process but not as a future reality.

     To summarize, the contribution by the classical economists to growth theory can be put in three points. First, the classical economists provide a list of crucial factors that are supposed to determine the pace of the output growth in the economy. The identified elements include factors of production--natural resources, capital, and labor--technology, and the institutional setting of economic activity. Second, they develop certain propositional relationships among the identified elements. One well-known proposition in this regard is the effects of diminishing returns resulting from the combination of capital and labor with limited natural resources. Third, they suggest "some ranking in the growth-promoting properties of the different elements, some crucial factors on which to focus" (Deane 1978, p. 41). Capital accumulation was identified as the single most important dynamic factor on the list.

HARROD AND DOMAR MODELS OF GROWTH

     The approach of the modern growth theory of the economy is derived directly from Keynes. For more than a century, the theory of economic growth fell largely outside the scope of orthodox economics. Economists were mainly concerned with problems other than economic growth--chiefly efficient allocation of resources at the

margin.   The topic of economic growth was intellectually neglected
partly because of relative prosperity for the economies in Western
Europe and North America despite the prediction of the stationary
state by the major classical economists.   Sir John Hicks (1966)
pointed out that it was Mill "who killed the Old Growth Economics
and paved the way for the Static Epoch which was to follow."

The modern growth theory differs from the earlier attempts in
that it is both less ambitious and more precise.   Postwar growth
theorists have been content to relegate theories of population
growth and of changes in the organizational or institutional framework, sometimes even of technological changes, to other disciplines
or to accept changes in these rather crucial dimensions as given,
rather than to be explained within the framework of the growth theory itself.   The development of macroeconomics as a result of the
Keynesian revolution created a demand for theoretical concepts that
were selected and defined in empirically measurable forms.

The beginning of modern growth theory, which is essentially an
attempt to extract the long-run dynamic implications of Keynes's
primarily static and short-run analysis for a mature, closed economy, is the work by Roy E. Harrod and Evsey D. Domar.   Basically,
their analysis deals with the relationship between the growth of
saving and investment and income under circumstances in which full
employment would be maintained.   They did not develop a full model
of economic growth.   Their aim was a limited one: to express a
certain relationship that must be achieved if an economy is to grow
smoothly with full employment.

As classical economists did, Harrod and Domar assign a crucial
part in the process of growth to capital accumulation resulting
from increased investment.   But they emphasize that investment has
a double role: on the one hand, investment generates income
through the multiplier process; on the other, it increases the productive capacity of the economy by enlarging its capital stock.
Classical economists gave attention to the productive capacity side
of capital accumulation but took for granted adequate demand; in
the earlier Keynesian literature, attention was given to the problem of adequate demand, but the problem of capacity increase was
ignored.   Net investment is, by definition, the rate of change of
the capital stock per unit of time.   The effects of net investment
on the expansion of capital stock can be ignored in the short run,
but the assumption of a constant stock of capital must be dropped
in the long-run analysis.   When the capital stock is expanded, it
is essential that the increment in capital be utilized.   Output
must expand to absorb the enlarged capital stock into production;
otherwise, idle capacity will emerge and act as a deterrent to future investment.

Though approaches by Harrod and Domar are lumped together to
obtain the Harrod-Domar model, the questions raised and the results
reached by each of them are different.   While Domar (1946, 1947,
1957) asks the question at what rate the investment must grow if
the economy is to keep fully utilized the growing capacity that results from an increasing capital accumulation, Harrod (1939, 1948)

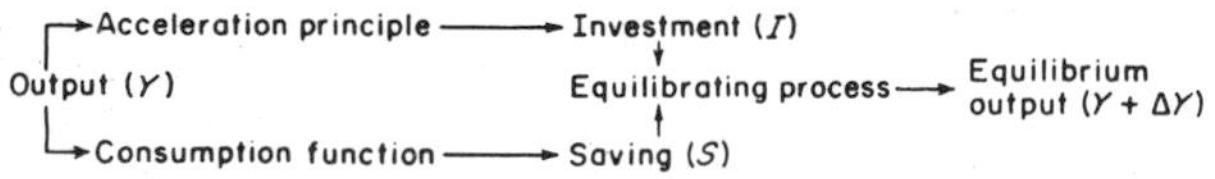

Acceleration principle ────────► Investment (*I*)

Output (*Y*)   Equilibrating process ───► Equilibrium
                                                                                                      output (*Y* + Δ*Y*)
Consumption function ──────► Saving (*S*)

Fig. 2.2. Harrod view of economic growth.

Capital coefficient ──────────► Potential output (*P*)

Investment (*I*)   Equilibrating process ───► Equilibrium
                                                                                                      investment
Multiplier ──────────────► Actual output (*Y*)

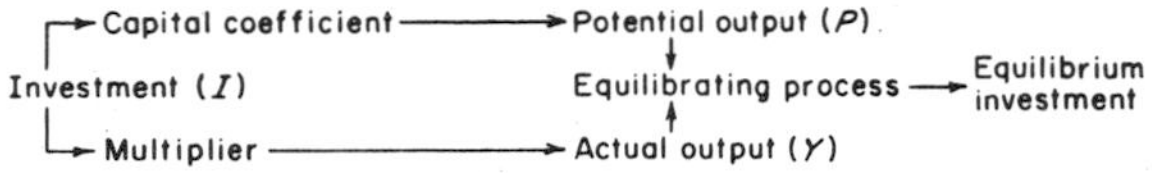

Fig. 2.3. Domar view of economic growth.

questions at what rate the economy must grow so that investors will
want to perpetuate their current rate of investment. Figures 2.2
and 2.3 present the key aspects of abstraction of the growth process by Harrod and Domar respectively. The simplest versions of the
Harrod and Domar models are outlined in equation form in Table 2.1.

Table 2.1. Summary of Harrod and Domar growth models

Harrod model		Domar model	
$I = \Delta K = C(\Delta Y)(K = CY)$	(H.1)	$\sigma = \Delta P/I$ or $\Delta P = \sigma I$	(D.1)
$S = sY$	(H.2)	$Y = (1/\alpha)I$ or $\Delta Y = (1/\alpha)\Delta I$	(D.2)
$I = S$	(H.3)	$\Delta Y = \Delta P$	(D.3)
$G_w = \Delta Y/Y = s/C$ or $C(\Delta Y) = sY$	(H.4)	$(\Delta I)/I = \alpha\sigma$ or $\sigma I = (1/\alpha)\Delta I$	(D.4)

Beginning with the concept of output, Harrod focuses on the
nature of the conditions of equilibrium between planned saving and
investment in a growing economy. Output is linked to saving
through a consumption function and to net investment through the
acceleration principle. Saving S is assumed to be a simple proportional function of the level of income, $S = sY$, in (H.2), whereas
investment I is assumed to be a constant proportion of the absolute
growth of income via the acceleration principle, $I = C(\Delta Y)$, in
(H.1); s is a constant average and marginal propensity to consume,
and C is a technical or required capital coefficient. By invoking
the familiar equilibrium condition that planned investment must be
equal to planned saving, $S = I$, in (H.3), we have the equilibrium
condition, $C(\Delta Y) = sY$ or $G_w = \Delta Y/Y = s/C$, in (H.4); the latter
Harrod calls the "fundamental equation." Therefore, the condition
for a continuous equilibrium between planned saving and investment
requires that the output grow at a constant rate of s/C. The equilibrium growth rate varies directly with s and inversely with C.

Harrod calls the rate of growth G_w the "warranted" rate and
defines it as that overall rate of advance which, if executed, will
leave entrepreneurs in a state of mind in which they will be prepared to carry out a similar advance. He distinguishes two other
growth rates: G_n, the natural rate of growth, is the maximum rate
allowed by the growth of labor force and the growth of labor productivity; and G_a, the actual rate of growth. If $G_w > G_n$, the
economy will move toward secular stagnation, the reason for this
trend being that the inability of the actual growth rate to equal
the warranted one in the face of the growth ceiling implies an in-
sufficiency of acceleration, so planned saving will persistently
exceed planned investment. The excess of saving over investment

will make for stagnation. If $G_a > G_w$, incomes will grow faster
than is warranted by the capital investment, the economy is stimulated to further expansion, and G_a will move farther from G_w. The
situation where $G_a = G_w = G_n$ is described as "The Golden Age" by
Joan Robinson (1970).

Domar chooses to focus on the dual nature of the rate of investment in a capitalist economy. As shown in Figure 2.3, investment is linked to aggregate demand through the familiar Keynesian
multiplier and to potential output through the capital coefficient.
From the Keynesian theory of the multiplier, the level of income is
determined by the level of investment or an increase in investment
brings about an increase in national income, $Y = (1/\alpha)I$ or $\Delta Y = (1/\alpha)(\Delta I)$, in (D.2), where $1/\alpha$ is the multiplier. Domar emphasizes
the significance of the capacity-creating aspect of net investment
and puts the relation involved in terms of $\sigma = (\Delta P)/I$ or $\Delta P = \sigma I$ in
(D.1) in Table 2.1, where σ refers to the rate of change of the potential capacity for the production of output associated with a
given level of output. (The coefficient σ is a productivity ratio,
the reciprocal of the technical capital-output ratio.) Equation
(D.1), $\Delta P = \sigma I$, represents a comprehensive description of the supply side of the economy. If initially, before the capacity-creating increment in investment occurred, aggregate demand Y and potential aggregate output P were equal, the full-capacity equilibrium
after the change in the economy's capital stock will prevail again
if the resulting change in potential output ΔP is matched by the
resulting change in aggregate demand ΔY, so that we have equilibrium condition, $\Delta Y = \Delta P$, in (D.3). By imposing full-employment equi-
librium initially and successively, we get $(\Delta I)/I = \alpha\sigma$ or $\sigma I = (1/\alpha)\Delta I$ in (D.4). According to the final result in (D.4), given the
productivity of new investment and the multiplier, investment must
grow at a constant rate of $\alpha\sigma$ to assure the full capacity utilization of a growing capital stock. Two things stimulate growth: an
increase in the productivity of capital and a higher multiplier
through an increase in the propensity to consume. The attempt to
do both at the same time leads to a conflict.

The growth process described above can be illustrated graphically by a slight elaboration of the ordinary short-run income determination diagram (Fig. 2.4). Since the average and marginal
propensities are assumed to be equal, we draw the saving function,

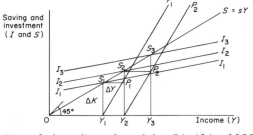

Fig. 2.4.   (Developed by Pivilin 1953)

$S = sY$, through the origin. The investment function is drawn in
the usual manner to show $I = f(Y)$, not $I = C(\Delta Y)$. The intersection
of the saving and investment functions determines the equilibrium
level of income. Now we impose a third function P depicting the
impact of investment on the economy's productive capacity. The
slope of the YP line is $\Delta K/\Delta Y = I/\Delta Y = C$, the marginal capital-output ratio. With respect to the saving function, Y is the independ-
ent variable; with respect to the P function, it is the dependent
variable. So C has the meaning of a productivity coefficient or a
marginal capital-output ratio.

Let us assume that OY_1 is the initial full-capacity equilibrium in year 1. This level of income generates a flow of investment
$S_1Y_1(I = S = \Delta K)$, which in turn increases productive capacity by an
amount equal to $S_1P_1 = Y_1Y_2 = \Delta Y$. Consequently, OY_2 represents the
economy's full-capacity income level in year 2. Unless income
grows to OY_2 in year 2, excess capacity will develop. Since equilibrium requires equality between saving and investment ex ante,
investment, with a given saving function, must rise to the level
represented by the investment schedule I_2. If Y_1Y_2 does induce the
shift from I_1I_2, we arrive at a new full-capacity income OY_2 at the
end of year 2, which generates investment equal to Y_2S_2. This
movement of the equilibrium income to the level OY_2 requires a
shift in the curve representing the productivity of investment coefficient from Y_1P_1 to Y_2P_2, because net investment results in further increase in the productive capacity by $S_2P_2 = Y_2Y_3$. Because
capital-output ratio C remains constant, Y_2P_2 is drawn parallel to
Y_1P_1. Once again, investment has to increase if full employment is
to be maintained. It is evident by inspection that $Y_3 - Y_2 > Y_2$
$- Y_1$, that is, full capacity is growing by increasing absolute
amounts, which implies that the investment schedule should rise by
increasing absolute amounts to prevent excess capacity.

The similarities and differences in the assumptions made and
the major results obtained between the models of Harrod and Domar
can be summarized as follows. First, both models are fundamentally
Keynesian in framework but extend the analysis to the long-run or
dynamic relationships. In particular, the capacity-creating effect
of investment is clearly recognized. Second, both obtain the economy, which grows at a constant rate, and suggest long-run difficulties in maintaining the equilibrium growth at full employment.
However, the reason for the long-run difficulty is different in the
two models. For Domar, the problem arises because of underinvest-
ment. In the Harrod model, the similar problem arises because
there is no mechanism that will ensure that the labor growth rate
and the warranted growth rate become equal. Third, both models depict instability of the equilibrium path. Once the economy is
pushed, however slightly, off its equilibrium growth path, it is
doomed to keep veering away from that path. Fourth, while Harrod
incorporates a theory of investment behavior in his model via a
simple accelerator hypothesis, Domar has no investment theory.
Domar's main concern is with finding the rate at which investment
would have to grow for expanding productive capacity to be fully

absorbed. He is concerned primarily with the essentially technical
question of the effect of present investment on future capacity.

The models of Harrod and Domar do serve as a starting point in
the dynamic analysis and they do constitute a major step forward as
far as dynamic economic theory is concerned. However, the two models face some criticisms. First, their very simplicity limits direct application to any economy. The models are too restricted by
assumptions made. Too many variables are exogenously determined,
and aggregation is carried to a high degree. Second, the Harrod-
Domar approach is a "price-less" one, i.e., the model does not include prices in it. While labor can be introduced into the system,
it must be at a constant ratio of capital to labor. Zero substitutability between labor and capital is not sustainable in the
analysis of long-run economic growth. Some amount of unemployed
resources always exists under zero substitutability between inputs
or under a fixed-price system. Third, the models have shortcomings
on empirical grounds. Observed growth rates have been faster than
can be accounted for by the savings ratio and the capital-output
ratio. Hans Brems (1973, pp. 33-41), using OECD data, estimates
Harrod-Domar capital coefficients and propensities to save for
eight advanced countries and uses the estimates to calculate the
growth rate according to $g = s/C$. The confrontation of the calculated growth rates with the actual growth rates produces a remarkable correspondence, not because of the merits but because of ap-
proximations in the calculation. The conclusions based on models
of Harrod and Domar conflict with a set of "stylized facts" proposed by Kaldor. The theory can be saved by allowing the capital-
output ratio to change, but then it ceases to be a theory and
lapses into the category of tautology. Last, but most important
from our point of view, the Harrod and Domar models are not theories of economic growth in the sense that they do not offer a hypothesis that purports to explain. None of these criticisms is
against the logic of the theories, only of their relevance to
analysis of growth problems.

From the launching of dynamic theory by Harrod and Domar
sprang an enormous literature on growth. The weakness of their
models led economists to explore more complex theories by relaxing
the highly simplified assumptions, examining the causes and consequences of changes in the parameters involved, and incorporating
institutional and structural elements in their new models. The exploration took two major directions, and the rift between the two
main groups of growth theory has been more than pronounced. On the
one hand there has been the neoclassical direction, which postulates an aggregate production function and assumes price flexibility generating full employment including the automatic equality between saving and investment. On the other hand a group of economists associated with Cambridge University takes a different direction along the line closer in inspiration to Keynes or Ricardo,
while they adopt the Harrod growth model as basic to the analysis
of long-run growth.

NEOCLASSICAL THEORY OF ECONOMIC GROWTH
     The weakness associated with the Harrod and Domar models of
economic growth in terms of the rigidities and instability problems
led economists to explore more complex theories by relaxing the
rigid assumptions of the Harrod and Domar models and making refinements to their simple models. The neoclassical approach to the
analysis of a growing economy has attracted substantial attention
since R. M. Solow (1956), T. W. Swan (1956), and J. E. Meade (1961)
worked out its implications.
     The neoclassical economists postulate a "well-behaved" aggre-
gate production function with flexible inputs that are smoothly
substitutable over the whole range determined by current technology
and assume that all inputs will be fully employed all the time
through complete flexibility in factor input prices. These postulates and assumptions enable neoclassicists to define a stable
equilibrium growth rate in which the warranted growth rate is tied
to the natural growth rate by factor price changes that induce appropriate variations in the input mix. In the neoclassical system,
the economy, if left alone, seeks out a steady-state equilibrium
growth path. Since full employment is assumed to be normally present, savings are continuously absorbed by employment. Unlike in
the Keynesian world where investment generates saving, in the neoclassical model of growth the rate of saving governs the rate of
investment. There is a similarity here to the monetarist approach
to the economy's behavior, for, like monetarists, the neoclassical
theorists are challenging the Keynesian notion that the economy is
inherently unstable. The automatic equality between saving and investment in the neoclassical economy led Robinson (1971, p. 111) to
protest that "the neo-neoclassicals seized upon Harrod's model and
thrust it into a pre-Keynesian mould."
     The substitutability between capital and labor plays a central
role in the neoclassical formulation. With variable factor proportions and flexible factor prices, the growth path is not inherently
unstable. If the labor force outgrew the supply of capital, the
price of labor would fall relative to the rate of interest, or vice
versa. Price flexibility and factor substitution mitigate the ter-
ror of the rigidity and instability in the models of Harrod and
Domar.
     Neoclassical growth in output can best be analyzed with the
production function, which relates output Y to inputs of capital K
and labor L as follows (except where it is absolutely necessary,
time subscript t is omitted to make our notations handy):

$$Y = F(K, L) \tag{2.1}$$

When the production is assumed to be subject to constant returns to
scale, i.e., F is linear homogeneous, the production function can
be written in terms of the capital-labor ratio as follows:

$$y = f(k) \tag{2.2}$$

where $y = Y/L$ and $k = K/L$. A "well-behaved" production function is characterized by

$$f(0) = 0 \qquad\qquad f(\infty) = \infty \qquad\qquad f'(k) > 0$$
$$f''(k) < 0 \qquad\qquad \lim_{k \to 0} f'(k) = \infty \qquad\qquad \lim_{k \to \infty} f'(k) = 0$$

$$(2.3)$$

If we assume that the saving ratio is constant as in the models of Harrod and Domar and that saving equals investment, we have

$$\dot{K} = dK/dt = I = S = sY \tag{2.4}$$

The labor force is assumed to grow at an exogenously determined constant proportional rate n, i.e.,

$$L_t = L_0 e^{nt}, \qquad \dot{L} = dL_t/dt = nL_0 e^{nt}, \qquad \dot{L}/L = n \tag{2.5}$$

since $k = K/L$, $\ln k = \ln K - \ln L$, where ln denotes the natural logarithm. By logarithmic differentiation we have

$$(1/k)(dk/dt) = (1/K)(dK/dt) - (1/L)(dL/dt) \quad \text{or} \quad \dot{k}/k = \dot{K}/K - \dot{L}/L \tag{2.6}$$

By assumption in (2.5), (2.6) can be written

$$\dot{k}/k = \dot{K}/K - n \tag{2.7}$$

Multiplying both sides of (2.7) by $k = K/L$ we obtain

$$\dot{k} = (\dot{K}/K)(K/L) - n(K/L) = \dot{K}/L - nk \tag{2.8}$$

or alternatively,

$$\dot{K}/L = \dot{k} + nk \tag{2.9}$$

Recalling that $\dot{K} = I$ and $y = f(k) = C/L + I/L$, we obtain

$$y = f(k) = C/L + \dot{k} + nk \tag{2.10}$$

Equation (2.10) states that output per worker is portioned off to three uses: (1) consumption per worker, C/L; (2) increase in capital-output ratio, $\dot{k}$--capital deeping; and (3) a portion of investment that maintains the capital-output ratio constant in the face of a growing labor force, nk--capital widening.

Equation (2.10) can be transformed into what is called the fundamental equation of neoclassical economic growth. Rearranging (2.10) we have

$$\dot{k} = f(k) - C/L - nk \tag{2.11}$$

Recalling that $f(k) - C/L = y - C/L = Y/L - C/L = I/L = S/L = sY/L = sy = sf(k)$, we obtain the fundamental equation, which corresponds to Equation (b) of Solow's original paper, which reads $\dot{r} = sF(r, 1) - nr$.

$$\dot{k} = sf(k) - nk \qquad\qquad (2.12)$$

Equation (2.12) is a differential equation involving the capital-labor ratio only. It states that the rate of change of the capital-labor $\dot{k}$ is the difference between the amount of saving (investment) per worker and the amount of investment required to maintain the capital-labor ratio unchanged as the labor force grows. Therefore, if the actual capital accumulation is greater than that required to equip the increase in labor with the same amount of capital as the existing labor force, capital per labor increases and vice versa.

The growth process of the neoclassical model can be studied in terms of Figure 2.5. The production function, $y = f(k)$, which has all the properties specified in (2.3), illustrates the quantity of output per worker y associated with any given level of capital per worker k. For example, the capital-labor ratio of k_0 in Figure 2.5 implies a flow of output per worker of $y_0 = Ak_0$. The curve $S = sy = sf(k)$ graphs the level of saving per worker associated with any level of the capital-labor ratio. When the capital per worker is k_0, saving (investment) per worker is Bk_0 while consumption per worker is AB. Given the exogenous constant rate of growth of the labor force, the investment requirement schedule to maintain the capital-labor ratio constant in the face of growing labor force is represented by line nk in the diagram. The investment requirement to maintain the capital-labor ratio unchanged at k_0 is equal to Ck_0.

It is apparent from Figure 2.5 that with a capital-labor ratio at k_0 we have a situation where saving and investment exceed the investment requirement. More is added to the capital stock than is required to maintain the capital-labor ratio constant. Saving and investment are sufficiently large not only to make up for population growth but also to raise capital per head. Accordingly, the capital-labor ratio grows. It should be noted that the increase in

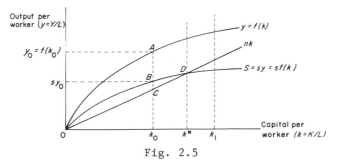

Fig. 2.5

the capital-labor ratio is equal to actual saving or investment
less the investment requirements and is thus given by the vertical
distance BC. It is clear from Figure 2.5 that with a somewhat
higher capital-labor ratio, the discrepancy between saving and the
investment requirement becomes smaller. Therefore, the increase in
the capital-labor ratio becomes smaller. The adjustment process
comes to a halt at point D. The point of intersection between the
investment requirement schedule nk and the actual saving and investment schedule, $sf(k)$, gives the equilibrium steady state value
of the capital-labor ratio k^*, since saving and investment associated with that capital-labor ratio exactly match the investment requirement. Given the exact matching of actual and required investment, the capital-labor ratio neither rises nor falls. We can make
the same argument by starting with an initial capital-labor ratio
in excess of k^*, say k_1. With the capital-labor ratio at k_1, the
investment requirement exceeds saving and investment. Accordingly,
not enough is added to the capital stock to maintain the capital-
labor ratio constant in the face of labor force growth. Thus the
capital-labor ratio falls until we get to k^*, the steady-state capital-labor ratio. In summary, whatever the initial capital-labor
ratio happens to be, a process of smooth convergence to balanced
growth can be expected in the neoclassical economy. We now turn to
a more detailed study of the characteristics of the steady-state
equilibrium and the adjustment process in the neoclassical model.

It can easily be shown that once the capital-labor ratio k^* is
attained, all the variables grow at the same constant rate--the
rate of growth of the labor force; output per worker, capital per
worker, consumption per worker, and saving per worker all remain
constant. At point D with k^*, the intersection of $sf(k)$ and nk implies that $\dot{k} = 0$ from the fundamental equation (2.12), $\dot{k} = sf(k)$
$- nk$. At point D, $\dot{k}$ is equal to zero and k remains constant at the
level of k^*. If $k = K/L$ is a constant and the labor force L is
growing at a given rate n, then the capital stock must grow at the
same rate. That is, constant capital-labor ratio with the labor
force growing at constant rate n implies that $\dot{K}/K = n$. By the production function, $y = f(k)$, the constant level of the capital-labor
ratio at k^* means a constant level of output per worker y^*. Since
$y = Y/L$, constant y^* implies that Y must grow at a rate n when the
labor force is growing at the constant exogenous rate, i.e., $\dot{Y}/Y$
$= n$. Therefore, at the constant equilibrium capital-labor ratio of
k^*, all the relevant variables grow at the natural rate of growth.
Since output and capital grow at the same constant rate n, output
per worker, capital per worker, consumption per worker, and saving
per worker all remain constant.

One interesting, seemingly paradoxical, proposition in the
neoclassical growth model is that the long-run rate of growth of a
neoclassical economy is the constant exogenous rate of growth of
the labor force and is entirely independent of the saving rate.
This proposition seems to contradict the commonplace observation
that an increase in the rate of growth requires more saving and investment. With the aid of Figure 2.6a we can show that an increase

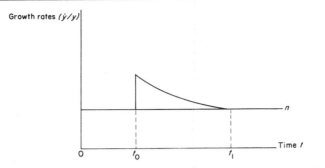

Fig. 2.6a. Equilibrium with a change in saving rate.

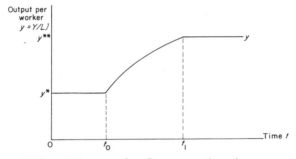

Fig. 2.6b. Time path of per capita income.

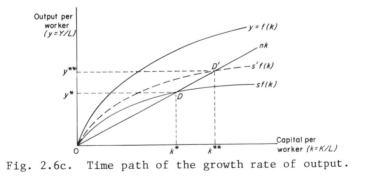

Fig. 2.6c. Time path of the growth rate of output.

in the saving rate (1) raises the growth rate of output in the
short run, (2) does not affect the long-run growth rate of output,
and (3) raises the long-run level of capital and output per head.
Consider an initial steady-state equilibrium at point D, where
saving precisely matches the required investment and the economy is
growing at the natural growth rate of the labor force. Assume that
for some reason people want to save a larger fraction of their income. The increase in the saving rate from s to s' is reflected in
an upward shift of the saving schedule, from $sf(k)$ to $s'f(k)$ in
Figure 2.6a. The exogenous rate of growth of the labor force re-

mains unchanged, so the new intersection of nk with the new saving curve, $s'f(k)$, is at the point D', with a higher capital-labor ratio at $k**$. Given the initial equilibrium capital-labor ratio at $k*$, saving per worker with the increased saving rate is greater than the required investment to keep capital per worker constant at that value of the capital-labor ratio. The capital-labor ratio must begin to rise, and it will continue to rise until $k**$ is reached. At point D', the higher amount of saving is just enough to maintain the higher stock of capital. At point D', both capital and output per worker have risen. Therefore, an increase in the saving rate raises the level of output and capital per worker, as shown in Figure 2.6a. In the transition from $k*$ to $k**$, the increase in the saving rate raises the growth rate of output because both increasing output and capital per worker during the "traverse" implies that the rates of growth of output and capital must be greater than the rate of growth of the labor force. Once the economy reaches the new steady state $k**$, saving equals the required investment and the capital-labor ratio again becomes constant. With the labor force growing at the constant natural rate, the constant capital-labor ratio implies that capital stock and national output must be growing at the same constant rate n. Therefore, the long-run rate of growth of output and the capital stock after the increase in the saving rate is the same as that prior to the increase in the saving rate, though in the short run an increase in the saving rate means faster growth in output and the capital stock. Figures 2.6b and 2.6c show the time path and growth rate of per capita income involved in the adjustment discussed above.

We may ask the question, What happens when the population growth rate increases say from n to n' and remains at that higher rate indefinitely? It can easily be shown that such an increase in the rate of population growth will raise the growth rate of output and lower the level of output per worker.

The simple neoclassical model of economic growth studied in this section provides for a consistent and coherent view of the world. Given the growth rate of the labor force and the saving habits, the rate of expansion of capital adjusts so as to provide the capital required to maintain full employment of the available labor force appropriate to a steady state. Steady growth at full employment is guaranteed by the assumptions that (1) firms are willing to carry out investment corresponding to whatever saving is going in, (2) techniques of production are sufficiently variable so as to allow for a choice of the appropriate technique, and (3) markets for labor and capital operate to ensure the wage and profit consistent with that technique.

Neoclassical models certainly have dominated the arena of growth theory and exerted pervasive influence on the way economists think about economic growth. The attractions of the neoclassical growth model are "its great simplicity, its use of Keynesian macroeconomic aggregates on the one hand and microeconomic technique on the other . . . and the fact that it seems to lend itself readily to empirical tests and predictions" (Deane 1978, p. 201).

The objections raised to the neoclassical growth model revolve around its choice of assumptions. The modern Cambridge school of economists are particularly critical of the measurement of capital and malleability of capital on which continuous substitutability between factors is postulated. The neoclassical vision of full employment and a smooth, long-run equilibrating process is inconsistent with Keynesian short-run vision of the possibility of unemployment. Unlike Keynesian analysis, the possibility of discrepancy between ex ante saving and ex ante investment does not exist in the neoclassical world. What is specific to the neoclassical approach to the theory of economic growth is the conception of growth as a form of adjustment to savings decisions and to factor supplies. Furthermore, it is presumed that there always exists a unique state of steady growth with full employment to which a neoclassical economy will adjust, given enough time. According to a simulation study by A. B. Atkinson (1969), convergence times to steady states are shown to be over a century.

The neoclassical approach to the theory of economic growth says nothing about the mutual interactions between growth and factor income distribution. The conception of income distribution in the neoclassical approach is one that relates to determination of the prices of inputs consistent with their relative scarcity and the given technology. To provide a determination of the distribution of income it is necessary to provide a specification of the ownership distribution of factors and a determination of factor prices. There is no specification of ownership distribution within the neoclassical conception. The ownership distribution is assumed to be given. Downward inflexibility of the wage rate and the possibility of zero marginal product of capital at some finite capital-labor ratio have not been adequately treated.

The evolution of the neoclassical analysis of economic growth since the mid-1950s has been characterized by an increased mathematical sophistication and complexity. A preoccupation with determining the mathematical properties of models has misled ensuing generations of economists in important respects. Economic growth theory developed under the spell of "technical" economic thinking, to the neglect of its empirical content. Neoclassical theory, in all its forms, shows a strong tendency to reduce the economic complexity of the analysis, doing so by holding the institutional framework constant. Little effort has been made to incorporate most of the important economic phenomena to be found in the real world. As a result, neoclassical growth theory has failed to develop in such a way as to answer the question such as why one country grows more rapidly than another.

NEO-KEYNESIAN THEORY OF ECONOMIC GROWTH

While neoclassical growth theory has dominated the journals and discussions during the postwar period, a small group of theorists, especially at the University of Cambridge, have attempted to develop, on the basis of the models of Michael Kalecki and John

Maynard Keynes, an alternative paradigm or view to the neoclassical traditions. Main contributions are by Nicholas Kaldor, Joan Robinson, Luigi Pasinetti, Piero Sraffa, and Richard F. Kahn. Others writing in the neo-Keynesian growth tradition include A. Asimakopulos, John Cornwall, Alfred S. Eichner, and J. A. Kregel.

The neo-Keynesian paradigm is described by a vastly different set of metaphysical beliefs and assumptions, values, and choice of techniques and problems. Although the development of neo-Keynesian growth theory has been an uneven one and there is no rigid orthodoxy, certain common elements have emerged that allow one at least to outline this neo-Keynesian conception of economic growth. Before we move to the discussion of works by two prominent contributors, Robinson and Kaldor, certain common features shared by different versions of neo-Keynesian growth are summarized and the distinctive features different from those of the neoclassical paradigm are pointed out.

First, neo-Keynesian growth theorists believe that the aggregate saving depends essentially on the distribution of income. It is necessary to distinguish between the propensities of workers and capitalists to save or between the propensities to save out of different kinds of income. For instance, a higher proportion of profits than wage income is saved. This is in sharp contrast to the neoclassical idea that the aggregate saving is independent of the distribution of income. Neo-Keynesian theory treats the distribution of income as a variable directly linked to the rate of economic growth, while in the neoclassical theory the distribution of income is ignored or assumed to be derived from the technical condition of the production relation. The neo-Keynesian explanation for the direct link between economic growth and income distribution is that both are determined by the same economic force, the rate of investment, whether measured against total income or viewed as the percentage change over time.

Second, neo-Keynesian growth theory avoids the use of a total stock of capital and objects to the neoclassical production function. The debate involved is the well-known "capital controversy." Neo-Keynesians reject the neoclassical assumptions necessary to treat capital and labor as continuously and smoothly substitutable, i.e., the assumption that real capital is like putty--homogeneous and malleable--as easily transformed from one use to another as putty. Robinson has been the most persistent and resourceful critic of the neoclassical production function. Her most influential allegation is that the neoclassical conception of capital, measured as a single number, simply could not be logically sustained because of the circularity involved. To measure capital, "we have to begin by taking the rate of interest as given, whereas the main purpose of the production function is to show how wages and the rate of interest (regarded as the wages of capital) are determined by technical conditions and the factor ratio" (Robinson 1953-54, p. 81). Most neoclassical economists probably agree that in general it is impossible to form a capital aggregate. Though they admit that the macroeconomic production function is not a justifiable concept, neoclassicists insist that it is an illuminating parable and that the usefulness of the concept depends on the purpose at hand.

Third, in place of the relative price variable, which is the focal point of a neoclassical analysis, neo-Keynesian theory makes investment the key determinant in economic growth. This follows from an underlying belief that in a dynamic, expanding economy, the income effects produced by investment and other sources of growth far outweigh the substitution effects resulting from price movements. In neo-Keynesian theory, investment depends on decisions made by entrepreneurs based on their expectations, and it is independent of the propensity to save. In neoclassical models the investment function is essentially nonexistent. The level of investment required to sustain full employment is determined by saving. The neo-Keynesian theory of investment, which is an explicit part of growth theory, is more sympathetic to Keynes's (1936, pp. 162-63) observation that "human decisions affecting the future, whether personal, or political or economic, cannot depend on strict mathematical expectation, since the basis for making such calculation does not exist; and that it is our innate urge to activity which makes wheels go round." Investment is determined by entrepreneurs, on the basis of expectations, the present capital stock, etc. How entrepreneurs form their expectations is extremely complex and essentially unknown. Since determinants of expectations and the interaction between all variables are unknown and complex, Robinson (1953-54, p. 161) summarizes all of this by saying that "animal spirits" determine the level of investment.

> Most, probably, of our decisions to do something positive, the full consequences of which will be drawn out over many days to come, can only be taken as a result of animal spirits--of a spontaneous urge to action rather than inaction and not as the outcome of a weighted average of quantitative benefits multiplied by quantitative probabilities.

In neo-Keynesian aggregative dynamic framework, the rate at which an economy moves is a function of the rate of investment, because the rate of investment is a measure of the rate at which profitable new industries are expanding their capacities. In the neoclassical view, an increase in the share of output-devoted investment cannot permanently increase the rate at which the economy grows. Neo-Keynesian growth theory maintains that a higher investment ratio, far from driving down the rate of return on capital, will lead on the average to more rapid rates of growth of productivity and per capita incomes. Neo-Keynesian theorists also emphasize that new technologies can seldom be introduced without large doses of investment. This causation of technological progress is left out in neoclassical models. Other things being equal, according to neo-Keynesian theory, the bigger the share of output devoted to investment, the more rapidly will this growth process unfold.

A fourth major characteristic to note is the direction of causality between the important variables involved. Neo-Keynesian

theory postulates that investment determines saving through the
multiplier and adjustment in the distribution of income and that
the rate of profit determines the marginal product of capital. If
there had been some saving out of wages, in the neo-Keynesian model, the distribution and marginal product would have had to be determined simultaneously. The same thing for the neoclassical model
will be that saving determines investment and the marginal product
determines the rate of profit. Robinson calls it the "pre-Keynesian theory after Keynes," because saving determines investment.

   The fifth distinguishing feature of neo-Keynesian theory is
that it regains the fundamental approach to a monetized production
economy outlined by Keynes. It is recognized that real commodity
and labor flows are expressed in the system as monetary flows, the
real aspects being reflected on the product side of the national
accounts and the monetary flows on the income side. Neo-Keynesian
theory describes an economic system with advanced credit and other
monetary institutions, all of which play a fundamental role in the
dynamic processes being analyzed. The role of financial institutions, the money wage rate independent of the real wage rate, distinction between discretionary and nondiscretionary expenditures,
etc., all have been paid adequate attention in the neo-Keynesian
models.

   A sixth important feature of the writings of neo-Keynesians is
their rejection of theories that imply that the rationality of an
individual is unbounded. The neo-Keynesian paradigm also shifts
emphasis toward the recognition of monopolistic and oligopolistic
elements and other forms of market imperfections. J. E. Stiglitz
and H. Uzawa (1969, p. 310) summarize the difference in fundamental philosophy between the neo-Keynesians and the neoclassicists as
follows: "The neoclassicists are committed to an economic theory
derived from some kind of rational behavior, while the Cambridge
economists believe that individuals are not calculating--in particular in a world of imperfect competition and uncertainty--and that
rules of thumb are used." In place of maximizing behavior in neoclassical theories, neo-Keynesians build behavioristic models in
which economic agents act according to some rules. The competitive
conditions assumed in neo-Keynesian theory are less restrictive
than those in the neoclassical analysis. The individual firm may
be a price maker with some ability to affect the prevailing price.
The neo-Keynesian formulation of a pricing model is based on a certain markup or margin above costs. This discarding of some of the
basic assumptions of neoclassical analysis is an effort by neo-
Keynesians of seeking to infuse the analysis with a "sense of history."

   Last, neo-Keynesians, particularly Robinson, concentrate on
the comparison of alternative steady-growth golden age equilibria
rather than on movements from one to another. For example, there
is a range of profit rates consistent with a given technology, and,
corresponding to this and to the given saving rates, we have a
range of possible warranted growth rates. Each may require a dif-

ferent composition of capital, and a shift from one equilibrium to another raises further problems of adjustment.

Since neo-Keynesian models are more general, take into account a much wider range of variables, tend to be explanatory rather than predictive, involve behavioristic rather than mechanistic assumptions, focus on the causes and mechanism of change rather than the conditions of equilibrium, try to construct "historical" causation, and link together a larger number of variables much less rigidly, it is not easy to describe the major features of a generalized neo-Keynesian growth model, as we did with the neoclassical growth model in the previous section. Each member of the neo-Keynesian camp tends to develop highly distinctive models of her or his own and puts different emphasis on various problems. Sometimes the same author develops a succession of different models. The growth theories of two neo-Keynesians may be as different as those of a neo-Keynesian and a neoclassicist. This being the case, it is not safe to speak of the neo-Keynesian growth theory. Following is an attempt to summarize the highlights of works of two major contributors--Robinson and Kaldor--in neo-Keynesian theories of economic growth.

Although both Robinson and Kaldor develop their model in Keynes's tradition, it must be noted that there are some important differences between their approaches. Kaldor's emphasis is more on the macroeconomic aspects while Robinson stresses the micro relationship. Whereas usually Kaldor's growth theory assumes that full employment is continuously maintained, Robinson's theory is not tied to the assumption of full employment. This second difference between Robinson and Kaldor can be ascribed to the fact that the former does not believe that any viable distinction can be made between "short-run" and "long-run" theory, while the latter does so. For Kaldor, stability is a natural property of long-period analysis; for Robinson it is a myth. Basic differences between Robinson and Kaldor with respect to methodology, the pricing mechanism, the determination of the profit rate, the analysis of technical progress, the valuation of capital, and the stability of the growth are well summarized by J. A. Kregel (1973, pp. 187-93).

The third difference to note is that Kaldor explicitly builds abstract models. Though he constructs them to correspond to what he calls "stylized facts," he does not have any particular qualms about analyzing changes over time in a particular economy, an exercise that Robinson treats with the utmost caution.

Robinson is quite prolific in her writings in many areas. Our presentation of her work on economic growth is based on the discussions in her two books, *The Accumulation of Capital*, 2nd ed., and *Essays in the Theory of Economic Growth*. An excellent summary of her intellectual genealogy, methodological preference, and criticisms of other theories is made by Henry Y. Wan, Jr. (1971, Chap. 3). Robinson's theory of growth represents an attempt to develop a causal model, operating in historical, not logical, time for a capitalist economy. In her own words, "The problem presented itself

to me as the generalization of *General Theory*, that is, an extension of Keynes's short-period analysis to long-run development"
(Robinson 1966, p. vi). To construct a causal model Robinson
(1962, p. 34) starts "not from equilibrium relations but from the
rules and motives governing human behavior. We therefore have to
specify what kind of economy the model applies to, for various
kinds of economies have different sets of rules." Robinson presents an analysis of long-run accumulation beginning with a simple
model and progressing to models of increasing complexity by varying
or relaxing the simplifying assumptions. (Since unlike her neoclassical counterpart, Robinson has carried through her argument in
verbal, analytical terms, it is not easy to put her system in mathematical formulation and much harder to detect errors in logic that
might have crept in at some state of the discussion.) Listing the
basic assumptions in her simple model may facilitate our discussion
of her theory of capital accumulation.

1.   There are two classes of income: profits and wages.
While wage earners spend all of their wage income on consumption,
profit takers save and invest all their profit income.
2.   Capital and labor are combined in fixed proportions to
produce a given output.
3.   Labor is homogeneous and there are no scarce natural resources.
4.   From one period to another the expected prices and rate of
profits are always realized and confirmed by experience, i.e.,
tranquility.
5.   The economy is a closed economy, with no government.
6.   Labor costs are the only variable costs, and prices are
determined by marking up unit prime costs.

Robinson (1962, p. 35) isolates determinants of equilibrium
and groups them under seven headings: (1) technical conditions,
(2) investment policy, (3) thriftiness condition, (4) competitiveness condition, (5) wage bargain, (6) financial conditions, and (7)
initial stock of capital goods and state of expectations formed by
past experience. The alternative models of equilibrium growth
processes in Robinson's system can be described with the different
cross-connections between the above determinants and with the basic
assumptions mentioned before.
At the core of Robinson's approach to the theory of economic
growth is the importance of investment in the growth process and
the "double-sided relationship between the rate of profit and the
rate of accumulation." Investment is important in Robinson's model
of growth because economic growth depends on investment to which
saving adapts. Saving adapts to investment through its dependence
on the share of profits, which rises with the level of investment
in relation to income. The basic idea here is that there is within
certain definite limits a distribution of income between profits
and wages to ensure that saving matches investment and demand absorbs output produced with growing productive capacity. This idea
is entirely that of Keynes because "firms are free, within limits,

to accumulate as they please, and that the rate of saving of the
economy as a whole accommodates itself to the rate of investment
that they decree" (Robinson 1962, p. 83).

The significance of the growth-investment or growth-profit relation is pointed out clearly by Donald J. Harris (1978, p. 183)
when he writes:

> The growth-profit relationship, viewed simply as an equilibri-
> um condition is consistent with any theory of growth and dis-
> tribution. What gives causal significance to this relation in
> the case of neo-Keynesian theory is the proposition that the
> rate of accumulation is an independent variable and there is a
> relation of dependence of the rate of profit on the rate of
> accumulation. This is one proposition about which all varie-
> ties of neo-Keynesian theory are in full agreement and one
> distinguishing that framework of analysis from others.

The direction of causation from investment to saving (profits), not the other way around, can be discussed using the distribution equation pivotal to Robinson's growth theory. Net income
per annum is exhaustively divided into wages and profits:

$$pY = W + P = wL + \pi pK \qquad (2.13)$$

where Y is real national income, p is the price of output as well
as of capital equipment, W is total wages, P is total profits, w is
the money wage rate, L is the amount of labor employed, π is the
gross profit rate, and K is the amount of capital employed. Dividing both sides of (2.13) by the average price index p, we have the
distribution equation in real terms

$$Y = (w/p)L + \pi K \qquad (2.14)$$

Equation (2.14) can be rearranged to yield the profit rate in the
form

$$\pi = \frac{Y}{K} - \frac{w}{p}\frac{L}{K} = \frac{Y - (w/p)L}{K} = \frac{Y/L - w/p}{K/L} \qquad (2.15)$$

Equation (2.15) shows that the profit rate depends on the technological condition, capital-labor ratio K/L, labor productivity Y/L,
and the real wage rate w/p.

On the assumption that all wages are consumed and that all
profits are invested, it can be shown that the rate of capital accumulation is equal to the rate of profit.

$$S = I = \pi K = \Delta K \quad \text{or} \quad \pi = \Delta K/K \qquad (2.16)$$

When we put together (2.15) and (2.16) we obtain

$$\frac{\Delta K}{K} = \pi = \frac{Y/L - w/p}{K/L} \qquad (2.17)$$

Equation (2.17) indicates that the rate of capital accumulation, in
Robinson's scheme of growth, depends on whatever determines the
profit rate, which is in turn dependent upon the capital-labor ra-
tio--real wage rate and labor productivity. If the capital-labor
ratio is fixed, equilibrium depends on the relation between wages
and profit. The main thrust of Robinson's model is that if entrepreneurs want to invest more, it is the variation in the profit
rate that provides the equilibrating mechanism. Investment can exceed planned saving through a change in the distribution of income.
But the crucial variable in the system is investment, which is determined by "animal spirits." The economy will grow only if entrepreneurs want to invest. Firms and entrepreneurs find themselves
to be influences on their plan for the future. A path of steady
growth in the Robinsonian framework is seen as a constant rate of
accumulation. The surprising similarity between the result in
(2.17) and the "magnificent dynamics" discussed previously should
be noted. The fact that the rate of growth of capital increases
when the return to capital ($Y/L - w/p$) rises in greater proportion
than the capital-labor ratio means in Ricardian terms that capital
accumulation is strengthened by a fall in the real wage rate and
weakened by a rise in the real wage rate when technological conditions remain unchanged.

What then determines the rate of accumulation? This question
leads us to discuss what Robinson (1962, p. 47) called "the double-
sided relationship between the rate of profit and the rate of accumulation." For a given state of animal spirits, the rate of accumulation planned by entrepreneurs can be expressed as an increasing function of the expected rate of profit. In the words of
Robinson, "The rate of investment they are planning for the future
is . . . higher the greater the rate of profit on investment."
This is Robinson's investment function. Entrepreneurs require a
higher level of profit to sustain a higher rate of accumulation
both because greater profits offer greater compensation for the
risks attached to investment and because greater profits make a
greater pool of internal funds available for further investment.
The other side of the double-sided relationship is the relation of
dependence of the rate of profit on the rate of accumulation. Unless there is investment, the rate of profit will be insufficient
to justify investment. Again in the words of Robinson, the "accumulation going on in a particular situation determines the level
of profits obtainable in it and thus . . . determines the rate of
profit expected on investment."

The nature of the two-edged investment (accumulation) relationship is illustrated in Figure 2.7, which reproduces Robinson's
diagram. The A curve represents the rate of profit that would be
realized at any rate of accumulation. When there is no saving out
of wages, it starts at the origin. Its slope depends on the saving
propensities associated with profit income. Under the tranquility
assumption the expected rate of profit is equal to the actual rate.
Thus the A curve gives the expected and actual rate of profit as a
function of the actual rate of accumulation. The I curve repre-

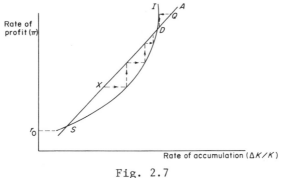

Fig. 2.7

sents the planned rate of accumulation as a function of the rate of profit that induces it. It is positively sloped, as discussed above. The position of the I curve reflects the state of animal spirits. There might be the minimum rate of profit (r_0) below which entrepreneurs are unwilling to undertake investment. As the planned rate of accumulation falls to zero, when the rate of profit reaches the minimum rate, the I curve becomes horizontal, as indicated by the dotted segment.

Given the conditions that determine the slopes and positions of the curves in the diagram, an equilibrium of steady growth can now be identified. Two situations of entrepreneurial equilibrium are indicated in Figure 2.7 by two points, D and S, where the I curve cuts the A curve. Each of these points represents that "a rate of accumulation is generating just the expectation of profit that is required to cause it to be maintained" (Robinson 1962, p. 49). At all other points, entrepreneurial expectations are shown by events to have been mistaken. Robinson uses the diagram to show that only equilibrium point D is stable. For all points to the left, as at X, the rate of profit generated by the current rate of accumulation and expected to continue into the future is such that the planned rate of accumulation exceeds the current rate. Entrepreneurs will try to increase the rate of accumulation. When they find themselves to the right of D, as at Q, the rate of accumulation going on is greater than would be justified by the rate of profit that it generates. Entrepreneurs will plan to reduce the rate of accumulation. Though point S is a situation where the realized rate of profit is just that required to induce entrepreneurs to maintain the same rate of accumulation as they are currently undertaking, it is a position of unstable equilibrium. Any deflection above this point would lead back toward D, while a deflection below this would mean that "the economy has fallen below its stalling speed and is heading toward even greater ruin and decay than it now suffers."

Even though the logically necessary sequence of the movement to the stable equilibrium position is traced by arrows in the diagram, the process by which an economy might adjust to the position in historical time, starting from a different initial position, cannot be shown, because the technical and behavioral conditions involved remain to be specified. Within a given set of conditions, there is no guarantee of the existence of a unique and stable equilibrium expansion in the actual capitalist economy. Suppose that the underlying conditions are such that the A curve lies entirely to the right of the I curve. Then no position of equilibrium can be maintained. The curves may also intersect more than once, thus giving rise to the existence of multiple equilibriums. Even if there is a stable equilibrium appropriate to a given set of conditions, this does not ensure that it would persist indefinitely, for "there may be influences within the existing situation which will cause changes in the immediate future" (Robinson 1962, pp. 49–50).

Robinson calls point D in Figure 2.7 the "desired rate of accumulation in the sense that it is the rate which makes the firms satisfied with the situation in which they find themselves." Recognizing the similarity between her "desired rate of accumulation" and Harrod's "warranted rate of growth" and their similar role in the analysis, she argues that "Harrod . . . has never removed the ambiguity as to whether the firms are supposed to be content with the stocks of productive capital that they are operating or with the rate at which it is growing" (Robinson 1962, p. 49).

When "tranquility" prevails and the underlying set of conditions, including technological progress, remains unchanged, the desired rate of accumulation will be maintained. Even the fulfillment of these special conditions does not guarantee the steady growth path of the capitalist economy, because we have said nothing about the availability of labor and the association between growth of the labor force and capital accumulation. When a desired rate of accumulation is equal to the rate of growth of the labor force plus the rate of neutral technical process, then the economy is maintaining the truly steady, smooth growth path. This case Robinson calls a "golden age." In a golden age the rate of profits and the capital–output ratio are constant, the real wage is increasing at the same rate as the technological progress rate, the shares of profits and wages in total income are constant, and the supply of labor is exactly matched by demand for labor. It should be noted that a golden age cannot be called an optimum; since the level of prevailing real wages depends partly upon the thriftiness condition, there is an element of interest conflict between workers and capitalists.

The point of Robinson's analysis is that even if there is an equilibrium with accumulation taking place at a steady rate, there is no guarantee that the available supply of labor will exactly match the requirement for continued accumulation, because the desired rate of accumulation and the natural rate, defined as the sum of the growth rates of the labor force and productivity, are determined by separate factors. According to Robinson, a golden age of full employment growth could only be the result of a historical accident in the capitalist economy. Once an economy is on the golden age path, the actual, warranted, and natural growth rates are all the same, as in Harrod's analysis. The relation between the Robin-

son and Harrod models can be shown as follows. Equation (2.15) can
be rewritten as:

$$\pi = \frac{Y - (w/p)L}{K} = \frac{Y}{K} \frac{Y - (w/p)L}{Y} \qquad\qquad (2.18)$$

Equation (2.18) shows that the profit rate π is proportional to
output-capital ratio Y/K times the share of profits in national income, $[Y - (w/p)L]/Y$. Note that Y/K is $1/C$ for Harrod (see Table
2.1). Since all profits are saved and invested by assumption in
the Robinson model $S = Y - (w/p)L$ and $s = S/Y = [Y - (w/p)L]/Y$.
When we put together (2.17) and (2.18) and the above relationships
we have

$$\Delta K/K = \pi = s/C = \Delta Y/Y \qquad\qquad (2.19)$$

However, it should be noted that there is more scope in Robinson's
approach than in Harrod's for the reconciliation between the warranted and natural rates. Robinson recognizes explicitly that the
investment activity of firms can influence the saving ratio and the
rate of technological progress, both of which are assumed as given
in Harrod's analysis.

As mentioned before, Robinson does not provide a predictive
model, only a framework for studying different types of growth.
Thus discussion of her taxonomy of possibilities of different gold-
en ages is helpful in understanding her framework designed to explain the concrete conditions of accumulation. A variety of adjec-
tives has been used to denote different golden ages that do not
have all the characteristics of the true golden age discussed
above. There is the "limping golden age" (a steady rate of accumulation with unemployment), where employment falls as time goes by.
The "leaden age" is when the proportion of unemployment is rising
because of an insufficient rate of accumulation. There is the "restrained golden age," with full employment but a desired rate of
accumulation exceeding the natural rate; the actual growth rate is
limited by the possible natural rate and kept down to it. A growth
path characterized by rising rates of accumulation and profit,
thereby speeding up the growth rate of employment, is called a
"galloping platinum age." The "creeping platinum age" is characterized by a growth path with decreasing rates of profits and accumulation and a gradually rising capital intensity of production,
with full employment being maintained. The phrase "bastard golden
age" is used to denote the case where the real wage is inflexible
downward in spite of unemployment, and this, in the absence of
technological progress, prevents a rise in rates of accumulation
and profits. If technological progress is going on, then even with
a constant level of real wages, acceleration of accumulation can
take place, and we are in a "bastard platinum age." (For details
of these different ages, see Robinson 1962, pp. 51-59.)

The above taxonomy is constructed to explain the concrete conditions of accumulation in capitalist economies. The framework

contains the general elements applicable to a broad range of historical conditions and particular elements applicable to a particular set of conditions. The taxonomy, however, does not provide the
possible connection or transition between one age and another or
the possible order these ages might occupy in the overall process
of growth of a particular economy.

To summarize our discussion of the Robinson model of economic
growth, her chief contribution lies in her integration of classical
value and distribution theory and modern Keynesian investment-sav-
ing theory in one coherent system. Robinson's theory brings to the
forefront of analysis the expansionary drive of firms and their
"technical dynamism" as basic forces governing the operation of the
capitalist economy. Interrelationships among identified forces are
clearly pointed out. Her theory emphasizes (1) the causal role of
investment decisions of entrepreneurs, (2) interconnection between
profits and accumulation, and (3) the dependence of income shares
on the rate of accumulation and saving propensities among classes
or income categories. While her model is capable of yielding a
stable equilibrium solution, there is no automatic equilibrating
mechanism to bring about continuous expansion at full employment.
Given the growth determinants mentioned above and their interactions, steady growth with full employment is unlikely and mythical.

Kaldor, in his attempt to build a model of economic growth,
begins with the basic requirement of any model designed to explain
the characteristic features of the economic progress. His theory
of economic growth has evolved over time in various writings
(Kaldor 1956, 1957, 1959, 1961; Kaldor and Mirrlees 1962). From
these we attempt to synthesize a model with the main emphasis on
his 1961 paper presented at the Corfu Conference of the International Economic Association. His suggestion is to (1) include the
influence of forces that are primarily responsible for the behavior
of the economic variable under investigation and (2) find the theory that does not lead to results contrary to what we observe in reality. In the words of Kaldor (1961, pp. 177-78), "Any theory must
necessarily be based on abstractions; but the type of abstraction
chosen cannot be decided in a vacuum; it must be appropriate to the
characteristic features of the economic process as recorded by experience." Instead of constructing a model that leads to results
contrary to our real observation and attributing the contrary movement to "the compensating influence of residual factors that have
been assumed away," in Kaldor's view, we should start off with a
"stylized view of the fact--i.e., concentrate on broad tendencies,
ignoring individual detail, and proceed on the 'as if' method."

Kaldor (1961, pp. 178-79) summarizes the broad facts about the
growth of advanced industrial economics in the form of six "stylized facts": (1) the continued growth in the aggregate volume of
production and in labor productivity, (2) a continued increase in
the amount of capital per worker, (3) a steady rate of profit on
capital, (4) a steady capital-output ratio over long periods, (5)
a high correlation between the share of profits in income and the
share of investment in output, and (6) appreciable differences in

the rate of growth of labor productivity and total output in different societies. As might be expected, Kaldor (1961, p. 179) maintains that "none of these 'facts' can be plausibly 'explained' by the theoretical constructions of neo-classical theory." For example, according to the neoclassical marginal productivity theory, one should expect a continued fall in the rate of profit with capital accumulation, not a steady rate of profit. Therefore, Kaldor's purpose is to present a model of income distribution and capital accumulation that is capable of explaining at least some of the above stylized facts.

Taking the well-known Harrod and Domar challenge to produce a growth theory as a starting point, Kaldor incorporates the guides laid down by Keynes and Kalecki and perceives capital accumulation along lines suggested by Ricardo, Marx, and von Neumann. At the foundation of his scheme are (1) the concept of the division of income into profits and wages, with the condition that "the proportion of profits saved is considerably greater than the proportion of wages saved," (2) the "Keynesian theory" of full employment, and (3) a technical progress function showing the relationship between the rates of growth of output per worker and capital per head. The conception of the first of the above major elements is from Ricardo, Marx, and von Neumann, whereas Kaldor translates competition and full employment in accord with the Keynesian techniques of analysis. With respect to the third element, the idea that technical progress is determined by forces within the economic system, not as "manna from heaven," is entirely his own, and he introduces his technical progress function as a means of representing his vision of the process of technical progress and as a replacement of the orthodox aggregate production function.

As with Robinson, Kaldor makes saving adjust to the desired level of investment through a rise in the share of profits in national income. Kaldor's approach to saving, which originally developed as a Keynesian "alternative theory of distribution," becomes a central element in all his subsequent models of economic growth. Since total income is the sum of wages W and profits P, we have

$$Y = W + P \qquad\qquad\qquad (2.20)$$

Kaldor decomposes saving into two components: saving out of profits S_p and saving out of wages S_w, and assumes that each of these savings will be proportional to the corresponding income, i.e., $S_p = s_p P$ and $S_w = s_w W$, where s_p and s_w are the propensity to save out of profits and wages respectively. Total saving S is given by

$$S = S_p + S_w = s_p P + s_w W \qquad\qquad (2.21)$$

By substituting (2.20) in (2.21), we have

$$S = s_p P + s_w (Y - P) = (s_p - s_w)P + s_w Y \qquad (2.22)$$

Since dynamic equilibrium requires that $I = S$, we obtain

$$I = (s_p - s_w)P + s_w Y \qquad (2.23)$$

Dividing both sides of (2.23) by Y and rearranging, we can obtain

$$P/Y = [1/(s_p - s_w)](I/Y) - s_w/(s_p - s_w) \qquad (2.24)$$

Equation (2.24) has a number of implications such that (1) the profit share and investment share vary directly, given the saving parameters, and (2) the profit share and the capitalists' saving propensity vary inversely. (In his paper on income distribution, Kaldor calls the second result a "widow's cruse" distribution theory, after a passage in Keynes's *A Treatise on Money*.) Kaldor believes that (2.24) constitutes a Keynesian distribution theory to supplant the marginal productivity theory of income distribution. Similarly, dividing (2.23) by K and rearranging, we obtain

$$P/K = [1/(s_p - s_w)](I/K) - [s_w/(s_p - s_w)]Y/K \qquad (2.25)$$

From (2.25), the profit rate P/K is related to the saving propensities out of wages and profits, the rate of capital accumulation, and the capital output ratio. In the special "classical" case, where the propensity to save out of wage income is zero, (2.25) reduces to

$$P/K = (1/s_p)(I/K) \qquad (2.26)$$

Equations (2.24), (2.25), and (2.26) show the requirement of steady growth under assumed conditions. What they essentially show is that profits will, at the expense of wage incomes, always provide the requisite saving.

Kaldor's saving and distribution theory provides an escape from the instability problem in the Harrod model, expressed as $G_w = s/C = n$. Dividing (2.22) by Y, the overall saving rate s is

$$s = S/Y = (s_p - s_w)(P/Y) + s_w \qquad (2.27)$$

or

$$s = s_w + (s_p - s_w)(P/K)(K/Y) \qquad (2.28)$$

Equations (2.27) and (2.28) show that the overall average propensity to save is no longer a constant. There always exist appropriate values of the profit share in income P/Y or the profit rate P/K that will ensure that the overall propensity to save is exactly that required to equate s/C to n.

As mentioned before, whereas Robinson's growth theory is not tied to the assumption of full employment, Kaldor assumes continuous full employment in his construction of growth theory. The justification for assuming full employment in long-run equilibrium

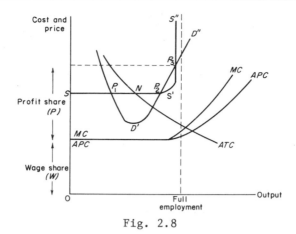

Fig. 2.8

analysis is discussed in his two papers (Kaldor 1959, 1961). To
analyze the conditions under which the forces equalizing saving and
investment determine the price-cost relationship at full employment, rather than the level of relationship at some given relationship of prices to cost, Kaldor employs "representative firm" with
price-making power. The cost structure and pricing decisions are
shown in Figure 2.8. Constant average and marginal prime costs are
assumed, up to a point, before they go up because of the limited
capacity of existing plants. Superimposed on that there is the
full employment barrier due to labor availability, as shown by the
dashed line in the diagram. Firms are assumed to fix prices by a
certain "minimum margin of profit" to their variable costs, up to
the full employment barrier, no matter what the state of demand in
the market. Therefore, the aggregate supply curve takes the form
of a reversed letter L, $SS'S''$. Kaldor then introduces the Keynesian demand function, which shows the demand price for each level of
output. Given constant money wages, each possible price suggests a
different relative distribution of income. The higher the price,
relative to prime costs, the greater the profits shares and the
greater the aggregate saving, since saving out of profits is larger
than saving out of wages. Therefore, the higher the price the
smaller the quantity of consumption goods demanded from the representative firm for any level of investment. Consequently, we obtain a downward sloping demand curve like DD'. However, our demand
curve has so far been based on the postulate that the rate of investment is invariant with respect to changes in output. Recall
that output growth governs investment demand. "Induced" investment
above and beyond the constant flow of autonomous investment will be
by above-normal profit, i.e., induced investment will come into
operation when receipts cover or more than cover total costs, including normal profits on the capital invested. In Figure 2.8 the
curve ATC represents average total cost with normal profits included and the point N indicates the level of production that
yields the normal rate of profits on the existing plant. When out-

put is carried beyond the point N(or D'), induced investment takes
place. When the increase in investment associated with an increase
in output exceeds the increase in saving for any given distribution
of income, the demand curve will slope upward. In this fashion,
Kaldor obtains a U-shaped aggregate demand function, cutting the
aggregate supply curve at P_1, P_2, and P_3. Application of the
Marshallian criterion of stability shows that P_1 and P_3 are stable
equilibriums, while P_2 is an unstable one. At P_1 there exists an
underemployment equilibrium with zero-induced investment. Since at
point P_1 nothing causes further investment, the economy, though
stable, is not moving and growing. In contrast, at P_3 induced investment is positive, the economy is stable, and the output is
growing. The basis for Kaldor's continued use of the assumption of
full employment in his formulation of growth theory is that only P_3
provides a stable equilibrium growth solution, while the stable but
less than full employment equilibrium like P_1 is incompatible with
long-run, steady expansion of investment and output. To repeat,
where Keynesian unemployment occurs, balanced growth is impossible
because there is no induced investment. It should be noted that "a
moving equilibrium of growth is only possible when, given the savings propensities, the profit margin resulting from the equilibrium
rate of investment is higher than the minimum profit margin indicated by the height of the horizontal section" (Kaldor 1961, p.
201) of the supply curve and that there must be sufficient competition to ensure this.
        The third element in Kaldor's scheme of economic growth is his
analysis of what the relations are among investment, growth, and
technical progress. While recognizing the influence of the expected rate of profit on investment decisions, Kaldor introduces an additional factor based on the concept of a desired capital-output
ratio. Firms are regarded as having some desired ratio of capital
to output, and their investment is geared to maintaining that ratio. Thus the rate of accumulation is equal to the expected rate
of output growth if the rate of profit on capital is constant. The
rate of accumulation is greater than this if the rate of profit is
expected to rise and less if it is expected to fall. Kaldor's explicit introduction of a technical progress function completes his
analysis of investment behavior. He believes that rate of technical progress is not exogenous to the economic system but depends on
the rate of capital accumulation. His technical progress function
can be represented by the TT curve in Figure 2.9, the shape of
which reflects Kaldor's basic assumptions regarding the nature of
technical progress and growth. The TT curve cuts the vertical axis
positively because "a certain rate of improvement would take place
even if capital per head remained unchanged." The technical progress function is convex upward and reaches a maximum at a certain
point because as more profitable innovations are exhausted, technical progress must taper off. The 45° line OX represents the rate
of accumulation that any given rate of growth of output would induce if the rate of profit were constant. At points on TT to the
left of Q such as point A, productivity per worker is rising faster

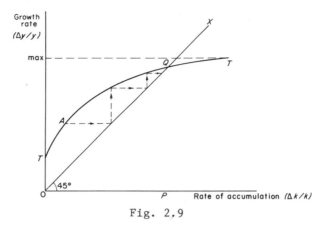

Fig. 2,9

than capital per worker, the rate of profit is expected to rise, and firms will plan to increase the rate of accumulation. The opposite result occurs at positions to the right of point Q. Only point Q is consistent with steady growth. At Q the capital-output and capital-labor ratios are constant, with a constant rate of profit, and the increase in productivity and capital accumulation proceeds at the same exponential rate.

We may pause to find out how consistent Kaldor's theoretical construction and results are with his stylized facts. At point Q in Figure 2.9, output per worker and the capital-labor ratio are growing exponentially, while the capital-output remains constant, proving his stylized facts (1), (2), and (4). With a capital-output ratio and the Keynesian demand function, an equilibrium at P_3 in Figure 2.8 means a constant profit share and investment share. This is his stylized fact (5). The same high correlation between profit share and invest-income ratio is expressed in (2.24). Dividing the constant profit share by the constant capital-output ratio proves his stylized fact (3) that there has been a steady rate of profit on capital despite the continued accumulation of capital. His stylized fact (6), appreciable differences in growth performance among countries, is explained by a varying technical progress function for each country.

In Kaldor's formulation there is no unique rate of growth of output at which alone steady growth can be maintained. The equilibrium rate of growth of output can be any point on the TT curve, and there are infinite numbers of such points. This is so because the growth of per capita output itself depends on the rate of accumulation in accordance with the technical progress function. Given the technical progress function, the growth rate of output will be determined by the rate of accumulation, which in turn depends on the conditions governing the demand for investment. In Kaldor's (1961, pp. 208, 209) view, "'technical dynamism,' meaning by this both inventiveness and readiness to change or to experiment," governs the height and slope of the technical progress function, and this technical dynamism is "responsible, in a capitalist economy, for making both the rate of accumulation or the rate of growth of output relatively small or relatively large."

A typical criticism against the neo-Keynesian growth models is that neo-Keynesian growth theorists have failed to "order their model" and, as a result, present the analysis of growth more in the form of a typology than a theory of economic growth. (One notable example contrary to this general statement is a model set out by Kaldor [1961, pp. 214-322]. His "final model V" presents a well-ordered model.) On one level, the reason for this is the ad hoc manner in which the conditions of competition, structure of the market, growth of firms, and process of technical progress are integrated into the overall conception of the capital accumulation, economic growth, and income distribution. Despite counterattack by neoclassicists, neo-Keynesian theory of growth represents an attempt to develop a causal model, operating in historical times, for capitalist economy along the line of Keynes, who "brought the argument down from the timeless stationary states into the present, here and now, when the past cannot be changed and the future cannot be known" (J. Robinson 1971, p. ix).

SOURCES-OF-GROWTH ANALYSIS

The sources-of-growth methodology, initiated by Moses Abramovitz (1956) and Robert M. Solow (1957), relies heavily on the neoclassical conception of an aggregate production function and highlights supply conditions for economic growth. Literature on growth accounting and factor productivity is too numerous to list all of it. Several other major contributors are John W. Kendrick (1961), E. F. Denison (1962, 1967, 1969), and D. W. Jorgenson and Z. Griliches (1967, 1972). The analysis is descriptive. It provides an accounting decomposition of input growth that must totally account for (but not necessarily explain) output growth. Although growth accounting of Abramovitz and Solow is based on some rather heroic simplifying assumptions, their study results and those of others are startling in that changes in capital and labor can account for only a very small fraction of the observed changes in output, leaving a substantial part of the growth rate unexplained.

The startling nature of these results has triggered numerous attempts to measure the growth in output that can be attributed to technological change, i.e., to shifts in the production function as opposed to mere movements along an existing production function. This constitutes a significant and long overdue change in the treatment by economists of technological change. Later studies swing back and forth between factor augmentation and technical change, leaving the situation confused. The three major contributions in the growth accounting literature are studies by Solow (1957), Denison (1962), and Jorgenson and Griliches (1967).

All three studies are very neoclassical and start with the standard production theory. They postulate a production function

$$Y = f(K, L, t) \qquad\qquad (2.29)$$

where Y is output, L is labor force, and K is capital stock, as before. The argument t (time) represents technological change and signifies that the form of the production function is changing over time. The rate of technical change α between the year 0 and the year T can be defined indirectly as

$$e^{\alpha t} = \frac{f(K_0, L_0, T)}{f(K_0, L_0, 0)} \qquad (2.30)$$

Therefore, the rate of technical change is the rate at which output would have increased over a given period, as it was observed to do, but factor inputs K and L remained the same. The differences in the three studies lie in the nature of the inputs accounted for and in the specification of the aggregate production function of (2.29).

Before we discuss the different formulations and results in the three studies, we obtain the following general results. Differentiation of the aggregate production function in (2.29) with respect to time t would give

$$\frac{dY}{dt} = \frac{\partial Y}{\partial K} \frac{\partial K}{\partial t} + \frac{\partial Y}{\partial L} \frac{\partial L}{\partial t} + \frac{\partial Y}{\partial t} \frac{\partial t}{\partial t} \qquad (2.31)$$

Equation (2.31) can be divided by Y to produce

$$\frac{1}{Y} \frac{dY}{dt} = \frac{1}{Y} \frac{\partial Y}{\partial K} \frac{\partial K}{\partial t} + \frac{1}{Y} \frac{\partial Y}{\partial L} \frac{\partial L}{\partial t} + \frac{1}{Y} \frac{\partial Y}{\partial t} \qquad (2.32)$$

Equation (2.32) can be rewritten as

$$\frac{1}{Y} \frac{dY}{dt} = \frac{f_K K}{Y} \frac{1}{K} \frac{\partial K}{\partial t} + \frac{f_L L}{Y} \frac{1}{L} \frac{\partial L}{\partial t} + \frac{1}{Y} \frac{\partial Y}{\partial t} \qquad (2.33)$$

When we define $g_Y = (1/Y)(dY/dt)$, $g_K = (1/K)\partial K/\partial t$, $g_L = (1/L)(\partial L/\partial t)$, $\alpha = (1/Y)(\partial Y/\partial t)$, $\beta_K = (f_K K)/Y$, and $\beta_L = (f_L L)/Y$, we have

$$g_Y = \beta_K g_K + \beta_L g_L + \alpha \qquad (2.34)$$

Needless to say, since in competitive conditions $f_K = \partial Y/\partial K$ and $f_L = \partial Y/\partial L$, the marginal products of capital and labor, equal the rental rate of capital and the wage rate respectively, then $\beta_K = (f_K K)/Y$ and $\beta_L = (f_L L)/Y$ equal the shares of capital and labor in national income. Note also that β_K and β_L are the elasticity of output with respect to capital and labor. According to the neoclassical production function, output growth depends on the growth of inputs, the elasticity of output with respect to each input, and technological change.

Solow (1957) investigated the extent to which the growth of the U.S. economy from 1909 to 1949 should be attributed to capital accumulation and the extent to which it has resulted from the technological change. The central equation of Solow's paper is

$$\alpha = g_y - \beta_K g_k \qquad\qquad (2.35)$$

where g_y is the growth rate of output per worker and g_k is the growth of capital per worker. Derivation of (2.35) is as follows: if the production is subject to constant returns to scale, $\beta_K + \beta_L = 1$. Thus $\beta_L = 1 - \beta_K$. Substitution of this final result into (2.34), $g_Y = \beta_K + (1 - \beta_K)g_L + \alpha$, which can be rewritten as $\alpha = g_Y - g_L - \beta_K(g_K - g_L)$; $g_Y - g_L = g_y$ and $g_K - g_L = g_k$ are nothing but the growth rates of per capita output and capital per worker respectively. Solow estimates (2.35) using available time series data on the growth rate of output per worker g_y, the growth rate of capital per worker g_k, and the relative share of capital in output β_K. Of the total increase in private nonfarm real gross national product per work hour of 104.6 percent, only 14.7 percent could be explained by capital formation, the remaining 85.3 percent being attributable by definition to technical change. (The numbers cited here are based on the correction made by W. P. Hogan [1958]. According to Solow's own calculation, an increase of 80.9 instead of 85.3 percent is due to technical change.) This finding was surprising and triggered more sophisticated analyses of the problem. Improvement on Solow's results has been made by employing more precisely defined inputs and taking into account the nature of technological progress.

Denison's approach is quite similar to that of Solow and can be summarized by an extended version of (2.34) as follows:

$$g_Y = \sum_{h=1}^{\ell} \beta_L^h g_L^h + \sum_{i=1}^{m} \beta_K^i g_K^i + \sum_{j=1}^{n} Z_j + \alpha' \qquad\qquad (2.36)$$

where g_Y is the growth rate of national income, β_L^h and β_K^i refer to shares of factors represented by g_L^h and β_K^i respectively, and Z_j refers to the growth rate of various disequilibrium factors. Denison specifies growth of labor input, g_L^h ($h = 1, \ldots, 4$), so as to reflect the effects of increasing educational attainments of the work force, changes in the age and sex composition of the labor force, improved utilization of women workers, and the assumed increase in work-hour output occasioned by a decline in the average number of hours worked. Denison also subdivides the growth of the total capital stock, g_K^i ($i = 1, \ldots, 5$), into inventories, nonresidential structure and equipment, dwellings and residential land, international assets, and nonresidential land. Z_j refers to adjustment factors resulting from improved resource allocation, adequacy of aggregate demand, adoption of best-practice technique, and economies of scale. Finally, α' is the residual after the total contribution of g_L^h, g_K^i, and Z_j is deducted from g_Y. Denison calls this term, α', "advances in knowledge."

Confusion over the use of some terms needs to be clarified.

The divergence in the growth of output relative to the growth of combined factor inputs has been called a "measure of our ignorance" by Abramovitz and simply "residual" by Domar. The whole unexplained part of the output growth is also referred to as "total factor productivity" by Kendrick and Denison and represents growth in output resulting from "technical change." To Denison, the term residual represents "advances in knowledge," an unexplained part of the total factor productivity that remains after quantifying contributions of other variables, which he believes explains the increase in total factor productivity.

Denison applies (2.36) to calculate the contribution by various factors to the growth of national income in the United States, nine Western European countries, and Japan. In his calculation Denison is not committed to any fixed pattern of adjustments, i.e., he allows the magnitude and numbers of $\beta_{T,}^h$, $\beta_{K,}^i$, $g_{T,}^h$, $g_{K,}^i$, and Z_i to differ over time as well as from one country to another, depending on the prevailing conditions. Denison's main results are summarized in Table 2.2. Between 1948 and 1969, national income of the United States grew at an annual rate of 4.00 percent. Of this total, 2.09 percentage points are attributable to the growth of the labor force and capital stock. The remaining 1.91 percentage points, 47 percent of the total, are attributable to increases in output per unit of input resulting from advances in knowledge and other factors. Only in two countries, Canada and the United States, does input growth account for more than half the growth in national income. Contribution to the output growth by capital accumulation is less than one-fourth of the total in all countries he examined. This insignificance of capital in influencing the growth of output is due to the failure in Denison's formulation to allow for the fact that an acceleration in the rate of investment brings with it an acceleration in the rate at which the efficiency of the capital stock increases. As in Solow's formulation, technical change is not assumed to be embodied in new investment.

Table 2.2. Sources of growth of total national income, 1950-1962

Country	Standardized growth rate of national income (g_y)	Contribution by labor $(\Sigma \beta_L^h g_L^h)$	Contribution by capital $(\Sigma \beta_K^i g_K^i)$	Total factor productivity $(\Sigma Z_i + a')$	Advances in knowledge (a')
	(A)	(B)	(C)	$(D = A - B - C)$	(E)
Belgium	3.03	0.76 (25)	0.41 (14)	1.86 (61)	0.84 (28)
Canada[a]	4.95	1.85 (37)	1.14 (23)	1.96 (40)	0.66 (13)
Denmark	3.63	0.59 (16)	0.96 (26)	2.08 (58)	0.75 (21)
France	4.70	0.45 (10)	0.79 (17)	3.46 (73)	1.51 (32)
Germany	6.27	1.37 (22)	1.41 (22)	3.49 (56)	0.87 (14)
Italy	5.60	0.96 (17)	0.70 (13)	3.94 (70)	1.30 (23)
Japan[b]	8.81	1.85 (21)	2.10 (24)	4.86 (55)	1.97 (22)
Netherlands	4.07	0.87 (21)	1.04 (26)	2.16 (53)	0.75 (18)
Norway	3.43	0.15 (4)	0.89 (26)	2.39 (70)	0.90 (26)
United Kingdom	2.38	0.60 (25)	0.51 (21)	1.27 (54)	0.79 (33)
United States[c]	4.00	1.30 (33)	0.79 (20)	1.91 (47)	1.19 (30)

Source: Denison and Chung 1976, pp. 40-41.

Note: Numbers in the parentheses represent the percentage contribution of each factor to the growth rate of national income in column A.

[a]For 1950-1967.
[b]For 1953-1971.
[c]For 1948-1969.

In fact, Solow (1962) later examined the effect of assuming
all technical change to be embodied in new capital. To construct
the model in this manner, Solow adjusts the capital stock data to
make newer, later additions to the capital stock more productive
than older, earlier additions. This is done by adjusting each
"vintage" of capital for depreciation and multiplying the surviving
capital by an improvement factor that grows steadily over time.
The resulting sum of the adjusted vintages of capital then represents a measure of the effective stock of capital. After these adjustments, Solow obtains results that suggest a much more important
role for capital in the growth process.

Despite the refinements made by Denison and Solow in the specification of factor input, a substantial portion of growth in output remained unexplained by input growth. An attempt to reduce the
magnitude of the residual (in the Domar sense) and to increase the
importance of factor inputs in the growth process was made by Jorgenson and Griliches (1967, 1972). They argue that when both labor
and capital inputs are measured in efficiency units that adjust for
improvements in quality, practically all the growth in output can
be explained by input growth without resorting to a technological
change residual. They adopt the usual neoclassical assumptions of
competition, a constant return to scale production function, equality of factor-price ratios to their ratio of marginal productivity,
and equality of marginal rates of substitution of goods to their
prices. Technical change is considered as a shift in the production function, as in Denison's work. Jorgenson and Griliches postulate a production possibility curve of the form

$$F(Y_1, Y_2, \ldots, Y_m; X_1, X_2, \ldots, X_n; t) = 0 \tag{2.37}$$

where Y_i are output, which may be consumption goods or new capital
goods, X_j are inputs of capital or labor, t is time, and F is homogeneous in degree zero in all Y_i and X_j. Differentiating (2.37),
the rate of technical change turns out to be a Divisia (variable-
weight) index

$$\alpha = \frac{1}{Y} \frac{\partial Y}{\partial t} = \sum_{i=1}^{m} w_i \frac{\dot{Y}_i}{Y_i} - \sum_{j=1}^{n} v_j \frac{\dot{X}_j}{X_j} \tag{2.38}$$

where w_i is the share of the i output in the national expenditure
and v_j is the share of the j input in national income.

The Jorgenson-Griliches approach differs from Denison in the
methods of handling the data and in perception of where adjustments
are needed, particularly in evaluating the contribution of the capital input. In using (2.38) to estimate technical change, they argue that it is necessary to distinguish between stocks and flows
and between stock prices and flow prices. They allege that capital
services, not capital stock, should enter the production function.
They adjust capital inputs for qualitative improvements and for

changes in the rates of capacity utilization, using the flow price
of capital services instead of the asset price of the capital
stock. They also correct for several other alleged errors in the
measurement of output and inputs. By all these adjustments they
reduce the residual or the increase in total factor productivity
almost to the vanishing point. Specifically, of the 3.59 percent
growth of output during 1941-1965, 3.47 percent can be explained by
growth of input, and only 0.10 percent (3 percent of the total) remains to be explained by technical change. The conclusion reached
by Jorgenson and Griliches was amended by Christensen and Jorgenson
(1969). Their results show that total factor productivity has
grown between 1948 and 1967 at an annual rate of about 0.31 percent
instead of the 0.10 percent reported by Jorgenson and Griliches.

There has been some attempt in the sources-of-growth analysis
to fit disequilibrium situations. In standard growth accounting,
wages are always equal to the marginal productivity of labor, i.e.,
$W = \partial Y/\partial L$. Upon his observation that wage and employment data from
Israel seem to be related linearly when plotted on a scatter diagram, Michael Bruno (1968) postulates that the relationship representing the demand for labor is

$$\partial Y/\partial L = b_0 + b_1 W \qquad (2.39)$$

instead of $\partial Y/\partial L = W$, which holds under perfect competitive equilibrium. Bruno's testing of (2.39) with the Israel data shows that
b_0 is negative, while b_1 is approximately unity. This result implies that in the real world the marginal product of labor is less
than the wage, while the marginal product of capital exceeds its
costs. Therefore, the growth accounting based on true marginal
products of inputs after adjusting the distortions in disequilibrium shows a substantial increase in contribution to growth by capital accumulation.

One interesting result is that the values of the residual as a
percentage of growth of national income are much smaller in developing countries (12-17 percent) than in advanced industrial countries (40-73 percent). This suggests that in developing countries
growth is much more dependent on the supply of inputs than in the
advanced countries (see Sherman Robinson 1971).

Despite the development of new theoretical models and the
availability of new and better data and estimation techniques, the
results in growth accounting studies do not lead to definite conclusions. Some recent studies make the case more confusing instead
of clarifying the whole matter. Some others like T. K. Rymes
(1972) claim that the whole problem is misconceived because capital
cannot be measured in real terms. According to S. Star (1974), the
attribution of technical change as an explanation of economic
growth is nothing but a failure on the part of economists to specify factors involved completely. Still others revise the definition
of technical change (Hulten 1975). In a new study incorporating
the broadest definition of income and capital, Kendrick (1976)
finds that a large part of observed economic growth is explained by

capital formation, but the residual cannot be eliminated altogether.

While the sources-of-growth literature has improved our conception of the production function and provides a useful first approximation of factors accounting for growth, efforts in growth accounting are bound to involve great uncertainties in view of measurement problems with respect to each input, misspecification or errors in estimating the parameters, and ambiguities resulting from the interdependencies among the identified factors. The role to be played by growth accounting in our furtherance of growth theory is well summarized by Richard Nelson (1973, p. 466) as follows:

> The principal purpose of growth accounting has been, and still is, the estimation of various magnitudes which our growth theory suggests are important, testing various propositions or alternative specifications of that theory, and illuminating better the phenomena that a growth theory must explain. Growth accounting is a complement to more traditional (regression) techniques of estimating and testing growth theory. . . . But some of the recent studies seem to imply that somehow the growth accounts really explain growth. I do not see how they can. A growth accounting is not a tested theory of growth.

Decomposing total factor productivity into various components is not the same as explaining it. The growth accounting technique is only the first stage toward the analysis of more ultimate causes. It is not enough to point out that the countries that have shown the highest growth rates have been those in which a certain factor turned out to have had a dominant role. The reasons why such a factor could play a dominant role in a certain country at a certain time, and the kind of causal relationship that links that factor to the growth rate, remain unknown. Instead of demonstrating a relationship, authors of growth accounting assume one. The sources-of-growth approach is very useful as a starting point; at some stage, however, it becomes necessary to consider causal factors of growth in practice.

CONCLUSIONS

We have discussed the achievements of the main lines of approach to economic growth, including their limitations and inadequacies. Perhaps it may be useful at this point to say something about what our survey has not included and what will not be included in the coming chapters. Marx's and Schumpeter's theories of economic growth are not discussed for the reasons indicated previously. Like other areas of economics, the field of economic growth can be subdivided into the positive and the normative branches. The theory of optimal growth examining the question of how the world should grow is not included in our discussion because we are primarily concerned with the positive theory of economic growth. Even two-sector models of economic growth, to say nothing of von

Neumann's multisector model of an expanding economy, have received
no attention. Despite the impressive literature, no consideration
has been given to the role of money in the context of economic
growth. The omission of these topics and many others arises from
the fact that they do not answer the questions being asked in this
study, the major one being, Why are some countries or regions growing faster than others?

With 200 years of cumulative theorizing and research, modern
growth theory has come of age. The major growth models we discussed above have great analytical power and considerable interest
for theoretical investigation of the growth process. In the early
stage of economic growth theory, it was quite sufficient to work
with rough aggregates and to show what the logical connections between them have to be if uninterrupted full employment is to be established in a simple model of a competitive capitalist economy.
Later, attempts were made to incorporate more economic variables
using advanced analytical tools, sometimes unnecessarily too sophisticated techniques. Intellectual fascination and curiosity
have led many economists to build highly abstract models based on
certain assumptions. Different contributors to the theory of
growth have differed a great deal in their views about the aims of
their exercise. This makes for difficulty in drawing conclusions
about how far their aims have been realized and in making a meaningful comparison among different models of growth. It is, however, clear that later refined models of growth have not proven as
successful in achieving their purpose as might have been hoped
when the first such models came to be constructed.

It is generally agreed that for all the investment in time and
energy that has gone into their construction, models of economic
growth are not currently sufficiently developed to illuminate many
important problems relating to real-world economic growth. Why is
it that economic science appears of such limited relevance in explaining economic growth of the real economy? Answers to this
question seem to lie in both endogenous and exogenous factors to
the discipline. On one hand, economists face many difficulties
and great complexities arising out of the rapid changes in the phenomenon they are trying to understand, theorize, and predict. On
the other hand, they are perhaps indulging in the narcissistic con-
templation of the beauties of their 200-year-old science. They enjoy constructing sophisticated and elegant models that have great
aesthetic appeal but have been built based on excessively unrealistic postulates and assumptions. Serious handicaps involved in developing a realistic growth theory are well summarized by Amartya
Sen (1970, p. 3) when he says:

> It is partly a measure of the complexity of economic growth
> that the phenomenon of growth should remain, after three dec-
> ades of intensive intellectual study, such an enigma. It is,
> however, also a reflection on our sense of values, particular-
> ly of the preoccupation with braintwisters. Part of the dif-
> ficulty arises undoubtedly from the fact that the selection of

topics for work in growth economics is guided much more by
logical curiosity than by a taste for relevance.

To be fair, it must also be pointed out that increasing pessi-
mism about the value of a whole range of growth models and the debate between opposing schools of thought should not bar us from realizing that it is these unrealistic models and controversies that
illuminate many important interrelationships in the process of economic growth, lead to a sharpening of theoretical concepts, and
provide insights into the problem of economic growth.

Given the meager, unsatisfactory results of the attempts to
build general growth models, several economists in recent years
have drawn attention to particular variables and have offered specific hypotheses or arguments to explain the differences in the
growth performance among countries. They emphasize one or more
specific factors as exerting the most influence in the growth process, thereby resulting in different growth performance among countries or regions.

REFERENCES

Abramovitz, M. 1956. Resources and output trends in the United
      States since 1870. *Am. Econ. Rev.* 46:5-23.
Atkinson, A. B. 1969. The timescale of economic models: How long
      is the long run? *Rev. Econ. Stud.* 36:137-52.
Baumol, W. J. 1970. *Economic Dynamics.* New York: Macmillan.
Brems, H. 1973. *Capital, Labor and Growth.* Lexington, Mass.:
      D. C. Heath.
Bruno, M. 1968. Estimation of factor contribution to growth under
      structural disequilibrium. *Int. Econ. Rev.* 3:42-62.
Christensen, L. R., and D. W. Jorgenson. 1969. The measurement of
      U.S. real capital input, 1929-1967. *Rev. Income Wealth* 15:
      293-320.
Cuyvers, L. 1979. Joan Robinson's theory of economic growth.
      Sci. Soc. 43:326-48.
Deane, P. 1978. *The Evolution of Economic Ideas.* Cambridge:
      Cambridge University Press.
Denison, E. F. 1962. *The Sources of Economic Growth in the
      United States and the Alternatives before Us.* New York: Com-
      mittee for Economic Development.
————. 1967. *Why Growth Rates Differ: Post-War Experience in
      Nine Western Countries.* Washington, D.C.: Brookings Institu-
      tion.
————. 1969. Some major issues in productivity analysis: An ex-
      amination of estimates by Jorgenson and Griliches. *Surv.
      Curr. Bus.* 49(pt. 5):1-28.
Denison, E. F., and W. K. Chung. 1976. *How Japan's Economy Grew
      So Fast: The Sources of Postwar Expansion.* Washington, D.C.:
      Brookings Institution.

Domar, E. D. 1946. Capital expansion, rate of growth and employment. *Econometrica* 14:137-47.

―――. 1947. Expansion and employment. *Am. Econ. Rev.* 37:34-55.

―――. 1957. *Essays in the Theory of Economic Growth.* New York: Oxford University Press.

Eltis, W. A. 1975. Adam Smith's theory of economic growth. In *Essays on Adam Smith,* ed. A. Skinner and T. Wilson. Oxford: Clarendon.

Harris, D. J. 1975. The theory of economic growth: A critique and reformulation. *Am. Econ. Rev.* 65:329-37.

―――. 1978. *Capital Accumulation and Income Distribution.* Stanford: Stanford University Press.

Harrod, R. F. 1939. An essay in dynamic theory. *Econ. J.* 49:14-33.

―――. 1948. *Towards a Dynamic Economics.* London: Macmillan.

―――. 1963. Themes in dynamic theory. *Econ. J.* 73:401-21.

―――. 1974. Pure theory of growth economics. *Z. Nationaloekon.* 34:241-47.

Hicks, J. R. 1965. *Capital and Growth.* London: Oxford University Press.

―――. 1966. Growth and anti-growth. *Oxf. Econ. Pap.* 18:260.

Higgins, B. 1968. *Economic Development.* New York: W. W. Norton.

Hogan, W. P. 1958. Technical progress and production function. *Rev. Econ. Stat.* 40:407-11.

Hulten, C. R. 1975. Technical productivity and the reproducibility of capital. *Am. Econ. Rev.* 65:956-65.

Jones, H. G. 1976. *An Introduction to Modern Theories of Economic Growth.* New York: McGraw-Hill.

Jorgenson, D. W., and Z. Griliches. 1967. The explanation of productivity change. *Rev. Econ. Stud.* 34:249-84.

―――. 1972. Issues in growth accounting: A reply to Denison. *Surv. Curr. Bus.* 52(pt. 2):65-94.

Kaldor, N. 1956. Alternative theories of distribution. *Rev. Econ. Stud.* 24(2):83-100.

―――. 1957. A model of economic growth. *Econ. J.* 67:591-624.

―――. 1959. Economic growth and the problem of inflation. *Economica* 26:212-26, 287-98.

―――. 1961. Capital accumulation and economic growth. In *The Theory of Capital,* ed. F. A. Lutz and D. C. Hague. London: Macmillan.

Kaldor, N., and J. A. Mirrlees. 1962. A new model of economic growth. *Rev. Econ. Stud.* 29:174-92.

Kendrick, J. W. 1961. *Productivity Trends in the United States.* Princeton: Princeton University Press.

―――. 1976. *The Formation and Stocks of Total Capital.* New York: National Bureau of Economic Research.

Keynes, J. M. 1936. *The General Theory of Employment, Interest and Money.* New York: Harcourt, Brace and World.

Kregel, J. A. 1972. *The Theory of Economic Growth.* London: Macmillan.

————. 1973. *The Reconstruction of Political Economy*. New York: Halsted.
Kuznets, S. 1952. Comment to Abramovitz, economic growth. In *A Survey of Contemporary Economics*, vol. 2, ed. B. F. Hailey, pp. 178–80. Homewood, Ill.: Irwin.
————. 1971. *Economic Growth of Nations*. Cambridge: Harvard University Press.
Lowe, A. 1954. The classical theory of economic growth. *Soc. Res.* 21:127–58.
————. 1975. Adam Smith's system of equilibrium growth. In *Essays on Adam Smith*, ed. A. Skinner and T. Wilson. Oxford: Clarendon.
Lutz, F. A., and D. C. Hague, eds. 1961. *The Theory of Capital*. London: Macmillan.
Meade, J. E. 1961. *A Neoclassical Theory of Economic Growth*. New York: Oxford University Press.
Nelson, R. R. 1973. Recent exercises in growth accounting: New understanding or dead end? *Am. Econ. Rev.* 63:462–68.
Nelson, R. R., and S. G. Winter. 1974. Neoclassical vs. evolutionary theories of economic growth: Critique and prospectus. *Econ. J.* 84:887–905.
O'Brien, D. P. 1975. *The Classical Economists*. Oxford: Clarendon.
Pivilin, H. 1953. A geometric analysis of recent growth models. *Am. Econ. Rev.* 42:594–99.
Richardson, H. W. 1973. *Regional Growth Theory*. London: Macmillan.
Robinson, J. 1953–1954. The production function and the theory of capital. *Rev. Econ. Stud.* 21(55):81–106.
————. 1962. *Essays in the Theory of Economic Growth*. London: Macmillan.
————. 1966. *The Accumulation of Capital*. London: Macmillan.
————. 1970. Harrod after twenty-one years. *Econ. J.* 80:731–36.
————. 1971. *Economic Heresies: Some Old-Fashioned Questions in Economic Theory*. New York: Basic Books.
Robinson, S. 1971. Sources of growth in less developed countries: A cross-section study. *Q. J. Econ.* 85:391–408.
Rymes, T. K. 1972. The measurement of capital and total factor productivity in the context of Cambridge theory of capital. *Rev. Income Wealth* 18:69–109.
Schumpeter, J. A. 1954. *History of Economic Analysis*. New York: Oxford University Press.
Sen, A. K., ed. 1970. *Growth Economics*. Baltimore: Penguin.
Smith, A. 1937. *An Inquiry into the Nature and Causes of the Wealth of Nations*. New York: Random House. (All references are made from the 1937 Modern Library edition, edited by Edwin Cannan.)
Solow, R. M. 1956. A contribution to the theory of economic growth. *Q. J. Econ.* 70:65–94.
————. 1957. Technical change and the aggregate production function. *Rev. Econ. Stat.* 39:312–20.

————. 1962. Technical progress, capital formation, and economic growth. *Am. Econ. Rev.* 52:76–86.

Star, S. 1974. Accounting for the growth of output. *Am. Econ. Rev.* 64:123–35.

Stiglitz, J. E., and H. Uzawa. 1969. *Readings in the Modern Theory of Economic Growth.* Cambridge: MIT Press.

Swan, T. W. 1956. Economic growth and capital accumulation. *Econ. Rec.* 32:334–61.

Vaciago, G. 1970. Alternative theories of growth in the Italian case. *Banca Naz. Lororo Q. Rev.*, June:180–211.

Wan, H. Y., Jr. 1971. *Economic Growth.* New York: Harcourt, Brace, Jovanovich.

3

Technological Change, Catch-up, and Economic Growth

During the past two centuries technological change has brought immense changes in the world, raising the standard of living and improving the quality of goods consumed. Technological change encompasses a highly complex and wide-ranging collection of human activities. Furthermore, not only does technology change over time, but numerous technologies coexist in a society at any moment. Despite various attempts in past decades to fully understand the complexities of technology, its interrelations with other components of the social system, and its social and economic consequences, much remains to be learned.

Even though little is known authoritatively about the role of technology and its change in the economy, one of the generally accepted beliefs or stylized facts is that technological change is the major source of growth of per capita income. We saw in Chapter 2 that sources-of-growth studies have usually concluded that the increase of aggregate inputs is able to explain only a small portion of the measured growth of output and that the bulk of that growth has to be explained by "residual" factors. Empirical studies have nominated many candidates to explain the residual in economic growth, i.e., that part of growth not accounted for by increases in the more traditional factor inputs. Early empirical works frequently assigned the residual to technical change by default. Later, as data and estimating procedures improved, other explanations were offered, such as economies of scale, improved resource allocation, structural change in production, and the degree of capacity utilization.

The growing body of research findings on productivity and sources of economic growth indicates the importance of technological change, though it is not the sole nonfactor input explanation of growth. What has puzzled many people is that in spite of the apparently greater capacity of the United States to innovate, the rate of growth in output is lower than in other industrialized countries. Despite higher research and development expenditures in

the United States than in other countries and U.S. technological
superiority in almost all (though not all) areas, the contribution
of technological progress to growth has not been higher in the
United States than in other advanced countries. This has led to an
increased effort to search for an answer to the puzzle.

Recent thinking of economists studying economic growth in developed countries suggests that since World War II, international
"technology gaps" have tended to even out through the migration of
knowledge, the activities of multinational companies, increasing
trade, and similar forces. So, it is expected that a country's
growth rate will tend to be faster the further it is behind. This
catching-up, later comer, or convergence hypothesis implies that
some countries--Germany, France, Italy, and Japan--have experienced
strong growth during the postwar period mainly because their economies grew so slowly or they had the opportunity to absorb a considerable amount of more advanced technology from the United States.

TECHNOLOGY, TECHNOLOGICAL CHANGE, AND ECONOMIC GROWTH

Technology and technological change are loose terms not clearly defined. The general discussion of these concepts is saddled
with a number of different meanings that have been attached to
them, and associated terms such as innovation, invention, or technical progress are confusedly intermingled in their usage. Thus
Jacob Schmookler (1966, p. 3) commented that "technological change
is the 'terra icognita' of modern economics. . . . We do not even
have an agreed upon set of terms."

Definition of technology varies with authors depending on the
purpose at hand. Schmookler (1966, p. 1) defines technology as
the "social pool of knowledge of industrial arts." According to
Edwin Mansfield (1980, p. 564), technology is made up of "knowledge
concerning physical and social phenomena, knowledge regarding the
application of basic principles to work in the relevant fields or
professions, and knowledge of the rules of thumb of practitioners
and craftsmen." To quote Nathan Rosenberg (1972, p. 18), technology refers to "man's capacity to control and to manipulate the natural environment in the fulfillment of human goals, and to make
the environment more responsive to human needs." In the definitions above and elsewhere, technology is a type of knowledge, the
know-how necessary for the creation of goods and services demanded
by economic society. Though there is no agreement on exactly what
types of knowledge are to be included under the rubric of technology, all economic knowledge should be included in the conception of
technology to encompass not only purely technical know-how, which
leads to new products and better processes, but also the know-how
associated with managerial practices in marketing, finance, and organization.

For our purpose we may define technology as the technically
feasible limits that allow a certain level of output for a given
level of the inputs. As the store of technical knowledge applied
to production advances, so do these limits. So our economic con-

cept of technological change is simply the notion that more output
can be produced, given the same quantities of the inputs.

Much of the early literature on the sources of shifts in the
production function distinguishes between technological and technical progress or advance. The former refers to the discovery of new
techniques, product design, or ideas (i.e., inventions) that have a
potential commercial value. The latter refers to the commercial
application of the invention in production. The notions "know why"
versus "know how" and invention versus innovation are often used to
capture the thrust of the distinction (see Kennedy 1971, p. 175).
The innovation (or technical change) stage occurs when the invention is first commercially introduced by a firm. But as the new
process or new product is recognized as superior to competing existing technologies, this results in its further application. In
this last stage, diffusion of the innovations occurs. So technological change in the industrial context can be conceived as comprising three more or less distinct stages--invention, innovation,
and diffusion. While this three-way distinction is not precise all
the time and can sometimes be misleading, it does provide a con-
ceptually useful framework in which the study of technology and
its impact on economic growth can operate. (The three-way distinction is due mainly to Joseph A. Schumpeter [1939, 1942], who was
primarily concerned with the effect of the introduction of new
technology upon the business cycle.)

In sum, maximum or potential output of an economy at some
point in time is a function of the state of knowledge. While inventive and innovative activities influence the "best-practice"
productive levels within an economy, diffusion is necessary if they
are to be translated into achieved productivity levels. In the
following discussion we use the terms technological change and
technical change interchangeably to represent changes in technology
resulting from a combination of research, invention, development,
and innovation. The spread of technology depends on its rate of
adoption and diffusion.

The interest of economists in technological progress or advance stems from the study of the process of economic growth. Most
economists would certainly agree that technological change is an
important source of economic growth. For example, Simon Kuznets
(1966, pp. 8-16) judges that the most distinctive driving force of
modern economic growth, what he calls the "epochal innovation," is
the extended application of science to the problems of economic
production or the emergence of modern science as the basis of an
advancing technology. Kuznets claims that since the second half of
the nineteenth century the major source of economic growth in the
developed countries has been science-based technology.

Before we examine the magnitude of contribution by technical
change to economic growth with available data, the importance of
technical progress in the long-run economic process can be shown
with the aid of the conventional production function:

$$Y = f(K, L; T) \qquad\qquad (3.1)$$

where Y, K, L, and T stand for output, capital, labor, and technology respectively. Assuming that the production function is subject to constant returns to scale, we obtain standard growth equation:

$$g_Y = \Pi g_K + (1 - \Pi)g_L + \lambda \tag{3.2}$$

where g_Y, g_K, and g_L are the growth rates of output, capital, and
labor respectively; Π is the elasticity of output with respect to
capital; and $\lambda = (\partial f/\partial T)(1/Y)$ is the productivity residual. Let c
$= K/Y$. Then,

$$g_c = g_K - g_Y \tag{3.3}$$

When (3.2) is rearranged to read

$$g_Y = \frac{\Pi}{1 - \Pi}(g_K - g_Y) + g_L + \frac{1}{1 - \Pi} \lambda \tag{3.4}$$

and (3.3) is substituted into (3.4) we obtain

$$g_Y = \gamma g_c + g_L + \alpha \quad \text{or} \quad g_Y - g_L = \gamma g_c + \alpha \tag{3.5}$$

where $\gamma = \Pi/(1 - \Pi)$ and $\alpha = 1/(1 - \Pi)\lambda$. Under the assumption of
constant or stable capital output ratio, $g_c = 0$. Hence it follows
that

$$g_Y = g_L + \alpha \quad \text{or} \quad g_Y - g_L = \alpha \tag{3.6}$$

From (3.6) it follows that the growth rate of labor productivity is
equal to the long-run rate of technical change. Recall that in the
neoclassical steady states (as examined in Chap. 2), output grows
at the same rate as the labor force, so the productivity of labor
is constant. To explain steady growth with rising per capita income, the neoclassical model has to introduce technical progress.

The growing interest in the role of technological change as a
contributor to economic growth has led to a considerable amount of
empirical research on technical change, roughly divided into two
areas: macroeconomic and microeconomic. The former attempts to
quantify the contribution of technological change to the growth in
long-term productivity; the latter examines the causes of the expansion of technical possibilities and studies the rate at which
new inventions, once made, were diffused throughout the economy or
a given industry. Micro studies are scarce compared with macro
studies mainly because micro studies have to be based upon company
data, which are always difficult to come by, with the further im-
pediment that any results must usually be published in such a way
that information about individual companies is not disclosed.
Those studies that do exist attempt, among other things, to relate
the interfirm rate of diffusion of a particular innovation to its
profitability, defined in terms of opportunity cost (Griliches
1957), and to specific economic or managerial variables such as

size of firm, market structure, or the ages of managers (Mansfield 1968a,b).

Empirical studies concerning technological change on the macro level have attempted to answer many interesting questions such as: Has technological change accelerated? How important is technical change in the process of economic growth? Is technological advance capital saving, neutral, or labor saving? Is technological progress embodied in new physical capital? In the following discussion we take up the first two questions, in turn.

The pace of technological progress related to the rate of advance of best-practice technology is not measurable directly. Perhaps the most frequently used procedure for identifying the growth component attributable to technological change and testing the hypothesis that technological change has accelerated is known as the method of residual. In view of the productivities of the physical inputs in some base period, we estimate the hypothetical increase of output that would have taken place since the base period if, given the level of technological knowledge of the period, the increase of output had been brought about merely by the growth of the quantity of physical inputs. The difference between the output actually observed and the so calculated hypothetical growth is then regarded as the result of productivity gains in the nature of technological and organization progress.

Though the United States is not the source of all technological progress, the trend in technological progress in the United States, as represented by the growth rate in total factor productivity or advances in knowledge, shows the opportunity for progress that is presented by the enlargement in technological and organization knowledge that has taken place over a long period. Crude indicators of technical changes are presented in Tables 3.1 and 3.2. The United States has been chosen to discuss the more rapid technological advance in this century than in the previous century and in years since World War II than in the previous years because "it seems unlikely that in the U.S. economy . . . the rate at which advances were incorporated departed much from the worldwide rate of new advances" (Denison and Chung 1976, p. 79).

As shown in Table 3.1 for successive subperiods since 1800, the rate of total factor productivity advances accelerated from an average of 0.3 percent a year during most of the nineteenth century to 1.7 percent between 1889 and 1919, 2.2 percent between 1919 and 1948, and 2.4 percent during the quarter century 1948–1973. A sim-

Table 3.1. U.S. growth rates of real gross product, real product per capita, and total factor productivity, 1800–1973

	Real gross product	Real product per capita	Total factor productivity
1800–1855	4.2	1.1	0.3
1855–1890	4.0	1.6	0.3
1889–1919	3.9	2.1	1.7
1919–1948	3.0	1.8	2.2
1948–1973	3.8	2.3	2.4

Source: Kendrick 1979, p. 23.

Table 3.2.   U.S. growth rates of total
factor productivity and advances in
knowledge

	Total factor productivity	Advances in knowledge
1902-1929	0.82	0.15
1929-1948	1.26	0.62
1948-1969	1.75	1.19

Sources: Denison 1962, 1974, p. 127.

ilar trend is found in Denison's growth accounting, as shown in Table 3.2. The growth rate of total factor productivity was 1.75 percent per year from 1948 to 1969 compared to 1.26 and 0.82 percent during the periods 1929-1948 and 1902-1929 respectively. The rate of 1.19 percent in advances in knowledge in 1948-1969 was almost double the rate of 0.62 percent in 1929-1948. The fact that the pace of technical progress in the recent period was more rapid than earlier is also found in the observations that there has been a speedup in the pace of scientific progress, levels of education are higher, more scientists and engineers are engaged in basic research and its application, and science-based industry has become more important.

Empirical evidence presented by a number of economists indicates that, apart from short-run fluctuations, by far the largest part of changes in productivity over time has been the result of technical progress. It would be useful to have the conventional facts of economic growth before us to learn something about the role of technical progress. Table 3.3 shows estimates of growth in total output and factor productivity assembled from various sources from which the relative importance of technological change as a source of growth can be delineated. A note of caution is in order: the data used to calculate total factor productivity are often subject to errors that are often believed to tend to overestimate the quantitative importance of total factor productivity growth. The definitions of output and inputs are seldom comparable, particularly among different authors. Thus international comparisons of total factor productivity should be made with considerable caution and the results obtained should be used as only rough measures.

It is important to bear in mind that serious difficulties associated with measurement of the contribution of technical change to economic growth by the residual method are avoided by inevitable but arbitrary assumptions. It is usually assumed that technical change is exogenous and neutral. One important point that has not received explicit mention is that the parameters of the ex ante production function cannot as a rule be identified on the basis of expost observations. A production function, postulated on the basis of expost observations of the production and the factors of production, should be carefully distinguished from the ex ante production function introduced into the theory for characterizing the technical possibilities, since the expost relationship depends also on some noneconomic factors.

Despite the problems associated with measurement, what is

Table 3.3. Comparative growth in total output (TO) and total factor productivity (TFP)

Country		Tinbergen 1870–1914	Domar 1948–1960	Barger 1950–1964	Denison 1950–1962	Kuznets 1913–1966	Christensen 1947–1960	Christensen 1960–1973
Belgium	TO				3.03			
	TFP				1.86			
Canada	TO		4.0		4.95	3.89[d]	5.2	5.1
	TFP		1.2		1.96	2.68[d]	1.7	1.8
Denmark	TO			3.97	3.63			
	TFP			1.62	2.08			
France	TO	1.9		4.58	4.70	2.33[e]	4.9[i]	5.9
	TFP	1.1		2.90	3.46	2.15[e]	2.9[i]	3.0
Germany	TO	3.4	7.2	6.90	6.27		8.2[i]	5.4
	TFP	1.5	3.6	3.46	3.49		4.7[i]	3.0
Italy	TO			6.32	5.60		6.0[j]	4.8
	TFP			4.01	3.94		3.8[j]	3.1
Japan	TO		8.5		8.81[b]		8.1[j]	10.9
	TFP		3.7		4.86[b]		3.4[j]	4.5
Netherlands	TO			4.86	4.07		5.0[k]	5.6
	TFP			3.20	2.16		2.3[k]	2.6
Norway	TO			3.83	3.43	2.80[f]		
	TFP			1.46	2.39	2.07[f]		
Sweden	TO			3.85				
	TFP			1.68				
United Kingdom	TO	1.6	2.4	2.72	2.38	1.93[g]	3.3[l]	3.8
	TFP	0.3	0.6	1.20	1.27	0.83[g]	1.5[l]	2.1
United States	TO	4.1	3.0	3.15[a]	4.00[c]	2.95[h]	3.7	4.3
	TFP	1.1	1.4	1.42[a]	1.91[c]	2.30[h]	1.4	1.3

Sources: Tinbergen 1959, p. 217; Domar et al. 1964, pp. 34, 39; Barger 1969, pp. 144, 146; Kuznets 1971, p. 74; Denison and Chung 1976, pp. 42–43; Christensen et al. 1980, p. 632.

[a]Private economy only   [g]Data for 1925–1963
[b]Data for 1953–1971   [h]Data for 1929–1957
[c]Data for 1948–1969   [i]Data for 1950–1960
[d]Data for 1926–1956   [j]Data for 1952–1960
[e]Data for 1913–1966   [k]Data for 1951–1960
[f]Data for 1899–1956   [l]Data for 1955–1960

brought out clearly in Table 3.3 is the importance of the total factor productivity growth in the growth rates of the advanced countries. Its contribution to total output growth was on average more than 50 percent, with two endpoint extremes being 19 percent (0.3 out of 1.6 percent) in the United Kingdom during 1870–1914 and 92 percent (2.15 out of 2.33 percent) in France during 1913–1966. With the exception of 9 out of 50 cases, total factor productivity growth accounted for more than 40 percent of the output growth rates in all countries for all periods examined. It is more important in its absolute magnitude in Japan, though not in its relative contribution. It is also noted that generally the growth rates of total factor productivity and total output are positively related.

Because of the complex interactions among the various factors on which the economic growth of a country depends, it is difficult to estimate from historical statistics the precise effect of a nation's rate of technological change on its rate of economic growth. Macro studies of technical progress that seek to estimate the rate of technical progress as a residual component of the growth of output almost invariably find that technical progress is the prime determinant of economic growth and has accelerated in recent periods, particularly since World War II. Even though the precise character of technical change associated with economic growth remains a "measure of our ignorance," it can be fairly unambiguously concluded that the association between technology and growth is indeed strong.

Saying that, as a measured source of growth, technological change estimated in terms of total factor productivity is a major source of the country's economic growth is not really explaining economic growth, because measuring sources of growth is not equivalent to explaining why this source or that grows most rapidly. The establishment of the quantitative importance of the residual throws crucial light on where to look for such an explanation. One of the various explanations of the residual recasts the residual rate of growth measured in terms of the hypothesis that some appreciable part of the residual can be explained by international transfer of technology.

CATCH-UP HYPOTHESIS

Theoretical Framework

Several economists have pointed out that the diffusion of technological knowledge resulting from relative technological backwardness could serve as an explanation for differential rates of economic growth. They assume that advanced industrial countries are sufficiently homogeneous for transfer and diffusion of knowledge to be a significant part of technological progress. The technologically less advanced countries will benefit from this and it will enable them to experience higher growth rates than the technological leader. These economists have assumed that technological lead and lag of an economy can be measured, as a proxy measure, by per capita income or relative per capita income. They generally hypothesize a significant negative correlation between the technology level of an economy, as measured by per capita income, and growth rate of the economy's overall productivity in a sector, usually manufacturing.

The process of the catch-up phenomenon will be better understood by distinguishing between two sources of the potential for productivity growth: those governing the potential for productivity growth and those controlling the pace at which the potential is exploited. (This distinction is credited to Moses Abramovitz 1979.) Productivity growth arises from rapid contemporaneous advances in technology resulting from the enlargement in technological and organizational frontiers that takes place during a period. The opportunity for productivity growth also exists when a country finds itself behind the technological leader in its level of achieved productivity and tries to narrow the gap between its level of technology and that of the leader.

Of the above two sources of the potential for productivity growth, the first--technological progress represented by the expan-

sion of the technological limits--helps to explain more rapid postwar productivity growth than before in almost all countries. The
second--the notion of a technological gap--has been employed to explain the fact that despite the leading role of the United States
in advancing technological frontiers through the expansion of research and development, Western European countries and Japan have
experienced much higher rates of economic growth.

Why and how is the existence of a technology gap among countries conducive to more rapid rates of growth in the technically
backward countries? What is generally argued is that productivity
growth will be higher if it is possible to borrow technology, because the elasticity of supply of inventions and innovations is
greater for imitators than for leaders. Productivity growth will
be higher for follower countries because knowledge is expensive to
produce but cheap to reproduce, and imitators will have greater
flexibility in their choice of technologies, other things being
equal. The advantage of borrowing technology by late starters can
be more rigorously formulated in the following way.

Suppose that the whole world consists of only two countries, A
and B. Both countries have already reached a certain level of economic development, in particular, a certain level of knowledge and
technology, which we will designate cardinal number T. Now let us
assume that country A is more advanced in technology than country
B, i.e., $T_A > T_B$. For country A, which as the world leader of
technology had exploited all profitable knowledge and technology at
the end of the last year, the rate of growth of total factor productivity would be constrained this year by $\alpha_A = dT_A/dt$, or the
rate of technical progress generated by its own research and development sector and/or through the process of learning by doing of
the working population.

Country B, which is backward in technology and did not catch
up completely at the end of last year, will be using technology,
some (or all) of which is inferior to the best technology attaina-
ble by country A. We can denote the lag in technology between
countries A and B by L, and it can be measured as $L = T_A - T_B$.
With the heroic assumptions of perfectly elastic world supply of
credit for any one country, and no social, cultural, institutional,
or political barriers preventing the flow of technology, the rate
of growth of total factor productivity in follower country B would
be $\alpha_B = L + \alpha_A$. For follower country B, the potential of technological progress is different from that of lead country A. Country
B does not have to break new ground. It will imitate rather than
innovate. It may not face the risks and problems faced by country
A. Furthermore, provided that patterns of industrialization are
such that countries go through a similar hierarchy of goods and
services, the follower will have a desire to borrow technology developed abroad.

The catch-up hypothesis emphasizes the technological gap between the lead country and the follower country and the diffusion
of technology from the former to the latter. A country's growth
rate will tend to be faster the further it is behind. Some coun-

tries--Germany, France, Italy, and Japan--have experienced strong
growth during the postwar period mainly because their economies
were behind in technology and they had the opportunity to absorb a
considerable amount of advanced technology from the United States.
As far as the lead country, the United States, is concerned, the
potential for productivity increase is constrained by its best
practical technology, which advances slowly. In the technologically leading country the pace of technical progress will be determined primarily by the research and development sector.

The early ideas of the catch-up hypothesis are found in the
writings of Thorstein Veblen and Alexander Gerschenkron. Veblen
(1915) explains why and how Germany, with its dynastic political
organization, made such rapid strides in machine technology as to
outstrip England, from where the modern industrial process emanat-
ed. German success lay in the fact that Germany avoided the "pen-
alty of taking the lead" in modern industry by virtue of its more
recent entrance among the great powers. Veblen, however, maintains
that Germany would in the long run come to behave more like England
as its industrial plants aged, standards of conspicuous waste rose,
and the cultural conditioning of modern machine technology had sufficient time to penetrate the German culture.

In dealing with problems of European industrial development in
the nineteenth century, Gerschenkron (1962, pp. 1, 44) put out the
general hypothesis that "very significant interspatial variations
in the process of industrialization are functionally related, to
the degree of backwardness that prevailed in the countries concerned on the eve of their 'great spurts' of industrial growth."
In Gerschenkron's view, the industrial history of Europe is not a
series of mere repetitions of industrialization but an orderly system of graduated deviations from industrialization because "the
more delayed the industrial development of a country, the more ex-
plosive was the great spurt of its industrialization, if and when
it came. Moreover, the higher degree of backwardness was associated with a stronger tendency toward larger scale of plant and enterprise and greater readiness to enter into monopolistic compacts
of various degrees of intensity. Finally, the more backward a
country, the more likely its industrialization was to proceed under
some organized direction." This statement was first made in 1957.

One of the most extensive treatments of the catch-up hypothesis is by Stanislaw Gomulka (1971, 1979), who in a study on the nature of inventive activity and diffusion of knowledge argues that
international differences in productivity growth can best be understood by starting from the notion of technological gap. He provides both rigorous theoretical arguments and empirical evidence to
suggest that the diffusion of technology from advanced to backward
countries is an important determinant of technical progress, which
in turn generates a concomitant increase in productivity.

Gomulka distinguishes five ways in which the technology level
of an economy can be raised. Two are by innovations produced do-
mestically by a country's own efforts and the other three are by
transfer of knowledge and technical innovations from abroad. The

increase in the technological level from internal sources is obtained either by applying labor and capital resources in a special sector that Gomulka calls the technological sector (research and development sector) (α_1) or through "learning by doing" by workers engaged in day-to-day activities (α_2). Transfer of knowledge and innovations from abroad to a given country occurs through three channels: diffusion associated with aimed import of licenses and patents (α_3), natural diffusion resulting from free exchange of scientific and technical information between countries (α_4), and embodied diffusion forced by imports of capital and intermediate goods (α_5).

According to Gomulka's scheme of five agents, the growth rate of technological change for a given economy will be the sum of each agent's contribution

$$\alpha = \sum_{i=1}^{5} e_i \alpha_i \tag{3.7}$$

where e_i is the share of ith agent's contribution to the total stock of accumulated technology. Though all five agents are contributing to the total, the relative importance of each agent usually varies in different economies at different stages of development. In the technologically leading country the rate of labor productivity is equal to the rate of progress generated by the technological sector, as in such an economy all other sources of technological changes are insignificant. Innovations of the learning-by-doing kind are by-products of the production process itself. This carrier of labor productivity growth is the principal one in the early state of development where international transfer of technology is low and the domestic technological sector is in its embryo. Two domestic sources of technological advance challenge the view that technical and technological progress are the result of manna from heaven and instead stress their endogenous character.

Foreign technology or innovations can be obtained by paying for licenses and patents. Government policy works as a key factor that makes this source of technology significant. Japan is the prime example of a country that has effectively geared its economic organization, public and private, to the acquisition of knowledge from abroad and has gained massive productivity increases as a result.

Natural diffusion—called "FG diffusion" by Gomulka—is forced by the technological gap. The strength of natural diffusion in influencing the technological level of a technologically backward economy depends on the magnitude of the gap between the technology leader and the given country and on the power of absorption, indicated by the technological level already achieved by that country. Technology absorption capability of an economy includes the educational level of the working population and the level of institutional development. It is easy to see that the impact of natural diffusion upon economic growth will be much less pronounced in

countries whose technology and development levels are very low or
very high.

   Importing modern equipment and plants from abroad has become
for many countries the main agent of their technological modernization. The embodied technical diffusion plays a significant role
not only in less developed countries but also in relatively well-
developed countries. Though the natural diffusion process seems to
be rather weak as a means of removing the existing technological
gap, the embodied diffusion, whether by import of licenses and patents or import of capital goods, can be considered a more effective and powerful means of removing the existing gap. It is also
noted that natural diffusion is costless, while the other two types
of diffusion require inputs of capital and/or labor.

   The gap in the technological level between technically more
advanced and less advanced countries is only a potential one, a
permissive but not sufficient condition for rapid technological
progress and thus for economic growth in technically less advanced
countries. There must be a number of other variables that jointly
characterize the extent to which the potential of technical change
present at a given relative technological gap is actually taken advantage of. Manoucher Parvin (1975) distinguishes two adaptation
sets, potential and available. He defines as the "potential adaptation set" (or technology gap) the set of all production functions
used to usable in more advanced countries but not effectively
availed of in a given country. A number of the elements of this
set are known to some economic agents of the adaptor country, and
they possess the technical know-how to put them to use. The collection of such production functions for a given country constitutes the "available adaptation set," which is a subset of potential adaptation sets.

   The distinction between potential and available adaptation
sets is important in view of the facts that there have been considerable variations in the productivity growth among countries at
similar technological levels and the labor productivity growth
rates of the follower countries have not declined as the gap between the lead and follower countries has been gradually reduced.

   What factors account for the variation between the potential
and available adaptation sets among different countries? The answer basically remains unknown. Various economic, cultural, and
institutional factors are mentioned as explanations. Reference has
been made to "X-efficiency," "degree of openness," or "institutional sclerosis" as umbrella terms covering a variety of factors.
(The various economic factors that might conceivably influence the
incidence of innovation and the speed of its diffusion include
among the most important, technical feasibility, profitability, finance, research and development activity, the labor market, size of
market, and resource endowment.) It seems that most believe that
cultural and institutional rather than economic factors account for
different degrees of diffusion. Examples of these factors include
receptive and innovative management willing to locate and adopt the
world's best technology, cooperating workers and unions ready to

accept technical change and its consequences, the high degree of
exposure to the competitive pressures, international agreements on
technical exchange, trade barriers and embargos, and strong government institutions that assist in the transfer of technology. In an
important contribution by an international consortium of economic
research institutes that have studied the diffusion of ten major
process innovations in six countries, considerable emphasis has
been placed on the role of "management factors" (Nabseth and Ray
1974). All this cultural and institutional basis for smoother diffusion of technology is not easy to create and certainly did not
exist to the same degree in every country.

     Once we accept that the process of technological diffusion has
permitted Japan and European countries to exploit the technological
potential and thus grow faster than the United States, it is necessary to examine what conditions and developments supported the rapid, general, and sustained exploitation of the large potential for
productivity growth during the postwar period. We also have to answer the question why the productivity gap became wider before
World War II and narrower after the war or why the follower countries waited so long to reduce the gap between themselves and the
leader.

     Abramovitz (1979) takes up the question under three subjects:
(1) improved facilities for technological innovation, diffusion,
and adaptation, (2) conditions facilitating structural change, and
(3) conditions encouraging and sustaining capital investment. A
number of developments favoring more rapid diffusion and adaptation
than had existed before World War II include higher general levels
of education, more engineers and technicians, growing professional-
ization of administrative and technical leadership in business,
liberalization of trade and capital movements, and the establishment of research facilities by industrial concerns and governments.

     Transformation in the composition of output and employment, so
much emphasized by Kuznets (1966, 1971) in his analysis of development process, emerges, according to Abramovitz, as a necessary concomitant of technological diffusion. The process of structural
change as governed by demand and supply conditions favored early
and rapid adaptation to the structural requirements of development
after World War II.

     One of the most important developments supporting more rapid
exploitation of opportunities for productivity advances was an investment boom of unprecedented size both with respect to the rates
of growth of stock and to the number of years these high rates were
sustained. Postwar conditions that encouraged and sustained capital investment included favorable financial development, strong
government support for investment, flexible labor supplies, successful monetary management (both domestic and international), and
the growth of output and productivity itself. All the above factors together worked as agents mediating between productivity potential and the pace of realization in the process of catch-up.
Angus Maddison's (1979a) answer to the question of why the opportunities to overcome backwardness open before the great productivity

spurt started after World War II is essentially the same as that by Abramovitz: the widening productivity gap before the war was due to the two world wars.

In an interesting article Edward Ames and Nathan Rosenberg (1963) examine whether we can expect technological leadership to rotate among different countries and formulate the catch-up hypothesis in three variants: weak, moderate, and strong theses. The weak thesis asserts that the latecomers will pass through any sequence of development more rapidly than early starters. The moderate thesis maintains that there will be a change in leadership because latecomers will ultimately reach higher levels of development than early starters, even though the latter do not cease developing. The strong thesis states that latecomers will surpass early starters because early starters develop rigidities and will cease to develop.

The validity of these theses depends upon a variety of empirical conditions. The weak thesis depends on the assertion that the latecomer need not repeat the mistakes of its predecessors and that mistakes do not contain useful experiences for those who make them. One real advantage of the later starter may be the clear perception of the advantages of standardization. The moderate thesis contains a logical weakness because it is partly based on the proposition that early starters are subject to retardation, which does not affect latecomers. The nature and sequence of technological change is important in justifying the moderate thesis because only discontinuities in the newly emerging technology will provide the early starter with no special advantages in skill, experience, and adaptability and allow the latecomer to catch up to the early starter. If technological change is a continuous, cumulative process, then there is a strong presumption that the latecomer will not surpass the early starter. The strong thesis depends upon the transition of costs. If the cost of moving from a low to a higher technology is an increasing function of the level of technology already reached, the rate of development will slow down as a country develops. When transition costs are an increasing function of output, but independent of technology, it can be argued that a more developed economy will fail to make a change to an advanced technology, while a less developed economy will.

As Ames and Rosenberg insist, even if there are some penalties for taking the lead in technology, it does not follow that, on balance, late starters are better off than early starters. It is important to make the distinction between factors that are alleged to be responsible for eventual retardation of growth and factors demonstrating the existence of penalties for taking the lead. Empirical evidence on the relative importance of the two different groups of factors is critical to the validity of the catch-up hypothesis and the three different versions of it. For example, if retardation is inevitable in a mature economy--the leader--it may be inevitable for the followers as well. Taking into account a time lag in diffusion and inevitable universal retardation, the removal of the technological gap would never be complete. Only the weak ver-

sion of the catch-up thesis is valid. Regardless of these different versions, the latecomer (follower) must grow faster than the
early starter (leader) as long as the former does not surpass the
latter in its technology level.

Empirical Findings

Several economists have sought to establish the empirical validity of the catch-up hypothesis. In general, their attempts have
been made by examining the inverse correlation between growth rates
of productivity in manufacturing or for the economy as a whole for
a given period and the levels of technology measured in terms of
per capita income at the beginning of that period.

One might have expected that in the decades during the twentieth century, countries in Western Europe, Japan, Australia, New
Zealand, and Canada would have enjoyed rapid economic growth and
the gap between their levels of productivity and that of the United
States would have been significantly reduced. As shown in Table
3.4, this expectation was balked by the effects of two world wars
and the Great Depression during the first half of the century.
However, Table 3.4 provides support for the narrowing gap in the
productivity level between the technological leader (the United
States) and the followers (other advanced countries) since World
War II.

Table 3.4 sets forth estimates of per capita real gross domestic product (GDP) based on the purchasing power parity, not on the
official exchange rates, in 12 or 13 European countries, Australia,
Canada, Japan, and New Zealand, all expressed as relatives of the
corresponding figures for the United States. By the turn of the
century the United States had become the productivity leader of the
developed world. Average labor productivity of 16 other advanced
countries at the turn of the century was about 60 percent of the
U.S. level. The variation in productivity level among the countries was high. Between 1901 and 1950 the average productivity
relative decreased by about 12 percent as a result of the combined

Table 3.4. Relative real per capita gross domestic product in 1970 U.S. dollars compared with the United
States (USA = 100)

Data	1901	1913	1920	1929	1938	1950	1955	1960	1965	1970	1975	1977	1978
Maddison													
16 countries (all)													
Mean	62	63	56	59	71	54	57	65	67	75	79		75
Standard deviation	21	20	18	15	16	17	15	14	12	10	10		9
Coefficient of variation	0.34	0.32	0.32	0.25	0.23	0.31	0.26	0.22	0.18	0.13	0.12		0.12
12 countries (European only)													
Mean	61	61	54	59	72	54	57	65	68	75	78		74
Standard deviation	17	14	14	13	14	13	11	11	11	10	10		9
Coefficient of variation	0.28	0.23	0.26	0.22	0.19	0.24	0.19	0.17	0.16	0.13	0.13		0.12
Summers, Kravis, and Heston													
17 countries (all)													
Mean						51		58	61	67	70	68	
Standard deviation						18		14	13	12	13	12	
Coefficient of variation						0.35		0.24	0.21	0.18	0.19	0.18	
13 countries (European only)													
Mean						48		58	60	67	70	67	
Standard deviation						12		12	12	13	13	12	
Coefficient of variation						0.25		0.21	0.20	0.19	0.18	0.18	

Sources: Maddison 1979b; Summers et al. 1980.

effects of two wars and the depression. There was a false appearance of an increase in productivity relative in 1938 because of higher unemployment in the United States than in other countries.

The strong potential, accumulated over half a century, burst into catch-up during the 30 years after World War II. According to Table 3.4, the mean productivity relative of other advanced countries increased from about 50 to around 70 percent of the U.S. level. The noticeable decrease in the coefficient of variation in relative per capita GDP implies that the gap narrowing has been accompanied by uneven growth among different economies.

In a study comparing the determinants of growth in the United States and Western Europe from 1950 to 1962, Denison (1967, Chap. 20) finds that "advances in knowledge" accounted for a compound annual growth rate of 0.76 percent in the United States out of a total annual compound growth rate of 3.32 percent. In nine advanced countries of northwestern Europe the residual was 1.32 percent out of a total annual compound growth rate of 4.78 percent. Because knowledge is an international commodity, the contribution made by advances of knowledge to growth was assumed to have been the same in the European countries as it was in the United States. The difference in the residuals, according to Denison, was the result of "changes in the lag in the application of knowledge and general efficiency." However, the conclusion derived from observations for the continental countries as a whole and the United States is misleading. A comparison of the general pattern of the residuals between the United States and each of the European countries suggests that, with the exception of France and Italy, the higher growth rates obtained by most European countries (compared to the United States) were not due in any large measure to a catch-up of technique. In contrast, Denison's study on the Japanese economy confirms the catch-up process (Denison and Chung 1976, Chap. 8). Advances in knowledge in Japan progressed at an annual rate of 1.97 percent from 1953 to 1971 as compared to 1.19 percent in the United States from 1948 to 1969. These estimates leave 0.78 points (about 10 percent of Japan's national income growth) in Japan for narrowing of the gap between actual and best practice.

The most frequently used method to test the catch-up phenomenon has been examining the inverse correlation between rates of economic growth and levels of technology. The correlation has been tested in various ways. Major previous empirical test results of the catch-up hypothesis are summarized in Table 3.5. Abramovitz (1979, pp. 1-30) measures the rank correlation between growth rates of labor productivity and the initial relative productivity levels for successive periods. The association, based on data from 11 advanced countries, is highest for the two decades 1950-1970 taken together, while the association of growth with initial standings is less for each decade in the 1950-1970 period.

The United Nations (1970), in its effort to analyze growth patterns in Europe, examined an association between manufacturing growth rates and the level of income per capita in the period 1953-1967. The association was tested by varying the collection of

Table 3.5. Summary of previous empirical results of the catch-up hypothesis
A. Abramovitz: Rank correlations (averages of three based on different data set)
    between labor productivity growth rates and relative productivity levels
      For 1950–1970, γ = -0.90   (1)
      For 1950–1960, γ = -0.81   (2)
      For 1960–1970, γ = -0.64   (3)

B. United Nations: Regression of manufacturing growth rate for 1953–1967 (Y_m) on
    the level of GDP per head in 1953–1955 (X)
    Market economies, excluding Japan
      Y_m = 4.24 + 1186.0771(1/X), γ = 0.88, σ = 1.00   (4)
    Industrial Western Europe, Canada, Japan, and the United States
      Y_m = 2.82 + 2888.3074(1/X), γ = 0.96, σ = 0.74   (5)
      Log Y_m = 0.40162 + 352.9573(1/X), γ = 0.90, σ = 0.77   (6)

C. Singer and Reynolds: Relation between growth of productivity in manufactur-
    ing (Y_m) and level of development (X)
    Rank-order correlation coefficient between Y_m and X (all coefficients sig-
    nificant at the 5 percent level)
      Using Kaldor data for 1953–1963, γ = -0.68   (7)
      Using Cripps/Tarling data for 1951–60, γ = -0.79   (8)
      Using Cripps/Tarling data for 1957–60, γ = -0.58   (9)
      Using Cripps/Tarling data for 1961–65, γ = -0.52   (10)
      Using Cripps/Tarling data for 1966–70, γ = -0.87   (11)
      Using Gomulka data for 1958–68, γ = -0.60   (12)
    Regression of Y_m on X (t-statistics and R^2 for regressions are not provided)
      Using Kaldor data for all countries, Y_m = 56.4527 - 1.88X (13)
      Using Kaldor data excluding Japan, Y_m = 47.7431 - 1.2390X (14)
      Using Gomulka data for all countries, Y_m = 68.5343 - 0.4141X (15)
      Using Gomulka data excluding Japan, Y_m = 63.2726 - 0.3297X (16)

D. Cornwall: Regressions of growth rate of manufacturing output (Y_m) on per cap-
    ita income (X), per capita income relative to the industrial leader (X_p), and
    ratio of investment to value added in manufacturing (I_{ym})
      Y_m = 0.185 + 1.09(1/X_p) + 0.173I_{ym} (17)
              (0.211)   (0.059) R^2 = 0.72
      Y_m = 0.078 + 2205(1/X) + 0.204I_{ym} (18)
              (449)   (0.062) R^2 = 0.69

E. Parvin: Regressions of growth rates of per capita income (Y) on an index of
    adaptation factor (A), net domestic capital formation as a percentage of net
    domestic product (s), percentage yearly change in human capital per capita
    (h), and yearly percentage population growth (n)
      Y = -0.0380 + 0.0728A + 0.1519s + 0.0604h (19)
             (0.0117) (0.0398)   (0.0251) R^2 = 0.95
      Y = -0.005 + 0.040A + 0.140s - 0.3261n (20)
            (0.007)   (0.031)   (0.209) R^2 = 0.91
      Sources: Abramovitz 1979, p. 11; UN 1970, pp. 62–63; Singer and Reynolds
1975, p. 844; Cornwall 1977, p. 141; Parvin 1975, pp. 26, 27.

countries and the specification form of the equation. When the
catch-up hypothesis is applied to 18 market economies, excluding
Japan, over 77 percent of the variations in growth rate are statistically explained by variations in per capita GDP at the beginning
of the period. But the standard error is too large for practical
use. Better results are obtained from equations restricted to the
observations of 12 industrial countries in Western Europe, Canada,
Japan, and the United States. Equation (4) (Table 3.5) explains
statistically about 90 percent of the intercountry variations in
manufacturing growth rates.

     H. W. Singer and L. Reynolds (1975, pp. 873–76) attempted to
test the catch-up hypothesis based on Gomulka's argument that among
industrial economies the growth rate of productivity in the manufacturing sector of a country is determined by relative technologi-

cal backwardness. As in all other studies, they measure technological leads and lags of an economy by per capita gross national
product (GNP). Their results also confirm the conclusion that
within the group of western style industrial economies the process
of catching up by those with initially low per capita GNP explains
a good deal of differential increases in the manufacturing sector.
The regression coefficients show that for every reduction in per
capita GNP of U.S. $100, the annual rate of productivity growth in
the manufacturing sector rises from 0.012 to 0.49 percentage points
depending on samples used.

John Cornwall (1977), who attempted to describe and explain in
some detail some of the more important developments that have taken
place under market capitalism since the end of World War II, offers
two reasons why low levels of per capita income are associated with
rapid rates of growth of manufacturing output. The first is that,
given the range of per capita income for the industrialized countries of the sample, the lower the level of income, the smaller the
proportion of consumer budgets allocated to services and the larger
the proportion spent on goods. The second reason is based on the
catch-up process; the lower the level of per capita income relative
to that of the industrial leader, the larger the stock of technological knowledge to be borrowed.

Since there is no a priori reason to expect that variables reflecting the two different factors above would move together, Cornwall includes both per capita income and the ratio of per capita
income of a country to that of the industrial leader in his model
to explain the growth of manufacturing output as an engine of economic growth. Among the various regression results obtained by
Cornwall, only two are presented in Table 3.5. Since the ratio of
per capita income of a country to that of the United States serves
to pick up the influence of income levels on demand patterns as
well as the technology gap, the result shows that the relative income variable performed a little better than the per capita income
variable. At the beginning of the postwar period, the ratio of per
capita income in Japan to that in the United States was 0.188 compared with a value of 0.255 for the ratio of German to U.S. per
capita income. Thus the late start in industrialization added 9.24
(1.09/0.118) percent to the Japanese growth rate in manufacturing,
while a 4.27 (1.09/0.255) percent growth resulted from the ability
to borrow technology.

The regression results of the catch-up hypothesis by Parvin,
rationalized by technology gap arguments, show that the adaptation
factor, along with capital accumulation and other factors, explains
a large portion of the variation of the per capita income growth
rate. In Parvin's test, the index representing the technology gap
G_i is defined as "the difference between the per capita income of
the most advanced economy Y_a and that of the ith economy Y_i; i.e.,
$G_i = Y_a - Y_i$." In addition, Parvin assumes that "the probability
of the discovery and usage of such production functions . . . is
directly related to the stock of human capital per capita, H_i,"
which he measures by the "percentage literacy rate in the popula-

tion aged 15 years and over as a first approximation" (Parvin
1975). Finally, Parvin defines the product of the two magnitudes,
$A_i = G_i H_i$, as an index of the adaptation factor and uses it in his
regression analysis to test the catch-up hypothesis. Parvin's result, which considers the adaptation factor as an index of the magnitude of technological windfall, supports the hypothesis that
countries with a large adaptation factor obtain more growth from an
increase in capital per worker than those with a smaller adaptation
factor.

The series of results discussed above support the catch-up hypothesis by establishing the existence of a relationship between
the level of income per head and the growth of manufacturing output
or the growth of per capita income. The relationship holds true
over a variety of samples based on a different group of countries.
However, the results examined are not without problems in data and
specification. Given the fact that per capita income is the only
available proxy for the technology or development level, however
unsatisfactory it may be, all used a measure of per capita income
in U.S. dollars derived from conversion of GNP or GDP of a country
into dollars at official exchange rates. This was inevitable because of the lack of data on per capita income based on purchasing
power parity.

The term "technological gap" refers to a phenomenon that tran-
scends the consequences of differences between countries in resource endowments either innate or developed through past investment. Therefore, differences in per capita income, which depend on
resource endowments, are not direct evidence of a technological
gap. One of the reasons the ratio of real per capita GDP in the
lead country to that in another country is used as an indicator of
the relative technological gap is that at a given constant capital-
output ratio the productivity level is proportional to the level of
technology. In growth theory the capital-output ratio as well as
labor's share of output has been frequently considered as stable.
A study by Ernst Helmstädter (1973) shows that in the long run the
capital-output ratio is not stable but follows a certain movement.

While it may be true that it is not possible to realize rapid
economic growth when per capita income is low, because there is so
much technology to be borrowed, using the level of absolute per
capita income (as Singer and Reynolds did) or the inverse of per
capita income (as the UN did) as the independent variable in the
regression is unsatisfactory on a priori grounds. Since the main
thrust of the catch-up process is the technological gap faced by
each country and its absorptive capacity, relative per capita income levels should be applied to measure the amount of technology
that can be borrowed by each country from the technology leader.
Parvin's attempt to allow for the existence of the technology gap
and the willingness and ability to exploit the gap in terms of human capital stock represent movement in the right direction. However, the index of adaptation factor, which is the product of two
factors, is an index difficult to interpret and does not carry the
meanings it intended. Finally, the sample included in the existing

test is not extensive in the number of countries employed and in the time period covered. The results are usually based on data from a dozen countries for about a decade.

An attempt to make better specifications of the hypothesis and utilize better and more extensive data must be made to establish the validity of the catch-up hypothesis. Among the various specifications, we choose the following six:

$$Y_1 = \alpha_1 + \beta_1(1/T), \qquad \alpha_1 > 0, \qquad \beta_1 > 0 \tag{3.8}$$

$$Y_1 = \alpha_2 + \beta_2(T/T_{US}), \qquad \alpha_2 > 0, \qquad \beta_2 < 0, \qquad \alpha_2 + \beta_2 > 0 \tag{3.9}$$

$$Y_1 = \alpha_3 + \beta_3(T_{US} - T)/T, \qquad \alpha_3 > 0, \qquad \beta_3 > 0 \tag{3.10}$$

$$Y_2 = \alpha_4 + \beta_4(T_{US}/T), \qquad \alpha_4 = 0, \qquad \beta_4 = 1, \qquad \text{or } \alpha_4 + \beta_4 = 1 \tag{3.11}$$

$$Y_3 = \alpha_5 + \beta_5(T_{US}/T), \qquad \alpha_5 + \beta_5 = 0 \tag{3.12}$$

$$Y_3 = \alpha_6 + \beta_6 \log(T_{US}/T), \qquad \alpha_6 = 0, \qquad \beta_6 > 0 \tag{3.13}$$

where Y_1 is the growth rate of each country, Y_2 is the growth rate of each country divided by that of the United States, Y_3 is the growth rate of each country subtracted from that of the United States, T is the technology level of each country at the beginning of the period, and T_{US} is the technology level of the United States at the beginning of the period.

The first two specifications, (3.8) and (3.9), are found in most of the previous studies. Essentially, the first equation is meant to test the "slow-down" hypothesis (that growth of advanced countries will eventually face retardation), while the second specification implies the "convergence" hypothesis (that the economic systems of the countries will be converging to a common path). Our third specification, (3.10), emphasizes the natural diffusion process discussed in the previous section and makes an explicit allowance for the fact that the magnitude of the diffusion of technology depends on the technological strength of a country in relation to that of the United States and on the power of absorption of the country. Natural diffusion depends on the technology gap and the level of technology already achieved. $Q = f(G, T)$, where $G = T_{US} - T$ is an absolute level of technology gap and T is the existing technology level representing conditions of absorption. When the function f is homogeneous of degree α, $f(G, T) = f(T_{US} - T, T) = (1/T)^{\alpha} f[(T_{US} - T)/T, 1] = (1/T)^{\alpha} g[(T_{US} - T)/T]$. This justifies the specification in (3.10) on the assumption that the growth rate depends on the technology gap.

The last three formulations, (3.11) to (3.13), are from Robin Marris (1977, 1978, 1980). As they indicate, Marris's version of the catch-up hypothesis is that relative growth rates (vis à vis the United States) are linearly or nonlinearly related to the initial ratio of the U.S. technology level to that of the country in question. According to Marris, a priori constraints on parameters in the regression equations are specific. In his first specification, (3.11), Marris considers two different versions of the general model. Whether or not it is possible for the follower to overtake the leader will put a different constraint on the model. The possibility of overtaking places a prior restriction that β_4 be positive while convergence without overtaking contains the prior expectation that α_4 and β_4 sum to one.

The catch-up hypothesis based on the above specifications is tested on data relating to three periods--1950 to 1960, 1960 to 1970, and 1970 to 1977--for 17 advanced countries plus the United States. (While Marris tests the hypothesis based on the 5-year interval, our testing uses a longer time interval because it has been found that the duration of the diffusion stage is fairly lengthy. For instance, from his pioneering study of the diffusion of 12 major innovations among the larger firms in four U.S. industries, Mansfield [1961] finds that the number of years of elapsing before half the firms introduced an innovation varied from 0.9 to 15, the average being 7.8. A similar picture emerges for the 22 innovations considered in the diffusion process study by Stephen Davis [1979], which shows that for 4 of the innovations, 50 percent diffusion was attained in 7 or fewer years, but for 7 others, over half of all potential adopters had still not adopted 14 years after the first appearance of the new innovation.) Time-series and cross-sectional data are pooled to make the number of observations sufficiently large, 54, for statistical purposes. Two proxy measures of an economy's level of technology are employed: real per capita GDP and per capita commercial energy consumption. Real GDP per capita figures are based on purchasing power parity exchange rates derived by Irving Kravis and his associates (Kravis et al. 1978a,b) rather than official exchange rates, which were used in almost all previous studies. Per capita commercial energy consumption is chosen not because there is a strong positive correlation between per capita energy consumption and per capita GDP but because energy consumption and economic growth are inextricably intertwined. Energy consumption for commercial and industrial use is more relevant for our purpose than energy consumption for residential use, because the latter is the result rather than the cause of economic growth.

The results of regression analysis of the different specifications of the catch-up hypothesis are shown in Table 3.6. These results are satisfactory in terms of relatively large t-values and high R^2s. Regressions with real per capita GDP as a proxy for technological level produce more favorable results to the hypothesis regardless of specification than those produced with per capita energy consumption. As expected, R^2s decrease noticeably when Japan is excluded from the sample, even though results without Japan are still statistically significant. In all cases, coefficients of regressions are consistent with our prior expectations. It can be concluded from the regression results shown in Table 3.6 that the catch-up process through the diffusion of technology has been one of the explanations for differential growth performance among ad-

Table 3.6. Tests of the catch-up hypothesis using cross-country data for 1950-1977

A. Using per capita income data

All countries, $n = 54$

$$Y = 1.2901 + 3762.64(1/X) \qquad (1)$$
$$(3.46) \qquad (5.55) \qquad R^2 = 0.37$$

$$Y = 6.4520 - 5.4327(X/X_{US}) \qquad (2)$$
$$(10.16) \qquad (5.45) \qquad R^2 = 0.36$$

$$Y = 2.0270 + 1.3401[(X_{US} - X)/X] \qquad (3)$$
$$(8.22) \qquad (6.02) \qquad R^2 = 0.41$$

$$Y/Y_{US} = -0.0886 + 0.9000(X_{US}/X) \qquad (4)$$
$$(0.44) \qquad (8.71) \qquad R^2 = 0.59$$

$$Y - Y_{US} = -1.6672 + 1.4989(X_{US}/X) \qquad (5)$$
$$(4.11) \qquad (7.26) \qquad R^2 = 0.50$$

$$Y - Y_{US} = -0.7892 + 3.4384 \, \log(X_{US}/X) \qquad (6)$$
$$(2.65) \qquad (7.26) \qquad R^2 = 0.50$$

Excluding Japan, $n = 51$

$$Y = 1.3771 + 3361.27(1/X) \qquad (7)$$
$$(3.41) \qquad (4.13) \qquad R^2 = 0.26$$

$$Y = 5.3778 - 3.9187(X/X_{US}) \qquad (8)$$
$$(8.79) \qquad (4.15) \qquad R^2 = 0.26$$

$$Y = 2.0447 + 1.2116[(X_{US} - X)/X] \qquad (9)$$
$$(7.96) \qquad (4.23) \qquad R^2 = 0.27$$

$$Y/Y_{US} = -0.1023 + 0.8992(X_{US}/X) \qquad (10)$$
$$(0.38) \qquad (6.00) \qquad R^2 = 0.42$$

$$Y - Y_{US} = -1.6260 + 1.4401(X_{US}/X) \qquad (11)$$
$$(3.32) \qquad (5.31) \qquad R^2 = 0.36$$

$$Y - Y_{US} = -0.5318 + 2.7571 \, \log(X_{US}/X) \qquad (12)$$
$$(1.78) \qquad (5.30) \qquad R^2 = 0.36$$

B. Using per capita commercial energy consumption data

All countries, $n = 54$

$$Y = 2.2475 + 1967.25(1/E) \qquad (13)$$
$$(0.28) \qquad (462.32) \qquad R^2 = 0.26$$

$$Y = 4.2556 - 2.9073(E/E_{US}) \qquad (14)$$
$$(10.46) \qquad (3.19) \qquad R^2 = 0.16$$

$$Y = 2.3918 + 0.2755[(E_{US} - E)/E] \qquad (15)$$
$$(9.38) \qquad (4.23) \qquad R^2 = 0.26$$

$$Y/Y_{US} = 0.8259 + 0.1974(E_{US}/E) \qquad (16)$$
$$(5.53) \qquad (6.14) \qquad R^2 = 0.42$$

$$Y - Y_{US} = -0.1043 + 0.3179(E_{US}/E) \qquad (17)$$
$$(0.36) \qquad (5.10) \qquad R^2 = 0.33$$

$$Y - Y_{US} = -0.6044 + 1.5103 \, \log(E_{US}/E) \qquad (18)$$
$$(1.57) \qquad (4.91) \qquad R^2 = 0.32$$

Excluding Japan, $n = 51$

$$Y = 2.3364 + 1413.17(1/E) \qquad (19)$$
$$(9.51) \qquad (3.14) \qquad R^2 = 0.17$$

$$Y = 3.6949 - 1.9257(E/E_{US}) \qquad (20)$$
$$(10.43) \qquad (2.48) \qquad R^2 = 0.11$$

$$Y = 2.4647 + 0.1891[(E_{US} - E)/E] \qquad (21)$$
$$(11.00) \qquad (2.98) \qquad R^2 = 0.15$$

$$Y/Y_{US} = 0.9312 + 0.1512(E_{US}/E) \qquad (22)$$
$$(6.31) \qquad (4.38) \qquad R^2 = 0.28$$

$$Y - Y_{US} = 0.0601 + 0.2330(E_{US}/E) \qquad (23)$$
$$(0.23) \qquad (3.77) \qquad R^2 = 0.22$$

$$Y - Y_{US} = -0.2589 + 1.0577 \, \log(E_{US}/E) \qquad (24)$$
$$(0.75) \qquad (3.65) \qquad R^2 = 0.22$$

Sources: UN 1976; Summers et al. 1980.
Note: Y = growth rate of per capita output for each country; Y_{US} = growth rate of per capita output for the United States; X = real GDP per capita for each country; X_{US} = real GDP per capita for the United States; E = per capita commercial energy consumption for each country; E_{US} = per capita commercial energy consumption for the United States.

vanced countries, at least for the years since World War II.

In fact, the concept of the catch-up (or convergence) process gained its popularity earlier in the regional growth context than in the national growth context. Two massive descriptive-analytical volumes (Kuznets et al. 1960; Perloff et al. 1960) on the process of interregional growth in the United States provided detailed empirical evidence of convergence tendencies in regional per capita income in the United States. Two main lines of theoretical explanation for the convergence trend in U.S. regional growth have been offered. The first is that of the technological gap and diffusion process emphasized throughout the chapter. Increases in regional output depend on the newly realized technical knowledge. New technical knowledge does not originate in all regions of a national economy at the same time or at the same rate. As the regions differ in the technical horizon, regions or areas face different potentials for technology and thus will exhibit differences in growth performance.

A new line of theoretical framework for the convergence hypothesis is the neoclassical model of regional growth. For example, George Borts and Jerome Stein (1964) argue that the most important explanation of convergence is an improvement in the efficiency of resource allocation within regions. The internal mechanics of the neoclassical model rely on the free resource mobility and on negative feedbacks in the movement of resources among regions. Rapid capital accumulation depresses capital yields, which, in turn, slows down the rate of capital accumulation. A theory predicting exactly opposite results is discussed in Chapter 5. The cumulative causation theory, which emphasizes positive feedbacks, states that growth rates are unstable. The region that got ahead acquires the means for additionally increasing its growth rate and the laggards fall even further behind. The neoclassical model itself can also predict divergence by allowing for increasing returns.

How does the catch-up or convergence hypothesis stand against U.S. regional data? The same specifications used to test the catch-up hypothesis among advanced countries are subjected to the data for 1958-1978 from the 48 contiguous states. The results are presented in Table 3.7. (The results based on total labor and proprietors' income exclude influences reflecting income transfers through government.) The regression results show that the states that have been experiencing rapid growth in recent years have been doing so because of the low levels from which they began. For the two decades under consideration, the convergence process is more pronounced in years 1968-1978 than in years 1958-1968. As in the cross-country case, all regression coefficients are consistent with a priori expectations.

Our result is in sharp contrast to that by Victor Fuchs (1962, p. 95), who reported that "the 'catching up' hypothesis is not supported by data. The absolute level of manufacturing is not significantly related to comparative growth when other variables are taken into account. . . ." The difference between the two results

Table 3.7. Tests of the catch-up hypothesis using U.S.
            regional data

A. For 1958-1978, $n = 96$

$$Y = 10.1643 - 6839.44(1/X) \qquad (1)$$
$$\quad (18.24) \qquad (6.83) \qquad \qquad R^2 = 0.33$$
$$Y = 9.2993 - 3.0020(X/\overline{X}) \qquad (2)$$
$$\quad (8.28) \quad (2.51) \qquad \qquad R^2 = 0.06$$
$$Y = 6.2536 + 2.3474[(\overline{X} - X)/X] \qquad (3)$$
$$\quad (28.38) \quad (2.42) \qquad \qquad R^2 = 0.06$$
$$Y/\overline{Y} = 0.6028 + 0.3703(\overline{X}/X) \qquad (4)$$
$$\quad (8.79) \quad (6.11) \qquad \qquad R^2 = 0.28$$
$$Y - \overline{Y} = -2.3455 + 2.2393(\overline{X}/X) \qquad (5)$$
$$\quad (5.72) \quad (6.18) \qquad \qquad R^2 = 0.29$$
$$Y - \overline{Y} = -0.0828 + 2.5037 \log(\overline{X}/X) \qquad (6)$$
$$\quad (1.01) \quad (6.05) \qquad \qquad R^2 = 0.28$$

B. For 1958-1968, $n = 48$

$$Y = 2.6990 + 3147.25(1/X) \qquad (7)$$
$$\quad (5.27) \qquad (4.13) \qquad \qquad R^2 = 0.27$$
$$Y = 6.0594 - 2.0251(X/\overline{X}) \qquad (8)$$
$$\quad (11.68) \quad (3.36) \qquad \qquad R^2 = 0.20$$
$$Y/\overline{Y} = 0.5547 + 0.3836(\overline{X}/X) \qquad (9)$$
$$\quad (5.27) \quad (4.13) \qquad \qquad R^2 = 0.27$$
$$Y = 4.5657 + 1.8667[(\overline{X} - X)/X] \qquad (10)$$
$$\quad (41.86) \quad (4.13) \qquad \qquad R^2 = 0.27$$
$$Y - \overline{Y} = -2.1671 + 1.8667(\overline{X}/X) \qquad (11)$$
$$\quad (4.23) \quad (4.13) \qquad \qquad R^2 = 0.27$$
$$Y - \overline{Y} = -0.2698 + 2.0137 \log(\overline{X}/X) \qquad (12)$$
$$\quad (2.46) \quad (3.76) \qquad \qquad R^2 = 0.24$$

C. For 1968-1978, $n = 48$

$$Y = 5.2273 + 7470.68(1/X) \qquad (13)$$
$$\quad (8.82) \qquad (5.20) \qquad \qquad R^2 = 0.37$$
$$Y = 11.3105 - 3.3082(X/\overline{X}) \qquad (14)$$
$$\quad (19.50) \quad (5.32) \qquad \qquad R^2 = 0.38$$
$$Y/\overline{Y} = 0.6635 + 0.3457(\overline{X}/X) \qquad (15)$$
$$\quad (8.82) \quad (5.20) \qquad \qquad R^2 = 0.37$$
$$Y = 7.9508 + 2.7235[(\overline{X} - X)/X] \qquad (16)$$
$$\quad (70.67) \quad (5.20) \qquad \qquad R^2 = 0.37$$
$$Y - \overline{Y} = -2.6507 + 2.7235(\overline{X}/X) \qquad (17)$$
$$\quad (4.47) \quad (5.20) \qquad \qquad R^2 = 0.37$$
$$Y - \overline{Y} = 0.0933 + 3.0583 \log(\overline{X}/X) \qquad (18)$$
$$\quad (0.85) \quad (5.30) \qquad \qquad R^2 = 0.38$$

Source: U.S. Department of Commerce 1979.
Note: Y = growth rate of per capita income for each
state; $\overline{Y}$ = growth rate of per capita income for the United
States as a whole; X = level of per capita income for each
state; $\overline{X}$ = level of per capita income for the United States
as a whole.

may be due to different periods examined (1929–1954 vs. 1958–1978),
economic activity covered (manufacturing value added vs. total labor and proprietors' income), method employed (multiple vs. simple
regression), or other factors. It must be noted that the secular
convergence trends observed among U.S. regions were occasionally
interrupted. The evidence suggests two periods of widening regional disparities: 1840–1880 and the 1920s and 1930s.
     Even though the convergence process among regions in the
United States is observed over the long run, and in particular over
the last three decades, some emphasize that influences other than
interregional resource reallocation and narrowing down of the technology (or income gap) are the causes. An analysis of the deter-

minants of state growth differentials finds that federal spending
in the form of redistributive expenditures in low-income states and
via locational bias in various government programs and amenities
explains much of the interstate variation in economic performance
(see Richardson 1974). The fact that the high-income regions tend
to be pulled down toward the national average rather than the low-
er-income regions being pulled up suggests the existence of growth-
retarding forces in the high-income regions. All these influences
will be examined in the coming chapters.

CRITICISMS AND CONCLUSIONS
        The technology gap (or diffusion of technology) approach is
based on the stylized fact that the residual is the single most important component in economic growth. It accepts the notion that
the rate of technical progress is the most important determinant of
growth rates. The thrust of the catch-up hypothesis is its emphasis on the importance of the international or interregional flow of
inventions and innovations in determining the rate of technical
progress and economic growth. A large stock of technology developed by the technological leader can be borrowed. The followers
(or latecomers) can avail themselves of the potential opportunity;
as a result output grows rapidly.
        Our discussion is based on the assumptions that a technology
gap exists between countries and that it can be clearly defined.
One of the theoretically and empirically knotty problems for investigators has been how to measure a technology gap. While no one
disputes the fact that there is a general, across-the-board technological gap between the United States and Ethiopia or Bangladesh,
for example, the gap between the United States and the United Kingdom or other advanced countries is not so clear. Furthermore, the
technology leader may fall behind other countries in certain industries and may be doing some catching up. In almost all cases, the
level of technology for a country has been approximated by its level of per capita income.
        At least two additional methods of measuring technological
level have been suggested by I. Dobozi (1974) and L. Nabseth and
E. F. Ray (1974). One is based on the simple assumption that a
country is considered to be technologically more developed than another if it produces a greater ratio of output in a given economic
activity by a technology held to be advanced on a worldwide scale.
Another method refers to the time interval between the initial
adoption of the production of a product or process by the innovator
and the initial adoption by the imitator.
        In our empirical investigation in the previous section, per
capita commercial energy consumption has been used as an alternative proxy for the technology level facing a country. Obviously,
per capita income or energy consumption is an imperfect measure of
the technology level. Therefore, any quantitative result using
these proxies in an effort to establish validity of the catch-up
hypothesis is bound to be approximate.

Despite the rather favorable regression results we obtained using the cross-country and U.S. interregional data in the previous section, the catch-up hypothesis does not enjoy utterly clear-cut empirical support. A simple view of the catch-up hypothesis leads one to expect that growth rates should decline as the measured productivity gap or technology gap narrows. Excluding unusual years in the 1970s, postwar experience displays no general marked retardation in growth. This might be because, contrary to the catch-up argument, capabilities rise as the gap narrows.

There are two conflicting views on whether the technology gap between the United States and Japan has been narrowed or widened. By noting the fact that Japan's technological imports have grown, Tuvia Blumenthal (1976) argues that the technological gap must have widened. There are massive imports of technological knowledge 30 years after the end of the war. A study by Mieko Nishimizu (1980) describes a very remarkable closing of the gap in technology between the United States and Japan over the period 1952-1974. Surprisingly, Nishimizu claims that between 1968 and 1973 the level of Japanese technology actually overtook that in the United States, and in 1974 the aggregate level of Japan stood ahead of that in the United States.

The catch-up hypothesis cannot explain the comparatively slow growth of some countries such as Luxembourg, the United Kingdom, Australia, Ireland, and New Zealand. According to the catch-up arguments, these countries ought to have been catching up because they, like Germany, France, and Japan, for example, had the opportunity to absorb a considerable amount of advanced technology from the United States. N. Kaldor (1966, p. 13) makes a strong case against the catch-up hypothesis:

> The usual hypothesis is that the growth of productivity is mainly to be explained by the progress of knowledge in science and technology. But in that case how is one to explain the large differences in the same industry over the same period in different countries? How can the progress of knowledge account for the fact, for example, that in the period 1954-1960, productivity in the German motor car industry increased at 7 percent a year and in Britain only 2.7 percent a year? Since large segments of the car industry in both countries were controlled by the same American firms, they must have had the same access to the improvements in knowledge and know-how.

Even though the catch-up thesis might well be true as historical fact, it is not a logical necessity. Theoretical construct of the catch-up hypothesis can be challenged on several grounds. The catch-up hypothesis (or latecomer thesis) depends upon some very special propositions about the nature and sequence of technological change. One must postulate sharp discontinuities and disjunctions such that the newly emerging technologies, at any time, are of such a nature that the current most technologically advanced economies possess no special advantages—in skill, experience, scientific

knowledge, or adaptability--in their development. If the technological change must be understood as a continuous process of cumulative synthesis emerging out of a perception of deficiencies in
existing techniques and knowledge, then there is a strong presumption that the technologically leading country will grow faster than
those following the leader.

Ames and Rosenberg (1973, p. 16) provide one interesting result. They assume that the concept of a state of technology can be
quantified. Three states of technology, A, B, and C, can be located in such a way that the distances A-B, B-C, and A-C can be measured. Ames and Rosenberg show that if all the points were on a
single line, and "technological change were thus one-dimensional,
all the interesting features of the catch-up hypothesis would auto-
matically be disproved."

The catch-up argument--that fundamental technical progress is
international and available to be used in all advanced countries--
assumes that the cost of adopting the results of much fundamental
research is not great and that technical and other capabilities of
the industrialized countries are uniform. There is no particular
reason for expecting U.K. firms to be slower to adopt new developments than firms in other countries. However, this argument is
based on a fallacy; it is like saying that all students can attend
the same lectures and read the same book and should therefore do
equally well on an examination. In terms of the distinction made
by Parvin between potential and available adaptation sets, the
catch-up hypothesis based on the potential adaptation set is not
sufficient to explain different growth performance among countries
unless an additional hypothesis is given to explain the difference
in the available adaptation set. The catch-up hypothesis emphasizes the determinants of growth as affected by supply. There is
no (or very little) discussion of effective demand as a determinant
of productivity growth. All this leads to the conclusion that the
technological gap, though very important, is not the only variable
determining the growth rate of productivity.

REFERENCES

Abramovitz, M. 1952. Economics of growth. In *A Survey of Contemporary Economics*, vol. 5, ed. B. F. Haley. Homewood, Ill.:
Irwin.
————. 1979. Rapid growth potential and its realization: The
experience of capitalist economies in the postwar period. In
Economic Growth and Resources, ed. E. Malinvaud. New York:
St. Martin's.
Abramovitz, M., and P. A. David. 1973. Reinterpreting economic
growth: Parables and realities. *Am. Econ. Rev.* 63:428-39.
Ames, E., and N. Rosenberg. 1963. Changing technological leader-
ship and industrial growth. *Econ. J.* 73:13-31.
Arrow, K. J. 1962. The economic implication of learning by doing.
Rev. Econ. Stud. 24:155-73.

Barger, H. 1969. Growth in developed nations. *Rev. Econ. Stat.* 51:143–48.

Blumenthal, T. 1976. Japan's technological strategy. *J. Dev. Econ.* 3:245–55.

Borts, G. H., and J. L. Stein. 1964. *Economic Growth in a Free Market.* New York: Columbia University Press.

Britto, R. 1973. Some recent developments in the theory of economic growth: An interpretation. *J. Econ. Lit.* 11:1343–66.

Christensen, L. R., D. Cummings, and D. W. Jorgenson. 1980. Economic growth, 1947–1973: An international comparison. In *New Developments in Productivity Measurement and Analysis*, ed. J. W. Kendrick and B. N. Vaccara. Chicago: University of Chicago Press.

Cornwall, J. 1977. *Modern Capitalism.* London: Martin Robinson.

Davis, S. 1979. *The Diffusion of Process Innovation.* Cambridge: Cambridge University Press.

Denison, E. F. 1962. *The Sources of Economic Growth in the United States and the Alternative before Us.* New York: Committee for Economic Development.

———. 1967. *Why Growth Rates Differ.* Washington, D.C.: Brookings Institution.

———. 1974. *Accounting for United States Economic Growth 1929–1969.* Washington, D.C.: Brookings Institution.

Denison, E. F., and W. K. Chung. 1976. *How Japan's Economy Grew So Fast: The Sources of Postwar Expansion.* Washington, D.C.: Brookings Institution.

Dobozi, I. 1974. A method for measurement and international comparison of technological levels. *East. Eur. Econ.* 12:17–25.

Domar, E. D., S. M. Eddie, B. H. Herrick, P. M. Hohenberg, M. D. Intriligator, and I. Miyamoto. 1964. Economic growth and productivity in the United States, Canada, United Kingdom, Germany and Japan in the post-war period. *Rev. Econ. Stat.* 46:33–40.

Fuchs, V. R. 1962. *Changes in the Location of Manufacturing in the United States since 1929.* New Haven: Yale University Press.

Gerschenkron, A. 1962. *Economic Backwardness in Historical Perspective.* Cambridge: Harvard University Press.

Gomulka, S. 1971. *Inventive Activity, Diffusion, and Stages of Economic Growth.* Aarhus, Denmark: Institute of Economics, Aarhus University.

———. 1979. Britain's slow industrial growth--increasing inefficiency versus low rate of technical change. In *Slow Growth in Britain--Causes and Consequences*, ed. W. Beckerman. Oxford: Clarendon.

Griliches, Z. 1957. Hybrid corn: An exploration in the economics of technological change. *Econometrica* 25:501–22.

Helmstädter, E. 1973. The long-run movement of the capital-output ratio and labor's share. In *Models of Economic Growth*, ed. J. A. Mirrlees and N. H. Stern. London: Macmillan.

Jorgenson, D. W., and Z. Griliches. 1967. The explanation of productivity change. *Rev. Econ. Stud.* 34:249–82.

Kaldor, N.   1966. *Causes of the Slow Rate of Economic Growth of
     the United Kingdom.* London: Cambridge University Press.
Kendrick, J. W.   1973. *Postwar Productivity Trends in the United
     States 1948-1969.*   New York: National Bureau of Economic Re-
     search.
————.   1979.   Productivity trends and the recent slowdown: His-
     torical perspective, causal factors, and policy options.   In
     Contemporary Economic Problems 1979, ed. W. Fellner.   Washing-
     ton, D.C.:   American Enterprise Institute.
Kennedy, C., and A. P. Thirlwall.   1972.   Surveys in applied eco-
     nomics: Technical progress.   *Econ. J.* 82:11-72.
Kennedy, K. A.   1971. *Productivity and Industrial Growth.*   Oxford:
     Clarendon.
Kravis, I. B.   1976.   Survey of international comparison of produc-
     tivity.   *Econ. J.* 86:1-44.
Kravis, I. B., A. W. Heston, and R. Summers.   1978a. *International
     Comparisons of Real Product and Purchasing Power.*   Baltimore:
     Johns Hopkins University Press.
————.   1978b.   Real GDP per capita for more than one hundred
     countries.   *Econ. J.* 88:215-42.
Kuznets, S.   1966. *Modern Economic Growth.*   New Haven: Yale Uni-
     versity Press.
————.   1971. *Economic Growth of Nations.*   Cambridge: Harvard
     University Press.
————.   1973.   Modern economic growth: Findings and reflections.
     Am. Econ. Rev. 63:247-258.
Kuznets, S., A. R. Miller, and R. A. Easterlin.   1960. *Population
     Redistribution and Economic Growth, United States, 1870-1950.*
     Philadelphia: American Philosophical Society.
Maddison, A.   1979a.   Long run dynamics of productivity growth.
     Banca Naz. Lavoro Q. Rev. 128:1-43.
————.   1979b.   Per capita output in the long run.   *Kyklos* 32
     (Fasc. 1/2):412-29.
Mansfield, E.   1961.   Technical change and the rate of imitation.
     Econometrica 29:745-66.
————.   1968a. *The Economics of Technological Change.*   New York:
     Norton.
————.   1968b. *Industrial Research and Technological Innovation--
     An Econometric Analysis.*   New York: Norton.
————.   1972.   Contributing of R & D to economic growth in the
     United States.   *Science* 175:477-86.
————.   1980.   Technology and productivity in the United States.
     In *The American Economy in Transition,* ed. M. Feldstein.
     Chicago: University of Chicago Press.
Marris, R.   1977.   Britain's relative economic decline: Some medi-
     um term facts and long term speculation.   Working paper 77-14,
     Department of Economics, University of Maryland.
————.   1978.   Some new results on catch-up.   Working paper 79-6,
     Department of Economics, University of Maryland.
————.   1980.   Catch-up, slow-down or convergence?   Statistical
     observations on 25 years of world economic growth in the light

of Kravis numbers. Draft, World Bank DPS Seminar.

Mirrlees, J. A., and N. H. Stern, eds. 1973. *Models of Economic Growth*. London: Macmillan.

Nabseth, L., and G. F. Ray, eds. 1974. *The Diffusion of New Industrial Process: An International Study*. Cambridge: Cambridge University Press.

Nishimizu, M. 1980. Technological superiority: A milestone in the postwar Japanese growth. In *Japan and the United States: Economic and Political Adversaries*, ed. L. Holleyman. Boulder, Colo.: Westview.

Parvin, M. 1975. Technological adaptation, optimum level of backwardness and the rate of per capita income growth: An econometric approach. *Am. Econ.* 19:23-31.

Perloff, H. S., E. S. Dunn, Jr., E. E. Lampard, and R. Muth. 1960. *Regions, Resources, and Economic Growth*. Baltimore: Johns Hopkins University Press.

Richardson, H. W. 1974. Empirical aspects of regional growth in the United States. *Ann. Reg. Sci.* 8:8-23.

Rosenberg, N. 1972. *Technology and American Economic Growth*. New York: Harper & Row.

Schmookler, J. 1966. *Invention and Economic Growth*. Cambridge: Harvard University Press.

Schumpeter, J. H. 1939. *Business Cycle*. New York: McGraw-Hill.

————. 1942. *Capitalism, Socialism and Democracy*. New York: Harper & Row.

Singer, H. W., and L. Reynolds. 1975. Technological backwardness and productivity growth. *Econ. J.* 85:873-76.

Sommers, P. M., and D. B. Suits. 1971. A cross-section model of economic growth. *Rev. Econ. Stat.* 53:121-28.

Summers, R., I. B. Kravis, and A. Heston. 1980. International comparison of real product and its composition: 1950-1977. *Rev. Income Wealth* 26:19-66.

Tinbergen, J. 1959. On the theory of trend movement. In *Jan Tinbergen Selected Essays*, ed. L. H. Klaassen, L. M. Koyck, and H. J. Witteveen. Amsterdam: North-Holland.

United Nations (UN). 1970. *Economic Survey of Europe, 1969. I. Structural Trends and Prospects in the European Economy*. New York: United Nations.

————. 1976. *World Energy Supplies 1950-1974*. New York: United Nations.

U.S. Department of Commerce. 1979. Computer printout. Regional Economic Information System, Bureau of Economic Analysis.

Veblen, T. 1915. *Imperial Germany and the Industrial Revolution*. New York: Macmillan. (Reprinted by Augustus M. Kelley, 1964.)

Williamson, J. G. 1976. Technology, growth, and history. *J. Polit. Econ.* 84:809-20.

4

The Investment-Led
Growth Hypothesis

Capital occupies a position so dominant in the economic theory of production and distribution that it is natural to assume that it should occupy an equally important place in the theory of economic growth. Whether economists approach the subjects--production, distribution, or growth--historically, analytically, or from the side of policy, the process of capital accumulation has occupied front stage.

One of the disturbing aspects of modern growth theory is the wide difference in opinion as to the importance of capital formation in growth. Theoretical models have been constructed that alternately show that changes in capital or investment can and cannot affect the long-term growth rate of an economy. While some claim there is no reason to suppose that capital accumulation exercises so predominant an influence on economic growth, others maintain that capital provokes or facilitates a more rapid rate of economic growth.

Viewed historically, the concept of capital and its role in economic growth is one of the controversial areas that dates back virtually to the birth of economics. Successive economic theories have changed the perception of the role. So-called classical models of economic growth, both those of the original authors of classical economics such as Adam Smith and Karl Marx and of their modern successors such as von Neumann, suggest that the decisive cause of high economic growth is a high investment ratio or a high rate of savings. For Smith, the accumulation of capital through saving or parsimony was essential to the division of labor and, therefore, to the productivity growth. For J. S. Mill, industry was limited by capital accumulation. Similar notions regarding the critical role of capital prevailed in all the mainstream works of classical economics.

J. M. Keynes, who was concerned primarily with the short-run employment question, removed saving and capital accumulation from the pedestal erected by the classical economists. However, R. F.

Harrod and E. D. Domar, in their effort to shed light on the long-run implication of the Keynes theme, put saving and investment back on the pedestal. In the Harrod-Domar models, growth rates are almost solely related to the propensity to save, assuming the capital-output ratio is constant.

The traditional view that accorded capital high priority as a causal factor in the growth process has been out of fashion since the mid-1950s, for empirical and theoretical reasons. Neoclassical models of growth demonstrated (as we examined in Chapter 2) that the rate of growth cannot be increased permanently by a higher rate of capital formation. Empirical studies along the line of neoclassical thinking showed that the quantity of capital and/or labor accounts for only a very small fraction of the increase in output. With no technological progress, capital accumulation could account for, at most, one-quarter of the recorded rate of economic growth. Attention then has been focused on the quality of labor and capital and technological change.

Although in the 1960s, following R. M. Solow's 1957 paper, the attention of economists who examined the process of economic growth in the industrialized developed countries was diverted from the effect of capital accumulation to that of technological change, economists who were concerned with growth and development of less developed countries continued to emphasize the importance of capital. According to T. Morgan (1969), 40 of 64 articles, notes, and communications dealing with economic growth published in *American Economic Review* and *Economic Journal* during 1964-1966 were devoted to investment as a cause of growth. Many empirical works confirm that there is a correlation between investment or savings ratios and the rates of economic growth. It is interesting to note that in recent years, as productivity growths lag and economic performances deteriorate in many advanced countries, capital formation has again moved to the forefront of national economic concerns.

The relationship between capital formation and economic growth is very complex. Viewed theoretically, the issue has been whether or not any change in policies that causes an increase or decrease in the investment ratio and the rate of growth of capital can have a permanent effect on the long-term growth rate. Variations in investment expenditure cause changes in aggregate demand as well as changes in productive capacity and technical progress embodied in new capital goods. Only when these important aspects of investment are expounded can we make reasonable conclusions on the relationship between capital accumulation and economic growth.

THEORETICAL EXPLANATIONS

The precise relationship between capital accumulation and economic growth is a matter of considerable debate. There are both empirical and theoretical arguments for and against the thesis that capital formation is the key to economic growth and therefore that differences in growth rates among countries, developed and developing, lie in differences in their savings or investment ratios. In

this section we review major theoretical explanations offered to
support or deny the investment-led growth hypothesis.

In general, neoclassical growth theories, which incorporate
the idea of savings providing a limit to investment (as was common
in the writings of pre-Keynesian or neoclassical economists), deny
that the rate of growth is directly dependent on the investment
(savings) ratio, as discussed in Chapter 2. The fact that the national product grows exponentially at a rate that is a function only of the growth rates of labor supply and technology, independent
of the national product devoted to saving and investment, can be
shown using a simple neoclassical model (see Hamberg and Schultze
1963; Hamberg 1969, 1971).

Let the following Cobb-Douglas production function represent
the economy:

$$Y_t = A_t K_t^\alpha L_t^{1-\alpha} \qquad (4.1)$$

Assume

$$L_t = L_0 e^{nt} \qquad (4.2)$$

$$A_t = A_0 e^{\delta t} \qquad (4.3)$$

$$I_t = \frac{dK}{dt} = S_t = sY_t \qquad (4.4)$$

It can be shown that the proportionate rate of growth of output is

$$\frac{1}{Y_t}\frac{dY_t}{dt} = a + ac\,\frac{\delta}{1-\delta}\,\frac{1}{c - [(c - \overline{K})/e^{at}]} \qquad (4.5)$$

where

$$a = \delta + n(1 - \alpha), \qquad c = \frac{s\overline{L}(1 - \alpha)}{a}$$

$$\overline{L} = L_0^{1-\alpha}, \qquad \overline{K} = K_0^{1-\alpha} \qquad (4.6)$$

From (4.5) it follows that as $t \to \infty$

$$\lim_{t\to\infty}\frac{1}{Y_t}\frac{dY_t}{dt} = a + ac\,\frac{\delta}{1-\delta}\,\frac{1}{c} = n + \frac{\delta}{1-\alpha} \qquad (4.7)$$

The golden age equilibrium growth rate in (4.7) is clearly independent of the proportion of the national product devoted to capital formation and saving. In the long run the capital-output ratio
will increase enough to offset the increase in the savings ratio
and restore the golden age equilibrium growth rate.

A caveat should be issued by observing the fact that even
though the long-run equilibrium growth rate appears to be independent of the savings ratio, the short-run relationship between the
investment ratio and the growth rate of output is positive. When

we rewrite (4.5) to include the savings parameter explicitly, we have

$$G = \frac{1}{Y_t}\frac{dY_t}{dt} = a + \frac{a\overline{L}se^{at}}{[(1 - \alpha)\overline{L}s/a](e^{at} - 1) + \overline{K}} \qquad (4.8)$$

where all notations are defined as before. Taking the partial derivative of the growth rate of output with respect to the savings rate, we obtain

$$\frac{\partial G}{\partial s} = \frac{\delta \overline{L}k}{e^{at}\{[(1 - \delta)s\overline{L}/a][1 - (1/e^{at})](\overline{K}/e^{at})\}^2} \qquad (4.9)$$

It is clear that $\partial G/\partial s > 0$ for all $t > 0$, implying that an increase in the savings ratio can raise growth rates in the short run. By plugging into (4.9) values for the various parameters within a plausible range, we can examine the length of time necessary before the equilibrium growth rate will be substantially restored following an increase in the savings rate or the extent to which increased saving leads to a higher growth rate for a given period of time.

In contrast to the neoclassical denial of savings and investment activities as a means to increase growth rates, at least for long periods of time, capital formation has been emphasized as a key to economic growth in many arguments. An early line of thinking showing that permanent changes in the investment share have permanent effects upon the rate of economic growth is that by Harrod and Domar. As we discussed in Chapter 2, they emphasize the dual nature of investment. Investment generates income through the multiplier process and increases productive capacity by enlarging the capital stock. The condition for continuous equilibrium in a growing economy between planned saving and investment requires that output and income grow at a rate:

$$G = \Delta Y/Y = s/C \qquad (4.10)$$

where s is an average or marginal propensity to save and C is the capital-output ratio, or the capital coefficient.

Equation (4.10) clearly shows that the rate of growth of income in any period is the product of the rate of saving, expressed as a ratio of income, and the reciprocal of the capital-output ratio. The equilibrium growth rate varies directly with the savings (investment) rate s and inversely with the capital coefficient C. If there is some reason for believing that the capital coefficient is stable at least for a certain period, it seems natural to conclude that the rate of growth depends upon the rate of capital formation. Under the formulation along Harrod and Domar's line of thinking, saving and investment are restored to their crucial role in determining the long-run rate of growth.

One of the attractive aspects of the Harrod-Domar model is
the magnificent simplicity of its variables. This is especially
true of the capital-output ratio, whose behavior and property are
crucial in accepting the conclusion that capital formation is a
key to economic growth. Harrod originally used the concept of the
capital coefficient primarily to analyze the conditions under
which aggregate demand will adjust to a growing productive capacity. Those who are inclined to view capital formation as the chief
agent of growth argue that the ratio of capital to output is governed essentially by technological considerations, and that for a
given state of technology the capital coefficient can be regarded
as a fundamental parameter that remains fairly constant.

Many have questioned the constancy of the capital-output ratio and the causality from investment or capital coefficient to
economic growth. For many reasons the capital coefficient can
vary. One reason is cyclical variation in the intensity of capital utilization. In periods of recession the average capital-output ratio will tend to be higher than its normal value because output will be depressed in relation to the size of the capital stock,
which is relatively fixed. The capital-output ratio may vary because capital intensity varies substantially from one sector to
another, and there is a certain tendency for new investment not to
be spread evenly over the whole economy. Furthermore, as a result
of technical progress and shifts in the pattern of demand, the
capital coefficient may be subject to change in one direction or
another (see Myrdal 1968, pp. 1941-2004).

Apart from the above considerations, what is perhaps more
worthwhile to note is the possibility of interrelatedness between
the capital coefficient and the investment ratio. Suppose, in the
spirit of neoclassical economics, the rate of technical progress is
more or less given worldwide datum and the rate of population
growth does not differ much. According to the principle of decreasing marginal productivity, an increase in capital per worker
would eventually lead to a lower marginal productivity of capital,
i.e., to a higher capital coefficient. Therefore, the higher the
investment ratio, the higher the capital coefficient. Since a
higher capital-output ratio leads to a slower rate of growth from a
given share of investment, it is not certain whether or not an increase in the savings ratio results in a higher growth rate. Another implicit conclusion from the interdependence between the capital coefficient and the investment share is that the capital coefficient may be a function of growth rather than the other way
around.

The fact that technical factors alone do not govern the capital-output ratio and therefore that the ratio varies widely from
country to country, from sector to sector, and through time--cou-
pled with the uncertainty in the causal direction among the variables involved--undermines the argument based on the Harrod-Domar
model that investment and saving are a key to economic growth.
However, it must be noted that the validity of the Harrod-Domar
model does not hinge on the assumption that the capital-output ra-

tio is constant. What is necessary is the assumption that changes in the capital coefficient do not occur quickly whenever more capital formation occurs.

The discussion so far leads us to conclude as follows: the limiting cases of the neoclassical and Harrod-Domar models give rise to opposing results. In the simplest formulations of both theories, the neoclassical theory predicts no relationship between the savings rate and the growth rate of output, while the Harrod-Domar model provides a direct link between the two. Relaxation of the assumption employed in each case and more realistic considerations make these contrasting conclusions less sharp. The short-run outcome of the neoclassical model is that there is a positive relation between the savings rate and the growth rate of output. The variability and volatility of the capital coefficient do not always lead to the conclusion that the growth rate will be raised by an increase in the savings rate.

In sharp contrast to the ambivalent results above, there are some strong reasons for believing that the rate of economic growth is influenced by the rate of capital formation. One important argument is that efficiency improvement and organizational change, which result in higher growth, result from new investment. Another important argument is that investment serves as a medium for technical progress. While the first of these two arguments has been neglected in almost all discussions of the role of investment in the growth process, the second has received some extensive examination in the literature. We discuss each of them in turn.

In much of the conventional theory, a more efficient system of allocation is deemed capable of securing only a once-and-for-all increase in output. Better allocation moves the production frontier closer to the production possibility frontier, and this gives a once-and-for-all increase in output and a temporary boost to the growth rate while it is occurring. If, however, investment is essentially a matter of incurring costs to reallocate resources, then the efficiency with which this is done must affect the yield of investment, and so the proportionate rate of growth in the long run. So long as new investment is occurring, reallocation of resources is occurring. It is not a once-and-for-all but a continuing process.

Organizational change in connection with new investment also generates dynamic forces conducive to economic growth. When a firm is growing rapidly through investment, there is a need to reorganize. In a growing concern it is much easier to shift workers around to the place of highest productivity and to avoid featherbedding or similar growth-retarding practices (see Chap. 8 for more detail). As long as investment continues to be occurring, organizational change for higher productivity will occur. Again, the result of this process is not a once-and-for-all increase but a continuous increase in the growth rate.

Since Solow's celebrated 1957 paper, technical progress has been accepted as the most significant source of economic growth. Many argued that a large portion of growth rates assigned to tech-

nical change must be ascribed to the capital formation because it
is through investment that new technologies are, in the main, introduced into the production process. When investment is married
to technology, which is what E. S. Phelps (1962) calls the "new
view" of investment, the role of investment is to modernize as well
as deepen and widen the capital stock. Many attempted to switch
back to the importance of capital accumulation by relating technical change to investment in the endogenous investment hypothesis.

Despite the intuitive appeal of the idea that if technical
change is treated as capital-embodied, with investment as the vehi-
cle for implementing technical change in production, change in investment will influence the equilibrium growth rate; no unequivocal
resolution has been made in the theoretical discussion of the matter. Some writers show that whether or not technical change is embedded in the processes of production through the medium of new investment, the long-run growth rate remains independent of the national product devoted to saving and investment. Others construct
growth models in which the share of investment affects the long-
term growth rate when technical progress depends on investment. We
examine these opposing views in turn, resorting to the simple
framework for each case.

Suppose every capital good embodies the latest technology at
the moment of its construction but does not participate in subsequent technical progress. The output rate at time t of capital
equipment of vintage v is assumed to be given by a Cobb-Douglas
production function

$$Y_v(t) = B_0 e^{\lambda v} K_v(t)^\alpha L_v(t)^{1-\alpha} \tag{4.11}$$

where $K_v(t)$ denotes the amount of capital stock of vintage v surviving at a time t, and $L_v(t)$ denotes the quantity of labor employed on that capital. It is assumed that technical progress is
neutral and the same for all vintages. Solow (1960) has shown that
if homogeneous labor is allocated efficiently across all vintages
of capital so as to maximize total output, aggregate output--the
sum of the homogeneous outputs of the various vintages--is given by

$$Y_t = B_0 J(t)^\alpha L(t)^{1-\alpha} \tag{4.12}$$

where $J(t) = \int_{-\infty}^{t} e^{(\lambda/\alpha)v} K_v(t)dv$. Equation (4.12) shows that capital-embodied technical change results in an aggregate production
function in total employment and what has been called the aggregate
"effective stock of capital."

We are now in a position to discuss our main question: whether or not the long-run growth rate depends on the proportion of the
national product devoted to saving and investment when technical
change is embedded in the production process through the medium of
new capital formation. The answer is deceptively simple. A comparison of (4.12) with (4.1) shows that they are identical in form.
Therefore, if we apply the same assumptions as those in (4.2)

through (4.4) and follow the same way in deriving the equilibrium
growth rate of aggregate output in the neoclassical model with disembodied technical change, the long-run growth rate in the vintage
model should be the same as the one we obtained in (4.5) or (4.7).
Therefore, the conclusion is that even when advances in technology
are associated with capital formation only, the long-run growth
rate is independent of the savings ratio. The limiting long-run
growth rate depends on the rate of technical progress but not on
the type of progress.

The explanation for this counterintuitive result from the vintage growth models lies in the constancy in the age distribution or
average age of the capital stock. Advances in technology associated with capital formation are a function of its age distribution.
Given the rate of technical change, the average level of technology
will be more up to date the lower the average age of capital, because more of the capital stock will embody the most recent technology. Apparently, it is overlooked that in exponential growth
the age distribution of capital depends on the growth rate of output and the rate of depreciation. All vintages of the capital
stock grow at the same rate. Since the rates of depreciation and
of growth itself are, under conditions of equilibrium growth, independent of the savings or investment ratio, all change in either
ratio can have no permanent influence on the age distribution of
capital and, therefore, on the golden age equilibrium growth of
output.

Some have modified slightly the neoclassical model with endogenous technical change and found that the equilibrium path of the
modified model differs in crucial ways from that of the usual neoclassical model discussed above. John Conlisk (1967, 1969) and
Walter Eltis (1973) are among those who successfully constructed
growth models in which technical progress is affected by investment
and the share of investment affects the long-term growth rate. We
rely on Conlisk's work for the following discussion.

Conlisk's model consists of the following three equations:

$$Y = F(K, L) \tag{4.13}$$

$$\dot{K} = dK/dt = sY - uK \tag{4.14}$$

$$\dot{L} = dL/dt = hY + nL \tag{4.15}$$

where Y, K, and L are respectively output, capital, and labor; $F(K,
L)$ is a neoclassical, linear-homogeneous production function; and
s, u, h, and n are constant parameters. It is noted that if $h = 0$
in (4.15), the model is a standard neoclassical growth model. Conlisk assumes that $h > 0$ to distinguish his model from the standard
neoclassical model.

As Conlisk interprets his model, the terms sY and hY in (4.14)
and (4.15) represent endogenous growth components, while the terms
uK and nL represent exogenous growth components. From the fact
that both inputs in the production function in (4.13) are specified

in their efficiency units, it follows that if there is capital aug-
menting technical progress, s represents both saving and endogenous
capital-augmenting technical change, while u represents both depreciation and exogenous capital-augmenting technical change.

By dividing both sides of (4.14) and (4.15) by K and L re-
spectively, and since $\dot{k}/k = \dot{K}/K - \dot{L}/L$ by definition, where $k = K/L$,
we obtain

$$\dot{k}/k = sY/K - u - hY/L - n$$

$$= sF(1, 1/k) - u - hF(k, 1) - n \qquad (4.16)$$

$$= sG(k) - hH(k) - (u + n)$$

Equation (4.16) involves the variables $\dot{k}/k$ and k alone. In-
vocation of the usual equilibrium conditions means that if K and L
grow at the same rate, then by the constant-returns assumption,
output also grows at this rate. Therefore, the equilibrium long-
term growth rate depends on the parameters s, u, h, and n. If the
savings rate increases, there will be an increase in the equilibrium value of k, which satisfies (4.16). The higher equilibrium value of k means a higher growth rate of labor and thus a higher equilibrium rate of growth of output. The result of Conlisk's model
shows clearly that the higher the rate of saving, the higher the
long-run proportionate rate of growth.

Our theoretical understanding of the effects of capital formation on economic growth is far from complete, as our discussion
above indicates. There are several reasons for the lack of some
definite conclusions on the relation between capital accumulation
and economic growth. One reason might be the complexity of the
process involved. It is also true that economists' indulgence in
beauty and elegance of the models they build does not allow them to
have some taste for the relevance of their models. In some cases
models are constructed in such a way that obvious conclusions can
be reached from them without any further serious thought.

Even when meaningful models are built, the conclusions reached
do not shed any light on real-world questions because they are
based on assumptions that are too restrictive. If we want to predict the likely effects of changes in the savings or investment ratio using the Harrod-Domar or neoclassical model with disembodied
or embodied technical change, we have to examine how robust the
model is with respect to many simplifying assumptions entering it.
Usefulness of a model can be questioned when a minor change in assumptions leads to a drastic change in conclusions. This was more
or less the case in the theoretical arguments on the relationship
between economic growth and capital formation.

It is recalled that all the models we discussed above assume
that the economy is operating at full capacity in the steady state
along the balanced growth path. It is inaccurate to try to predict
the rate of growth that would follow from a greater share of investment in the GNP of an economy with unemployment by looking at

the theoretical results of the effects on the rate of growth of a
similar share of investment of an economy with full employment.
Some account must be taken of the unbalanced nature of growth not
only on the supply side, but also on the demand side. It is necessary to know where on its growth path an economy is at the time an
increase in the savings or investment rate is contemplated. Much
of the analysis of the effect of investment on economic growth is
about steady state. As Solow (1970, p. 7) once remarked, "The
steady state is not a bad place for the theory of growth to start,
but may be a dangerous place for it to end."

Before we accept the conclusions reached in our discussion of
theoretical studies, we have to bear in mind the important forces
and factors that may have great significance but have been left out
in most cases. Surprisingly there is little or no discussion about
the influence of economic growth on investment or saving. In some
cases the capital accumulation may be little more than a symptom of
growth and economic development rather than its cause. It is more
likely that the growth rate and savings or investment rate are mu-
tually determined.

EMPIRICAL EVIDENCE

Survey of Empirical Studies
Theories of comparative economic growth are concerned with explaining why some countries or regions grow faster than others.
The investment-led growth hypothesis is one of the most widely discussed explanations. Since the theoretical prediction regarding
the relationship between capital formation and economic growth is
not conclusive, many authors have resorted to empirical testing
for the answer. In this section we will first review major empirical studies dealing with economic growth and capital formation and
then present empirical evidence based on more comprehensive data.

Table 4.1 summarizes the results of previous major empirical
studies of the investment-led growth hypothesis. One of the earliest investigations of the relationship between capital formation
and economic growth is that by Simon Kuznets (1961, pp. 17-21). An
enormous quantity of data gathered enabled him to examine the relationship for 10 countries for the period from the midnineteenth
century to World War I and for 13 countries from the end of the
nineteenth century through the midtwentieth century. Kuznets cal-
culates Kendall's rank correlation between the rate of growth of
output and the investment ratio for each of two samples he considers. In each case, four rank correlation coefficients were obtained depending on the alternate selection of net or gross figures for investment and output to calculate the share of investment. None of the eight coefficients exceeded 0.33 nor was statistically significant. Kuznets's preference for rank correlation
was the desire to avoid the appearance of significant correlation
that might result in a regression merely from one or two extreme
outlying cases.

Table 4.1. Summary of empirical tests of the investment-led growth
hypothesis

A. Kuznets: Rank correlation between growth rate of output and
investment ratio
$$r = 0.33 \sim -0.07$$

B. United Nations: Linear correlation between rate of growth of
GDP and gross fixed investment to GDP
$$r = 0.20 \sim 0.69$$

C. Hill: Regressions of growth rates on investment ratios

$G = -6.11 + 0.58I$	$R^2 = 0.96,$	$n = 5$	(C.1)
$g = -3.57 + 0.38I$	$R^2 = 0.67,$	$n = 5$	(C.2)
$G = -2.26 + 0.51I_m + 0.19I_c$	$R^2 = 0.59,$	$n = 12$	(C.3)
$g = 0.69 + 0.35I_m - 0.05I_c$	$R^2 = 0.37,$	$n = 12$	(C.4)

D. Conlisk: Regression of growth rates on gross savings rates and
population growth rates

$$G = 0.005 + 0.155S + 0.700L \qquad\qquad\qquad\qquad (D.1)$$
$$(0.009)\ (0.038)\quad (0.185)\quad R^2 = 32, \qquad n = 56$$

E. OECD: Regressions between growth rates of GDP and investment
ratio

$G = 1.91 + 0.13I$			(E.1)
$(1.1)\quad(1.7)$	$R^2 = 0.09,$	$n = 20$	
$g = 0.77 + 0.15I$			(E.2)
$(0.3)\quad(1.4)$	$R^2 = 0.07,$	$n = 15$	
$G = 1.97 + 0.16I_{-d}$			(E.3)
$(1.3)\quad(1.9)$	$R^2 = 0.13,$	$n = 18$	
$g = 1.01 + 0.17I_{-d}$			(E.4)
$(0.5)\quad(1.6)$	$R^2 = 0.11,$	$n = 13$	
$G_a = 2.31 - 0.04I_a$			(E.5)
$(2.8)\quad(0.8)$	$R^2 = 0.03,$	$n = 14$	
$g_a = 6.47 - 0.07I_a$			(E.6)
$(4.4)\quad(0.9)$	$R^2 = 0.02,$	$n = 10$	
$G_i = -1.21 + 0.35I_i$			(E.7)
$(0.3)\quad(1.8)$	$R^2 = 0.36,$	$n = 14$	
$g_i = 1.61 + 0.12I_i$			(E.8)
$(1.0)\quad(1.4)$	$R^2 = 0.10,$	$n = 10$	
$G_s = 3.35 + 0.05I_s$			(E.9)
$(4.4)\quad(1.5)$	$R^2 = 0.08,$	$n = 14$	
$g_s = 3.05 + 0.01I_s$			(E.10)
$(1.7)\quad(0.3)$	$R^2 = 0.13.$	$n = 10$	

Sources: Kuznets 1961; UN 1964; Hill 1964; Conlisk 1967; OECD
1970; Pesmazoglu 1972; Thirlwall 1974; Modigliani 1970; Massell
1962; Feldstein and Horioka 1980.
Note: G = rate of growth of total output; g = rate of growth
of per capita output; G_i = rate of growth of investment; S = gross
domestic savings ratio; I = ratio of gross domestic fixed investment
to GNP or GDP; I_m, I_c, I_a, I_i, and I_s = investment ratio in machinery and equipment, construction, agriculture, industry, and services respectively; Ime and Ims = expenditures on equipment and
structures respectively divided by the capital stock in the manufacturing sector; I_{-d} = total fixed investment less dwellings divided by GDP; L = growth rate of population; Z = ratio of foreign
and government saving to total income; Am = level of technology in
the manufacturing sector; t = time.
Numbers in parentheses in studies by OECD and Massell indicate
the t-statistics, while others are the standard error of each coefficient.

Table 4.1. *(continued)*

F. Pesmazoglu: Associations between growth and investment and saving

$$G = 1.16 + 0.27G_i + 0.07I \tag{F.1}$$
$$(1.20)\ (0.12)\quad (0.04)\qquad R^2 = 0.31,\qquad n = 14$$
$$G = 0.93 + 0.22G_i + 0.08S \tag{F.2}$$
$$(1.18)\ (0.12)\quad (0.05)\qquad R^2 = 0.35,\qquad n = 14$$

G. Thirlwall:

$$G = 4.124 + 0.0436S \tag{G.1}$$
$$(0.0723)\qquad R^2 = 0.20,\qquad n = 20$$
$$G = -0.680 + 0.240I \tag{G.2}$$
$$(0.072)\qquad R^2 = 0.377,\qquad n = 20$$
$$G = 1.300 + 0.1081S \tag{G.3}$$
$$(0.0659)\qquad R^2 = 0.130,\qquad n = 20$$
$$G = -1.012 + 0.1994I \tag{G.4}$$
$$(0.0757)\qquad R^2 = 0.378,\qquad n = 20$$

H. Modigliani: Testing of the life cycle hypothesis

$$S = 4.5 + 1.43G \tag{H.1}$$
$$(1.3)\ (0.25)\qquad r = 0.67,\qquad n = 36$$
$$G = 0.52 + 0.265I \tag{H.2}$$
$$(0.72)\ (0.042)\qquad r = 0.73,\qquad n = 36$$
$$S = 9.2 + 0.44Z \tag{H.3}$$
$$G = 3.2 + 0.33Z \tag{H.4}$$
$$S = 4.9 + 1.35G \tag{H.5}$$
$$G = 1.1 + 0.23I \tag{H.6}$$

I. Massell: Time-series and cross-industry analysis of the effects of capital formation on technical change

$$\ln Am(t) = 0.123 + 0.069t + 0.649 \ln Am(t - 1) \tag{I.1}$$
$$(2.78)\quad (5.82)$$
$$- 0.058 \ln I_m(t - 1)$$
$$(0.94)\qquad\qquad n = 40$$

$$\ln Am(t) = 0.103 + 0.068t + 0.631 \ln Am(t - 1) \tag{I.2}$$
$$(2.68)\quad (5.43)$$
$$+ 0.005 \ln Ime(t - 1) - 0.050 \ln Ims(t - 1)$$
$$(0.05)\qquad\qquad (0.82)\qquad n = 40$$

$$Am = 0.20 + 0.07Im + 0.99W - 0.09J - 0.06R \tag{I.3}$$
$$(3.69)\quad (5.31)\quad (2.51)\quad (1.40)\qquad n = 19$$

J. Feldstein and Horioka: Study of international capital mobility

$$I = 0.035 + 0.887S \tag{J.1}$$
$$(0.018)\ (0.074)\qquad R^2 = 0.91,\qquad n = 20$$

The Secretariat of the Economic Commission for Europe of the United Nations explores the relationship between conventional capital inputs and growth rates for 22 western countries in the 1950s (UN 1964, pp. 16-18). For all 22 countries the correlation coefficient is 0.2. When, for more homogeneity, the 11 most industrialized countries are selected out, the correlation coefficient is nearly as low. It rises to 0.69 when Norway, an extreme deviant, is also excluded from the sample.

In his effort to elucidate the effects of capital accumulation, Thomas Hill (1964) examines the relation between the ratios of investment to GNP and the rate of growth of GNP on the one hand and GNP per person employed on the other. His regression, shown in (C.1) of Table 4.1, indicates that the rates of growth of GNP

achieved by the United States and the four largest European coun-
tries--France, Italy, the United Kingdom, and West Germany--have
been quite strongly associated with the shares of national product
devoted to investment. When the correlation is obtained for the
relation between investment ratios and growth rates of GNP per person employed (C.2) or when the sample is extended to include 12
western countries (not shown), Hill finds much weaker or almost no
relationship between growth and investment.

     In addition to showing that high growth rates might be associ-
ated with high investment ratios, Hill demonstrates the need to
distinguish between different types of capital and output if much
progress is to be made in understanding the relation between economic growth and investment at the level of the economy as a whole.
There are reasons for expecting different types of investments to
have different impacts on the growth of measured output. As between two projects with the same initial outlay on capital, but involving assets with very different lengths of life, the project
with the longer lived assets will tend to yield a smaller flow of
output because the total output derived from it is spread over a
longer period over time. Hill's result more or less confirms the
different influences of different types of capital. As the sizes
of the coefficients in (C.3) and (C.4) show, the correlation of
economic growth with investment in machinery and equipment is higher than that with capital invested in construction.

     As discussed in the preceding section, Conlisk (1967, 1969)
built a model showing that the equilibrium growth rate is positively related to the value of the savings rate. Conlisk provides statistical evidence to support his model over the standard neoclassical model via the significant relationship between the propensity
to save and the long-run rate of growth. He uses data from 56
countries over the period 1950-1963. The positive significance of
the savings coefficient, though the R^2 is low as shown in (D.1),
has led him to conclude that the cross-country data favor his modified model over the standard.

     OECD (1970) extends Hill's analysis both to include data for a
longer period and to examine the relationships in each of the three
major sectors--agriculture, industry, and services. As seen in
(E.1) through (E.10) regression results are not favorable to investment-led growth, whether the dependent variable is the growth
rate of total output or that of productivity. It is worthwhile to
note that when dwellings are excluded in the calculation of the
investment share, the results are hardly affected--(E.3) and (E.4).
Turning to the evidence for sectors, it appears that the hypothesis
is completely inapplicable to the agricultural sector--(E.5) and
(E.6)--as the association is negative though not statistically significant. This might be the result of other predominant influences such as climate and natural fertility peculiar to the agricultural sector.

     A fuller and more revealing finding emerges from the analysis
by John Pesmazoglu (1972), who investigated patterns of relationships between investment and economic growth by different groups

of countries and by periods covered in the analysis. As an effort
to take into account the effect of technical progress on economic
growth, Pesmazoglu introduces rates of growth of real gross fixed
capital formation into his equation, while most investigators before him used only average gross fixed capital investment ratios
in their analyses. The association between technical progress and
the growth rate of gross fixed investment is based on the analysis
by Kaldor and Mirrlees, although their precise conception is not
statistically testable because of the lack of employment statistics on new investment.

The general finding by Pesmazoglu is that investment is particularly important in the long run and that this is especially
true in economics at an intermediate stage of development. The
regression results shown in (F.1) and (F.2) indicate that varying
growth rates of GNP over the period 1957-1968 appear to be more
closely associated with the growth rate of investment or saving in
GNP over the period, confirming the influence of investment as a
carrier of technical progress on output growth.

In his effort to examine the relation between saving and inflation, A. P. Thirlwall (1974) takes up the relationship between
economic growth and saving or investment. Using the sample of 20
developed countries, he finds a positive association between the
growth rate of income and the savings rate. The association is
slightly stronger when the growth rate of output is related to the
investment ratio. The correlation of growth rates of total income
with the savings or investment ratio is stronger than that of
growth rates of per capita income with either of them. One possible explanation for the stronger association of saving or investment with the growth of total income than with the growth of per
capita income, as found not only by Thirlwall but also by Hill and
OECD, is that the use of capital depends on the availability of labor.

Franco Modigliani (1970) has made an effort to find out what
light his well-known life cycle theory of consumption can shed on
the relationship between the savings ratio and the rate of output
growth for the economy as a whole. He attempts to take into account the interaction between saving, investment, and the growth
rate of income. The life cycle model leads him to postulate

$$S = \alpha_1 + \alpha_2 G + \alpha_3 (1/Y) + w \tag{4.17}$$

where S, G, and Y represent the savings ratio, the growth rate of
output, and per capita income respectively, and w is the disturbance term. Estimation of (4.17) using data from 36 countries over
the period 1951-1960 produces a coefficient of the per capita income variable that is statistically insignificant. Knowing that
the savings ratio is independent from per capita income, Modigliani
drops the term and reformulates (4.17) into

$$S = \alpha_1 + \alpha_2 G + u \tag{4.18}$$

where u is an error term and S and G are as defined above. The estimated result of (4.18) is shown in (H.1) of Table 4.1.

While the regression result of (H.1) provides support for the
life cycle model, in which Modigliani's prime interest lies, he
further examines other mechanisms that might influence the relationship of (4.18). He notes the dependence of the rate of growth
on the rate of investment and the identity of saving and investment, both implied in the Harrod model. So he hypothesizes:

$$G = \beta_1 + \beta_2 I + v \tag{4.19}$$

where new terms I and v denote the investment ratio and disturbance
term respectively. Equations (4.18) and (4.19), together with the
identity, $S = I$, are a system of simultaneous equations. Unfortunately, as long as the rate of capital formation I is identical
with the savings rate S the system is underidentified, and therefore the parameters of the system cannot be estimated.

To overcome the identification problem, Modigliani resorts to
the fact that domestic investment and saving differ because of the
existence of two sectors in the economy--government and foreign.
The rate of domestic capital formation differs from the domestic
savings rate by two major components--the net foreign deficit on
current account, i.e., net capital imports, and government surplus
on current account, i.e., excess of government capital formation
over government borrowing. Denoting by Z the sum of these two components, divided by total income or output, implies

$$I = S + Z \tag{4.20}$$

Modigliani uses (4.20) to untangle the causal mechanism underlying the observed association between the growth rate of output on
the one hand and savings and investment ratios on the other. Substitution of (4.20) into (4.19) gives rise to

$$G = \beta_1 + \beta_2 (S + Z) + v \tag{4.21}$$

Now the system of two simultaneous equations, (4.18) and (4.21),
has two endogenous variables, G and S, and the exogenous variable
Z. The system is identifiable, and when solved it yields the reduced form equations

$$S = r_1 + \gamma_2 Z + u' \tag{4.22}$$

$$G = \delta_1 + \delta_2 Z + v' \tag{4.23}$$

Estimated results of the reduced forms are shown in (H.3) and (H.4)
in Table 4.1.

The coefficients of the reduced forms in (H.3) and (H.4) imply
the structural estimates shown in (H.5) and (H.6) respectively.
Comparison of (H.5) and (H.6) with (H.1) and (H.2) clearly demonstrates that the structural estimates do not differ much from those

obtained by the least squares method. Modigliani's result, though
based on a simple simultaneous equation approach, renders some assurance to those who rely on the simple formulation of the relationship between economic growth and saving or investment with no
regard to the interaction between them. Modigliani also confirms
that there is an interdependence between saving and growth. Growth
determines saving according to the life-cycle hypothesis, and
growth partly depends on saving as a determinant of the rate of
capital accumulation.

Despite the common belief that the rate of technical change is
influenced by the rate of capital formation, no supporting evidence
had been put forth until B. F. Massell (1962) investigated the hypothesized relationship between technical change and gross investment using time-series data for the manufacturing sector of the
U.S. economy for the period 1919–1958. Based on output per work
hour, capital per work hour, and property share of the product,
Massell first computes the technology index $A(t)$, the dependent
variable in the regression. For the independent variable he uses
expenditure by manufacturing firms on equipment Ime and structures
Ims. The results by Massell, based on the time-series data, do not
lend support to the hypothesis that investment has acted as a vehi-
cle for improvements in technology. Whether total investment is
subdivided into equipment and structure, (I.2), or not, (I.1), the
coefficients indicating the effects on the level of technology of a
higher rate of investment are not significantly different from zero
at the 5 percent level.

As Massell himself acknowledged, the data used for the time-
series analysis might be too crude to be of value in investigating
the hypothesized complementarity between investment and technical
improvements, mainly because of the difficulty of obtaining appropriate capital input measurements. He turns to cross-sectional industry data for help. Instead of relating the aggregate level of
technology to the age composition of the capital stock, Massell
tries to explain the interindustry variations in the level of technology in a given year in terms of differences in the age composition of the capital stock among industries. The level of technology is expected to be highest in those industries with relatively
new stock. Massell uses the ratio of gross investment to net capital stock as an index of the "newness" of the stock. Since the
technology level is a resultant of many other forces, Massell includes in his estimation some of these forces, important among
which are the ratio of equipment to structure R, the ratio of fixed
capital to variable capital J, and the average wage rate W as a
measure of labor quality. The regression result based on data from
19 standard industrial classification, two-digit manufacturing industries over the 1949-1957 period is shown in (I.3) of Table 4.1.
The coefficient associated with the newness of the capital stock is
positive and statistically significant, confirming our initial hypothesis that the level of technology is related to the age of capital, which in turn changes with new capital formation. Because of
the inadequacy of the data used in the time-series analysis, Mas-

sell is more inclined to accept the result of the cross-sectional industry study. So the tentative conclusion is that advances in technology are partially a result of investment activity.

As briefly touched on in our discussion of the result by Modigliani, domestic saving and domestic investment are not identical. Investments have to be financed in one way or another. Two major sources of financing domestic investments are domestic saving and inflow of capital from abroad. In this connection, Martin Feldstein and Charles Horioka (1980) offered two hypotheses and tested them. One hypothesis is that with perfect world capital mobility there is little or no relation between the domestic investment in a country and the amount of saving generated in that country. In contrast, if the flow of long-term capital among countries is impeded, for whatever reasons, increases in domestic saving will be reflected primarily in additional domestic investment. The conclusion reached by Feldstein and Horioka, based on the statistical evidence from the 21 OECD countries for the period 1950-1974, is more favorable to the latter view than to the former. As shown in (J.1) of Table 4.1, differences in domestic savings rates among major industrial countries have resulted in almost equal corresponding differences in domestic investment rates.

The empirical tests reviewed above provide mixed results for the investment-led growth hypothesis, which maintains that differences in growth rates can be accounted for primarily by differences in the volume and structure of capital accumulation. Because of the limited availability of data, some who have wrangled in a sophisticated manner over the theoretical issues have used far laxer standards when it comes to empirical tests of their theories. We can question comparability and consistency in data among sample countries even though each study used the best data available at the time of the empirical investigation.

Given these and other limitations in the existing empirical tests, evidence based on small homogeneous samples confirms the investment-led growth hypothesis. However, when the sample is extended to include a large number of countries or to cover a longer period of time, the relationship between economic growth and capital formation becomes less close. The magnitude of the size of the regression serves as a coefficient of the investment ratios, which approximation of the marginal output-capital ratio or the marginal productivity of capital varies so much from study to study as to work against the hypothesis.

New Tests of the Hypothesis
The remaining part of this section will test the investment-led growth hypothesis using more comprehensive sets of data than employed in previous tests. By way of introduction, we begin with an examination of comparative statistics on investment and saving since World War II. The data presented in Tables 4.2 to 4.4 will, on the one hand, give a general idea of the developments in savings and investment patterns in the advanced industrial countries and, on the other hand, form the basis on which the hypothesis of in-

Table 4.2. Percentage of real gross domestic income devoted to domestic capital formation

Country	1950	1960	1965	1970	1975	1977
Australia	30	30	29	29	36	25
Austria	25	27	27	29	27	30
Belgium	17	20	23	25	24	24
Canada	26	26	28	24	29	27
Denmark	24	27	28	29	24	28
Finland	22	29	29	33	39	27
France	21	24	26	30	28	28
Germany	26	33	34	34	27	29
Ireland	19	17	23	24	22	25
Italy	20	26	22	26	24	24
Japan	22	30	30	37	33	31
Netherlands	28	29	29	31	24	26
New Zealand	26	26	28	27	32	27
Norway	29	30	30	32	39	41
Sweden	21	28	30	29	29	24
Switzerland	20	30	31	34	24	22
United Kingdom	15	22	22	22	21	21
United States	22	20	21	20	18	20

Source: Summers et al. 1980.

Table 4.3. Gross national saving as a percentage of gross domestic product

Country	1950	1955	1960	1965	1970	1975
Australia	25.9[a]	23.5	24.7	24.4	25.7	24.3
Austria	20.5	25.3	27.7	27.1	30.1	26.1
Belgium	14.8[b]	19.2	19.3	23.5	27.1	23.2
Canada	23.4[b]	21.1	19.6	23.3	21.7	21.0
Denmark	19.4[b]	16.8	22.1	22.4	22.4	18.7
Finland	25.1[a]	28.5	29.2	26.9	30.7	29.0
France	13.6[b]	20.5	25.8	26.6	27.2	23.9
Germany	25.0[b]	28.0	29.9	28.4	29.9	23.4
Ireland	7.8	10.6	13.5	17.3	18.2	16.6
Italy	18.6	21.1	23.9	22.8	24.1	19.8
Japan	34.0	25.6	34.7	33.4	39.9	32.5
Netherlands	20.1	27.5	30.4	27.4	26.9	24.0
New Zealand	29.3	21.9	20.3	23.3	23.8	19.7
Norway	28.5[a]	26.2	26.2	27.7	28.6	27.5
Sweden	19.2	21.9	24.3	25.9	24.5	22.8
Switzerland	17.3	27.2	31.1	31.8	34.2	29.0
United Kingdom	na	na	18.1	20.2	21.9	17.1
United States	21.6	21.7	19.6	21.3	18.3	17.2

Source: World Bank 1980, pp. 228-69.
[a]For the year 1952.
[b]For the year 1953.

Table 4.4. Average annual growth rates of gross domestic investment

Country	1950-1960	1960-1970	1970-1977	1950-1965	1965-1977	1950-1977
Australia	7.7	7.0	-0.4	7.7	2.4	5.3
Austria	6.3	6.1	0.3	6.2	2.8	4.5
Belgium	4.9[a]	6.2	2.1	6.0	3.3	4.8
Canada	5.6	4.6	5.6	6.4	3.8	5.2
Denmark	7.4	6.8	0.1	7.5	2.6	5.3
Finland	8.7	4.8	1.7	7.5	2.8	5.4
France	6.1	7.9	1.9	6.8	4.2	5.6
Germany	10.8	4.9	-1.0	8.9	1.3	5.5
Ireland	0.9	11.0	1.7	5.0	4.7	4.9
Italy	9.6	5.5	-0.2	7.1	3.5	5.5
Japan	12.9[b]	10.8	2.0	12.7	9.1	11.1
Netherlands	4.7	6.6	-0.4	5.1	2.9	4.1
Norway	2.9	4.8	6.2	4.2	4.8	4.5
Sweden	6.2	5.4	0.3	6.5	1.7	4.4
Switzerland	8.7	5.4	-5.0	7.7	-0.8	3.9
United Kingdom	7.7	4.8	-0.3	7.1	1.4	4.6
United States	1.6	4.2	0.7	3.5	0.8	2.3

Sources: OECD 1980; World Bank 1980, p. 382.
[a]For the period 1953-1960.
[b]For the period 1952-1960.

vestment-led growth is formulated and tested. Tables 4.2 and 4.3
show the investment and savings ratios respectively, while Table
4.4 summarizes growth rates of investment for the last three decades or so.

Table 4.2 sets out gross domestic investment as a percentage
of gross domestic income at constant real prices. Most exercises
that investigated the relation of investment to growth generally
have failed to allow for relative differences in the price of capital goods and output in intertemporal and intercountry comparisons.
Since an adjustment to real terms is made possible by the efforts
of Irving Kravis and his associates, the figures in Table 4.2 can
be taken with much more confidence. Except for Norway, which shows
an increasing trend in the investment ratio, investment as a proportion to total income remains unchanged for all countries during
the period under examination.

The share of capital formation in gross domestic income varies
from 15 to 30 percent in 1950 and from 20 to 41 percent in 1977.
The variation among countries narrowed during the 1950s and 1960s
and has been getting wider since 1970. A comparison of Table 4.2
with Table 1.1 shows that the variation among countries in their
share of capital formation is much sharper than that for the annual
rate of growth of GDP. The very fast growing economies--West Germany and Japan--did a great deal of investing. The very slow growing economies--the United States and the United Kingdom--did much
less investing than the other countries. But Table 4.2 also shows
that no simple generalization will quite describe the facts, because besides these extreme cases the connection between economic
growth and the investment share is loose. France has invested
rather less and Norway and Canada rather more than their growth
rates might have led one to expect.

The process of capital formation involves three distinct, if
interdependent, activities: saving, finance, and investment. Saving is the activity by which resources, which might be exercised in
favor of current consumption, are set aside and so become available
for other purposes. Until resources are actually committed to the
production of capital goods through investment activity, the intermediate step involved is finance, the activity by which claims to
resources are either assembled from those released by domestic saving or obtained from abroad and then placed in the hands of investors. Table 4.3 shows, as a percentage of GDP, gross national savings, which is the amount of gross domestic capital formation financed from national output. The overall pattern in Table 4.3 is
similar to that of Table 4.2. The savings rate in Ireland has been
the lowest throughout, while that in Japan has been the highest.

Table 4.4 sets out the growth rates of gross domestic investment, which as can be seen, varied over a wide range in individual
countries over time. There is a drastic decrease in average growth
rates of investment since 1970. Besides the fact that Japan has
maintained an unusually high rate of investment growth, about 11
percent for the period 1950-1977, the variation in the average
growth rate of investment among countries under study is not wide.

The difference in average rate of investment growth between the
second fastest and the second slowest growing country is 1.7 percentage points, compared with 2.4 percent difference in the corresponding figures for the growth rate of per capita GDP.

Having discussed the major existing empirical studies of the
investment-led growth hypothesis and historical statistics on investment and savings, we now examine how well the hypothesis of investment-led growth explains the growth performance among 18 industrial countries since 1950.   The same hypothesis is also subjected
to empirical testing using the data from the 48 contiguous states
and from 20 U.S. manufacturing industry groups.   It should be noted
that this testing is constrained by data availability.   Since the
proponents of the investment-led growth hypothesis are not unani-
mous in their specification of the hypothesis, various specifications of the hypothesis are tried.   We use simple regressions; the
results are summarized in Table 4.5.   Overall, the hypothesis fits

Table 4.5. Regressions for the investment-led growth hypothesis
A. Using cross-country data for 1950-1977, $n = 51 \sim 53$

$$G = 2.5557 + 0.3593G_i \tag{1}$$
$$(7.99) \qquad\qquad R^2 = 0.57$$

$$g = 2.0810 + 0.3374g_i \tag{2}$$
$$(7.36) \qquad\qquad R^2 = 0.52$$

$$G = 0.5169 + 0.1389S_i \tag{3}$$
$$(2.52) \qquad\qquad R^2 = 0.12$$

$$g = 0.3082 + 0.1141S_i \tag{4}$$
$$(2.15) \qquad\qquad R^2 = 0.09$$

$$G = 0.2641 + 0.1602S_s \tag{5}$$
$$(3.84) \qquad\qquad R^2 = 0.22$$

$$g = -0.3197 + 0.1459S_s \tag{6}$$
$$(3.49) \qquad\qquad R^2 = 0.19$$

$$G = 2.4551 + 1.4338INV \tag{7}$$
$$(10.19) \qquad\qquad R^2 = 0.68$$

$$g = 7.9955 + 1.3614inv \tag{8}$$
$$(8.89) \qquad\qquad R^2 = 0.62$$

B. Using U.S. regional data for 1958-1972, $n = 144$

$$G_{mv} = 6.0011 + 0.1124G_{mi} \tag{9}$$
$$(4.47) \qquad\qquad R^2 = 0.12$$

$$G_{mv} = 5.6464 + 0.1484S_{mi} \tag{10}$$
$$(2.34) \qquad\qquad R^2 = 0.04$$

$$G_{mv} = 6.2630 + 0.0096INV_m \tag{11}$$
$$(3.99) \qquad\qquad R^2 = 0.10$$

C. Using U.S. manufacturing industry data for 1948-1973, $n = 60$

$$G_m = 3.0229 + 0.2665G_c + 0.5406G_l \tag{12}$$
$$(2.36) \qquad (3.34) \qquad R^2 = 0.43$$

Sources: Tables 4.2, 4.3, 4.4; Bureau of Census 1962,
1967, 1972, 1977; Kendrick 1976b.
Note: Numbers in parentheses represent t-statistics. G
= growth rate of GDP; g = growth rate of per capita GDP; G_i
= growth rate of gross domestic investment; g_i = growth rate of
per capita gross domestic investment; S_i = percentage of real
gross domestic income devoted to domestic capital formation; S_s
= gross national saving as a percent of GDP; $INV = G_iS_i$; inv
= g_iS_i; G_{mv} = rate of growth of value added by manufacture; G_{mi}
= rate of growth of new capital expenditures in manufactures;
S_{mi} = ratio of new capital expenditures to value added in manufactures; $INV_m = G_{mi}S_{mi}$; G_m = growth rate of real gross product
of manufacturing industry groups; G_c = growth rate of gross capital; and G_l = growth rate of the number of persons engaged.

well, given the fact that economic growth is a consequence of the
interaction among so many factors. Since the sample is related to
cross-sectional data, where typically the R^2 obtained is not large,
the explanatory power of the hypothesis for the variation in rates
of growth for each case is discernible enough.

The investment-led growth hypothesis has received strong support from the data from 18 advanced countries over the three intervals 1950-1960, 1960-1970, and 1970-1977, as indicated by regressions (1) through (8) of Table 4.5. Estimation of the most widely
used specification, relating economic growth to the savings or investment ratio--(3) to (6)--produces significant results consistent
with the investment-led growth hypothesis. Based on the argument
that there is association between technical progress and the growth
rate of gross fixed investment, as analyzed by Kaldor and Mirrlees,
and that growth rates differ because of differences in the technical progress among countries, an attempt is made to examine the relationship between economic growth and the growth rate of gross investment. Regressions (1) and (2) show clearly that there is a
very close association between economic growth and the growth of
gross investment, confirming the role of gross investment in fur-
thering technical progress, thus helping the economy grow fast.

The specifications in (1) and (2) of Table 4.5, as a way of
demonstrating the importance of investment as a carrier of technological change in the growth process, are susceptible to attack.
As mentioned earlier in our discussion of Pesmazoglu's empirical
testing in a similar fashion, regression of economic growth against
investment growth is a very rough way of relating technical change
to capital accumulation. One may also object on the grounds that
running the regression of a part (investment) of the total (total
output) against the total will yield a high association regardless
of the underlying theoretical relationships between them. This
criticism, which is valid by itself, will lead one, in the extreme,
to pursue consumption-led or government expenditure-led growth.
However, on many grounds, one is likely to believe that so long as
investment continues to grow, investment is a more influential
force in economic growth than any other component of aggregate demand.

It is argued that the relative size of a country's investment
to its GDP is not taken into account in estimating regressions like
(1) and (2) of Table 4.5. According to this view, the proper way
of testing is to run a regression of economic growth on investment
growth adjusted by the relative size of investment to GDP. The
product of the growth rate of investment and its share to GDP is
taken as the independent variable in regressions (7) and (8).
Quite a statistically significant association is found between this
new variable and economic growth. Again, one strong objection to
the above procedure might be that whether or not the relative size
of a part to the whole is taken into consideration, the association
between growth rates of a part and the whole is bound to be strong.
In the extreme case of a stationary state, where all variables are
growing at the same rate and the proportion among them is not

changing at all, the correlation between a part and the whole would
be perfect.

A comparison of the regression results for the investment-led
growth hypothesis with those for the export-led growth hypothesis
demonstrates that the above criticism is not always valid. As will
be discussed in detail in the next chapter, when a statistical association is sought between economic growth and the growth rate of
exports adjusted by the relative size of exports to GDP, we find a
very weak relation between them--(7) and (8) in Table 4.5--even
though exports are, on the average, higher in relative size and
growth rates than investment. The close association between economic growth and investment growth shown by (7) and (8) confirms
the investment-led growth hypothesis. Otherwise, an answer must be
sought to explain the fact that the same procedure applied to both
the export-led and investment-led growth hypotheses produces quite
different statistical results.

The basic specifications for the cross-country case are repeated using data on manufacturing value-added and its capital expenditures, pooled for the 48 contiguous states over three component time periods, 1958-1963, 1963-1967, and 1967-1972. Pooling
gives 144 data points. Three regressions, (9) to (11) in Table
4.5, relate growth rate of value-added by manufacture to that of
new capital expenditures, the share of new capital expenditures in
value-added, and the product of these two variables respectively.
Though the coefficients of determination in the three regressions
are not high, estimated coefficients are statistically significant.

Several of the specifications of the investment-led growth hypothesis are incomplete because of the absence of capital stock
data among countries or regions. There are no signs of any immi-
nent solution to this problem. Analysts faced with hard reality
try to generate some approximate empirical results that might increase their understanding of the growth process. Thanks to the
painstaking efforts by John Kendrick (1961, 1973, 1976a, b, 1980),
time-series and cross-industry data on the capital stock in the
United States are available. For our purpose, we employ one of
Kendrick's cross-industry data series to examine the relationship
between economic growth on the one hand and the growth of capital
and labor on the other. Regression (12), Table 4.5, shows that the
growth of real capital stock and labor force engaged in production
contributes positively to economic growth, the coefficients associated with both variables being statistically significant.

To summarize, the regression results based on three different
sets of data provide support for the investment-led growth hypothesis. To be sure, the regressions are very simple, omitting a great
deal of the complications, lags, and interactions of the real
world, and much needs to be done in the way of getting better data,
employing more sophisticated estimating techniques, and the like.
Better availability of data, particularly for the capital stock, in
the future should lead one to the investigation of other theoretical specifications of the hypothesis. It might be fair to say that
while the sources-of-growth accounting unduly downgrades the impor-

tance of capital and investment in economic growth, the regression
results obtained above may provide an upward bias to the investment-led growth hypothesis.

CONCLUSIONS

The investment-led growth hypothesis states that the rate of
growth in national product depends directly on how fast real capital increases. This consideration has led policymakers aiming at
economic growth to concentrate on actions designed to increase investment. The results of such policies have not always been up to
expectations. The explanation for such failures can be sought in
several ways. First, almost all economists agree with Ragnar
Nurkse (1953), who stated: "Capital is a necessary but not a sufficient condition of progress." High investment does not guarantee
rapid growth, but low investment does constitute a bar to rapid
economic growth. Historical statistics suggest that in general no
country has achieved very fast growth without a high rate of investment, whereas a large number of countries that were investing
substantially failed to grow rapidly.

Second, the composition of investment may be just as important
as its magnitude. Once investment takes place, there are important
problems of ensuring that it finds its way into the most productive
lines leading to further output and growth. The analysis by Hill
examined earlier, for example, shows that growth is much less sensitive to certain types of investment than to others, providing a
simple explanation of why some countries appear to have grown slowly in relation to their investment. Indeed, much of the discussion
of the investment-led growth hypothesis assumes the optimality of
investment decisions.

Third, one may argue that policies to promote economic growth
through higher investment failed simply because there was no connection between them, anyway. Out of the welter of confusing en-
tanglements in which we find our theory and data, it is difficult
to draw any clear-cut conclusion directly. Our vision is blurred
by the miasma of complexity surrounding the theoretical explanations and constrained by the availability of data necessary to dis-
entangle the complexity.

Edward Denison (1980) is one of several writers who have persistently criticized the preoccupation by growth analysts with the
investment ratio. While he accepts that "capital is an important
growth source" and that "it has sometimes contributed importantly
to differences in growth rates between periods and places," he argues that gross investment ratios have little value for analyzing
the relationship between capital and growth and for explaining differences in growth rates among countries. He advances several
points in justification of his negative view (Denison 1967, pp.
117-22).

First, he maintains that insofar as capital is a source of
growth, it is the growth of the stock of capital that is relevant,
and this is neither measured nor determined by investment ratios.

This criticism makes the whole investigation of the relationship
between rates of investment and economic growth unnecessary and redundant. The validity of the criticism depends on whether or not
one accepts the theoretical result of neoclassical analysis that
the long-run equilibrium rate of growth of both output and capital
stock is insensitive to differences in the investment ratio. Colin
Clark (1962) is also critical of the role of capital in the process
of economic growth because he believes the main factor of growth is
the human factor, not the material factor.

To leap from the neoclassical theoretical conclusion to the
belief that historical investigation of investment ratios is unnecessary appears to be an unwarranted step. In the first place,
the process of adjustment by which rates of growth of output and
capital fall back to the long-term equilibrium may be very slow,
allowing long intervals during which the increase in investment
does generate an appreciable, if always diminishing, increment to
growth rates.

The speed of adjustment to equilibrium in the neoclassical
growth model depends on many factors, such as the size of the natural growth rate, where on its growth path an economy is at the time
investment or saving is increased, and many others. R. Sato (1963,
1964) finds that it takes about 100 years for the adjustment of the
actual to the equilibrium growth rate to be 90 percent complete.
(For a criticism of R. Sato, see K. Sato [1966].) Daniel Hamberg
(1969) predicts a much shorter adjustment period of about 20 to 25
years. It may take less time to do so if the vintage capital approach is fully appropriate. As long as the adjustment process is
slow, investigation of the relationship between growth and investment is not unwarranted.

It is also noted that the neoclassical result is based on the
assumption of perfect substitutability of one factor of production
for another. If the economy is characterized by a production function in which factors can only be combined in a certain proportion,
the growth of the economy is limited by the rate of growth of the
factor in inadequate supply. Suppose a country's growth is constrained by the inadequate supply of capital; then an increase in
investment share will raise the rate of growth and the level of
output. To the extent that the elasticity of substitution is low,
Denison's first criticism is not valid. Of course, the extent to
which factors are substitutable is a question of fact, not of theory.

The second argument by Denison against the investment-led
growth hypothesis is that capital is only one source of growth, not
the sources of growth. As shown in Table 2.2, capital's contribution to growth ranges from 14 to 26 percent in the advanced developed countries Denison examined. The figures in the table imply
that an increase of the range from 7 to 4 percentage points in the
net investment ratio would have been required to add 1 full percentage point to the growth rate.

To justify his viewpoint of the unimportance of investment,
Denison asks the question how much more investment or savings Amer-

icans should make to match the growth rate of the United States to
that of Japan. To add 5 percentage points to the growth rate,
which is required to match Japan, the investment ratio of the
United States has to be raised five times, from 7.6 percent of net
output to 45 percent. Needless to say, it is not correct to say
that if the United States would invest only as large a fraction of
her national income as Japan, it would grow as rapidly. The truth
might be that even when the United States saves and invests as much
as Japan it will not grow as rapidly or that probably nothing Amer-
icans do will make the United States grow as fast as Japan unless
the two countries become similar in many other respects.

Third, Denison downgrades the investment-led growth hypothesis
by noting that the effects of embodiment of technical progress in
new capital are negligible. As we examined above, the embodiment
effects operate through the age distribution of the gross capital
stock of the economy. Denison argues that the reduction in average
age of capital will not be realized because of the offsetting effects between obsolescence and quality improvement. The return on
replacement is highest, and hence the incentive to invest greatest,
for types of investments that have suffered the most obsolescence
as a result of quality improvement in new vintages. Furthermore,
even when there are changes in the average age, according to Denison, they cannot account for a large portion of the growth rate.

The validity of the above criticism again depends on the speed
of adjustment and the rapidity by which new innovations occur.
Once it is understood that one main innovative effect of investment
is caused by the reorganization of enterprises as a result of the
introduction of investments into the productive process, it becomes
clear that it takes considerable time before the full amount of
technical progress due to a given amount of investment is realized.
An increase in investment does not yield an instant growth impulse.
Innovation rarely stands still when capital deepening is accompanied by capital quickening.

Denison's (1980) last point of criticism touches upon the causality question of the relationship between investment and economic
growth. He says that "raising investment may also be the least
fundamental part of the problem of growth and productivity because
the observed setback to capital growth was . . . more the consequence of other problems than their cause." So Denison believes
that the causation runs from growth to investment rather than vice
versa.

With regard to the controversy on the causation between investment and growth, it is not correct to simply say that it merely
expresses a shortcoming of any simple correlation. It is as sensi-
ble to say that capital accumulation results from growth as it is
to say that it is the cause of growth. It is more correct to say,
according to the former view, that a fast rate of capital accumulation is a symptom of a fast rate of growth rather than a cause of
it. Because savings and capital accumulation in a capitalist economy do not represent independent variables, the truth might be that

investment and growth proceed side by side and the causation between them runs in both directions.

Our theoretical and empirical understanding of the effects of capital formation on economic growth is far from complete. Despite the above arguments against the investment-led growth hypothesis, we can still maintain that investment is a major, if not the primary, contributor to economic growth. The importance of capital accumulation can be seen vividly when we ask the question whether anything like the observed expansion in productivity since the Industrial Revolution would have occurred in the absence of capital formation. When investment is prized as the carrier of technical progress, productivity can hardly be expected to grow without positive investment.

REFERENCES

Aukrust, O. 1959. Investment and economic growth. *Prod. Meas. Rev.* 16:35-50.

Bureau of Census. 1962. *County and City Data Book.* Washington, D.C.: U.S. Government Printing Office.

————. 1967. *County and City Data Book.* Washington, D.C.: U.S. Government Printing Office.

————. 1972. *County and City Data Book.* Washington, D.C.: U.S. Government Printing Office.

————. 1977. *County and City Data Book.* Washington, D.C.: U.S. Government Printing Office.

Clark, C. 1962. *Growthmanship: A Study in the Mythology of Investments.* London: Institute of Economic Affairs.

Conlisk, J. 1967. A modified neoclassical growth model with endogenous technical change. *South. Econ. J.* 34:199-208.

————. 1969. A neoclassical growth model with endogenously positioned technical frontier. *Econ. J.* 79:348-62.

Cornwall, J. 1970. The role of demand and investment in long-term growth. *Q. J. Econ.* 84:48-69.

Denison, E. F. 1964. The unimportance of the embodied question. *Am. Econ. Rev.* 54:90-94.

————. 1967. *Why Growth Rates Differ.* Washington, D.C.: Brookings Institution.

————. 1980. The contribution of capital to economic growth. *Am. Econ. Rev.* 70:220-24.

Eltis, W. A. 1963. Investment, technical progress, and economic growth. *Oxf. Econ. Pap.* 15:32-52.

————. 1973. *Growth and Distribution.* New York: John Wiley and Sons.

Ghali, M., M. Akiyama, and J. Fujiwara. 1978. Factor mobility and regional growth. *Rev. Econ. Stat.* 60:78-84.

Feldstein, M., and C. Horioka. 1980. Domestic savings and international capital flows. *Econ. J.* 90:314-29.

Hamberg, D. 1969. Saving and economic growth. *Econ. Dev. Cult. Change* 17:460-82.

————. 1971. *Models of Economic Growth*. New York: Harper & Row.

Hamberg, D., and C. L. Schultze. 1963. Investment and economic growth. *Metroeconomica* 15:1-16.

Hill, T. P. 1964. Growth and investment according to international comparisons. *Econ. J.* 74:287-304.

Humphries, J. 1976. Causes of growth. *Econ. Dev. Cult. Change* 24:339-53.

Johnson, D. W., J. S. Chiu, and T. P. Hill. 1965. Growth and investment according to international comparisons: Comment and reply. *Econ. J.* 75:626-32.

Kendrick, J. W. 1961. *Productivity Trends in the United States*. Princeton: Princeton University Press.

————. 1973. *Postwar Productivity Trends in the United States 1948-1969*. New York: National Bureau of Economic Research.

————. 1976a. *The Formation and Stocks of Total Capital*. New York: National Bureau of Economic Research.

————. 1976b. *The National Wealth of the United States by Major Sector and Industry*. New York: Conference Board.

————. 1980. *Productivity in the United States*. Baltimore: Johns Hopkins University Press.

Kuznets, S. 1961. Quantitative aspects of the economic growth of nations. VI. Long term trends in capital formation proportions. *Econ. Dev. Cult. Change* 9(pt. 2).

Lamfalussy, A. 1961. *Investment and Growth in Mature Economy*. New York: Macmillan.

Massell, B. F. 1962. Is investment really unimportant? *Metroeconomica* 14:65-85.

Modigliani, F. 1970. The life cycle hypothesis of saving and intercountry differences in the savings ratio. In *Induction, Growth and Trade*, ed. W. A. Eltis, M. F. Scott, and J. N. Wolfe. Oxford: Clarendon.

Morgan, T. 1969. Investment vs. economic growth. *Econ. Dev. Cult. Change* 17:392-414.

Myrdal, G. 1968. *Asian Drama*, vol. 4. New York: Twentieth Century Fund.

Nurkse, R. 1953. *Problems of Capital Formation in the Underdeveloped Countries*. Oxford: Blackwell.

Organization for Economic Cooperation and Development (OECD). 1970. *The Growth of Output, 1960-1980*. Paris: OECD.

————. 1980. *National Accounts of OECD Countries, 1950-1978*. Paris: OECD.

Pesmazoglu, J. 1972. Growth, investments, and savings ratio: Some long and medium term associations by groups of countries. *Bull. Oxf. Univ. Inst. Econ. Stat.* 34:309-28.

Phelps, E. S. 1962. The new view of investment: A neoclassical analysis. *Q. J. Econ.* 76:548-67.

Preston, E. 1969. Growth and investment in the market economies. *Econ. Rec.* 45:544-62.

Sato, K. 1966. On the adjustment time in neo-classical growth models. *Rev. Econ. Stud.* 33:263-68.

Sato, R. 1963. Fiscal policy in a neo-classical growth model: An
    analysis of time required for equilibrating adjustment. *Rev.
    Econ. Stud.* 30:16-23.
————. 1964. The Harrod-Domar model vs. the neo-classical growth
    model. *Econ. J.* 74:380-87.
Scott, M. FG. 1976. Investment and economic growth. *Oxf. Econ.
    Pap.* 28:317-63.
Smith, D. M. 1975. Neoclassical growth models and regional growth
    in the United States. *J. Reg. Sci.* 15:165-81.
Solow, R. M. 1959. Investment and economic growth: Some com-
    ments. *Prod. Meas. Rev.* 19:62-68.
————. 1960. Investment and technical progress. In *Mathematical
    Models in the Social Sciences,* ed. K. J. Arrow, S. Karlin, and
    P. Suppes. Stanford: Stanford University Press.
————. 1970. *Growth Theory: An Exposition.* New York: Oxford
    University Press.
Stein, J. L. 1965. Economic growth in the west. *Economica* 32:
    74-87.
Summers, R., I. B. Kravis, and A. Heston. 1980. International
    comparisons of real product and its composition, 1950-1977.
    Rev. Income Wealth, ser. 26:34-66.
Thirwall, A. P. 1974. *Inflation, Saving, and Growth in Develop-
    ing Countries.* New York: St. Martin's.
United Nations (UN). 1964. *Some Factors in Economic Growth in
    Europe during the 1950's.* Geneva: UN.
Wilson, G. W. 1970. The concept of capital and its role in eco-
    nomic growth. In *Essays in Economic Analysis and Policy,* ed.
    F. Gehrels, H. M. Oliver, Jr., and G. W. Wilson. Bloomington:
    Indiana University Press.
World Bank. 1980. *World Tables,* 2nd ed. Baltimore: Johns Hop-
    kins University Press.

5
The Export-Led
Growth Hypothesis

For many years economists have suspected that there is a significant relationship between a country's international trade and its economic performance. The relationship between exports and economic growth has long held a fascination for those seeking to explain major influences bearing upon economic growth. A large body of theoretical literature, accompanied by a substantial number of empirical investigations (using the advantage of statistical simplicity), emphasizes the role of exports in leading the economy. Despite a quite extensive discussion of the question of how exports and economic growth are related and a relatively easy availability of relevant data, up to now there has been no general agreement as to the role of exports in economic growth.

The view that economic growth is export led has a long history and many interpretations. (The term "export-led growth" was introduced by Charles P. Kindleberger [1962b].) Adam Smith stressed the importance of trade as a vent for surplus and a means of widening domestic markets, thereby improving the division of labor and the level of productivity. Though John S. Mill (1964) rejected Smith's vent-for-surplus argument on the grounds that resources are mobile, he did accept the importance of the dynamic effects of trade--"indirect effects," as called by Mill.

Alfred Marshall (1959, p. 255) believed that the causes of economic growth must be sought in the theory of international trade when he said that "the causes which determine the economic progress of nations belong to the study of international trade." Marshall's view and D. H. Robertson's (1938) well-known phrase about trade being an "engine of growth" show the awareness of the relationship between trade and growth by neoclassical writers.

Later, Ragnar Nurkse (1961a,b) revived and elaborated the same theme. His reading of nineteenth-century history led him to conclude that "trade was an 'engine of growth' in the 19th century" (Nurkse 1961b, p. 14). A modern version of the export-based model of economic growth is the staple theory of growth (Watkins 1963).

Previously idle or undiscovered resources are brought into use, creating a return to those resources, which is consistent with venting the surplus through trade. The export of primary products affects the rest of the economy by inducing a higher rate of domes-- tic saving, attracting an inflow of factor inputs into the expand- ing export sector, and establishing linkages with other sectors of the economy. Although the rise in exports is induced by greater demand, there are supply responses within the economy that increase the productivity of the exporting economy.

It should be noted that indirect benefits, higher productivi- ty effects, and dynamic gains from trade result not from the as- sumptions of a perfectly competitive world, as in the static neo- classical theory of trade, but from the very removal of these as- sumptions. With perfect competition--homogeneous and divisible resources, no economies of scale, and a full utilization of re- sources--there is no scope for the indirect benefits and dynamic gains from trade to contribute to growth and development. There is the possibility of a greater contribution by trade to the growth of real income beyond the increase from direct gains from trade and the reinvestment of the increase in income. The gains-from-trade approach is ill-adapted to capture the dynamic interaction between trade and rising productivity.

The main purpose of this chapter is to analyze the view that economic growth is export led in some sense. It is different from other chapters in that there is no discussion and empirical exami- nation of the main theme of the chapter in the U.S. regional con- text. As far as theory is concerned, the regional analog of the export-led growth theory is the export-base theory, much discussed in regional economics. That theory, formulated by Douglas North (1955) and Charles Tiebout (1956), stresses the importance of openness in the analysis of subnational economies and the interde- pendence among different areas of a country. Data availability does not allow us to undertake a serious empirical testing of the theory throughout regions in the United States.

THEORETICAL EXPLANATIONS AND MECHANISMS

Many economists have argued that export growth has been the key variable in explaining the variations in economic growth among countries. Although most of the discussions have concentrated on the relationship between growth and exports for countries in the process of development, several interesting hypotheses and differ- ent mechanisms purport to explain the growth-export nexus for ad- vanced countries. If a country's growth of exports can be shown to be related to its growth performance, the next question becomes, Through which mechanisms are they related? Answers assume particu- lar importance when one looks ahead to testing the explanatory pow- er of the export-led model against models embodying other hypothe- ses concerning the determinants of economic growth.

Since 1960 several export-led models of economic growth have appeared in the literature. They differ in their points of empha-

sis, the degree to which they have been articulated, and their
amenability to empirical verification. The most noteworthy recent
contributions to the subject are by Kindleberger, A. Lamfalussy, W.
Beckerman, W. M. Corden, J. Black, and Richard E. Caves.

Kindleberger (1962b, pp. 196–98; 1964, pp. 264–77) is one of
the first modern economists to discuss the impact of foreign trade
on economic growth (see also Kindleberger 1961, 1962a). Kindleberger first distinguishes three possible ways in which exports and
economic growth are related. He then goes on to discuss the specific probable connections between growth and exports in each case.
Three main models of the relationship between exports and economic
growth are posited. In the first, exports are a leading sector
serving to accelerate the rate of domestic expansion. In the lagging model, growth is primarily generated internally, and trade may
slow down domestic expansion. Finally, exports may serve to balance the economy during a time when domestic output is expanding
but internal demand is insufficient to absorb all the output.

The basic characteristic of Kindleberger's export-led growth
model is that an increase in foreign demand for a country's exports, however it occurs, will stimulate the country's domestic
growth. When the economy is at full employment, export expansion
increases income, which will be further expanded through greater
saving and investment along Harrod–Domar lines. If the economy is
operating below the full employment level, expanded exports will
allow resources to be drawn into productive uses. With or without
full employment, expanded exports permit firms to take advantage
of decreasing costs through economies of large-scale production.
If exports increase continuously over time, they serve to raise
the growth rate of the economy. Thus export-led growth may establish a "virtuous circle" with the economy.

Kindleberger points to the economic growth of Britain in the
nineteenth century as the classic example of exports leading
growth. Japan, in the very early stages of industrialization, also seems to have developed mainly through the expansion of exports. Other examples quoted by Kindleberger are Sweden and Denmark after 1880; Switzerland, the Low Countries, and Canada from
1900 to 1913; and Canada after 1945.

In contrast to the foregoing possibility of exports as the
leading sector, Kindleberger also discusses the case where increased exports may retard growth when a nation is not able to
adapt or transform its domestic resources to foreign trade. The
expansion of exports may alter the distribution of income in favor
of groups whose consumption and savings patterns do not contribute
significantly to economic growth. Expanded exports may require
heavy domestic investment, which, in turn, increases demand for
capital equipment from abroad and for basic raw materials. Increased imports will lead to a strain on the country's balance of
payments. Much of the interest in trade as a lagging sector has
centered on the transformation problems of less developed countries. The industrialization of such economies requires the establishment of new industries, but their development may be re-

tarded by the competition of existing foreign imports. A forced
reduction in imports may foster the expansion of certain domestic
industries. But the removal of the competitive stimulus provided
by imports may well lower incentives to innovate and invest.

Kindleberger's contribution is significant in that he emphasizes the importance of the mechanisms involved in the export-
growth nexus, although the mechanisms mentioned by him are not precise nor articulated in great detail. According to Kindleberger,
more or less trade is neither a necessary nor sufficient condition
for growth or nongrowth. Exports can be either growth promoting or
growth retarding. In these circumstances we should be careful not
to attribute growth or stagnation to changes in exports without
specifying the precise mechanisms through which they operate.

In his attempt to explain the differences in the postwar performance of the United Kingdom as compared to member countries of
the Common Market, Lamfalussy (1963) emphasizes the role played by
exports. He explicitly assumes that all countries concerned have
abolished controls over imports, or are in the process of liberal-
izing their import controls and tariffs, and that the primary goal
of government economic policy is to maintain full employment and
stimulate economic growth without inflation and external disequilibrium. The first assumption is clearly in line with Western
European history, while the second implies that external disequilibrium would necessitate government policies to restrict home demand, with the result that the level of employment and the rate of
growth might be adversely affected.

Lamfalussy takes up several potential factors that might have
limiting influences on economic growth. Two stand out: labor on
the supply side and the balance of payments on the demand side.
With regard to the argument that an inadequate rise in the supply
of labor has been one of the factors responsible for the difference
between the British and Continental rates of growth, Lamfalussy
claims that available statistical evidence refutes the argument.
He says that the common feature of the growth pattern of the Common
Market countries relative to the United Kingdom is not connected to
faster rise in employment in these countries. Rather, the part
played by the rate of growth seems to have been more important than
differences between the rates of increase in the labor supply of
the two parties. (The importance of the availability of surplus
labor and the controversy surrounding this factor are discussed in
detail in Chapter 6.)

So Lamfalussy turns to the demand side and analyzes the influence of the balance of payments on the British and Continental
rates of growth. The achievement of equilibrium or a surplus in
the balance of payments is of great importance, according to Lamfalussy, because it enables governments to follow expansionist policies. If exports grow rapidly, this helps overcome the balance-
of-payments problem. Furthermore, increases in exports stimulate
investment through accelerator effects. The increases in investment would have the consequence of increasing internal demand and
at the same time would lead to favorable effects on productivity

and a strengthening of a country's international competitive position.

Lamfalussy also stresses the response of saving to a sudden quickening of the rate of growth of income, especially in the corporate sector through the retention of a large share of the short-run increase in profits and in the government sector through a rise in tax revenues not immediately matched by increased expenditures or offset by reduced tax rates. So long as exports keep rising, there would be a self-reinforcing tendency for a country to maintain its competitive position and to continue its rapid rate of economic growth.

In Lamfalussy's framework, the notion of a virtuous circle of growth describes how a rapid growth of exports allows an economy to find itself in a situation of rapid, sustained growth of demand, maximum output, and productivity while staying free of balance-of-payment difficulties. The association between rapid growth in exports, investment, productivity, and declining relative export prices can be cited as the essence of the export-led growth hypothesis by Lamfalussy. His model is an important contribution to the theory of growth in an open economy since it encompasses many major aggregative forces that affect a country's growth and balance of payments and specifies in its own logical way the mechanisms involved. While it is very likely true that a failure of exports to grow rapidly will choke off booms, it is open to question as to whether balance of payment considerations by themselves determine long-run growth rates.

In his review of the massive Twentieth Century Fund study, *Europe's Needs and Resources* (Dewhurst 1961), which relies upon a "convergence" model according to which there are some long-run historical rates of growth from which substantial deviations must be of a temporary nature, Beckerman (1962) observes that, contrary to the Twentieth Century Fund assumption, the relative growth experience of European countries during the 1950s showed a substantial dispersion of the growth rates of individual countries around the overall average and followed a "divergence" rather than a "convergence" theory of growth process.

Beckerman's interpretation of the growth experiences of European countries is that the expectation of the business community concerning long-term demand prospects is the key variable that determines both the level of investment and the rate of productivity change; demand expectations thereby differentiate the output growth rates of advanced industrial countries. Beckerman believes that the expansion of exports is the variable that helps businesspeople form more confident expectations. The ability to expand exports is in turn linked to the degree of competitiveness, which is defined basically by prices and technological superiority. Rapid productivity growth, resulting from high rates of capital formation based on favorable demand expectations, deters the upward movement of the price level on the assumption that while money wages respond positively to the rate of productivity growth, the net relation between productivity growth and unit labor costs remains negative. A lower rate of price inflation will have favorable effects on the trade balance. Faster growth will not have to be choked off to protect the balance of payment so long as it is accompanied by the favorable trade balance.

To help clarify the foregoing relationships and make more explicit the significance of the various parameters, Beckerman puts out a very simple algebraic formulation of his model in which X = exports, O = labor productivity, W = money wages, P = domestic prices, P_f = foreign prices, and x, o, w, and p represent correspondingly the proportionate rates of change in the variables per unit of time for a given country:

Export equation	$x = a + b(1 - P/P_f)$	$(b > 0)$	(5.1)
Productivity equation	$o = c + dx$	$(d > 0)$	(5.2)
Wage equation	$w = m + no$	$(1 > n > 0)$	(5.3)
Price equation	$p = w - o$		(5.4)

Beckerman states that the constant term in (5.1) can be taken to represent the rate of increase in world trade. If a country's position of international price competitiveness is favorable, i.e., if $P/P_f < 1$, its exports will rise faster than world trade. Equation (5.2) assumes that rate of increase of productivity is positively correlated with the rate of increase of exports. Less than a proportional increase in wages relative to productivity is given by the condition that $0 < n < 1$, in (5.3). Equation (5.4) is designed to measure "wage drift," based on the assumption of constant distributive shares.

From (5.3) and (5.4) it follows that

$$p = m + o(n - 1) \tag{5.5}$$

From (5.1) and (5.2) for a given country we obtain

$$o = (c + ad) + bd(1 - P/P_f) \tag{5.6}$$

Thus if a given country has a competitive advantage, e.g., if $P/P_f < 1$, its rate of productivity growth o will exceed the average rate $(c + ad)$ by $bd(1 - P/P_f)$. Since by assumption $n < 1$ in (5.5), price p will rise less, the greater is the growth rate of productivity o. It therefore follows that an initial disparity in international price competitiveness will tend to become accentuated and will bring about a growing disparity in relative growth rates. This is, according to Beckerman, consistent with the European experience of the 1950s.

Beckerman's model has the virtue of simplicity in focusing on productivity and wage as determinants of prices and exports. At the same time the simplicity of the model necessitates the introduction of unverified empirical assumptions, leaves unexplained and untouched some important mechanisms involved, and subjects some parameters of the model to different interpretation.

Both Corden and Black examine the effects of foreign trade on

the rate of economic growth and compare the growth paths of income
in countries with and without foreign trade. In his effort to mar-
ry modern trade theory with neoclassical growth theory, Corden
(1971) uses a model of the economy with two factors, capital and
labor, and two types of final output, consumption goods and investment goods. He argues that an opening of trade affects the rate of
economic growth through (1) the impact effect, (2) the capital accumulation effect, (3) the substitution effect, (4) the income distribution effect, and (5) the "factor-weight" effect.

The opening up of trade gives rise to gains from trade. A
permanent, once-and-for-all increase in real income results, raising the rate of growth temporarily, which will fall back in the
subsequent year. In the medium run the growth rate of income may
be temporarily increased via the increase in accumulation made possible by the increased real income resulting from the initial gain
from trade. Despite these favorable impacts of trade on the growth
rate of output in the short and medium runs, the conclusion reached
by Corden on the effect of trade on the long-term growth rate of
any country is that the system will move toward the steady state as
determined by the given rate of growth of labor, because the capital accumulation rate declines as the capital-output ratio is rising and keeps on declining until capital is growing at the same
rate as labor.

In two countries whose incomes are growing at different rates,
the growth rate of the faster-growing country will eventually approximate that which it would have attained without trade, since
its trade must ultimately become negligible relative to its output.
The gains from trade will eventually vanish. Therefore, Corden is
pessimistic about the long-run effects of trade on growth rates.

Though it is not likely in practice that trade will allow a
complete merging of two different economies, Black (1970) examines
how the natural rates of economic growth of countries may be affected by a complete integration of two separate economies with
similar production functions but different rates of factor input
growth. Whether the natural rate of growth of the combined econo-
ies will exceed that of either economy alone depends on the characteristics of the production function in terms of degrees of elasticity of substitution and returns to scale. In the generalized
Cobb-Douglas case, in the long run the natural rate will be dominated by the growth rate of the natural factor input in whichever
country it was growing faster. When the economies are characterized by decreasing returns to scale and low elasticities of input
substitution, the natural growth rate of the combined economies
will tend to approach zero; on the other hand, with very high elasticities of substitution and increasing returns the combined economies will grow very rapidly. In the generalized high-substitution
case, the natural growth rate of the combined economies will tend
to converge to the same level as that of its faster-growing component. In the generalized low-substitution case, the natural growth
rate of the combined economies is set by whichever country's natural input grows most slowly. Whenever substitutes for slow-grow-

ing factors can be obtained via foreign trade, economies can attain long-run growth at natural growth rates set by their faster-growing factors.

Which of these outcomes is more likely to occur in the real world is, of course, an empirical question. Even when an economy exhibits decreasing returns to scale with low elasticities of substitution, the outlook is not necessarily pessimistic so long as foreign trade can stimulate technical progress. Though much remains to be done in this area, and the present expositions are sometimes heuristic and based on rigid assumptions, the studies by Corden and Black constitute an important contribution to the exploration of the relation between trade and economic growth.

In seeking to examine some of the theoretical properties of the export-led growth models by Beckerman and Lamfalussy, Caves (1965, 1970, 1971) elaborates and enriches the general structure of the export-led growth model. He looks at a number of theoretical issues: whether the functional relations in Lamfalussy and Beckerman lead to equilibrium growth paths, whether these paths are stable or imply positive rates of income change. His discussion is imbedded in two simple models similar to those by Lamfalussy and Beckerman: an export-assisted growth model and an export-led growth model.

Caves's export-assisted model can be represented by the following equations:

Investment function	$I = a\Delta Y + bY$	(5.7)
Savings function	$S = c\Delta Y + dY$	(5.8)
Balance-of-payments function	$X - M = eI - fY$	(5.9)
Equilibrium condition	$S = I + (X - M)$	(5.10)

where I = investment, S = savings, Y = income, X = exports, and M = imports.

The investment function is of the Harrod-Domar type, with the increment to output related to the level of investment through the incremental capital-output ratio. The function also has a term allowing for investment induced by the attained level of income. The savings function postulated depends also on the rate of growth in income. It is different from the more common formulation employed in growth models of a constant savings ratio that is independent of the growth rate of income. Caves's justification for a variable savings ratio is the possibility that export-based growth of demand may stimulate an increase in the proportion of income saved. The balance-of-payment function postulates that the trade balance is inversely related to the level of income and positively related to the level of investment; the reason for the latter relationship is that rapid productivity growth will be induced by a high level of investment.

Substitution of (5.7), (5.8), and (5.9) into the equilibrium condition in (5.10) gives

$$g_1 = \Delta Y/Y = [b(1 + e) - f - d]/[c - a(1 + e)] \qquad (5.11)$$

Under this formulation, neither the magnitude nor the sign of the numerator and the denominator can be determined unless the values of the parameters are specified. This means there is no assurance that a growth rate that satisfies the conventional conditions will be positive. The stability of the model cannot be predicted a priori. Even if values of the parameters are such that they give rise to a positive growth path, no assurance can be drawn about one of the central questions of the export-led growth models: whether or not the balance of payments on current account will remain favorable in the face of higher economic growth.

In this model of export-assisted growth, trade expansion responds passively to favorable productivity growth. In his second version of the model (export-led growth) Caves considers the case where export expansion exerts an influence on the rate of investment. So the investment function in (5.7) changes to

$$I/Y = u(X/Y) + b \tag{5.12}$$

Substitution of (5.12) for (5.6) necessitates some change in (5.9). Caves's choice is

$$M/Y = v(\Delta Y/Y) - f \tag{5.13}$$

Solving by substituting (5.8), (5.12), and (5.13) into (5.10) gives

$$g_2 = \Delta Y/Y = (b - f - d)/(c + v) + [(u + 1)/(c + v)](X/Y) \tag{5.14}$$

Equation (5.14) clearly shows the positive relation between the growth rate of income and the share of exports to income. As before, a growth path satisfying the equilibrium conditions need not be positive. The overall relation of the trade balance to the growth rate of income cannot be determined. The stability properties of the model require further specification of the parameters involved.

Our discussion so far suggests various mechanisms by which exports can exercise positive influence on economic growth. However, it is an easy matter to demonstrate as well a negative relationship between the proportion of exports to total product and the rate of growth of domestic output. Assuming a fixed-proportion production function, constant proportions of saving and imports in income, and exogenously given growth rates of exports, we can arrive at a negative relationship between the rate of income growth and the share of exports in income. (See also Ball 1962; Voivodas 1973.)

A simple extension of the basic Harrod–Domar model to an open economy will do the job. Assume that the economy is characterized by the following five equations:

Investment function	$I = c\Delta Y$	(5.15)
Savings function	$S = sY$	(5.16)
Import function	$M = mY$	(5.17)

Export function $X = X_0(1 + e)^f$ (5.18)
Equilibrium condition $I - S = M - X$ (5.19)

Relationships (5.16), (5.17), and (5.19) give

$$I = sY + mY - X \qquad\qquad\qquad (5.20)$$

Substitution of (5.20) into and division of both sides by Y give

$$\Delta Y/Y = (1/c)[s + m - (X/Y)] \qquad\qquad (5.21)$$

Equation (5.21), based on a simple model, shows that there can be a negative relationship between the rate of growth of domestic output and the proportion of exports to total product.

This unexpected result is due, however, to some very restrictive assumptions included in the model. Capital formation is the only source of growth. There is no distinction between domestic and foreign capital. Imports are made solely for consumption purposes. Since investment has no import component, exports and domestic investment are essentially competitors for available saving. Under these special conditions, a rise in exports will necessarily give rise to a fall in the rate of income growth. The model makes no reference to the country's balance-of-payment position.

The above survey shows that all the authors who support the hypothesis that exports are a key factor in the growth process point to the direct and indirect benefits from a high export growth rate in promoting general economic growth. The effects of exports on growth can be interpreted in terms of their effects on demand and supply. The firms in a country with a favorable export position will be faced with a wide and expandable market. This will have a beneficial effect on employers' expectations and stimulate output and investment. Though a shift in the demand function for exports can increase gains from trade and real income, this is likely to be a once-and-for-all effect and not the cause of long-run increases in growth rates.

Proponents of the export-led growth view generally emphasize favorable influences of exports resulting from not only the demand side but also the supply side. The acceleration of investment will increase productivity, partly because embodied technical progress can be fostered and partly because with faster expansion of capacities, economies of scale can be achieved. Productivity will also be fostered by the competitive pressure emanating from international competitors. The necessity of remaining competitive in international markets tends to maintain pressure on export industries to keep costs low and to constantly strive for more efficient operations. The increase in exports due to international competitiveness will stimulate demand and outputs, and the circle is virtuously closed through further productivity gains.

Moreover, export-led growth ensures that balance of payments will not cause a slowing of growth rate. Of course, aggregate demand can be maintained by a policy of stimulating any part of aggregate demand, but with a policy emphasizing, say, consumption, governments will find themselves in a dilemma. If a government tries to shift resources from consumption to investment, it will, by reducing consumption, weaken the inducement to invest. Export-led growth frees the government from this dilemma. Consumption can be restrained while exports, and therefore investment in export industries, expands. The continuing expansion of exports prevents the occurrence of balance-of-payment crises. Government will not be obliged to put a brake on economic growth for balance-of-payment reasons.

HISTORICAL TRENDS AND EXISTING EMPIRICAL STUDIES

Historical Trends in Foreign Trade

The importance of foreign trade in a national economy and its contribution to economic growth differ from country to country and vary over time for a given country. In this section we examine the trend of foreign trade in developed countries over the last century or so and review the major empirical studies dealing with the export-led growth hypothesis.

One statistic most frequently used by economists to measure the importance of foreign trade in a nation's economy is what is often called the foreign trade ratio, usually defined as the proportion of total foreign trade (exports plus imports) to either gross national product (GNP) or gross domestic product (GDP). One of the controversies surrounding the foreign trade ratio is whether or not there is a rising trend in the ratio as economies grow and develop.

Karl Deutsch and Alexander Eckstein (1961) argue that a declining trade ratio is a normal accompaniment to economic growth. One commonsense judgment is that, other things being equal, small countries are likely to have bigger trade ratios than large countries. If the size of a country is inversely related to its trade ratio, an increase in the size of an economy accompanying economic growth should mean, other conditions being equal, a downward trend in the foreign trade ratio. Deutsch and Eckstein buttress their claim by presenting statistics from 14 predominantly industrialized countries for four benchmark years from 1928 to 1957 and from 11 such countries from 1913 to 1957. They also collect estimates of the export-income ratio for a smaller number of countries for much earlier periods.

Their evidence is not sufficient to justify the formulation of a law of declining foreign trade shares. For 8 out of the 14 countries surveyed by Deutsch and Eckstein, the export-income ratio was lower in 1957 than in 1928. However, in 6 other countries the ratio was higher. The import-income ratio split evenly, 7 up and 7 down. A comparison of the data from 11 countries shows that 7 out of the 11 experienced a smaller trade-income ratio in the later years than in the earlier years for the period 1913-1957.

Kuznets (1967) is somewhat skeptical about the law of declin-

ing foreign trade and presents a summary of the volume of world
foreign trade in commodities over a long period extending back to
the mideighteenth century. His evidence suggests three broad conclusions. First, the share of foreign trade in the older developed countries rose markedly over the decades before World War I
because of a great revolution in transportation and a marked relaxation of trade barriers. Second, the foreign trade proportions
for the younger countries like the United States, Australia, and
Canada do not show the same consistent, significant upward trend
from the nineteenth century to World War I found in the developed
countries of Europe and Japan. The failure by the younger developed countries to produce an upward trend in their foreign trade
proportions may have been due partly to the much higher rates of
domestic growth, bolstered by immigration, and partly to the
transportation revolution that made a greater impact on the growth
of domestic output than on foreign trade.

Third, foreign trade proportions declined after 1913 until
the late 1950s, while the volume of international trade continued
to grow despite wars and depressions. This implies that the aggregate output of developed countries grew at rates well above
those of foreign trade and that the major developments during the
post-1913 period had a far more disturbing and retarding effect on
foreign trade than on national output.

Tables 5.1 and 5.2 show that foreign trade has become more
important in the decades since 1950. The ratios of exports and
imports to GDP have increased in all developed countries except
two, Australia and New Zealand, where the export-GDP ratios have
declined somewhat. Exports rose faster than the rest of the economy and export growth was faster in the 1960s than in the 1950s or
1970s. The most spectacular growth of exports was in Japan during
the 1960s and in Germany and Italy during the 1950s. The rate of
growth of exports in the two slowest-growing countries, the United

Table 5.1. Exports (EX) and imports (IM) as a percentage of gross domestic product

Country	1950 EX	1950 IM	1955 EX	1955 IM	1960 EX	1960 IM	1965 EX	1965 IM	1970 EX	1970 IM	1975 EX	1975 IM
Australia	23.0[a]	15.9	16.5	18.8	14.9	17.8	15.3	17.7	15.2	15.4	15.3	16.0
Austria	14.5	19.5	19.6	23.0	24.6	25.1	25.7	26.2	32.4	31.5	33.7	38.7
Belgium	23.7	28.1	32.1	31.3	32.9	33.9	36.3	36.2	43.9	41.6	46.2	47.9
Canada	21.8[a]	19.7	19.4	20.3	17.5	18.7	19.2	19.4	23.3	20.6	23.3	24.0
Denmark	31.3[b]	30.6	34.0	33.0	33.9	34.9	30.8	32.1	28.2	31.3	30.3	32.9
Finland	24.1[a]	25.1	21.7	20.1	23.5	24.2	21.3	23.2	27.4	28.8	25.4	29.1
France	13.4[b]	13.1	13.7	12.6	15.0	12.9	13.8	12.9	16.3	15.8	19.6	21.7
Germany	13.6[b]	10.6	15.9	13.7	19.0	16.5	18.1	17.8	21.1	19.0	24.8	23.5
Ireland	29.9	44.8	29.2	41.4	31.8	37.3	34.8	43.9	37.0	45.0	44.1	60.4
Italy	11.9	13.5	10.9	12.1	15.1	15.3	17.2	14.4	19.3	18.7	24.8	27.4
Japan	7.2	7.1	10.7	10.1	11.0	10.5	10.7	9.3	10.8	9.5	12.7	11.4
Netherlands	41.2	48.4	47.9	47.0	50.5	48.6	45.4	46.1	47.2	49.0	52.2	49.4
New Zealand	30.5	25.1	28.4	30.6	23.4	25.6	21.6	24.3	23.1	25.0	24.0	29.7
Norway	42.9[a]	43.6	41.6	45.5	41.9	44.6	40.9	41.9	41.8	43.1	41.8	51.0
Sweden	21.9	21.3	22.4	23.3	22.9	23.5	21.7	22.5	24.3	24.8	28.7	30.3
Switzerland	25.5	25.9	27.6	26.9	29.3	29.6	28.7	29.6	32.8	34.5	31.4	34.1
United Kingdom	20.1	17.3	22.8	22.6	21.3	22.6	19.6	20.3	23.5	22.6	26.7	30.5
United States	4.3	4.7	5.0	4.3	5.1	4.4	5.1	4.4	5.7	5.5	8.6	9.5

Source: World Bank 1980, pp. 228-69, 389.

[a]For the year 1952.

[b]For the year 1953.

Table 5.2. Average annual growth rates of exports

Country	1950-1960	1960-1970	1970-1977	1950-1965	1965-1977	1950-1977
Australia	5.0	7.4	3.3	5.2	6.3	5.7
Austria	12.1	9.0	6.8	10.3	8.6	9.5
Belgium	7.6[a]	9.4	5.7	7.9	7.7	7.8
Canada	3.0	9.8	3.6	4.6	6.6	5.5
Denmark	7.2	6.6	4.2	7.3	4.9	6.2
Finland	7.1	7.7	2.7	6.4	5.8	6.1
France	6.0	8.5	8.6	6.0	9.6	6.4
Germany	14.8	8.2	6.6	12.0	7.9	10.2
Ireland	3.1	7.8	6.4	4.7	7.0	5.7
Italy	14.4[b]	10.9	7.4	13.3	8.6	11.2
Japan	11.0[c]	15.0	12.7	12.4	13.8	13.0
Netherlands	9.6	8.8	5.8	8.7	7.8	8.3
New Zealand	4.6[d]	5.6	4.1	4.3	5.4	4.8
Norway	6.7	8.2	6.1	7.3	6.8	7.1
Sweden	5.5	7.8	2.9	6.8	4.9	6.2
Switzerland	7.7	7.3	3.6	7.3	5.5	6.5
United Kingdom	2.4	5.1	5.0	2.8	4.7	4.1
United States	4.1	6.2	6.0	4.7	6.2	5.4

Sources: World Bank 1980, p. 383; OECD 1980.
[a]For the period 1953-1960.
[b]For the period 1951-1960.
[c]For the period 1952-1960.
[d]For the period 1954-1960.

States and the United Kingdom, has been high by historial standards and has not diminished. The balance of trade in these two countries is good both by historical standards and compared to other developed countries. Note also that high export growth since 1950 has been accompanied in most countries by an equivalent spurt in imports.

The most important finding for our purpose--from Table 5.1 as well as from observations from studies by Kuznets and Deutsch and Eckstein--is that there is a marked difference among developed countries in the ratios of exports and imports, or the sum of the two, to gross domestic produce. Export-GDP ratios for the postwar years range from 5.0 and 8.6 percent in the United States to 47.9 and 52.2 percent in the Netherlands in 1955 and 1975 respectively. Substantial and consistent differences in the trade proportions are of long standing and have not tended to narrow through time. The degree of reliance on foreign trade differs more widely and more consistently between countries than it does for individual countries at different times.

What significance can be attached to the change in trade ratio over time or in intercountry differences in the level of trade ratios? Though Kindleberger (1962b, p. 178) has drawn up an interesting table that schematically presents the likely direction of the influence on trade of factors conditioning economic growth at various stages of development, there is not likely to be any simple functional relationship, invariant over time, between trade and income levels. The most frequently cited of the more permanent characteristics explaining intercountry differences in the trade ratio is the size of countries. Several statistical tests have confirmed the commonsense judgment that, other things being equal, small countries are likely to have bigger trade ratios than large countries. Physical size seems to be a more important aspect of size than population (Kindleberger 1962b, pp. 32-37).

Previous Empirical Studies

The above observations on the historical trends in the growth rates of foreign trade and the shares of foreign trade in national output and the discussion of the theoretical explanations for the export-led growth hypothesis lead us to question how well the hypothesis stands against historical experience. The empirical studies of export-led growth are of two types: time-series for individual countries and cross sections of samples of countries at points in time. The statistical evidence from existing studies is not always unequivocal in supporting the hypothesis. Table 5.3 summarizes the results of major empirical studies based on cross-sectional samples.

Table 5.3. A summary of empirical testings of the relation between exports and economic growth

A. Emery: 50 countries for 1953-1963

$$Y = 0.6630 + 0.32952X \tag{1}$$
$$(1.1557)\ (0.03316) \qquad R^2 = 0.67$$

B. Syron and Walsh: 13 developed countries for 1953-1963

$$Y = -0.1599 + 0.3718X \tag{2}$$
$$(0.3718)\ (0.0448) \qquad R^2 = 0.86$$

35 less developed countries for 1953-1963

$$Y = 0.8128 + 0.3327X \tag{3}$$
$$(0.3067)\ (0.0447) \qquad R^2 = 0.62$$

C. Crafts: 18 countries for 1960-1966

$$Y = -0.489 + 0.040X \tag{4}$$
$$(7.984) \qquad R^2 = 0.80$$

D. Voivodas: 33 less developed countries for 1957-1968

$$Y = a + 0.200 S_X \tag{5}$$
$$(2.303) \qquad R^2 = 0.206$$
$$S_I = a - 0.053 S_X \tag{6}$$
$$(0.207) \qquad R^2 = 0.248$$
$$S_M = a + 0.266 S_X \tag{7}$$
$$(3.722) \qquad R^2 = 0.603$$
$$Y = a - 0.013 S_F \tag{8}$$
$$(0.201) \qquad R^2 = 0.182$$
$$C = a + 5.552 S_F \tag{9}$$
$$(5.219) \qquad R^2 = 0.221$$
$$C = a + 5.940 S_F - 0.774 S_I \tag{10}$$
$$(5.504)\ \ (1.792) \qquad R^2 = 0.235$$

Sources: Emery 1967; Syron and Walsh 1968; Crafts 1973; Voivodas 1973; Lubitz 1973; Balassa 1978; Smith 1975.

Note: Numbers in parentheses in the first three equations indicate the standard error; the remaining ones are values of t-statistics. Y = rate of growth of GDP or income; X = rate of growth of exports; S_X = proportion of exports to total product; S_I = proportion of domestic investment to total product; S_M = proportion of imports to total product; S_F = proportion of foreign capital inflow to total product; C = incremental capital-output ratio; X_m = rate of growth of manufactured exports; I = investment ratio; K_D and K_F = growth rate of domestic and foreign capital respectively; L = growth rate of labor force; PPX = rate of growth of exports based on the purchasing power; IXR = incremental export-GNP ratio.

Table 5.3. *(continued)*

E. Lubitz: 1 developed country for 1954-1969

$$Y = 1.22 + 0.43X$$
$$(4.64) \qquad\qquad R^2 = 0.64 \qquad\qquad (11)$$
$$Y = 2.02 + 0.31X_m$$
$$(3.23) \qquad\qquad R^2 = 0.43 \qquad\qquad (12)$$
$$Y = -1.62 + 0.29X + 0.23I$$
$$(3.15) \quad (2.42) \qquad R^2 = 0.77 \qquad\qquad (13)$$
$$Y = -1.78 + 0.18X_m + 0.29I$$
$$(2.02) \qquad (2.59) \qquad R^2 = 0.65 \qquad\qquad (14)$$
$$Y = 1.05 + 0.81X - 0.34X_m$$
$$(2.73) \quad (1.35) \qquad R^2 = 0.67 \qquad\qquad (15)$$
$$Y = -2.17 + 0.42I$$
$$(3.82) \qquad\qquad R^2 = 0.53 \qquad\qquad (16)$$

F. Balassa: 10 less developed countries for 1960-1966 and 1966-1973

$$Y = a + 0.15K_D + 0.23K_F + 0.97L + 0.04X$$
$$(3.33) \quad\; (2.40) \quad\; (3.57) \quad (1.99) \quad R^2 = 0.77 \qquad (17)$$
$$Y = a + 0.16K_D + 0.24K_F + 0.92L + 0.05PPX$$
$$(3.59) \quad\; (2.44) \quad\; (1.82) \quad (3.34) \quad R^2 = 0.75 \qquad (18)$$
$$Y = a + 0.14K_D + 0.26K_F + 0.98L + 0.006IXR$$
$$(2.32) \quad\; (2.32) \quad\; (1.66) \quad (1.86) \quad R^2 = 0.65 \qquad (19)$$

G. Smith: 17 developed countries for 1961-1972

$$X = 0.6009 + 1.4116Y$$
$$(2.346) \quad (11.037) \qquad\qquad R^2 = 0.81 \qquad\qquad (20)$$

One of the most comprehensive tests dealing with the association between export growth and growth rates of the economy is in Robert F. Emery's (1967) study, which covers 50 countries, developed as well as developing, over the period from 1953 to 1963. According to Emery's regression of (1) in Table 5.3, growth of exports accounts for about two-thirds of the variation in the growth rates of the included economies.

In an attempt to extend Emery's work, Richard F. Syron and Brendan M. Walsh (1968) divide the original sample of 50 countries into two subsets: developed and less developed. They find that the association between exports and the rate of growth of per capita GNP is greater for the developed countries--R^2 = 0.86 in (2)--than for the less developed countries--R^2 = 0.62 in (3). One explanation for the difference might be that in general the stimulation provided by exports to the domestic economy may be expected to be lower in the less developed countries than in the advanced industrial countries because of the weakness in the underdeveloped economy of the institutional framework that transmits various favorable mechanisms involved.

While debating with Irving Kravis (1970) over the proper interpretation of Nurkse's (1961a) exposition of the export-led growth hypothesis, N. F. Crafts (1973) examines the relationship between export growth and economic growth. His sample consists of 18 less developed countries over the period 1960-61 to 1965-66. His regression result of (4) in Table 5.3 and an examination of the partial correlation coefficients between competitiveness, diversification, and growth (not shown in the table) lead Crafts to favor the "exports as an engine of growth" hypothesis.

In his effort to ascertain the links in the chain of causation
for a positive association between the rate of growth of exports
and that of total production, C. S. Voivodas (1973) examines the
theoretical and empirical relationships between exports and domestic growth inherent in the open economy Harrod-Domar and two-gap
models. Voivodas's empirical examination is based on data from 22
less developed countries over the period 1956-1967. Equation (5)
in Table 5.3 indicates a positive and statistically significant relationship between the ratio of exports to total product and its
rate of growth. The positive and significant relation between exports and capital goods imports--(7)--and a weak negative association between exports and domestic investment resources--(6)--indi-
cate that trade exercises a beneficial effect on growth through the
ability of countries with high export receipts to import the capital goods necessary for development.
     From the facts that there is no significant correlation be-
tween the proportion of foreign capital inflow to total product and
its rate of growth--(8)--and that foreign capital inflow is positively associated with a higher overall incremental capital-output
ratio--(9)--Voivodas argues that the ordinary beneficial effect of
foreign capital inflow on growth is generally neutralized by either
a substantial spillover of foreign capital to consumption or an increase in the incremental capital-output ratio or both.
     Raymond Lubitz (1973) makes a critical examination of two im-
portant elements of export-led growth that are essential links in
the model. First, export growth will stimulate industries with
significant economies of scale; second, export growth, by ensuring
a strong balance of payments, will encourage investment. Lubitz
tests the export economies-of-scale argument by comparing total exports and manufacturing exports as explanatory variables of economic growth to see whether manufacturing exports, the carrier of
economies of scale, are more closely related to growth than total
exports. The export-investment link is investigated by including
an investment variable in the export-growth equations to see if exports operate on growth through their effect on investment or if
investment has an independent effect on growth. Using data for the
period 1954-1969 for 11 leading manufacturing exporters, Lubitz obtains the regression results shown in (11) through (16).
     With these results, Lubitz denies the two mechanisms of ex-
port-led growth (via manufactured exports and balance-of-payments
effect on investment), suggesting that "exports may be the handmaiden rather than the engine of growth." His argument for this
conclusion, based on the above regression results, runs as follows.
If export-led growth works through economies of scale in the manufacturing sector, we should expect that manufacturing exports will
be more closely correlated with economic growth than total export
growth. Since variable X, total exports, outperforms X_m, manufactured exports--(11) and (12)--the manufacturing-economies-of-scale
argument can be rejected. In (15), where X and X_m are run together, X_m takes on a negative sign, indicating that it contributes
negatively rather than positively to growth. If exports are sup-

posed to promote growth because of the encouragement to investment, this effect should be accounted for by the investment variable. The fact that investment has an independent significant effect in (13) and (14), where exports are also in the equations, implies that the export-growth correlation would not be due to export stimulus to growth working through investment.

In investigating the effects of exports on economic growth, all of the authors whose work we have discussed so far examine the relationship using simple regression analysis, thereby assuming that causality runs from exports to growth. Bela Balassa (1978) attempts to remedy one deficiency by using domestic and foreign investment and labor as explanatory variables together with exports in regressions designed to explain intercountry differences in GNP growth rates. His regression results in (17) to (19) indicate that export growth favorably affects the rate of economic growth over and above the contributions of domestic and foreign capital.

David Smith (1975) is one of the few researchers who questions the causal direction of the relationship between export growth and economic growth and the mechanisms involved in the export-led growth process. Smith postulates a hypothesis that the rate of growth of a country's exports is largely determined by that country's growth, and he tested the hypothesis. He argued that the direction of causation is from growth to exports, not the other way around, because "when considering the long term factors . . . supply factors are likely to be of major significance." With data from 17 developed countries over the 1961-1972 period, he obtains the result in (20). Needless to say, simple regression cannot solve the question of causality.

According to Michael Michaely (1977), all of the studies we have examined so far share a common fault in that they correlate growth, measured by change in GNP, with changes in exports. The high R^2s obtained in most regressions result simply from the presence of autocorrelation. Because exports are themselves part of GNP, a positive correlation of the two variables is almost inevitable, whatever their true relationship to each other. Since Michaely believes that "the variable used to represent export performance must indicate the extent of export bias," he suggests that the rate of change of the proportions of exports in the national product be used as a proxy for the rate of expansion of exports.

Michaely uses this new definition of export expansion to test the export-led growth hypothesis for a sample of 41 less developed countries for the years 1950-1973. He finds the coefficient of the Spearman rank correlation between the average size of the annual changes in the ratio of exports to GNP and the average annual change in per capita GNP to be 0.38, significant at the 1 percent level. Michaely also tests a different version of the export hypothesis: the higher the export ratio in a country, the more rapid the country's growth. The coefficient of Spearman's rank correlation of these two variables is negative, significant at the 2.5 percent level.

From our survey of empirical studies we can conclude that

there are more or less strong positive correlations between exports
and economic growth across countries, providing support to the export-led growth hypothesis. However, there are at least two strong
arguments against this general conclusion. One is the argument by
Kravis (1970) that exports are the handmaiden, not the engine, of
growth, and the other is the results of various studies investigating the export-led growth hypothesis against the Japanese experience over time.

If exports are the engine, Kravis asserts, we should expect to
find one or more of the following features in the economic history
of periphery countries: (1) large and/or growing shares of exports
in domestic production, (2) an accelerated increase in GNP following the increase in exports, (3) a concentration of exports in sectors that are growing relatively rapidly and/or rapid growth in industries linked to the export industries, and (4) the attraction of
foreign capital to export industries or to industries supported by
them.

Kravis surveyed the data of 7 newly developing countries in
the nineteenth century; none of the countries were characterized by
the features above. He also examined the exports of 58 less developed countries during the period 1959-61 to 1964-65, confirming no
dependence of export performance on world demand.

Many students of the Japanese economy argue against the popular belief that Japan's high economic growth is a result of rapid
export expansion (see Kanamori 1968; Blumenthal 1972; Monroe 1973;
Rosovsky and Ohkawa 1973). By any standard, the expansion of Japanese exports has been rapid. However, most researchers agree that
the rapid increase of exports in Japan was made possible by domestic factors such as increased domestic investment and enlarged home
markets. Growing domestic demand and new investments lead to mass
production, which in turn reduces costs, strengthening the competitive position of products in international markets. Once the expansion of domestic demand and investment begins to promote exports, a kind of circular action begins. Industries whose markets
were enlarged through growing exports attract more investment and
thus strengthen their competitive positions.

Those who argue against the export-led growth position and favor the homespun growth view for the Japanese economy provide some
simple statistics to support their argument. As a study by H.
Kanamori (1968) suggests, the growth of exports in Japan seldom exceeded the growth of the home market. The proportion of Japanese
output devoted to export was low (around 10 percent) during the
postwar period. While this proportion is larger than that for the
United States, it is only half or less of the corresponding figures
for all Western European countries, as shown in Table 5.1. The ratio of exports to GDP is low not only in relation to other countries but also when compared to that of prewar Japan. The export
ratio was much higher in prewar Japan, e.g., 24 percent in 1934-
1936. These findings and others lead most students of the Japanese
economy to conclude that exports were relatively unimportant in Japan's postwar economic growth.

SOME ADDITIONAL TESTS

The numerous empirical studies conducted to test the export-
led growth hypothesis (surveyed in the preceding section) do not
lead to definitive conclusions concerning the validity of the hypothesis. Despite the best efforts put into each study, most existing tests are deficient in several ways. An examination of the
samples used indicates they are limited in the number of countries
included as well as in the length of time covered. Most of the
previous tests are based on data for only a decade or so. The combination of heterogeneous groups of developing and developed countries in the sample may not be the best way of testing the hypothesis, even though the sample size is enlarged by the combination.
Some believe that tests of the export-led growth must intrinsically
involve case studies of individual countries. All of these considerations suggest that it is appropriate to subject the hypothesis
of export-led growth to additional and rather more comprehensive
sets of data.

The data used in our regressions come from 18 industrial countries, covering three subinterval periods: 1950–1960, 1960–1970,
and 1970–1977. Time-series and cross-sectional data are pooled to
make the number of observations sufficiently large for statistical
purposes. Time-series data for two extreme cases, in terms of
openness of the economy involved and measured by foreign trade volume, are also employed to test the export-led growth model. It is
hoped that tests based on the time-series data will provide us with
some clues of the causal direction of the relationship between exports and economic growth. Since theoretical considerations are
not clear on the exact specification of the functional relationship
between export performance and growth performance, various specifications are alternately used in our investigation. Regression results are summarized in Table 5.4. (Alternate regressions including and excluding Japan in our sample do not produce significantly
different results. Therefore, we present and discuss regression
results with Japan included.)

The first two regressions show the statistical relation between export growth and economic growth; the next two show the association between economic growth and the share of exports to GDP.
A very strong correlation is found between growth of exports and
growth of the overall economy. The regression results in (3) and
(4) (Table 5.4) indicate there is a negative association between
economic growth and the proportion of exports to output, though the
association is not statistically significant. This result suggests
that the more open a country, the slower the growth of the economy
--contrary to intuition and contrary to the Voivodas finding of a
positive association between the export ratio and growth of total
output for a group of less developed countries--(5) of Table 5.3.

Recall that Michaely made a strong objection to the specification of the export-led growth model as employed in (1) or (2) (Table 5.4) on the grounds that since exports are themselves part of
the GDP, autocorrelation is present and therefore a positive correlation between the two variables is almost inevitable. Equations
(5) and (6) test Michaely's argument by using the rate of change of

Table 5.4. Regressions for the export-led growth hypothesis
A. Using cross-country data for 1950-1977, $n = 50 \sim 53$

$$G = 1.0010 + 0.4454 G_x \tag{1}$$
$$(9.10) \qquad\qquad R^2 = 0.61$$

$$g = 0.5125 + 0.4415 g_x \tag{2}$$
$$(10.13) \qquad\qquad R^2 = 0.66$$

$$G = 5.2481 - 4.2022 S_x \tag{3}$$
$$(2.00) \qquad\qquad R^2 = 0.07$$

$$g = 3.9439 - 0.2741 S_x \tag{4}$$
$$(1.30) \qquad\qquad R^2 = 0.03$$

$$G = 3.9893 + 0.1963 g_{sx} \tag{5}$$
$$(1.41) \qquad\qquad R^2 = 0.04$$

$$g = 2.9188 + 0.3347 g_{sx} \tag{6}$$
$$(2.55) \qquad\qquad R^2 = 0.11$$

$$G = 3.4407 + 0.4220 EXP \tag{7}$$
$$(1.69) \qquad\qquad R^2 = 0.05$$

$$g = 2.2887 + 0.5459 exp \tag{8}$$
$$(2.27) \qquad\qquad R^2 = 0.09$$

$$G = 1.0520 + 0.2896 G_x + 0.2347 G_i \tag{9}$$
$$(5.75) \qquad (5.69) \qquad R^2 = 0.77$$

$$g = 0.6234 + 0.3105 g_x + 0.2010 g_i \tag{10}$$
$$(6.71) \qquad (5.06) \qquad R^2 = 0.77$$

$$G = 2.4342 + 0.0305 EXP + 1.4339 INV \tag{11}$$
$$(0.20) \qquad (10.00) \qquad R^2 = 0.69$$

$$g = 1.7154 + 0.2194 exp + 1.3206 inv \tag{12}$$
$$(1.29) \qquad (8.46) \qquad R^2 = 0.65$$

$$G_i = -0.0003 + 0.6374 G_x \tag{13}$$
$$(4.39) \qquad\qquad R^2 = 0.28$$

$$g_i = -0.0093 + 0.5892 g_x \tag{14}$$
$$(4.17) \qquad\qquad R^2 = 0.26$$

$$INV = 0.8130 + 0.2328 EXP \tag{15}$$
$$(1.61) \qquad\qquad R^2 = 0.05$$

$$inv = 0.5850 + 0.2582 exp \tag{16}$$
$$(1.75) \qquad\qquad R^2 = 0.06$$

$$g = 3.8996 - 0.1152 INF \tag{17}$$
$$(1.81) \qquad\qquad R^2 = 0.06$$

B. Using U.S. time-series data for 1950-1978

Year by year for both dependent and independent
variables, $n = 28$
$$G = 2.7038 + 0.1452 G_x \tag{18}$$
$$(1.94) \qquad\qquad R^2 = 0.13$$
With economic growth by 1-year lag, $n = 27$
$$G = 4.1661 - 0.1221 G_x \tag{19}$$
$$(1.66) \qquad\qquad R^2 = 0.10$$
With export growth by 1-year lag, $n = 27$
$$G_x = 3.2724 + 0.5289 G \tag{20}$$
$$(1.06) \qquad\qquad R^2 = 0.04$$

C. Using Dutch time-series data for 1950-1978

Year by year for both dependent and independent
variables, $n = 28$
$$G = 1.3840 + 0.3804 G_x \tag{21}$$
$$(5.00) \qquad\qquad R^2 = 0.49$$
With economic growth by 1-year lag, $n = 27$
$$G = 3.1509 + 0.1709 G_x \tag{22}$$
$$(1.64) \qquad\qquad R^2 = 0.10$$
With export growth by 1-year lag, $n = 27$
$$G_x = 8.7249 - 0.1206 G \tag{23}$$
$$(0.32) \qquad\qquad R^2 = 0.00$$

Sources: Same as in Tables 5.1 and 5.2; UN 1980.
Note: Numbers in parentheses are values of t-statis-
tics. G = rate of growth of GDP or GNP; g = rate of growth
of per capita GDP or per capita GNP; G_x = rate of growth of
total exports; G_i = rate of growth of total fixed investment; g_x = rate of growth of per capita exports; g_i = rate of
growth of per capita fixed investment; S_x = share of exports
to GDP; S_i = share of total investment to GDP; g_{sx} = rate of
growth of export share; $EXP = S_x G_x$; $exp = S_x g_x$; $INV = S_i G_i$;
$inv = S_i g_i$; INF = inflation rate, measured by GDP deflator.

the proportion of exports in the national product as the independent variable in the regression. The outcome is not impressive by the usual standards of regression analysis. The correlation between economic growth and the growth of export shares is slightly higher when economic growth is measured on a total basis than on a per capita basis.

Another suggestion for the proper specification of the export-led growth model is contained in the regressions represented by (7) and (8), where the product of export shares and the growth rate of exports is employed as the explanatory variable. It is argued that the level of GNP, Y, should be a function of the level of exports, X (see Severn 1968); i.e.,

$$Y = a + bX \tag{5.22}$$

When this relationship is expressed in differential form, (5.22) becomes

$$\Delta Y = c + b\Delta X \tag{5.23}$$

Normalization to avoid the effects on different currency units and sizes of countries is achieved by dividing both sides of (5.23) by y; this gives

$$G = \Delta Y/Y = d + b(\Delta X/Y) \tag{5.24}$$

The explanatory variable in (5.24) is $\Delta Y/Y$, not $\Delta X/X$, the rate of growth of exports.

It is in this sense that some agree that the proper specification of the export-led growth model is not between growth rates of exports and economies. Equation (5.24) can be rewritten as

$$G = \Delta Y/Y = d + b(\Delta X/X)(X/Y) \tag{5.25}$$

As shown in (5.25), the proper way of testing the model is to regress the rate of economic growth on the rate of export growth while incorporating the "openness" coefficient X/Y.

The validity of this argument depends on whether or not the original specifications and arguments for export-led growth have been made in terms of relationships between rates of growth of two variables or levels of the two variables. The theoretical discussions are not clear on this point. In any case the specification in (5.25) is subject to empirical testing with our more comprehensive set of data. As the regression results of (7) and (8) in Table 5.4 show, these results are not significant by conventional criteria. As discussed in Chapter 4, in sharp contrast to the results for the export-led growth hypothesis, a similar specification for the investment-led growth hypothesis yields a very strong association between investment growth and economic growth (see (7) and (8) in Table 4.5).

Our empirical testing so far is confined to the direct asso-

ciation between export performance and economic growth without considering the mechanisms by which the relation between them is supposed to operate. As stated earlier in this chapter, many proponents of the export-led growth hypothesis emphasize different mechanisms concerning the export-growth nexus. One of the major links
in export-led growth is the association of the accumulation of capital with the rapid growth of exports. Of course, investment depends upon changes in demand, both domestic and foreign. The hypothesis that changes in investment are related to changes in exports is tested, and the results are shown in (13) through (16) in
Table 5.4.

Equations (13) and (14) show that the correlation between the
growth rates of investment and exports is high enough to confirm a
close association between them, though the causal direction cannot
be determined by a simple regression such as ours. However, when
each of the shares of investment and exports in GDP is taken into
account, no relation is found between export and investment performances among developed countries during the period 1950-1978, as
the results in (15) and (16) show. The quest for evidence concerning the relation between trade performance and capital formation
does not provide decisve results.

Given the fact that both capital formation and export performance have their own separate influences, whether small or large, on
economic growth, it seems interesting to examine how they together
exercise influence on the growth performance of economies. This is
done by putting variables representing export performance and capital formation as explanatory variables in the same regression, as
shown in (9) to (12) in Table 5.4. It is interesting to note that
the coefficients associated with exports and investment in (9) and
(10) are statistically significant despite multicollinearity between the mere growth of investment and exports, as evidenced by
the results in (13) and (14). When each share of investment and
exports in total output is taken into account to measure their performance, the coefficients associated with investment are found to
be statistically significant, while the export coefficients are
not. The significance of the investment coefficients and the insignificance of export coefficients in our multiple regressions of
(11) and (12) cannot be attributed to multicollinearity between the
two variables because (15) and (16) clearly show that the correlation between the two independent variables is weak. This result
may be interpreted as suggesting the relative superiority of the
investment-led growth over the export-led growth.

Another link emphasized in the virtuous circle mechanisms of
the export-led growth models is the relation of changes in wages
of prices to the growth rate of productivity or capital stock on
the presumption that a negative partial relation will favor the
trade balance and allow the virtuous circle to be sustained. The
negative, though not significant, relation between productivity
growth and inflation rate in regression (17) of Table 5.4 provides
at least partial evidence to this link.

Some authors believe that a cross-sectional analysis is not

adequate to confirm or deny the export-led growth hypothesis, but that such an analysis can work to rule out any broad and systematic inconsistency of predictions of the hypothesis with the facts (Caves 1971). According to this view, a better way of testing the model of export-led growth is to use case studies of relevant countries for a given period of time or time-series data for regression analysis. Robert M. Stern (1967) examined models of export-led growth against the Italian experience during the period 1951-1963. His results at an aggregate level are not encouraging, but he did find that at an industry level those industries that were Italy's most important exporters recorded the most rapid increases in total output.

For our regression analysis based on time-series data, only two countries are chosen. They are the United States, whose economy depends least on the foreign sector, and the Netherlands, which, among advanced industrial countries, relies most heavily on the foreign sector, as shown in Table 5.1. Annual growth rates of exports and the overall economy are obtained for each country during the period 1951-1978. From a statistical point of view, the results are not very satisfactory since the correlation coefficients are low. From an economic point of view, the results are informative and interesting. The general message of the regression results is that export growth plays an important role in the growth process of open economies, while it does not in nearly closed economies. A comparison of (18) with (21) indicates that the correlation between growth rates of the economy and exports is stronger in the more open economy, the Netherlands, than in the less open economy, the United States.

We obtain more interesting results when we investigate lagged relationships between economic growth and export growth. One hard decision facing the researcher who investigates lagged causal relationships concerns the determination of the appropriate lag to be used. As a matter of convenience, we employ a one-year lag between variables. The regression of the preceding year's export growth on the current year's economic growth produces a negative correlation for the United States, as shown by (19), and a positive association for the Netherlands, as shown by (22), while the regression between economic growth of the preceding year and export growth of the current year yields a positive relation for the United States --(20)--and a negative correlation for the Netherlands--(23).

On the presumption that what precedes is the cause rather than the effect of what follows, our regression results suggest that the growth of the overall economy has been propelled by export growth in the open economy, while in the closed economy the growth is homespun. In countries like the United States, a healthy domestic economy leads to more rapid export growth. But as the economy becomes more dependent on the foreign sector, the role of exports in the growth process becomes more important. This conclusion is consistent with various studies of Japanese economy that more or less reject the export-led growth view, favoring the homespun growth position.

CONCLUSIONS

The relationship between foreign trade and economic growth has been much discussed in the postwar literature. Earlier attention on the effect of export expansion on income growth was confined to the simple, short-run multiplier analysis. On the other hand, much of the attention was directed to the effects of economic growth on the volume and terms of trade and the resulting adjustments required to maintain international equilibrium. From the early sixties, attention has been increasingly diverted to new discussions on the role of exports in promoting economic growth. The export-led growth hypothesis attempts to explain the significant differences in the rate of growth of advanced industrialized countries by postulating the rapid growth of exports as a necessary and perhaps sufficient condition for the rapid growth of income.

There are substantial grounds for believing that exports are a key factor in promoting economic growth. The tenet of the export-led growth hypothesis is in line with economists' general conception of the nature of economic growth. They have singled out at one time or another a variety of causes of the wealth of nations. Among them are three that have been accorded particular emphasis: the progress of technology, the accumulation of capital, and the growth of markets. The first two causes as factors responsible for different growth performances have been discussed in the preceding two chapters. The growth of markets, which puts emphasis on the demand side, can be growth of home markets or foreign markets or both at the same time. The export-led growth hypothesis singles out the growth of foreign markets as a key variable in economic growth.

A big challenge to the export-led growth hypothesis comes not only from those who emphasize other economic and noneconomic factors as causes for explaining different growth performances among countries but also from those who put emphasis on the export-growth nexus, giving rise to different conclusions. What is known as the theory of homespun growth or "trade as the handmaiden of growth" theory interprets the close association between growth performance and export performance from different lines of causation. Rapid increase in exports is made possible by domestic factors such as increased domestic investment or economies of scale or both. Once home markets expand sufficiently to allow for economies of scale, the resulting decrease in average cost of production strengthens the competitive position in the international market. Once domestic factors begin to promote exports, a kind of circular action begins. Unlike the export-led growth model, the model of homespun growth has no explanation of what factors generate growth of demand.

The relationship between trade and economic growth is not unique and is one of mutual interdependence rather than unilateral causation. In studying the two-way interaction between growth and exports, it has to be noted that the two are not themselves independent variables. There are many factors that influence these two variables independently. Complexities of the problem are illus-

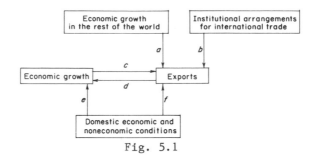

Fig. 5.1

trated in Figure 5.1. The upper two boxes represent variables that
are exogenous with respect to the growth performance of the economy
in question. The factors in the bottom box exert influences on economic growth and exports independently or simultaneously.

A delineation of each link is necessary to pinpoint the relation between economic growth and export performance. If neither c
nor d is strong, economic growth and exports are separate problems.
If c is strong but d is weak, better growth would help with exports. The converse is true when d is strong but c is weak. If
both c and d are strong, we may have a mutual causation. When e
and f exercise dominant influences at the same time, output and exports move in parallel fashion, though there may in fact be no direct relationship between them.

Complex and ever-changing interactions make it difficult to
pinpoint the path an economy is following, to say nothing of making
comparisons between countries. An assessment of the gains a country can make from foreign trade is not straightforward. In this
context, R. S. Sayers (1965) makes a useful distinction between
"complementary" and "competitive" aspects of the effects of expansion of the world economy on a given country's growth through exports. Economic growth elsewhere is complementary to the extent it
raises the demand for exports, but it becomes competitive in so far
as it leads to the development of alternative sources of supply,
which may compete with the country's home market. From the point
of view of a particular country, an expansion of the world economy
provides a changing balance between complementariness and competitiveness. All this illustrates the point that the relation between
exports and economic growth is not unique and is most likely to be
one of mutual interdependence rather than unilateral causation.

The relatively extensive set of empirical evidence does not
support any generalization concerning the role of exports in economic growth. This is not surprising at all, given the rather significant number of difficult theoretical and empirical questions
involved in testing the export-led growth hypothesis. One simple
but important problem relating to the selection of dependent and
explanatory variables in regressions has remained unsolved. Which
specific indicator of growth performance and export performance
should be employed? It is not clear whether the hypothesis applies
to the growth of aggregate or per capita output. As seen above,

different indicators of export performance produce quite different results in the regressions. All the regressions that include the export growth rate as the independent variable provide statistically significant results, while empirical results based on other specifications do not support the hypothesis. Further discussion of the hypothesis must be specific as to the choice of the dependent and explanatory variables in the regressions.

The question of whether or not the growth of an economy is export led, and whether or not differences in growth performance among countries can be accounted for by differences in export performances, is not capable of being answered with a simple "yes" or "no." As Kindleberger noted, foreign trade can work as either a leading, a balancing, or a lagging sector for the performance of the whole economy. Only when demand is right abroad and supply and other conditions are right at home can growth be export led. In all other cases the relation between export and economic growth becomes equivocal. Perhaps it is for this reason that empirical studies of our own as well as others provide only partial support for the export-led growth hypothesis.

REFERENCES

Balassa, B. 1963. Some observations on Mr. Beckerman's "export-propelled" growth model. *Econ. J.* 73:785-87.
———. 1964. Some observations on Mr. Beckerman's export-propelled growth model: A further note. *Econ. J.* 74:740-43.
———. 1978. Exports and economic growth: Further evidence. *J. Dev. Econ.* 5:181-89.
Ball, R. J. 1962. Capital imports and economic development: Paradoxy or orthodoxy. *Kyklos* 15(3):610-23.
Beckerman, W. 1962. Projecting Europe's growth. *Econ. J.* 72:912-27.
———. 1964. Professor Balassa's comments on my "export-propelled" growth model. *Econ. J.* 74:738-40.
———. 1966. The determinants of economic growth. In *Economic Growth in Britain*, ed. P. H. Henderson. London: Weinfeld & Nicolson.
Berrill, K. 1960. International trade and the rate of economic growth. *Econ. Hist. Rev.*, ser. 2, 12(3):351-59.
Black, J. 1970. Trade and the natural growth rate. *Oxf. Econ. Pap.* 22:13-23.
Blumenthal, T. 1972. Export and economic growth in postwar Japan. *Q. J. Econ.* 86:617-31.
Caves, R. E. 1966. Vent for surplus models of trade and growth. In *Trade, Growth and the Balance of Payments*. Chicago: Rand McNally.
———. 1970. Export-led growth: The post-war industrial setting. In *Induction, Growth and Trade*, ed. W. A. Eltis, M. F. Scott, and J. Wolfe. Oxford: Clarendon.
———. 1971. Export-led growth and the new economic history.

In *Trade, Balance of Payments and Growth*. Amsterdam: North-Holland.

Cooper, R. N. 1964. Growth and trade: Some hypotheses about long-term trends. *J. Econ. Hist.* 24:609–28.

Corden, W. M. 1971. The effects of trade on the rate of growth. In *Trade, Balance of Payments and Growth*. Amsterdam: North-Holland.

Crafts, N. F. 1973. Trade as a handmaiden of growth: An alternative view. *Econ. J.* 83:875–84.

Deutsch, K. W., and A. Eckstein. 1961. National industrialization and the declining share of the international economic sector, 1890–1950. *World Polit.* 13:267–99.

Dewhurst, J. F. 1961. *Europe's Needs and Resources*. New York: Twentieth Century Fund.

Emery, R. F. 1967. The relation of exports and economic growth. *Kyklos* 20(Fasc. 2):470–86.

―――. 1968. The relation of exports and economic growth. *Kyklos* 21:757–60.

Hanson, J. R. II. 1977. More on trade as a handmaiden of growth. *Econ. J.* 87:554–57.

Heller, P. S., and R. C. Porter. 1978. Exports and growth: An empirical re-investigation. *J. Dev. Econ.* 5:191–93.

Kanamori, H. 1968. Economic growth and exports. In *Economic Growth: The Japanese Experience since the Meiji Era*, ed. L. Klein and K. Ohkawa. Homewood, Ill.: R. Irwin.

Kindleberger, C. P. 1961. Foreign trade and economic growth: Lessons from France and Britain, 1850–1913. *Econ. Hist. Rev.* 14:289–91.

―――. 1962a. Foreign trade and growth: Lessons from British experience since 1913. *Lloyd's Bank Rev.* July.

―――. 1962b. *Foreign Trade and the National Economy*. New Haven: Yale University Press.

―――. 1964. *Economic Growth in France and Britain, 1851–1950*. Cambridge: Harvard University Press.

Kravis, I. B. 1970. Trade as a handmaiden of growth: Similarities between the nineteenth and twentieth centuries. *Econ. J.* 80:850–72.

―――. 1973a. Trade as a handmaiden of growth: Reply to Mr. Adams. *Econ. J.* 83:212–17.

―――. 1973b. A reply to Mr. Crafts' note. *Econ. J.* 83:885–89.

Kuznets, S. 1967. Quantitative aspects of the economic growth of nations. Level and structure of foreign trade: Long term trends. *Econ. Dev. Cult. Change* 15(2, pt. 2):1–140.

Lamfalussy, A. 1963. *The United Kingdom and the Six: An Essay on Economic Growth in Western Europe*. Homewood, Ill.: R. Irwin.

Lubitz, R. 1973. Export-led growth in industrial economies. *Kyklos* 26(Fasc. 2):307–21.

Marshall, A. 1959. *Principles of Economics*, 5th ed. London: Macmillan.

Matthew, R. C. 1973. Foreign trade and British economic growth. *Scott. J. Polit. Econ.* 23:195-209.

Michaely, M. 1977. Export and growth: An empirical investigation. *J. Dev. Econ.* 4:49-53.

Mill, J. S. 1964. *Principles of Political Economy*, collected ed., vol. 1. Toronto: University of Toronto Press.

Monroe, W. 1973. The contribution of Japanese exports to growth in output. *Neb. J. Econ. Bus.* 12:11-21.

North, D. C. 1955. Location theory and regional economic growth. *J. Polit. Econ.* 63:243-48.

Nurkse, R. 1961a. *Equilibrium and Growth in the World Economy: Economic Essays.* Cambridge: Harvard University Press.

————. 1961b. *Patterns of Trade and Development.* Oxford: Blackwell.

Organization for Economic Cooperation and Development (OECD). 1980. *National Accounts of OECD Countries.* Paris: OECD.

Robertson, D. H. 1938. The future of international trade. *Econ. J.* 48:1-14.

Rosovsky, H., and K. Ohkawa. 1973. *Japanese Economic Growth: Trend Acceleration in the Twentieth Century.* Stanford: Stanford University Press.

Sayers, R. S. 1965. *The Vicissitudes of an Export Economy--Britain since 1880.* Sidney: University of Sidney Press.

Severn, A. K. 1968. Exports and economic growth: Comment. *Kyklos* 21(Fasc. 3):546-48.

Smith, D. 1975. Public consumption and economic performance. *Natl. Westminster Bank Q. Rev.*, November:17-30.

Stern, R. M. 1967. *Foreign Trade and Economic Growth in Italy.* New York: Praeger.

Syron, R. F., and B. M. Walsh. 1968. The relation of exports and economic growth: A note. *Kyklos* 21(Fasc. 3):541-45.

Tiebout, C. M. 1956. Exports and regional economic growth. *J. Polit. Econ.* 64:160-64.

United Nations (UN). 1980. *Yearbook of National Accounts Statistics 1979.* New York: United Nations.

Voivodas, C. S. 1973. Exports, foreign capital inflow and economic growth. *J. Int. Econ.* 3(3):337-49.

Watkins, M. H. 1963. A staple theory of economic growth. *Can. J. Econ. Polit. Sci.* 29:141-58.

World Bank. 1980. *World Tables*, 2nd ed. Baltimore: Johns Hopkins University Press.

6

The Kaldor Approach, the Verdoorn Law, and the Dual Economy Model

In addition to a series of theoretical papers on growth theory, which proceeded by way of deductive reasoning from "macroeconomic axioms" of a rather general character, as we examined in Chapter 2, Nicholas Kaldor has recently tried to find certain regularities involved in economic growth and discover some testable hypotheses that can explain observed regularities and provide solutions for real growth problems. In his search for an explanation of why Britain's rate of economic growth was so much lower than that of other industrial countries, Kaldor, in the course of writing and lecturing since the mid-1960s, has suggested several hypotheses on comparative economic growth.

In a lecture in 1966, Kaldor (1966, 1978b) suggests that it would be better to view economic growth as a process of the reallocation of resources that leads to improved efficiency in production; he maintains that economic growth cannot be properly analyzed until one takes account of the crucial differences, in terms of behavioral assumptions, between the sectors of the economy. The main message of his lecture is that on the basis of empirical findings, the slow rate of economic growth of the United Kingdom is due mainly to the "economic maturity" reached by the United Kingdom. To Kaldor, an economy reaches economic maturity when the mechanism that enables the manufacturing industry to expand by drawing labor from the other sectors in response to demand ceases to function. The expansion of manufacturing output in the United Kingdom was limited by the labor shortage resulting from the elimination of the earnings difference between sectors. In sum, the rate of growth slows down when the economy reaches economic maturity, defined as the end of the dual economy, or when "growth with unlimited supplies of labor," to use an Arthur Lewis phrase, is no longer possible.

Kaldor (1975a, p. 895), in a subsequent rejoinder to R. E. Rowthorn's criticism, abandons the above reasoning and emphasizes the extraordinarily close correlation between the rates of growth of manufacturing and the gross domestic product (GDP)--the relationship that suggests that the rate of the economic growth of a country will depend on how much faster its manufacturing output grows than the rest of the economy. He asserts that a key element in explaining the close relationship between the growth rates of manufacturing output and the overall economy is Verdoorn's Law, which says that the growth of productivity in manufacturing depends largely upon the growth of manufacturing output. Kaldor establishes the support for the principles of Verdoorn's Law in manufacturing and other industrial sectors using data drawn from 12 advanced countries. This new observation and perspective leads Kaldor to conclude that the key to an explanation of slow and fast growth rates must be sought in demand factors, in particular in the growth of demand for the products of the manufacturing sector.

Kaldor's new view on economic growth is different from his earlier view, which maintains that "in a growing economy the general level of output at any one time is limited by available resources, and not by effective demand" (Kaldor 1980, p. 262). Before he changed his theoretical perspective, around the mid-1960s, Kaldor believed that steady state growth is determined by exogenously given factors such as technical progress and labor force growth. Kaldor (1978b) now believes that economic growth is demand-constrained when he says that "it is the growth of demand for the products of manufacturing industries, and not the constraints on supply, which determines how fast overall productivity and hence total output will grow in an advanced industrial economy." Another important change in Kaldor's theoretical perspective on economic growth is that his new theory consists of a two-sector model of agriculture and industry, where the latter is subject to increasing returns while the former is not, as discussed below.

Theoretical arguments in the new Kaldorian macrodynamics gave rise to heated and interesting interchanges among a group of economists, particularly between Kaldor and Rowthorn, and most of the hypotheses in Kaldor's new theory have successfully withstood empirical testing by himself and several others. What has been controversial in the subsequent debates is the flaw in the line of logical reasoning and the empirical obscurities in the causal relationships. The whole discussion by participants in the controversy was complicated by the emphasis put on different aspects of the statistical argument, by statistical tests based on divergent data, and by different theoretical formulations.

TWO-SECTOR MODEL OF MACRODYNAMICS:
MANUFACTURING AS AN ENGINE OF GROWTH

One big issue raised by Kaldor in his search for an explanation of why growth rates differ is whether the growth of manufacturing is in some sense the key to growth and transformation of the whole economy. That the manufacturing sector plays a key role in the process of development and growth is a view widely accepted among economists studying the less developed economies and has been

supported by causal empiricism and theoretical considerations. Its
importance on growth in other sectors has been associated with concepts of backward and forward linkage effects and the leading sector (see Hirschman 1958, Chap. 6). What has been attempted by Kaldor is to make the case that the manufacturing sector continues to
play the key role for economies well after modernization and industrialization are achieved.

The recognition that different productive activities exhibit
different characteristics and the empirical finding that there is
an extraordinarily close correlation between the rates of growth of
manufacturing output and of GDP lead Kaldor to conclude that a
thorough understanding of the nature of the growth process can only
be gained on the basis of a two-sector model of agriculture and industry. Unfortunately, though he developed the features of a two-
sector model, no work dealing with the model explicitly has been
published yet because Kaldor (1978b, p. xxii) "has never felt that
the new theory has reached a sufficiently mature stage to merit
publication without further work on it."

The major themes and implications of Kaldor's two-sector macrodynamic model are provided in several papers written in the years
1970-1976 (Kaldor 1970, 1971, 1972, 1975b, 1976, all reprinted in
1978b). Kaldor makes use of the principle of circular and cumulative causation, which he borrowed from Gunnar Myrdal (1957), and
the notion of increasing returns, which he borrowed from Allyn
Young (1928). Under the principle of circular and cumulative causation, success breeds success while failure begets more failure.
Therefore, Kaldor's two-sector model explains not only the differences in growth rates but also the persistence of a discrepancy in
growth rates among different economies and regions in a country.

Kaldor (1967, p. 7) asserts that "fast rates of growth are almost invariably associated with the fast rate of growth of the secondary sector, mainly manufacturing." The evidence supporting the
above assertion is summarized in Table 6.1. Kaldor emphasizes that
the correlation between the growth rates of GDP and manufacturing
production is much closer than could be explained simply on the
grounds that the manufacturing sector is a fairly large component
of GDP.

An important property contained in the regression results
(showing the relationship between the growth of GDP and the growth
of manufacturing output--(1), (6), (7), and (8) in Table 6.1) is
that all regressions produce the positive constant, and the coefficient of the growth of manufacturing production X_m is significantly
less than unity. The positive constant and the regression coefficient (which is considerably less than unity) imply, according to
Kaldor, that there is a positive correlation between the overall
rate of economic growth and the excess of the rate of growth of
manufacturing output over that of the nonmanufacturing sectors.
This fact is shown by a separate regression equation, (1), which is
statistically significant. This result can be shown graphically in
Figure 6.1. Using (6) as an illustration, the relationship states
that a rate of growth of total output above 3.26 percent a year is

Table 6.1. Manufacturing as the engine of
growth
_____
A. Kaldor:

$$Y = 1.153 + 0.614X_m \qquad (1)$$
$$(0.040) \qquad R^2 = 0.959$$
$$X_{nm} = 1.42 + 0.550X_m \qquad (2)$$
$$(0.080) \qquad R^2 = 0.824$$
$$Y = 3.351 + 0.954X_{em} \qquad (3)$$
$$(0.267) \qquad R^2 = 0.562$$
$$Y = -0.188 + 1.060X_s \qquad (4)$$
$$(0.092) \qquad R^2 = 0.930$$
$$X_s = 1.283 + 0.597X_i \qquad (5)$$
$$(0.0805) \qquad R^2 = 0.846$$

B. Cripps and Tarling:

$$Y = 1.295 + 0.603X_m \qquad (6)$$
$$(0.031) \qquad R^2 = 0.899$$

C. United Nations:

$$Y = 1.12 + 0.6002X_m \qquad (7)$$
$$(n.a.) \qquad R^2 = 0.97$$

D. Stoneman:

$$Y = 0.010 + 0.386X_m \qquad (8)$$
$$(0.025) \qquad R^2 = 0.715$$
$$Y = 0.019 + 0.135X_a \qquad (9)$$
$$(2.62) \qquad R^2 = 0.067$$
_____
Sources: Kaldor 1967, pp. 8-9, 73-75;
Cripps and Tarling 1973, p. 22; UN 1970;
Stoneman 1979, p. 311.
Note: Numbers in parentheses are the
standard errors. Y = rate of growth of GDP;
X_m = rate of growth of manufacturing output;
X_{nm} = rate of growth of nonmanufacturing output; X_{em} = excess of rate of growth of manufacturing over rate of growth of nonmanufacturing production; X_s = rate of growth of GDP
in service; X_i = rate of growth of industrial
production; X_a = rate of growth of agricultural output.

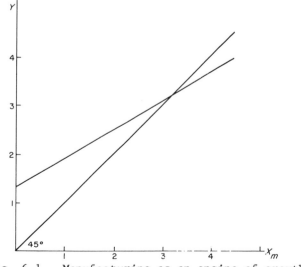

Fig. 6.1. Manufacturing as an engine of growth.

found in cases where the rate of growth in manufacturing is in excess of that of the nonmanufacturing sectors.

The significance of the above findings is subject to further testing by examining the relationship between the growth of GDP and the growth of output in other branches of production. The result indicating the relationship between the growth of GDP and that of GDP in services is shown in (4), while the relationship between the rate of growth of GDP and that of the agricultural sector is shown in (9). The fact that in (4) the coefficient is near unity and the constant is negative suggests that it is the rate of growth of GDP that determines the rate of growth of the service sector. It is notable that the correlation with the growth of GDP, as measured by the coefficient of determination R^2, is as close for manufacturing as for services. The very close correlation in the latter is interpreted to mirror the growth of production in the economy as a whole (Cripps and Tarling 1973, p. 22). Equation (9), based on time-series data from the United Kingdom over the period 1865-1965, shows that there is no significant relationship between the growth of agricultural output and that of GDP. The results discussed so far, and others, lead us to conclude that there is strong support for the relationship between the growth of GDP and the growth of the manufacturing production, and that in no other branch of production does the growth of output exhibit such a close correlation with the growth of GDP; if it does, the causal relationship may be the other way around.

As Kaldor himself acknowledges and discusses, one should not attribute causal significance to a statistical relationship unless general hypotheses can be offered explaining the phenomenon under consideration. Is there any reason to believe that the rate of growth of manufacturing output influences that of total output, with the causation running from the former to the latter, not vice versa? In his search for the answer to this question, Kaldor (1967, pp. 11-13) first notes that differences in overall growth rates are largely accounted for by differences in the rates of growth of productivity, because changes in the labor force have not been large enough to explain differences in the rate of growth of GDP. He then considers three possible explanations for the close correlation between productivity growth for the economy as a whole and the rate of growth of manufacturing production.

Kaldor finds the first explanation in the fact that the level of productivity in manufacturing activities is higher than that in the rest of the economy. Therefore, a faster expansion of the high-productivity manufacturing sector pulls up the average. The second explanation concerns the incidence of technical progress in the manufacturing sector as compared with other sectors. The argument goes that since the incidence of technical progress is higher in manufacturing activities than in others, a greater concentration of labor in the manufacturing sector brings about a higher average rate of productivity growth for the economy as a whole. However, Kaldor rejects these two explanations as unsatisfactory, citing evidence against them: (1) only a small part of the observed dif-

ferences in productivity growth has been accounted for by changes
in the distribution between high and low productivity sectors and
(2) there are some sectors whose growth rate of productivity is
higher than in manufacturing activities.

The third possible explanation offered by Kaldor himself for
the strong association between the growth rate of manufacturing
output and the rate of overall productivity growth is that productivity increases in response to increases in total output because
of economies of scale or increasing returns. To Verdoorn's Law--
the positive correlation between the growth of productivity and the
growth of production--Kaldor (1967, p. 15) gives the particular interpretation that "the relationship is peculiarly associated with
industrial activities (manufacturing, public utilities, construction) rather than with the primary or tertiary sectors of the economy," because industrial activities are subject to economies of
scale or increasing returns, while the activities of the other sectors are not. Kaldor emphasizes a dynamic relationship between
productivity change and output change involving both technical
progress and economies of large-scale production, not a static relationship relating the level of productivity to the scale of output.

To understand Kaldor's two-sector model of growth, which emphasizes the dynamic relationship between output growth and productivity growth, it should be remembered that to Kaldor the key to an
explanation of slow and fast growth rates is in the demand factors,
in particular in the growth of demand for the products of the manufacturing sector. As the demand for manufacturing output increases, the resulting greater supply carries with it a productivity increase. The extent to which the application of the tendency
of diminishing returns in the primary sector can be postponed depends on the growth of manufacturing output, since agricultural
productivity growth results mainly from increasing mechanization.
The increasing capital intensity in agricultural production is a
function of manufacturing output. Growth in agricultural productivity and the change in capital intensity in agriculture due to
the growth in manufacturing output serve two purposes: they free
labor that can be employed in manufacturing, while at the same time
the higher per capita agricultural incomes generate a strong demand
for manufacturing output. Thus to maintain a high growth rate of
GDP, a country must increase its manufacturing output, provided
there is a strong demand for it and human and nonhuman resources
can be transferred from the other sectors of the economy to be employed in manufacturing.

To justify a causal relationship emanating from the rate of
manufacturing output growth to productivity growth Kaldor emphasizes the fact that manufacturing activities are subject to the law
of increasing returns and that output growth in manufacturing is
important in inducing technological progress that is embodied in
the capital goods used by other industries. Kaldor (1978b, p. 143)
uses the term increasing returns to scale or economies of scale in
the broadest sense. Increasing returns to scale "are not just the

economies of large-scale production, but the cumulative advantages
accruing from the growth of industry itself--the development of
skill and know-how; the opportunities for easy communication of
ideas and experience; the opportunity of ever-increasing differentiation of process and of specialization in human activities."

Kaldor regrets the economists' neglect of the existence of increasing returns to scale even though the concept was first emphasized by Adam Smith in the first three chapters of the *Wealth of
Nations*. According to Smith (1937, pp. 3, 17), "The greatest improvements in the productive powers of labor . . . seem to have
been the effects of the division of labor." The division of labor,
according to Smith, gives rise to (1) an improvement of the dexter-
ity of the worker, (2) saving of time lost in passing from one part
of work to another, and (3) an application of machinery. However,
"the division of labor is limited by the extent of the market."
Therefore an increase in the size of the market or the growth of
output would contribute to the growth of productivity.

Similar arguments were used by J. S. Mill (1923, p. 701) to
foster the case of free commodity and factor movements between different territories. The mainstream of recent neoclassical theory
has neglected the prominent role played by increasing returns because of the difficulty of fitting them into the prevailing framework of perfect competition and marginal productivity factor pricing. Increasing returns gives rise to problems with the steady
growth of neoclassical theory because steady growth is not compati-
ble with increasing returns (see Eltis 1973, Chap. 11). Kaldor
notes that Alfred Marshall and Allyn Young stressed the interplay
of static and dynamic factors in causing returns to increase in response to an increase in the scale of industrial activities.
Marshall is of the opinion that an increase in the aggregate volume
of production gives rise to internal and external economies, resulting in increasing returns for the economy as a whole. Marshall
(1920, p. 382) says that "the Statical theory of equilibrium is only an introduction . . . to the study of the progress and development of industries which show a tendency to increasing return."

Since Marshall went no further to explicate the notion of increasing returns and made only scattered remarks on the problem of
increasing returns, Kaldor turns to Young (1928), who pointed out
the far-reaching consequences of the law of increasing returns on
the manner of operation of markets and on the behavior of an economic system. Young examines the interrelationship of industries
in the process of growth, the emergence of new industries as a result of specialization and standardization in a large market, and
the impact of an increase in the market size on technological
change, although he realizes that the causation between technological change and an increase in market size runs in both directioni.
He shows that the main function of a market is to transmit impulses
to economic change and thereby create more sources through enlarging the scope for specialization and the division of labor, rather
than to secure an optimum allocation of a given quantum of resources. According to Young (1928, p. 533), continual change with

increasing returns is self-generated and "propagates itself in a cumulative way."

In elaborating on industrial operations as an "interrelated whole" and continual change as a self-generating cumulative process, Young (1928, p. 534) relies heavily on the notion of the demand for any one commodity being elastic "in the special sense that a small increase in its supply will be attended by an increase in other commodities which can be had in exchange for it." In a later paper Kaldor (1972) demonstrates that elastic demand is neither a necessary nor a sufficient condition for economic progress to be cumulative under conditions of increasing returns. What is necessary, according to Kaldor, is that any initial change, whether it arises on the side of supply or demand, should induce additional investment. Kaldor's conclusion is simply that "the essential element missing from Young's presentation, and which can only be supplied on the basis of Keynesian economics, is the addition to incomes resulting from the accumulation of capital (in other words, from investment expenditure) combined with the induced character of such investment which arises more or less as a by-product of changes in organization of production."

The long search for a "better insight of how the world really works," combined with important though incomplete contributions by eminent economists such as Marshall and Young, has convinced Kaldor that the function of markets is not allocation but creation and that creative functions are related to the dominating role of increasing returns in industry. Economies of scale or increasing returns, which is a "macrophenomenon," are responsible for continuous endogenous change in the manner of Myrdal's principle of circular and cumulative causation.

In conclusion, Kaldor emphasizes the self-sustained nature of growth based on two important notions: the economies of scale in manufacturing and the relationship known as Verdoorn's Law. In addition to dynamic interactions among the variables involved as discussed above, Verdoorn's Law is also a crucial element in Kaldor's macrodynamics, a detailed discussion of which follows in the next two sections.

VERDOORN'S LAW

Empirical Evidence

In his famous article, P. J. Verdoorn (1949) presents empirical evidence on the constancy of the ratio between productivity growth and output growth in industry in the long run. The empirical, positive relationship between output growth and productivity growth is usually referred to as Verdoorn's Law. In 1966 Kaldor rediscovered and made famous the Verdoorn Law, which is a very critical element in his new macrodynamics. From the examination of a historical series on production for industry as a whole and for individual sectors of industry in a number of countries, Verdoorn concludes that the average value of the elasticity of labor produc-

tivity with respect to output is around 0.45, the upper and lower
limits being 0.41 and 0.57. This means that over the long period a
change of 10 percent in the volume of production tends to be associated with an average increase in labor productivity of 4.5 percent.

Since Kaldor returned Verdoorn's Law to the attention of economists in 1966, different interpretations and statistical testings
have been made of the causal mechanism that underlies the law. As
Verdoorn himself did, we first present empirical evidence on the
relationship between the growth of labor productivity and that of
output. The theoretical rationale behind the relationship is discussed next.

The data used to test Verdoorn's Law are of two types: a
cross section of industrial subsectors within a country and a
cross section of industrial sectors of different economies. A significant positive association between the growth of output and labor productivity was found by Solomon Fabricant (1942) for 51 manufacturing industries in the United States over the period 1899–
1937, seven years before Verdoorn published his paper. In fact, he
examines rank correlation between changes in output and employment
per unit of output (i.e., the inverse of labor productivity) and
finds the coefficient of -0.73. Fabricant's result has been confirmed in subsequent studies of the National Bureau of Economic
Research. John Kendrick (1961) presents rank correlation coefficients between relative changes in productivity and output for different groups of industries in the United States over the period
1899–1953. His coefficients of rank correlation are 0.68, 0.67 and
-0.10 for 33 industry groups, 80 manufacturing industries, and 12
farm groups respectively. Kendrick's 33 industry groups comprise 1
farming group, 5 mining groups, 20 manufacturing groups, and 7 ser-
vice-type groups in transportation and communications and public
utilities. In his most recent study, Kendrick finds a simple correlation coefficient of 0.601 between rates of growth of total factor productivity and rate of change in output for 20 manufacturing
industries in the United States during the period 1948-1976 (Kendrick and Grossman 1980, p. 4). Victor R. Fuchs (1968, p. 90) examines data for subsectors in the service industry in the United
States over the period 1939-1963. For 17 service industries, Fuchs
finds a rank correlation coefficient of 0.93 between the growth of
output and output per unit of labor.

In addition to the evidence supporting the high positive association between the long-term growth rates of output and labor productivity based on the rank correlation or simple correlation techniques (see Kennedy 1971, pp. 105-11), numerous investigators using
the regression technique have found statistically significant results on Verdoorn's Law. The results of the cross-sectional and
time-series studies utilizing the manufacturing sectors and others
within a country, or for different countries as observations, are
summarized in Table 6.2. Kaldor examines data from 12 developed
countries for the period 1953-1964. In the industrial sector as a
whole, (4), and in its subsectors, (1) to (3), Kaldor finds statis-

Table 6.2. Verdoorn's Law

A. Kaldor:

$$P_m = 1.035 + 0.484X_m \qquad (1)$$
$$(0.070) \qquad R^2 = 0.826$$

$$P_{pu} = 2.707 + 0.419X_{pu} \qquad (2)$$
$$(0.154) \qquad R^2 = 0.451$$

$$P_c = -0.543 + 0.572X_c \qquad (3)$$
$$(0.092) \qquad R^2 = 0.810$$

$$P_i = 0.888 + 0.446X_i \qquad (4)$$
$$(0.060) \qquad R^2 = 0.847$$

$$P_a = 2.700 + 1.041X_a \qquad (5)$$
$$(0.155) \qquad R^2 = 0.812$$

$$P_{mg} = 4.0714 + 0.671X_{mg} \qquad (6)$$
$$(0.153) \qquad R^2 = 0.705$$

$$P_{tc} = 2.314 + 0.224X_{tc} \qquad (7)$$
$$(0.252) \qquad R^2 = 0.102$$

$$P_{co} = -1.751 + 0.953X_{co} \qquad (8)$$
$$(0.098) \qquad R^2 = 0.932$$

B. United Nations:

$$P_m = 0.67 + 0.64X_m \qquad (9)$$
$$(n.a.) \qquad R^2 = 0.90$$

$$P_{nm} = -0.60 + 0.97X_{nm} \qquad (10)$$
$$(n.a.) \qquad R^2 = 0.79$$

C. Kennedy:

$$P_m = -0.085 + 0.489X_m \qquad (11)$$
$$(0.0492) \qquad R^2 = 0.897$$

D. Kendrick:

$$P_m = 2.113 + 0.287X_m \qquad (12)$$
$$(0.087) \qquad R^2 = 0.539$$

E. Stoneman:

$$P_m = 0.0013 + 0.655X_m \qquad (13)$$
$$(0.159) \qquad R^2 = 0.514$$

$$P_a = 0.0094 + 0.953X_a \qquad (14)$$
$$(-0.2708)* \qquad R^2 = 0.653$$

F. Dixon and Thirlwall:

$$P_m = 2.116 + 0.512X_m \qquad (15)$$
$$(0.147) \qquad R^2 = 0.573$$

Sources: Kaldor 1967, pp. 76–78; United Nations 1970, pt. 1, p. 84; Kennedy 1971, p. 139; Kendrick 1974, p. 112; Stoneman 1979, p. 311; Dixon and Thirwall 1975, p. 185.

Note: Numbers in parentheses are the standard errors. Growth rates of productivity P and output X are the dependent and independent variables respectively. Subscripts denote the following industries: m = manufacturing; pu = public utilities; c = construction; i = industry; a = agriculture; mg = mining; tc = transportation and communications; co = commerce; nm = nonmanufacturing.

*t-statistic for the test of the hypothesis that the regression coefficient is equal to unity.

tically significant results for the relationship between productivity growth and output growth. Agriculture and mining show a different picture. In agriculture, (5), the regression coefficient is not significantly different from unity, and in mining, (6), produc-

tivity growth involves a large trend factor (constant term) that is
independent of the output growth. In the case of transportation
and communications, (7), Kaldor finds no correlation whatever between productivity growth and output growth. Though there is a
high correlation between productivity growth and output growth in
commerce, (8), a regression coefficient not significantly different
from unity and the negative trend rate of productivity growth indicate that different factors other than those assumed in Verdoorn's
Law are working. From these results Kaldor contends that the close
relationship between output growth and productivity growth is associated with the secondary industrial sector rather than with the
primary or tertiary sectors of the economy. The UN study based on
15 industrial countries during the period 1953-1967 produces the
same results as those obtained by Kaldor. Verdoorn's Law holds
well in the manufacturing sector, while it does not work in the
nonmanufacturing sector.

The remaining results in Table 6.2 are based on time-series or
cross-sectional data for a given country. Kennedy obtains the result of regressing the growth rate of labor productivity on the
growth rate of output, (11), using the 26 Irish manufacturing industry data for 1938-1962. Kendrick's study for the 21 two-digit
manufacturing groups for the period 1948-1966 in the United States
yields a significant statistical result, though the regression coefficient lies outside the boundary suggested by Verdoorn. Stoneman and Dixon and Thirlwall examine Verdoorn's Law against British
growth performance. The time-series analysis by Stoneman using
data for more than a century and a half, from 1800 to 1969, produces results consistent with Verdoorn's Law. Using the manufacturing sector data from 11 regions in the United Kingdom over the
period 1958-1968, Dixon and Thirlwall obtain (15), which shows a
Verdoorn coefficient significantly different from zero and unity.

We conclude from the above empirical evidence based on rather
extensive sources of data that there is strong support for Verdoorn's Law, particularly in manufacturing though not necessarily
in other sectors of the economy. It is noted that most empirical
studies of the Verdoorn coefficients yield estimates between 0.4
and 0.7, around the limits originally obtained by Verdoorn.

Theoretical Explanations

The mere fact that there is a statistically significant relationship between productivity growth and production growth says
nothing about the cause and effect. The question that arises naturally is why such a marked pattern should emerge from the statistical analysis. Quite obviously, powerful mechanisms must be at
work to produce a consistent pattern of experience in industries
with such diverse technical, economic, and institutional backgrounds. Many writers have commented on the factors that account
for the causal mechanisms underlying the Verdoorn statistical relationship. The very first question concerns whether high rates of
growth of output cause high rates of growth of productivity or
whether it is rapid productivity growth that causes rapid output

growth. In principle, either sequence is possible. The examination of this causation itself is discussed later in connection with the controversy between Kaldor and Rowthorn over the appropriate test of Verdoorn's Law. Our discussion proceeds on the premise that the direction of causation is from growth of output to growth of productivity.

The theoretical underpinning of the constancy of the ratio between productivity growth and output growth given by Verdoorn himself is brief and relies on roundaboutness in the production process that is permitted by the expansion of output. Specifically, Verdoorn (1949, p. 3) says:

> In fact, one could have expected a priori to find a correlation between labor productivity and output, given that the division of labor only comes about through increases in the volume of production; therefore the expansion of production creates the possibility of further realization which has the same effects as mechanization.

In the appendix to the paper Verdoorn demonstrates the theoretical possibility of the constancy of the elasticity using a Cobb–Douglas production function and the "normal assumptions of long period analysis."

Verdoorn defines the elasticity of labor productivity with respect to output as

$$V = \frac{\dfrac{d(Q/L)}{dt}}{\dot{Q}/Q} \Big/ \frac{Q}{L} = \frac{L}{Q} \frac{L\dot{Q} - Q\dot{L}}{L^2} = \frac{\dot{Q}}{Q} - \frac{\dot{L}}{L} \tag{6.1}$$

where Q is the volume of production, L is the quantity of labor, and a dot denotes the first derivative with respect to time t. From (6.1),

$$V = 1 - (\dot{L}/L)/(\dot{Q}/Q) \tag{6.2}$$

Verdoorn derives an expression for $(\dot{L}/L)/(\dot{Q}/Q)$ from the Cobb–Douglas production function, $Q = L^\alpha K^\beta$, by totally differentiating with respect to time and dividing the result by $\dot{L}/L$:

$$(\dot{Q}/Q)/(\dot{L}/L) = \alpha + \beta \; (\dot{K}/K)/(\dot{L}/L) \tag{6.3}$$

Substitution of (6.3) into (6.2) gives the following Verdoorn coefficient:

$$V = 1 - \frac{1}{\alpha + \beta \; (\dot{K}/K)/(\dot{L}/L)} \tag{6.4}$$

From (6.4) it is clear that Verdoorn's coefficient depends upon partial elasticities of output with respect to each input, α and β --which together determine returns to scale in production--and on the rate at which capital is growing relative to labor. This re-

economies of plant, firm, and industry scale.

In seeking to explain the strong positive association between
the rates of growth of output and labor productivity in manufacturing industries, Kieran Kennedy (1971) considers the same explanatory factors as Salter, but in greater depth and detail. He finds
it unsatisfactory to account for differences in productivity movements among industries in terms of substitution of other factor in-
puts--capital or material. To Kennedy the differences in labor
productivity cannot be satisfactorily accounted for by the differences in the rate at which labor improves its skill and efficiency
in different industries, though increases in the personal efficiency of labor may be important in realizing productivity gains
attributable to other causes.

When Kennedy considers technological progress or advances in
knowledge as a cause explaining the association between output
growth and productivity growth, he examines two different types of
technological progress: exogenous and endogenous. He then pursues
the implications of both types on relative movements in productivity, prices, costs, and output to find out whether correlations between movements are consistent with the evidence. If technological
progress were exogenously determined, in order to explain the close
association between growth in output and productivity, it is necessary to show, first, that relative productivity increases are accompanied by relative price reductions and, second, that the price
elasticities of demand, given the relative price reductions, would
be such as to generate relative output increases of the order observed. If technological progress is conceived of as determined
exogenously, the causation behind the association between the
growth of output and productivity has to work from productivity
growth to output growth via relative price changes. Even though he
finds evidence supporting the two mechanisms mentioned above--nega-
tive correlation between changes in productivity and prices and
positive correlation between changes in prices and output--Kennedy
(1971, p. 185) concludes that "if technological progress were exogenously determined, differential price movements among industries,
resulting from differential productivity movements, would be unlikely to bring about a strong positive correlation between the
growth of output and productivity, though they might make for some
degree of positive correlation."

One way of explaining the Verdoorn Law, even when technological advances are determined exogenously, emerges if technical progress depends on the rate of growth. Kennedy (1971, p. 175) makes a
distinction between technological progress and technical progress.
He associates technological progress with the discovery of new
technological knowledge and technical progress with the application
of new knowledge. He suggests three possibilities for expecting
that technological advances will be quicker or greater in rapidly
growing industries. The first is the case where the relatively
greater additions of new and superior capacity are likely to take
place in industries with a faster rate of growth of output. The

second possibility is that the time lag in the application of new
technological advances will be shortened by a more rapid growth of
output. The third possible way is that the introduction of new
techniques may result in the exploitation of economies of scale
only when output of the industry is expanding rapidly.

Kennedy believes that endogenous technological progress provides a much more convincing explanation of the generality of the
association between the growth of output and productivity. Following the theories of Kenneth Arrow and Jacob Schmookler, Kennedy
suggests that endogenous technological change depends on the relative rate of growth of output or on relative changes in other variables that are determined to a great extent by relative rates of
growth of output. According to Arrow's (1962) learning-by-doing
model, technological knowledge is acquired by experience, which is
in turn a function of the volume of cumulative gross investment.
Since over a reasonably long period the increase in output in an
industry is a principal factor in determining the volume of investment, Arrow's argument suggests that there will be a close association between the rates of growth of output and productivity.

Schmookler (1966) advances a somewhat different theory of endogenous technological change. He is concerned with the determinants of invention and finds that demand factors are more important
determinants of invention than supply factors. Schmookler stresses
the rate of gross investment because the current rate per time period in an industry is a guide to the future amount of capital
goods sales to the industry and, therefore, to the rate of return
on effort devoted to making improvements in capital goods used in
the industry. So the causal chain is, according to Schmookler,
from investment to invention. The dependence of invention or technical progress on investment, combined with the fact that there is
a close relationship between output growth and rate of investment,
suggests that the relative rate of advance in knowledge is endogenously determined and depends on the relative rates of growth of
output.

The last cause Kennedy discusses in great detail to explain
the strong positive correlation between the growth of productivity
and output is economies of scale. He considers the different possible types, distinguishing between internal and external and between static and dynamic economies of scale, and examines how far
economies of scale might be expected to explain differences in
productivity movements and their association with differences in
output movement. To Kennedy (1971, p. 219), "the most plausible
explanation of the association between the rates of growth of output and labor productivity, consistent with the associated movements in relative costs and prices, is one that allows for the interrelations between changes in scale and technological progress."
At this stage Kennedy and Kaldor share the view that the dynamic
relationship between productivity change and output change involving economies of large-scale production and technical progress is
the key to the growth of capitalist economies.

CONTROVERSY BETWEEN KALDOR AND ROWTHORN

The most critical review of Kaldor's explanation of why growth rates differ has been made by Rowthorn. He questions Kaldor's view on the grounds that Kaldor's estimation method is misleading and his sample is biased. The exchanges between Kaldor and Rowthorn brought out "the importance of interaction and simultaneity in the economic processes concerned" and led to a better understanding of the principle of Verdoorn's Law and its empirical testing.

One of the problems arises from the fact that Kaldor has abandoned the main message of his lecture, that the slow growth of the United Kingdom was due mainly to the shortage of labor resulting from "economic maturity." Until Kaldor (1975a, p. 891) changed his mind "as a result of fresh statistical evidence as well as further historical experience" and stated his new views on the issue, there had been a misunderstanding by Rowthorn and several others of the main message of Kaldor's lecture. For example, John Cornwall (1976) summarizes Kaldor's model in the form of three equations, which can be written: $Y = a_0 + a_1 X_m$; $X_m = b_0 + b_1 E_m$; and $E_m = c_0 + c_1 E$; where Y and X_m represent the rates of growth of total output and manufacturing output respectively and E_m and E represent the rates of growth of employment in manufacturing and total labor supply. As interpreted by Cornwall, growth is "supply-determined." "Total labor supply determines manufacturing labor supply, manufacturing labor supply determines manufacturing output and the latter determines total output." This interpretation is in sharp contrast to Kaldor's current view, which emphasizes the "demand-constrained" note of the growth process. Kaldor (1975a, p. 895) admits that he "was wrong in thinking in 1966 that the United Kingdom had attained the stage of 'economic maturity' . . . and that her comparative poor performance was to be explained by an inability to recruit sufficient labor in the manufacturing industry rather than poor market performances due to lack of international competitiveness."

The major controversy between Kaldor and Rowthorn revolves around establishing and testing the validity of Verdoorn's Law. While Kaldor maintains that it is important to show the existence of statistically significant relationships between productivity growth (P_m) and output growth (X_m) and between employment growth (E_m) and output growth, Rowthorn argues that the whole argument depends crucially on the existence of a positive relationship between P_m and E_m and suggests that it is more natural to examine this relation directly by regressing P_m on E_m rather than indirectly, as Kaldor has done, by regressing P_m and E_m on X_m. Since there is an identity relationship, $P_m = X_m - E_m$, the three regressions involved are not independent of each other.

Kaldor believes that the existence of a significant relationship between E_m and X_m is the main test to determine whether the Verdoorn Law asserts something significant about the real capitalist economies or whether it is simply a statistical illusion, even though he does not suggest that a statistically significant positive association between P_m and E_m is a necessary test of the Verdoorn Law. The reason for this belief lies, as we discussed earlier, in the fact that Kaldor (1975a, p. 892) "regards output as being in general the exogenous variable (determined by demand)." As long as economic growth is to be explained by the growth of demand, which is exogenous to the manufacturing sector, and not by exogenously given growth rates of labor and capital, accompanied by exogenously given technical progress over time, any error or disturbance would be associated with E_m. This theoretical perspective and statistical requirement led Kaldor (1975a, p. 895) to conclude "that a 'sufficient' condition for the presence of static or dynamic economies of scale is the existence of a statistically significant relationship between $e(E_m)$ and $p(P_m)$, with a regression coefficient which is significantly less than 1." Equations (1) through (4) in Table 6.3 confirm Kaldor's arguments. The regression coef-

Table 6.3. Summary of regressions by Kaldor, Cripps and
        Tarling, and Rowthorn
A. Kaldor:

Including Japan for 1953-54 to 1963-64 (N = 12)

$$P_m = 1.035 + 0.484X_m \quad (0.070) \qquad R^2 = 0.826 \tag{1}$$

$$E_m = -1.028 + 0.516X_m \quad (0.070) \qquad R^2 = 0.844 \tag{2}$$

Excluding Japan for 1953-54 to 1963-64 (N = 11)

$$P_m = 1.359 + 0.417X_m \quad (0.129) \qquad R^2 = 0.536 \tag{3}$$

$$E_m = -1.331 + 0.574X_m \quad (0.130) \qquad R^2 = 0.685 \tag{4}$$

B. Cripps and Tarling:

Including Japan for 1951-1965 (N = 32)

$$P_m = 3.178 + 0.549E_m \quad (0.133) \qquad R^2 = 0.362 \tag{5}$$

$$X_m = 3.178 + 1.549E_m \quad (0.133) \qquad R^2 = 0.818 \tag{6}$$

Including Japan for 1965-1970 (N = 12)

$$P_m = 4.855 + 0.101E_m \quad (0.757) \qquad R^2 = 0.002 \tag{7}$$

$$X_m = 4.855 + 1.101E_m \quad (0.757) \qquad R^2 = 0.175 \tag{8}$$

C. Rowthorn:

Including Japan for 1953-54 to 1963-64 using Kaldor data (N = 12)

$$P_m = 2.632 + 0.626E_m \quad (0.220) \qquad R^2 = 0.447 \tag{9}$$

Excluding Japan for 1953-54 to 1963-64 using Kaldor data (N = 11)

$$P_m = 3.237 + 0.183E_m \quad (0.267) \qquad R^2 = 0.050 \tag{10}$$

Excluding Japan for 1951-1965 using Cripps and Tarling data (N = 29)

$$P_m = 3.590 + 0.186E_m \quad (0.145) \qquad R^2 = 0.057 \tag{11}$$

Excluding Japan for 1965-1970 using Cripps and Tarling data (N = 11)

$$P_m = 5.211 + 1.405E_m \quad (0.556) \qquad R^2 = 0.415 \tag{12}$$

Sources: Kaldor 1967, p. 76; 1975a, p. 892; Cripps and Tarling 1973, p. 23; Rowthorn 1975a, p. 14.
Note: Standard errors are in parentheses; N represents numbers of observations. P_m = rate of growth of productivity in manufacturing; X_m = rate of growth of manufacturing output; E_m = rate of growth of employment in manufacturing.

ficients for both P_m on X_m and E_m on X_m are around 0.5. The findings do not depend on whether or not Japan is included in the sample, even though the exclusion of Japan reduces the closeness of
the fit somewhat.

According to Rowthorn (1975a), a more appropriate method of
establishing the validity of Verdoorn's Law and of arguing that the
potential growth of industrial productivity is limited by the supply of labor is to regress P_m on E_m directly, expressed as:

$$P_m = a + bE_m \qquad (6.9)$$

Rowthorn views (6.9) as a reformulation of the original Verdoorn
Law:

$$P_m = c + dX_m \qquad (6.10)$$

For appropriate values of a, b, c, and d, the two equations are
mathematically equivalent. Making use of the identity, $X_m = P_m$
$+ E_m$, shows that the two equations are equivalent when $a = c/(1-d)$
and $b = d/(1-d)$. Rowthorn refers to the alternative formulation
in (6.9) as "Kaldor's Law."

When Rowthorn uses this direct method, he finds that the association depends on the particular period employed and the presence
of one extreme observation, Japan. Kaldor's Law is valid only when
Japan is included in the sample and only for the first two decades
since World War II--(5) and (9) in Table 6.3. When Japan is excluded from the sample--(10), (11), and (12)--or when the data for
the period 1965-1970 is employed--(7) and (12)--the estimated coefficients become statistically insignificant and the coefficient of
determination drops sharply. When Japan is omitted for the period
1965-1970--(12)--there appears a strong negative and significant
relationship between growth of productivity and employment.

In his reply to Kaldor's comment, Rowthorn (1975b, p. 900)
claims that the exogeneity of output growth is implausible because
causality from output to productivity and employment is not unidi-
rectional, with a significant feedback in both directions, and
maintains that:

> his [Kaldor's] method of estimating the productive relations
> between $p[P_m]$, $e[E_m]$, and $q[X_m]$ is appropriate only when (1)
> there is an "unlimited" supply of labor in virtually every
> country in his sample and (2) demand is not significantly af-
> fected by the movement of productivity or employment. Under
> these conditions it is formally correct to take q as the inde-
> pendent variable and to interpret the result as evidence about
> technology. If these stringent conditions are not met, how-
> ever, Kaldor's method is incorrect.

Different interpretations can be made of the causal mechanism
that underlies the Verdoorn Law. The controversy between Kaldor
and Rowthorn can be settled only when the nature of technological

progress and employment growth is identified. When they are of the endogenous type, Kaldor's position is upheld, while exogenous technological progress and employment growth independent of demand support Rowthorn's view. Whether technological change is exogenous or endogenous or whether the rate of growth of employment is exogenously or endogenously determined cannot be settled without some information in addition to the statistical results provided by Kaldor and Rowthorn. The existence of this identification problem has been clearly observed in the literature.

As we discussed earlier, the evidence obtained so far indicates that endogenous technological progress provides a much more convincing explanation for the movements in major variables involved. With regard to the question whether or not the rate of growth of employment in manufacturing is exogenously determined, independent of demand, Cornwall's (1976) answer is that whenever demand for labor in manufacturing is strong, labor supply is forthcoming. A. Parikh (1978), in his effort to remove the simultaneous equations bias and the misspecification bias involved in both Kaldor's and Rowthorn's estimates, finds support for the view that the rate of growth of employment in the manufacturing sector is determined by the rate of growth of manufacturing output. All of these theoretical arguments and empirical evidence, though incomplete and inconclusive, lead us to lean toward Kaldor's interpretation.

DUAL MODEL OF ECONOMIC GROWTH

It has long been recognized that important insights into the growth and development process of economies can be gained by explicitly emphasizing structural difference between key sectors in the economy. To this end, two major approaches have been developed. One of these deals with the relationships between economic structure and economic performance demonstrated in a number of studies, going back to the work of Allen Fisher (1935, pp. 25-43) and Colin Clark (1940, pp. 337-73). Put simply, the Fisher-Clark hypothesis is that if economic activities are classified as "primary," "secondary," and "tertiary," then the level of per capita income will rise as the major sources of an economy's employment or income move from primary through secondary to tertiary activities. The other is the dual economy model whereby the economy is divided into two sectors according to the chosen criterion. Even though the Fisher-Clark theory of structural transformation, when tested at a sufficient level of industrial detail, provides useful information, the theoretical content of various hypotheses relating economic structure to economic performance has been the subject of considerable criticism. If a theory requires that one begin with a set of propositions about the economic behavior of decision making units, then most hypotheses in the Fisher-Clark theory do in fact have little theoretical content. Despite the explanatory and predictive power based on empirical analysis, the Fisher-Clark hypothesis "offers no insight into the causes of economic growth itself" (Richardson 1979, p. 34).

The dual economy approach has emerged out of an attempt to understand the transformation of nonwestern, underdeveloped economies as they emerge from a state of backwardness to that of modernity. According to Arthur Lewis (1954), with whom the model originated, a dual economy has an advanced modern sector coexisting with a backward nonmonetized sector, which is usually thought of as agriculture. There are a number of possible definitions of the term dualism. In the main, dualism refers to economic and social divisions in an economy, such as differences in the level of technology and productivity between sectors or regions, differences in demographic pattern and social development, and differences in social customs and consumer behavior. Alternative labels representing the two sectors have been applied, such as subsistence and modern, traditional and capitalist, or agricultural and industrial. The backward sector is usually considered to be underemployed, so labor can be taken out of it without adversely affecting the output in the sector. The importance of the backward sector in Lewis's model is that it provides the more modern sectors of the economy with a supply of labor over time. Furthermore, real wages in industry are kept low because there is an abundance of labor available for the industrial sector. The mechanism of growth is that profits that arise in industry are reinvested and increase the growth of industry. Labor is always available, and since the real wage is low because of the existence of the low-productivity sectors, profits in industry rise over time. The rising profits generate a rapid and accelerating growth process, which ends when so much labor has been taken out of the low-productivity sectors that they are no longer underemployed. At this point, wages start to rise, cutting into profits and slowing the growth process.

The dual economy theory has been the subject of numerous extensions and modifications, most notably by John Fei and Gustav Ranis (1964), Dale Jorgenson (1961, 1967), and Lewis (1958, 1979) himself. Recently, it has been argued by several writers that real insight can be gained into the nature of the growth of the transformation process of countries with incomes well above the subsistence level by stressing the absence or presence in these economies of certain dualistic elements heretofore associated only with underdeveloped countries. Writers analyzing western, more developed economies differ in their emphasis from those concerned with nonwestern, less developed economies, but the similarity of the models suggests that models of growth and development stressing dualism may have wider applicability than originally thought.

Charles Kindleberger (1967) and John Cornwall (1977a) conceptualize the problem of the fast rates of economic growth achieved by some industrialized countries in the postwar period in terms of the dual economy model. Both emphasize the presence in one sector of a dual economy of surplus labor or elastic labor supply as an engine of rapid growth in other sectors. (Kaldor, in a lecture given in 1966, also stressed the importance of shifts in the disposition of the labor force in his explanation of the poor growth performance in the United Kingdom. To Kaldor, the absence of sur-

plus labor is the result of the United Kingdom having reached a
stage of maturity. Kaldor changed his position and relies on other
mechanisms to explain the difference in growth performance among
countries and regions, as we discussed earlier. So our discussion
here is based on works of Kindleberger and Cornwall.) In applying
the dual economy model to European experience, Kindleberger assumes
a dualistic structure, both for the group of countries under consideration and within each country. Though he admits that the
Lewis model may not account for all the divergences in Europe from
country to country or from industry to industry and notes instances
where data do not conform to the model, he argues that the expansion of the 1950s in European countries followed the Lewis model of
"growth with unlimited supplies of labor." The essential characteristic here is an infinitely elastic supply of labor. Thus it
has been possible to satisfy high demand in the capitalistic sector
under stable conditions as long as an abundant labor reserve force
existed. Excess labor is permissive rather than initiating.
Whether the initiating mechanism arises from the demand or the supply side, higher rates of growth or "super-growth" continue so long
as the supply of labor remains elastic. When the labor reserves
are used up, the supply of labor reaches a limit, and the extra demand generated by the system encounters a less than infinitely
elastic supply of labor. When the advanced sector approaches a
turning point in the form of a rapid fall in the elasticity of labor supply, wages and prices rise and profits and investment are
reduced, so the growth rate slows down and becomes irregular.

As evidence of his claim that the process of dualistic economic growth is behind the supergrowth experience of some Western European countries, Kindleberger (1967, p. 3) examines the labor supply situation in a number of countries in some detail and remarks:

> The major factor shaping the remarkable economic growth which
> most of Europe has experienced since 1950 has been the availa-
> bility of a large supply of labour. The labour has come from
> a high rate of natural increase (the Netherlands), from trans-
> fers from agriculture to services and industry (Germany,
> France, Italy), from the immigration of unemployed and under-
> employed workers from the Mediterranean countries (France,
> Germany and Switzerland). Those countries with no substantial
> increase in the labour supply--Britain, Belgium and the Scan-
> dinavian nations--on the whole have grown more slowly than the
> others.

Given the diversity of the problems under consideration, Lewis
and Kindleberger naturally differ in the emphasis they place on
certain factors. Lewis is interested in explaining how a growth
mechanism based on the accumulation of capital works when there is
an infinitely elastic supply of labor. Kindleberger, on the other
hand, assumes a high level of demand in the industrial countries
and aims at explaining the differentials between growth rates by
the differences in the elasticity of the labor supply.

    In his attempt to get to the heart of the matter of why growth
rates differ, by incorporating the main thrusts of important theoretical and applied work in many different areas in economics,
Cornwall presents a framework of macrodynamics with a "sense of
history," emphasizing (1) the unbalanced nature of growth, (2)
qualitative change, (3) perpetual disequilibria downgrading changes
in relative factor prices as an allocative mechanism, (4) the critical role assigned to the manufacturing sector, (5) the importance
of flexibility in the factor movement among sectors, and (6) the
importance of entrepreneurship, all together with a stress on the
importance of demand pressures. One of the notable features from
detailed examination of comparative data from advanced, developed
countries for the postwar period is differences in sectoral growth
rates over time, whether the economy is viewed in terms of output
or input. Cornwall relies on the "classical" model of dual economy
to explain the unbalanced growth experienced by developed economies.

    In discussing the relevance of dualism in explaining develop-
ment in advanced, capitalist economies, Cornwall (1977a, pp. 46–47)
identifies three conditions necessary for the existence of surplus
labor: (1) the existence of a substantial number of workers willing to undertake complex mobility patterns; (2) a rather rigid interindustry wage structure that persists in spite of the fact that
members of the labor force are willing and able to undertake complex mobility strategies; this has partly to do with the growth of
productivity and the elasticities of demand for the output of the
low wage sector; and (3) the existence of an allocative mechanism
in the labor markets that does not reflect some sort of equaliza-
tion of net benefits for workers. Cornwall maintains that if these
three conditions are present and if the demand for industrial output and the derived demand for labor by industry are strong enough
so that the rate of growth of output and employment in industry exceeds that in the economy, then such an economy conforms to the
workings of a dual economy.

    Detailed theoretical and empirical attempts have been made to
discern the presence or absence of the above conditions during the
postwar period. Because of high wage differentials between agricultural and nonagricultural jobs, incentives for a labor movement
from the former to the latter existed for most, though not all, of
the industrialized market economies. So, when the demand for industrial labor was strong, employment patterns were such as to conform to the working of the dual economy. One important question
now is whether movements of labor out of agriculture produced any
pronounced narrowing of wage differentials. Cornwall and others
find a very strong stability and rigidity in the interindustry wage
structure, which is in sharp contrast to the neoclassical view that
wage differentials would narrow as the market mechanism induced labor and capital to reallocate until factor returns are equalized
across industries. Relatively large shifts in industry employment
along with relatively small changes in relative wages are the result of an increase in demand pressures in reallocating labor as
revealed in the opening and closing of job vacancies.

Cornwall (1977a, p. 68) adopts the following criterion, in addition to the existence of surplus labor, for the applicability of the model of the dual economy: "If in some country in the postwar period the rate of growth of manufacturing output and employment was greater than the overall rate of growth of output and the employment, it will be said that this country's development showed characteristics of growth of a dual economy." According to this criterion, of 12 countries examined, Austria, Denmark, France, Germany, Italy, Japan, and Norway conform to the working of the dual economy for the period covering the early 1950s to the late 1960s. Growth performance in Belgium, Canada, the Netherlands, the United Kingdom, and the United States does not follow the dual economy model. In these countries the rate of growth slowed down because the economy reached the mature stage. Cornwall's data indicate less conformity with the dual model for the recent period in most countries. The dual model, from the point of view of output, implies that growth of manufacturing output exceeds that of total output. In terms of the output criterion, all countries in Cornwall's sample confirm the working of the dual model.

The distinguishing feature of the dual theory is its systematic nature, which tries to conceptualize the process of economic development and growth over time. It isolates what are considered to be the key elements of the situations, makes specific assumptions about the shapes of relationships regulating the interactions, and predicts the resultant path through time of the key variables by deductions based on the extremely parsimonious assumptions. The dualistic theory is a composite body of many analytically distinct hypotheses. While a falsification of one deduced implication would mean falsification of the model as an integral unit, all the constituent hypotheses provide useful insights. The dual economy model, as interpreted by Kindleberger and Cornwall, is mainly intended to shed light on historical changes. They have to call upon history to explain the model as much as they call upon the model to explain history. They show clearly that dualism continues to be an appropriate model of analysis, well beyond the initial stages of industrialization until cessation of population growth and immigration create a market for labor.

FURTHER EVIDENCE AND CONCLUSIONS

One of Kaldor's major contributions to the theory of comparative economic growth is to provide a framework for analyzing the dynamic nature of the growth process for capitalist economies. His framework negates the use of the neoclassical paradigm to explain both the allocation of resources within the advanced countries and their growth, based on what he considers to be the untenable assumption of constant returns to scale and the postulate that labor or any other factor of production is the limiting factor in the growth process. Most of the hypotheses in Kaldor's new macrodynamics have successfully withstood empirical testing, as we examined earlier and will examine next with a rather comprehensive set of data. Though it still remains to be seen whether or not Kaldor is

mistaken in his arguments as to the determinants of economic
growth, his strong insistence that for economic analysis to be
fruitful it must be firmly grounded in empirical generalizations or
"law" deserves commendation.

A full evaluation of the theoretical construct of Kaldor's new
macrodynamics of economic growth and a thorough investigation of
the empirical validity of his hypotheses may have to wait until he
himself puts out a complete model. Before we examine a few arguments brought against Kaldor's view in general and Verdoorn's Law
in particular, we provide some additional tests of the major hypotheses, using a different, comprehensive set of data. The regression results utilizing the various sectors of advanced market
economies as observations are shown in Table 6.4, while the results

Table 6.4. Empirical testing of Verdoorn's Law, Kaldor's Law, and
the dual hypothesis using cross-country data

A. Manufacturing sector:
Based on data from 12 industrialized countries for 1950-1955,
1955-1960, 1960-1965, 1965-1970, and 1970-1975 (N = 56)

$$P_m = 2.0811 + 0.4648X_m \tag{1}$$
$$(6.90) \quad (8.53) \qquad\qquad R^2 = 0.57$$

$$E_m = -2.0811 + 0.5352X_m \tag{2}$$
$$(6.90) \quad (9.83) \qquad\qquad R^2 = 0.64$$

$$P_m = 4.1018 + 0.1982E_m \tag{3}$$
$$(15.34) \quad (1.63) \qquad\qquad R^2 = 0.05$$

$$LC_m = 6.0704 - 0.5568P_m \tag{4}$$
$$(6.71) \quad (2.83) \qquad\qquad R^2 = 0.13$$

B. Various industries:
Based on data from 7 European countries for 1955-1960, 1960-1964,
1964-1969, and 1969-1973 (N = 28)

Agriculture, forestry, and fishing
$$P_{aff} = 4.4321 + 0.7290X_{aff} \tag{5}$$
$$(12.26) \quad (4.65) \qquad\qquad R^2 = 0.45$$

$$E_{aff} = -4.4321 + 0.2710X_{aff} \tag{6}$$
$$(12.26) \quad (1.73) \qquad\qquad R^2 = 0.10$$

$$P_{aff} = 3.4268 - 0.6199E_{aff} \tag{7}$$
$$(3.85) \quad (2.82) \qquad\qquad R^2 = 0.23$$

Mining and quarrying
$$P_{mq} = 4.3257 + 1.1761X_{mq} \tag{8}$$
$$(6.05) \quad (9.26) \qquad\qquad R^2 = 0.77$$

$$E_{mq} = -4.3257 - 0.1761X_{mq} \tag{9}$$
$$(6.05) \quad (1.39) \qquad\qquad R^2 = 0.07$$

$$P_{mq} = -1.0264 - 1.3909E_{mq} \tag{10}$$
$$(0.63) \quad (4.93) \qquad\qquad R^2 = 0.48$$

Sources: Table 3.3; OECD 1969, 1978; World Bank 1980, pp. 268-
69, 394-95, 464; U.S. Department of Labor 1977, Tables B-1, B-3, B-5;
Jones 1976, pp. 80-81.

Note: Numbers in parentheses are t-statistics. Growth rates of
productivity, output, and employment are denoted by P, X, and E respectively. Subscripts denote industries as follows: m = manufacturing; aff = agriculture, forestry, and fishing; mq = mining and
quarrying; egw = electricity, gas, and water; c = construction; i
= industrial production; and s = service. In addition, TFP = growth
rate of total factor productivity; TO = growth rate of total output;
Y = growth rate of GDP; SE_a = share of civilian employment in agriculture; SE_i = share of civilian employment in industry; SE_o = 1
$- SE_a - SE_i$; P_{ia} = ratio of productivity in industry to productivity
in agriculture; and LC_m = growth rate of labor cost in manufacturing.

Table 6.4. *(continued)*

Manufacturing

$$P_m = 1.9062 + 0.5461 X_m \tag{11}$$
$$\quad (2.28) \quad (3.88) \qquad\qquad R^2 = 0.37$$
$$E_m = -1.9062 + 0.4539 X_m \tag{12}$$
$$\quad (2.27) \quad (3.22) \qquad\qquad R^2 = 0.29$$
$$P_m = 5.3101 - 0.3706 E_m \tag{13}$$
$$\quad (18.89) \quad (1.90) \qquad\qquad R^2 = 0.12$$

Electricity, gas, and water

$$P_{egw} = 0.8027 + 0.7819 X_{egw} \tag{14}$$
$$\quad (0.58) \quad (5.02) \qquad\qquad R^2 = 0.49$$
$$E_{egw} = -0.8027 + 0.2181 X_{egw} \tag{15}$$
$$\quad (0.58) \quad (1.40) \qquad\qquad R^2 = 0.07$$
$$P_{egw} = 8.0157 - 0.6785 E_{egw} \tag{16}$$
$$\quad (13.41) \quad (2.95) \qquad\qquad R^2 = 0.25$$

Construction

$$P_c = 0.3762 + 0.5951 X_c \tag{17}$$
$$\quad (0.63) \quad (5.22) \qquad\qquad R^2 = 0.51$$
$$E_c = -0.3762 + 0.4049 X_c \tag{18}$$
$$\quad (0.63) \quad (3.55) \qquad\qquad R^2 = 0.33$$
$$P_c = 3.3302 - 0.1928 E_c \tag{19}$$
$$\quad (6.12) \quad (0.85) \qquad\qquad R^2 = 0.03$$

Industrial production

$$P_i = 1.5703 + 0.5964 X_i \tag{20}$$
$$\quad (1.95) \quad (4.25) \qquad\qquad R^2 = 0.41$$
$$E_i = -1.5703 + 0.4036 X_i \tag{21}$$
$$\quad (1.95) \quad (2.87) \qquad\qquad R^2 = 0.24$$
$$P_i = 5.1289 - 0.4016 E_i \tag{22}$$
$$\quad (17.22) \quad (1.93) \qquad\qquad R^2 = 0.13$$

Service

$$P_s = -0.4868 + 0.7175 X_s \tag{23}$$
$$\quad (0.91) \quad (6.28) \qquad\qquad R^2 = 0.60$$
$$E_s = 0.4868 + 0.2825 X_s \tag{24}$$
$$\quad (0.91) \quad (2.47) \qquad\qquad R^2 = 0.19$$
$$P_s = 3.3091 - 0.3267 E_s \tag{25}$$
$$\quad (6.22) \quad (1.20) \qquad\qquad R^2 = 0.05$$

C. Total factor productivity and total output ($N = 50$)
$$TFP = 0.1415 + 0.4807 TO \tag{26}$$
$$\quad (0.66) \quad (11.18) \qquad\qquad R^2 = 0.72$$

D. Economic growth and share of civilian employment by sector
    ($N = 47$)
$$Y = 2.0261 + 0.0854 SE_a \tag{27}$$
$$\quad (4.69) \quad (3.56) \qquad\qquad R^2 = 0.22$$
$$Y = 5.0137 - 0.0439 SE_i \tag{28}$$
$$\quad (3.31) \quad (1.12) \qquad\qquad R^2 = 0.03$$
$$Y = 7.5100 - 0.0904 SE_o \tag{29}$$
$$\quad (5.19) \quad (2.92) \qquad\qquad R^2 = 0.16$$

E. Economic growth and relative productivity between industry and
    agriculture ($N = 32$)
$$Y = 2.0159 + 0.7668 P_{ia} \tag{30}$$
$$\quad (3.38) \quad (2.60) \qquad\qquad R^2 = 0.18$$

based on data from the U.S. manufacturing sector and the 48 contiguous states are presented in Table 6.5. It is noted that our data base is quite extensive in that it covers longer periods than most of the previous studies.

The results based on data from various industries of developed market economies—(1) to (25) in Table 6.4—illustrate:

Table 6.5. Empirical testing of Verdoorn's Law and Kaldor's Law
using U.S. manufacturing sector and regional data

A. Manufacturing sector:
Based on data from 20 two-digit SIC industries for 1948-1966 and
1966-1976 ($N = 40$)

$$P = 1.4899 + 0.3834X \qquad\qquad (1)$$
$$\quad (5.52) \quad (5.03) \qquad\qquad R^2 = 0.40$$
$$E = -1.4899 + 0.6116X \qquad\qquad (2)$$
$$\quad (5.52) \quad (8.09) \qquad\qquad R^2 = 0.63$$
$$P = 2.6115 - 0.0260E \qquad\qquad (3)$$
$$\quad (13.22) \quad (0.20) \qquad\qquad R^2 = 0.00$$
$$TFP = 0.7274 + 0.4216X \qquad\qquad (4)$$
$$\quad (2.95) \quad (6.06) \qquad\qquad R^2 = 0.49$$
$$TFP = 1.9227 + 0.1444E \qquad\qquad (5)$$
$$\quad (9.99) \quad (1.17) \qquad\qquad R^2 = 0.03$$

B. 48 contiguous states for 1958-1968 and 1968-1978:

Total labor and proprietor's income ($N = 96$)
$$P = 0.1045 + 0.8280X \qquad\qquad (6)$$
$$\quad (0.31) \quad (20.20) \qquad\qquad R^2 = 0.81$$
$$E = -0.1045 + 0.1720X \qquad\qquad (7)$$
$$\quad (0.31) \quad (4.16) \qquad\qquad R^2 = 0.16$$
$$P = 6.6384 - 0.0965E \qquad\qquad (8)$$
$$\quad (20.00) \quad (0.44) \qquad\qquad R^2 = 0.00$$

Manufacturing ($N = 96$)
$$P = 2.0150 + 0.4711X \qquad\qquad (9)$$
$$\quad (3.34) \quad (6.31) \qquad\qquad R^2 = 0.30$$
$$E = -2.0150 + 0.5289X \qquad\qquad (10)$$
$$\quad (3.34) \quad (7.09) \qquad\qquad R^2 = 0.35$$
$$P = 6.4072 - 0.3415E \qquad\qquad (11)$$
$$\quad (23.99) \quad (3.68) \qquad\qquad R^2 = 0.13$$

Construction ($N = 84$)
$$P = 4.0258 + 0.1794X \qquad\qquad (12)$$
$$\quad (11.61) \quad (4.56) \qquad\qquad R^2 = 0.20$$
$$E = -4.0258 + 0.8206X \qquad\qquad (13)$$
$$\quad (11.61) \quad (20.84) \qquad\qquad R^2 = 0.84$$
$$P = 5.4354 + 0.0251E \qquad\qquad (14)$$
$$\quad (28.34) \quad (0.51) \qquad\qquad R^2 = 0.00$$

Transportation and public utility ($N = 84$)
$$P = 1.7994 + 0.5970X \qquad\qquad (15)$$
$$\quad (6.11) \quad (16.69) \qquad\qquad R^2 = 0.77$$
$$E = -1.7994 + 0.4030X \qquad\qquad (16)$$
$$\quad (6.11) \quad (11.26) \qquad\qquad R^2 = 0.61$$
$$P = 5.7233 + 0.5073E \qquad\qquad (17)$$
$$\quad (21.23) \quad (3.79) \qquad\qquad R^2 = 0.15$$

Wholesale, retail, and finance ($N = 84$)
$$P = 0.4825 + 0.4917X \qquad\qquad (18)$$
$$\quad (1.35) \quad (11.03) \qquad\qquad R^2 = 0.60$$
$$E = -0.4825 + 0.5083X \qquad\qquad (19)$$
$$\quad (1.35) \quad (11.40) \qquad\qquad R^2 = 0.61$$
$$P = 3.5518 + 0.2062E \qquad\qquad (20)$$
$$\quad (9.02) \quad (1.94) \qquad\qquad R^2 = 0.04$$

Service ($N = 80$)
$$P = -0.8623 + 0.5630X \qquad\qquad (21)$$
$$\quad (1.54) \quad (9.34) \qquad\qquad R^2 = 0.53$$
$$E = 0.8623 + 0.4370X \qquad\qquad (22)$$
$$\quad (1.54) \quad (7.25) \qquad\qquad R^2 = 0.40$$
$$P = 4.6461 - 0.0783E \qquad\qquad (23)$$
$$\quad (7.31) \quad (0.62) \qquad\qquad R^2 = 0.00$$

Sources: Kendrick and Grossman 1980, pp. 39-40; U.S. Department of Commerce 1979; U.S. Department of Labor 1979.
Note: Numbers in parentheses are t-statistics. P = rate of growth of productivity in each industry; X = rate of growth of output in each industry; E = rate of growth of employment in each industry; TFP = rate of growth of total factor productivity in each industry.

1. The cross-country data provide empirical support to Verdoorn's Law, yielding estimates of the Verdoorn coefficient around 0.5 for the manufacturing sector—(1) and (11)—and higher values for all other sectors.

2. The results are consistent with Kaldor's Law for all sectors except for the mining and quarrying sector, where the expansion of output requires a reduction rather than a simultaneous expansion of employment, as (9) shows.

3. The above two conclusions are not influenced by the exclusion of Japan. Dropping Japan from the sample—(1) to (4) vs. (5) to (25)—does lead to a reduction in the explanatory power, but the results are not appreciably affected.

4. Verdoorn's Law, as reformulated by Rowthorn (the third regression in each industry group), does not receive any significant statistical support. There appears a negative, and sometimes statistically significant, relationship between growth of productivity and employment. As discussed above, this negative result may confirm the fact that technological change is endogenous or that growth of employment is endogenously determined, or both.

5. Regression (4) shows an inverse association between the increase in labor cost and the growth of productivity. This result renders support to the possible mechanism, in the principle of circular and cumulative causation, on which Kaldor put emphasis for his new macrodynamics.

While the positive association between output growth and productivity growth has been examined for subsectors of the economy, results of the sources-of-growth accounting enable us to investigate the relationship between output growth and total factor productivity for the whole economy. Regression (26) of Table 6.4 shows that output growth is a significant factor in total factor productivity growth, confirming the working of macrodynamics of the Kaldor type or the mechanism of cumulative causation of Myrdal.

Regressions (27) to (30) are the results of an attempt to test the dual model of economic growth. Operationally, there are two elements in the concept of dualism. The first is simply the relative size of the various sectors of the economy, in particular the size of the agricultural sector. The larger the primary sector relative to industry, the stronger is the dualism of the economy. The second element is the relative levels of wages and productivity in the various sectors of the economy. The greater the differential in favor of manufacturing, the more immature is the economy and the stronger is the dualism in the economy.

The above two operational elements in the concept of dualism lead us to use the relative share of employment by sector and the ratio of productivity in industry to productivity in agriculture as two alternative measures of the explanatory variable in our empirical testing of the dual model. Regression (27) in Table 6.4 shows a statistically significant positive relationship between economic growth and the relative size of agricultural employment, while (28) and (29) indicate that economic growth is inversely associated with the relative size of employment in industry and service respective-

ly. The last regression result in Table 6.4 clearly demonstrates
that higher economic growth is related to a stronger dualistic nature of the economy in the sense that the spread in productivity
between industry and agriculture is higher.

     Verdoorn's Law and Kaldor's Law, of the same type as in Table
6.4, were fitted to the data from 20 industries in the manufacturing data from 1948 to 1976 and from the 48 contiguous states from
1958 to 1978 in Table 6.5. The results are quite similar to those
based on the cross-country data in Table 6.4. The manufacturing
sector and regional data provide very strong empirical support to
Verdoorn's Law and Kaldor's Law. However, the relationship between
productivity growth and employment growth, which Rowthorn regards
as a more appropriate and direct method of establishing the validity of Verdoorn's Law, produces mixed results in terms of changing
signs of regression coefficients and varying sizes of t-statistics
for the estimated coefficients.

     In spite of forceful theory, strongly supported empirically by
diverse sets of data, several arguments can and have been brought
against Kaldor's two-sector model of macrodynamics in general and
Verdoorn's Law in particular. One important question has something
to do with how Kaldor, without getting involved in a circular argument, would account for differences in growth rates between countries. If the rate of expansion of the national market dominates
the growth in productivity, and if the growth in productivity explains why the national market is expanding at a given rate, what
leads to differences in output growth between countries in the
first place? Kaldor's theory does not really explain why some
countries enjoy high growth rates but, rather, given that they have
high growth rates, why these growth rates persist.

     In an open economy, Kaldor (1970) points out, the growth of
export demand is the most important exogenous component of the demand for the product of the manufacturing sector in particular.
But as we examined in the previous chapter, export growth may or
may not be exogenous and exports may lead or retard the growth of
an overall economy.

     In Kaldor's theory, the supply side is almost neglected and
technological change is exclusively of the endogenous type. As
Cornwall (1970, 1976, 1977b) extends Kaldor's theory to develop a
model (for explaining why growth rates differ) that is essentially
a demand-determined model, the amount of labor available to manufacturing is always sufficient to meet the demand for labor, which
is, in turn, derived from the demand for manufacturing output.
Whether growth is supply constrained or demand constrained is an
important question, to which an answer is not easily found but must
be sought, not only to settle some theoretical controversies but
also to provide meaningful policy suggestions. The evidence provided by this chapter's empirical testing is conflicting. Empirical results of the dual model of economic growth provide indirect
support to the possibility of insufficient labor supply as a growth
constraint. On the other hand, the observation--that there exists
a very close correlation between the growths of manufacturing out-

put and of GDP and at the same time a strong correlation between
the rate of productivity growth in the economy as a whole and the
change in the structure of employment between manufacturing and
nonmanufacturing--provides favorable support to the demand-constrained growth of Kaldor and Cornwall.

If it is assumed that technological progress is purely an exogenous phenomenon, falling at random across industries within a
country or across manufacturing sectors of different countries, it
is possible to assert that in the relationship between the growth
of productivity and that of output the causal direction is from the
higher rates of growth of productivity to higher rates of growth of
outputs, which is the opposite causal chain assumed in Verdoorn's
Law. Given the fact that the rate of growth of employment in manufacturing is endogenously determined, depending on demand, and that
most technical progress over time is also endogenously determined,
one is more inclined to favor Kaldor's view that productivity expands as the market expands. The increase in productivity resulting from a large market in turn enlarges the market for other
things and, by the same token, causes productivity to rise in others.

REFERENCES

Arrow, K. J. 1962. The economic implication of learning by doing.
    Rev. Econ. Stud. 29:155-73.
Clark, C. 1940. *The Conditions of Economic Progress.* London:
    Macmillan.
Cornwall, J. 1968. Postwar growth in Western Europe: A re-evalu-
    ation. *Rev. Econ. Stat.* 50:361-68.
———. 1970. The role of demand and investment in long-term
    growth. *Q. J. Econ.* 84:48-69.
———. 1976. Diffusion, convergence and Kaldor's Law. *Econ. J.*
    86:307-14.
———. 1977a. *Modern Capitalism.* London: Martin Robinson.
———. 1977b. The relevance of dual problems for analyzing de-
    veloped capitalist economies. *Kyklos* 30(Fasc. 1):51-73.
Cripps, T. F., and R. J. Tarling. 1973. *Growth in Advanced Capi-
    talist Economies 1950-1970.* London: Cambridge University
    Press.
Dixon, R. J., and A. P. Thirlwall. 1975. *Regional Growth and Un-
    employment in the United Kingdom.* London: Macmillan.
Eltis, W. A. 1973. *Growth and Distribution.* New York: Halsted.
Fabricant, S. 1942. *Employment in Manufacturing, 1899-1939.* New
    York: National Bureau of Economic Research.
Fei, J. C., and G. Ranis. 1964. *Development of the Labor Surplus
    Economy, Theory and Policy.* Homewood, Ill.: Irwin.
Fisher, A. G. 1935. *The Clash of Progress and Security.* London:
    Macmillan.
Fuchs, V. R. 1968. *The Service Economy.* New York: National
    Bureau of Economic Research.

Hirschman, A. O. 1958. *The Strategy of Economic Development*. New Haven: Yale University Press.

Jones, D. T. 1976. Output, employment and labor productivity in Europe since 1955. *Natl. Inst. Econ. Rev.* 77:72–85.

Jorgenson, D. W. 1961. The development of a dual economy. *Econ. J.* 71:309–34.

Kaldor, N. 1966. *Causes of the Slow Rate of Growth of the United Kingdom: An Inaugural Lecture*. London: Cambridge University Press.

————. 1967. *Strategic Factors in Economic Development*. Ithaca: Cornell University Press.

————. 1968. Productivity and growth in the manufacturing industry: A reply. *Economica* 35:385–91.

————. 1970. The case for regional policies. *Scott. J. Polit. Econ.* 17:337–49.

————. 1971. Conflicts in national economic objectives. *Econ. J.* 81:1–16.

————. 1972. The irrelevance of equilibrium economics. *Econ. J.* 82:1237–55.

————. 1975a. Economic growth and the Verdoorn Law—A comment on Mr. Rowthorn's article. *Econ. J.* 85:891–96.

————. 1975b. What is wrong with economic theory? *Q. J. Econ.* 89:347–57.

————. 1976. Inflation and recession in the world economy. *Econ. J.* 86:703–14.

————. 1977. Capitalism and industrial development: Some lessons from Britain's experience. *Camb. J. Econ.* 1:193–204.

————. 1978a. *Further Essays on Applied Economics*. New York: Holmes & Meier.

————. 1978b. *Further Essays on Economic Theory*. New York: Holmes & Meier.

————. 1980. *Essays on Economic Stability and Growth*, 2nd ed. London: Duckworth.

Katz, J. M. 1969. *Production Functions, Foreign Investment and Growth*. Amsterdam: North-Holland.

Kelly, A. C., J. G. Williamson, and R. J. Cheetham. 1972. *Dualistic Economic Development, Theory and History*. Chicago: University of Chicago Press.

Kendrick, J. W. 1961. *Productivity Trends in the United States*. Princeton: Princeton University Press.

————. 1974. *Postwar Productivity Trends in the United States, 1948–1969*. New York: National Bureau of Economic Research.

Kendrick, J. W., and E. S. Grossman. 1980. *Productivity in the United States*. Baltimore: Johns Hopkins University Press.

Kennedy, K. A. 1971. *Productivity and Industrial Growth—The Irish Experience*. Oxford: Clarendon.

Kindleberger, C. P. 1967. *Europe's Postwar Growth: The Role of Labor Supply*. Cambridge: Harvard University Press.

Leeson, P. F. 1979. The Lewis model and development theory. *Manchester Sch. Econ. Sociol.* 47:198–210.

Lewis, W. A. 1954. Economic development with unlimited supplies of labor. *Manchester Sch. Econ. Soc. Stud.* 20:139-92.

————. 1958. Unlimited labor: Further notes. *Manchester Sch. Econ. Soc. Stud.* 26:1-32.

————. 1979. The dual economy revisited. *Manchester Sch. Econ. Soc. Stud.* 47:211-29.

McCombie, J. S. L. 1981. What still remains of Kaldor's Law? *Econ. J.* 91:206-16.

Marshall, A. 1920. *Principles of Economics.* London: Macmillan.

Mill, J. S. 1923. *Principles of Political Economy,* Ashley ed. London: Longman, Green.

Myrdal, G. 1957. *Economic Theory and Underdeveloped Regions.* London: Duckworth.

Organization for Economic Cooperation and Development (OECD). 1969. *Labor Force Statistics 1956-1967.* Paris: OECD.

————. 1978. *Labor Force Statistics 1965-1976.* Paris: OECD.

Parikh, A. 1978. Differences in growth rates and Kaldor's Laws. *Economica* 45:83-91.

Richardson, H. W. 1979. *Regional Economics.* New York: Praeger.

Rowthorn, R. E. 1975a. What remains of Kaldor's Law? *Econ. J.* 85:10-19.

————. 1975b. A reply to Lord Kaldor's comment. *Econ. J.* 85:897-901.

Salter, W. E. G. 1966. *Productivity and Technical Change.* London: Cambridge University Press.

Schmookler, J. 1966. *Invention and Economic Growth.* Cambridge: Harvard University Press.

Singer, H. 1970. Dualism revisited. *J. Dev. Stud.* 7(1):60-80.

Singer, M. 1961. Cumulative causation and growth economics. *Kyklos* 14(Fasc. 4):533-45.

Smith, A. 1937. *An Inquiry into the Nature and Causes of the Wealth of Nations.* New York: Random House.

Stoneman, P. 1979. Kaldor's Law and British economic growth: 1800-1970. *Appl. Econ.* 11:309-20.

Thirlwall, A. P. 1980. Rowthorn's interpretation of Verdoorn's Law. *Econ. J.* 90:386-88.

United Nations (UN). 1970. *Economic Survey of Europe 1969.* New York: UN.

U.S. Department of Commerce. 1979. Computer printout. Regional Economic Information System, Bureau of Economic Analysis.

U.S. Department of Labor. 1977. *Comparative Growth in Manufacturing Productivity and Labor Costs in Selected Industrialized Countries.* Bull. 1958. Washington, D.C.: USGPO.

————. 1979. *Employment and Earnings, State and Areas, 1939-1978.* Bull. 1370-13. Washington, D.C.: USGPO.

Vaciago, G. 1970. Alternative theories of growth and the Italian case. *Banca Naz. Lavoro Q. Rev.* June:180-211.

————. 1975. Increasing returns and growth in advanced economies: A re-evaluation. *Oxf. Econ. Pap.* 27:232-39.

Verdoorn, P. J. 1949. Fattori che regolano lo sviluppo della producttivita' del lavoro. *L'Industria* 1:3-11. [Factors that determine the growth of labor productivity.] Trans. G. and A. P. Thirlwall.

————. 1980. Verdoorn's Law in retrospect: A comment. *Econ. J.* 90:382-85.

Wolfe, J. N. 1968. Productivity and growth in the manufacturing industry: Some reflections on Professor Kaldor's inaugural lecture. *Economica* 35:117-26.

World Bank. 1980. *World Tables*, 2nd ed. Baltimore: Johns Hopkins University Press.

Young, A. A. 1928. Increasing returns and economic progress. *Econ. J.* 38:527-42.

7
The Public Sector
as a Growth Retardant

Even though in detail there have been considerable differences between countries, an important characteristic of all the advanced economies in the postwar era has been the rapid expansion in each of them of the public sector. The seemingly marked increase in the size of the public sector in all industrial countries has given rise to a great deal of comment, mostly adverse, in the popular media. The common perception is unquestionably that government and bureaucracy are too big, too costly, and too powerful and the government of the day has acted imprudently or unwisely. A growing number of people, the conservatives whether professional economists or laymen, tend to regard any government intervention as undesirable, to attribute all evils to the government, and to evaluate new proposals in the ideal market system as they might work perfectly if guided by the invisible hand alone. This is a restatement of Milton Friedman's (1962, p. 197) remark in the opposite direction.

The rise in government expenditure as a proportion of GNP or GDP in Western industrial countries is one of the economic phenomena that are now producing a concomitant growth in professional comment and discussion. Until recently, the interest of economists was confined almost exclusively to the analysis of the economic effects of budgetary policy and development of normative theories seeking to provide criteria that should determine the revenue and expenditure policies of a government rather than to the examination of the overall impact of the growing public sector, along with the private sectors, on the performance of the economy. The economics profession has sadly neglected the analysis of the government sector. In almost all textbook discussions, the modern government sector is simply viewed as an exogenous black box whose basic characteristics are never examined in depth. In economics the theory of government behavior has not been developed as far as comparable to the established theories of consumer and firm behavior.

Where economic analysis requires that some recognition be given to the role of the public sector, government is usually treated

181

as an exogenous factor outside the particular model's area of mutual interdependence or is incorporated into it by postulating simple
relationships between such magnitudes as government expenditure and
other variables in the model.   In the latter case, the relationship
assumed appears usually to be determined by analytical convenience
rather than by the facts.   R. F. Harrod (1948, p. 20) states:

> Government is the most troublesome of the three [forms of
> expenditure] because we have no theory of government expendi-
> ture.   In its absence we may dump government expenditure on
> the top of the other two as an exogenous factor, merge it with
> consumer expenditure . . . or assume it away altogether.   This
> last suggestion is certainly the most convenient of all and
> such treatment of a troublesome factor is richly supported by
> precedents in economic theory.

Recently, because of considerable broadening of the impact of
the public sector upon the economy and the continuing poor performance of the economy in many important policy areas, particularly
with regard to inflation and economic growth, some interest has
been directed toward studying the behavior of government activities
on the basis of empirical and historical facts, with a view to discovering whether generalizations can be made about their impact on
the economic performance.   In particular, a number of recent studies raise the strong suspicion that a large and growing public sector actually causes slower economic growth in Western industrialized countries.

STATISTICAL FINDINGS ON THE GROWTH OF THE PUBLIC SECTOR
No single, absolute measure summarizes the multidimensional
term, "the size of the public sector."   On an a priori basis, one
may suggest a number of possibly relevant variables indicating the
importance of the public sector with a view of government as (1) a
consumer, (2) a producer, (3) an employer, (4) a redistributor,
and (5) a reallocator of resources.   Since there remain many unre-
solved questions concerning the appropriate definition of government and there is no one magic number that measures the importance
of government activity in any country at any time, the appropriate
measure of government activity depends in theory on the purpose for
which we are interested in measuring it and in practice on the
availability of data.   Several measures have been suggested.
The ratio of exhaustive expenditure to GNP, which measures the
extent to which government uses up resources that would otherwise
be available for use in the private sector, can perhaps serve as a
measure of government as a consumer.   One may compare the size of
government employment to that of the total labor force when focusing on the measurement of government activity as an employer.
Though government is very important in the production process of
the whole economy, not even a rough measure of its scope as a producer is readily available, one of the primary reasons being that

the government produces intermediate inputs for the production
process in the private sector, inputs that are also provided free
of charge. Practically, the size of transfers will measure the
scope of the public sector as a redistributor of income. To measure government's relative importance as a reallocator of resources
we need to answer the big question to what extent resources in the
private sector are employed in ways different from those in a hypothetical market untouched by government taxes and subsidies. It is
impossible to formulate the above question in a manner that is con-
ceptually or statistically tractable, because we have no idea of
what an economy without a public sector would look like.

The discussion of these familiar difficulties indicates that
there are a number of ways in which the size of the public sector
can be measured and that there is a substantial element of arbi-
trariness in any measure and definition. After a long attempt to
find ideal measures of government activity, Richard M. Bird (1970,
p. 206) concludes:

> While there is no one measure of government's importance
> that is satisfactory for all purposes, the best single ratio
> indicating the "importance" of government appears, under mod-
> erately reasonable assumptions, to be the ratio of total gov-
> ernment expenditure (including transfer payments) to gross na-
> tional product at market prices.

A useful starting point for studying government expenditures
growth is G. Warren Nutter's recent study, *Growth of Government in
the West*. Based on national accounts data published by OECD for
the period 1950-1974, Nutter measures government spending as a
fraction of GNP evaluated at factor cost (Table 7.1). His result
confirms the well-known observation that in Western industrial

Table 7.1. Government expenditures as a percentage of national income

Country	Total government expenditure			Defense expenditure			Transfer expenditure		
	1955	1965	1974	1955	1965	1974	1955	1965	1974
Australia	28.6[a]	33.0	38.9	3.1[a]	4.4	3.0	7.6[a]	8.1	10.4
Austria	35.2	44.5	49.2[b]	0.2	1.6	1.3[b]	12.0	16.3	17.5[b]
Belgium	29.8	40.2	48.3	4.1	3.7	2.9	11.7	15.7	18.3
Canada	35.2	40.2	51.3	9.0	4.1	2.7	8.5	8.7	13.2
Denmark	28.9	37.9	58.7	3.8	3.4	2.8[a]	8.4	11.1	18.8
France	42.4	48.1	50.3	6.5	6.9	4.9	18.2	22.9	25.4
Germany	38.4	45.5	54.1	4.3	5.0	4.0	16.7	17.5	19.9
Italy	34.7	41.3	48.5[b]	3.5	3.1	2.5[b]	11.8	16.8	20.9[b]
Japan	18.8	24.8	29.3	2.0	1.2	1.0	5.2	5.6	7.0
Luxembourg	34.9	43.7	50.9[c]	3.2	1.9	1.2[c]	13.5	17.9	22.0[c]
Netherlands	35.4	48.7	61.0	6.9	4.5	3.7	9.1	17.1	30.3
Norway	35.3	47.3	62.9	4.6	4.7	4.2	8.3	12.9	22.6
Sweden	38.5[a]	45.1	63.6	5.0[a]	5.1	4.5[b]	10.5[a]	12.5	22.3
Switzerland	21.3	29.7	31.6	3.0	2.9	2.8[d]	6.2	8.9	14.7
United Kingdom	39.6	43.4	55.3	9.4	7.2	6.3	7.1	10.7	13.8
United States	30.7	34.1	40.2[b]	11.9	9.2	7.3[b]	5.0	6.7	10.8[b]

Source: Nutter 1978, pp. 58-73.
[a]Data for 1960.
[b]Data for 1973.
[c]Data for 1972.
[d]Data for 1967.

countries, government spending rose quite rapidly after World War II. For the sample of 16 OECD countries, the median percentage of national income accounted for by government expenditures was about 35 in 1955 and rose steadily to reach 50 in 1974. Table 7.1 also shows the growth of two major components of government expenditures. Transfer payments grew at a much faster rate than expenditures on goods and services. Transfers as a percentage of GNP, taking the median, rose from about 8.8 in 1955 to 18.6 in 1975. The relative importance of defense spending declined, though not steadily for all countries in the sample. Though not shown in the table, Nutter has found that there is an inverse relation between the size of government in the early 1950s and the growth in government over two decades since then. For the sample countries included in Nutter's study we note that the largest public sectors are found in France, Germany, and the United Kingdom in the 1950s, but in the Netherlands, Norway, and Sweden in the 1970s. Total government expenditure in the latter three countries is over 60 percent of national income. Milton Friedman (1976, pp. 5, 8-14) has recently set the limit of the public sector size at 60 percent of GNP, and among the consequences he predicts are the deterioration of traditional Western values and the ending of democracy. Japan and Switzerland have maintained the two smallest governments throughout the period under review.

The size of the public sector, as revealed in Nutter's study, is startling in the sense that government spends more than half the national income in more than half the countries under study. It should be noted that in the calculation of the size of government, Nutter uses the national income evaluated at factor cost based on current prices.

Table 7.2 shows the size of the public sector on a different basis. It is measured by general government consumption as a percentage of the GDP evaluated at current market prices. As shown in Table 7.2, the role of government, when measured in terms of the

Table 7.2. General government consumption as a percentage of gross domestic product at current market prices

Country	1955	1960	1965	1970	1977
Australia	10.0	9.7	11.6	12.6	16.7
Austria	12.4	12.7	13.4	14.7	17.4
Belgium	11.6	12.8	13.1	13.7	17.4
Canada	14.0	13.6	14.9	19.2	20.3
Denmark	12.6	12.3	15.1	20.0	24.0
Finland	11.5	12.6	14.6	15.9	20.4
France	12.8	13.0	13.1	13.4	14.9
Germany	13.3	13.5	15.3	15.9	20.0
Ireland	12.4	12.5	13.6	14.8	18.6
Italy	11.8	12.2	14.5	12.7	13.7
Japan	10.4	8.8	8.5	7.4	9.9
Netherlands	14.5	13.4	15.5	16.3	18.3
New Zealand	12.6	12.9	13.3	15.4	18.7
Norway	11.2	12.4	14.3	15.8	18.7
Sweden	15.1	15.8	17.6	21.3	28.5
Switzerland	9.2	8.8	10.5	10.5	12.9
United Kingdom	17.2	16.5	16.8	17.7	20.8
United States	16.0	17.2	17.0	19.1	18.4

Source: World Bank 1980, p. 388.

resources it absorbs, has not grown so dramatically. Most of the
Western industrialized countries exhaust or use up less than 20
percent of the goods and services that would otherwise be available
to the private sector. The public sector has grown in all countries, but the growth rates are not so drastic and the size of government is not so large as in Nutter's study when transfer payments
are excluded from the calculation. The difference in results between Tables 7.1 and 7.2 is because, in addition to exclusion or
inclusion of transfers, different choices have been made with regard to capital consumption and taxes. Bird (1970, pp. 197-208)
has demonstrated quite clearly that the use of factor cost or market price measures of aggregate output depends on the views taken
about the shifting of indirect taxes. Both Tables 7.1 and 7.2
show clearly that a rising share of government expenditure does
not necessarily mean an increased allocation of resources to government. Higher public spending consists mainly of an increase in
transfer payment, which does not involve the movement of resources
to the public sector.

Nominal size of the public sector, represented by a simple ratio of government expenditure to some measure of total economic activity, has been the dominant concern of most writers. Recent
studies by Morris Beck (1976, 1979a, b, c) indicate the importance
of developing a measure of the public sector that takes into account relative price changes. The main point is that there is no
reason why the deflator for GNP should be the same as for government expenditure, given the fact that the input mix for government
goods and services may be different from the aggregate input mix
for all economic activities. If the prices of the goods and services purchased by the government rise relatively more quickly than
the general price level, the relative size of the public sector
must increase in nominal terms to maintain the same size in real
terms.

Most studies of long-term expenditures growth have largely ignored differential effects of inflation on government's ability to
provide public services. Separate deflation of the major components of total government expenditure has enabled Beck to estimate
the deflated value of total government expenditure, which, when expressed as a percentage of real GDP, measures the real size of the
public sector. The major result of Beck's study is summarized in
Table 7.3. Although the details of his calculation can be contest-
ed, the general message is clear. In all 12 countries the real
size of the total public sector has expanded but has not grown as
much as with the current prices data. The share of government in
real GDP in no country exceeds 50 percent. Government consumption
expenditure, which involves the direct use of resources by government, tells a singular story. In 6 cases--those with income elasticity below unity--price movements produced an actual decline in
the ratio of real consumption to real GDP over the period studied.
The coefficients of income elasticity of transfer expenditure confirm our previous observation that higher government spending is
mainly the result of an increase in transfer payments. On the av-

Table 7.3. Public sector ratios and income elasticity of government spending in constant prices, 1950-1977

Country	Total government expenditure				Consumption expenditure				Transfer expenditure			
		1977		Income elasticity 1950-1977		1977		Income elasticity 1950-1977		1977		Income elasticity 1950-1977
	1950	Current price	Constant price		1950	Current price	Constant price		1950	Current price	Constant price	
Austria	21.2	39.8	33.7	1.80	11.3	17.4	7.5	0.54	9.9	22.4	26.2	3.23
Canada	19.0	36.9	32.3	1.96	10.3	20.3	11.0	1.17	8.7	16.6	20.6	2.90
Denmark	18.1	40.0a	31.9a	2.25b	10.2	24.0	14.4	1.54	7.9	16.0a	18.2a	3.09b
Finland	20.4	35.6	30.4	1.70	11.1	20.3	12.7	1.20	9.3	15.3	17.7	2.30
France	26.7	41.8	38.5	1.61	12.8	14.9	9.2	0.60	13.9	26.9	29.3	2.54
Germany	28.3	41.3	38.3	1.46	14.3	20.0	12.8	0.87	14.0	21.3	25.5	2.06
Ireland	23.0	43.3a	44.7a	2.47b	13.7	18.6	15.5	1.21	9.3	24.3a	27.9a	4.33b
Netherlands	23.9	52.3	48.3	2.46	12.2	18.3	9.0	0.63	11.7	34.0	39.3	4.38
Sweden	23.7	55.6	48.1	2.70	13.7	28.5	17.2	1.42	10.0	27.1	30.9	4.43
Switzerland	19.3	30.4	29.8	1.89	11.2	12.9	9.7	0.79	8.1	17.5	20.0	3.41
United Kingdom	30.2	40.8	35.8	1.37	16.3	20.8	14.4	0.77	13.9	19.9	21.4	2.07
United States	20.0	32.6	28.8	1.74	12.1	18.5	13.4	1.18	7.9	14.2	15.4	2.59

Source: Beck 1979.
aFor 1976.
bTerminal year is 1976.

erage, the percentage increase in transfer--nonexhaustive outlays
--is nearly three times that of real GDP. In all cases the income
elasticity of transfer expenditure is substantially larger than
that of government final consumption expenditure.

     Another important study showing the share of total output de-
voted to public consumption based on the real terms and constant
prices is that by Irving Kravis, Alan Heston, and Roy Summers.
They undertook a major research project on international comparisons of real product during the middle of the decade 1970-1980; the
results of their investigation have been in the process of publication since mid-1975. In one of their most recent works (Summers
et al. 1980), they develop a table of real gross product and shares
of GDP devoted to private and public consumption and investment for
each of over 100 countries in the years 1950 and 1960-1977 based on
structural relationships estimated from data obtained in a benchmark study of expenditures and prices of 16 countries (Kravis et
al. 1978). Kravis et al. use an indirect method for estimating the
results that could have been expected for GDP and its major components if all the countries included had been intensively studied by
the direct method. Their study differs from Beck's in that in
theirs the expenditure components are valued at the same relative
prices (at international prices to use the language in their previous work) for all countries.

     Table 7.4 summarizes, among many important data produced, only
that share of real GDP devoted to public consumption. The figures
confirm the general observation that the share of public consumption to the aggregate output--when measured in real terms, particularly in constant international relative prices--has not grown as
much as usually supposed over the last three decades. Taking the
median for the sample of 18 OECD countries, the percentage of real
GDP accounted for by government consumption rose by only 1 percent,
from 14 percent in 1950 to 15 percent in 1977. In all countries
except Sweden and the United Kingdom the ratios of public consumption to GDP are less than 20 percent. In Sweden, which saw the

Table 7.4. Percentage of real gross domestic income devoted
to public consumption

Country	1950	1960	1965	1970	1975	1977
Australia	9	11	12	12	13	15
Austria	15	15	15	15	16	16
Belgium	14	15	14	14	15	16
Canada	10	12	12	15	14	14
Denmark	12	13	14	16	18	19
Finland	14	14	15	14	15	17
France	15	14	13	12	12	13
Germany	13	10	11	11	13	12
Ireland	16	16	16	16	19	18
Italy	12	12	13	11	12	12
Japan	14	12	11	9	10	10
Netherlands	14	14	14	14	15	16
New Zealand	9	10	11	12	14	15
Norway	12	13	14	13	14	16
Sweden	12	13	14	15	17	21
Switzerland	12	10	10	10	11	12
United Kingdom	17	17	17	18	21	20
United States	12	17	17	19	19	18

Source: Summers et al. 1980, pp. 34-66.

largest increase, the government share rose by 7 percent, while in
5 countries--France, Germany, Italy, Japan, and Switzerland--the
shares of the public sector consumption have remained the same or
been reduced over the period under investigation.

The huge government bureaucracy in all industrial countries
has become a particular symbol of the wasteful use of labor by government. Unfortunately, no comparable data on public employment or
size of bureaucracy covering all major industrial countries over
some time period is available. Relative public sector employment,
shown in Table 7.5, illustrates the postwar trend in the United
States and Canada. Although the data are not strictly comparable
either in coverage or definition, the differences do not seem great
enough to vitiate the overall impression that the patterns and
trends over time in both countries are remarkably similar. In both
cases total public employment as a percentage of the total working
population has increased over the whole period. The growth in employment at lower levels of government greatly exceeds that of
higher levels. In both the United States and Canada, employment in
the federal government as a percentage of the total labor force has
remained stable or been reduced slightly very recently.

Another frequently mentioned measure of the size of the public
sector is the ratio of tax revenues to various macroeconomic indicators. Tables 7.6 and 7.7 show the general trend of total tax

Table 7.5. Public employment as a percentage of total employment in the
United States and Canada

	United States		Canada		
	Federal civilian employee	State or local government employee	Federal government employee	Provincial or municipal government employee	Total public employment
1950	3.32	6.16[a]	3.72	4.67	12.23
1955	3.49	6.59	3.70	5.19	13.40
1960	3.35	7.72	3.76	6.10	16.20
1965	3.35	8.98	3.45	7.15	19.20
1970	3.35	9.92	3.18	7.62	20.92
1975	3.11	12.76	2.99	7.77	19.31

Sources: McGrath 1978, pp. 100, 110; Foot 1979, pp. 68-69.
[a]For the year 1952.

Table 7.6. Total revenue as a percentage of gross
domestic product

Country	1955	1960	1965	1970	1975
Australia	na	na	27.3	28.1	31.6
Austria	29.5	31.4	34.9	36.7	39.1
Belgium	23.7	26.2	30.7	35.2	40.6
Canada	26.3	28.4	28.1	35.2	37.1
Denmark	25.8	27.5	31.2	41.9	44.5
Finland	na	na	33.5	36.0	39.8
France	33.2	34.4	39.1	39.0	40.5
Germany	34.8	35.9	35.3	37.5	41.0
Ireland	24.8[a]	24.1	26.9[b]	35.3	36.8
Italy	27.7	31.2	32.1	32.9	35.2
Japan	20.4	22.0	20.7	22.0	23.6
Netherlands	28.4	33.1	37.1	44.0	52.6
Norway	31.0	34.9	37.1	43.5	49.7
Sweden	32.4	36.2	39.1	46.2	52.6
Switzerland	24.8	28.1	25.1	26.5	32.1
United Kingdom	30.4	29.6	33.4	40.9	41.2
United States	24.9	27.3	27.1	30.5	30.6

Sources: OECD 1966, 1967, 1978.
[a]For the year 1958.
[b]For the year 1964.

Table 7.7. Tax revenue as a percentage of gross domestic product

Country	Total tax revenue			Taxes on income and profits (corporate income)			Social security contribution			Taxes on property			Taxes on goods and services		
	1965	1970	1975	1965	1970	1975	1965	1970	1975	1965	1970	1975	1965	1970	1975
Australia	24.7	25.9	29.7	12.4(4.0)	13.9(4.3)	16.6(3.6)	...	...	...	2.9	3.0	2.8	7.4	7.1	7.5
Austria	34.7	35.9	38.7	8.8(1.8)	9.1(1.6)	10.0(1.6)	8.7	9.1	10.7	1.3	1.3	1.2	12.1	13.0	13.2
Belgium	30.8	35.3	41.2	8.5(1.9)	11.0(2.4)	16.3(3.1)	9.7	10.7	13.1	1.2	1.2	1.0	10.8	11.9	10.4
Canada	25.9	32.0	33.0	10.2(3.9)	14.3(3.6)	15.8(4.5)	1.5	3.1	3.3	3.4	4.2	3.1	9.2	8.8	8.6
Denmark	30.1	40.3	40.6	13.8(1.4)	20.6(1.1)	23.7(1.3)	1.6	1.6	0.6	2.4	2.4	2.4	11.5	14.7	13.0
Finland	30.6	33.1	37.6	13.5(2.5)	15.7(1.8)	19.7(1.6)	2.5	3.0	4.1	1.2	0.8	0.8	13.1	13.5	13.0
France	35.0	35.6	37.4	5.6(1.8)	6.5(2.2)	6.6(2.0)	11.9	12.9	15.3	1.5	1.3	1.3	13.1	13.2	12.0
Germany	31.6	32.8	35.7	10.7(2.5)	10.6(1.9)	12.3(1.6)	8.5	10.0	12.2	1.5	1.4	1.1	9.8	9.8	9.0
Ireland	26.0	31.2	32.6	6.7(2.4)	8.5(2.7)	9.8(1.8)	1.7	2.6	4.5	3.9	3.8	3.2	12.8	15.4	14.5
Italy	29.2	30.3	31.6	5.2(2.1)	5.3(2.0)	6.8(2.0)	10.0	10.8	14.5	2.2	2.0	1.1	10.7	10.9	8.8
Japan	18.1	19.6	20.9	7.2(3.2)	8.1(4.0)	8.3(3.4)	3.5	4.4	6.1	1.5	1.5	1.9	4.7	4.1	3.1
Netherlands	35.5	39.9	45.7	12.6(2.9)	13.3(2.7)	15.9(3.5)	10.9	14.0	17.6	1.7	1.5	1.3	9.6	10.4	10.2
New Zealand	25.6	27.8	31.7	15.6(5.3)	17.1(5.1)	20.6(4.2)	...	...	0.9	2.7	2.7	2.6	6.8	6.9	7.1
Norway	33.6	39.3	44.9	14.6(1.3)	15.1(1.3)	18.3(1.3)	4.0	6.3	8.3	1.0	0.9	1.0	13.6	16.6	16.8
Sweden	35.6	40.5	46.2	19.4(2.2)	22.0(1.8)	23.2(2.0)	4.3	6.1	9.0	0.6	0.6	0.5	10.7	10.7	10.8
Switzerland	20.7	23.8	29.6	7.9(1.5)	9.7(1.8)	13.0(2.3)	4.7	5.6	8.6	1.8	2.1	2.1	5.9	5.9	5.4
United Kingdom	31.0	37.8	37.0	11.3(1.8)	15.1(3.2)	16.3(2.0)	5.0	5.5	6.8	4.5	4.7	4.6	9.5	9.9	8.6
United States	26.5	30.1	30.2	12.3(4.2)	14.4(3.8)	13.2(3.3)	4.4	5.8	7.4	4.2	4.2	4.1	5.1	5.1	4.9

Source: OECD 1979, pp. 81–94.

revenue since 1955 and a detailed comparative tax structure and its
trend since 1965 respectively. As shown in Table 7.6 and the first
three columns of Table 7.7, over the study period the ratio of total taxes to GDP has been increasing fairly regularly in all countries. The Netherlands, Norway, and Sweden are at the top of the
list, while Australia, Japan, Switzerland, and the United States
have the lowest ratios. Colin Clark (1945) believes there is a
limit to the level of taxation that any economy can absorb, putting
it at about 25 percent of net national income at factor cost, not
of GDP at market prices. Changing the denominator to follow Clark
will produce higher rates than shown above. When the tolerable
level of taxation is exceeded, according to Clark, a decline in the
state of the economy and perhaps even of the social and political
fabric of society itself would result. (For a later statement see
Clark 1970.) In all of the countries examined, taxation exceeds
the 25 percent limit set by Clark more than 35 years ago. Countries with the highest tax ratios in 1975 have gradually increased
their tax ratios relative to most other countries. The largest increase was in the Netherlands over the 1955-1975 period. At the
other extreme, the smallest increases were observed in Japan, the
United States, and France.

     Table 7.7 shows the relative importance of the main tax fields
and their trend over the period 1965-1975. Comparisons of tax
structures reveal the relative dependence of countries on different
types of taxes. Taxes on income and profits account for more than
half the total tax revenue in Australia, New Zealand, and Sweden.
In France, Italy, and the Netherlands social security contributions
are the most important source of revenue, while Austria and Ireland
rely mainly on taxes on goods and services. There is not much difference among countries in the dependence of tax revenue on corporate income and property. It should be noted that during the period covered, receipts from corporation taxes, as a proportion of total tax revenue as well as GDP, declined in most countries.

     This section has had the limited purpose of presenting data on
the growth of the public sector in major industrialized countries
over the last 30 years. The broad expenditure and tax comparisons
appear to suggest that the public sector has been growing. However, the growth of government in the economy is not as large as
most people have thought, particularly so when the size of the public sector is measured in terms of its demand on real resources.
Since disaggregation of total public expenditure into its components produces different results, a more detailed comparison is
necessary in order to understand the substantive variations between
countries.

THE GROWING PUBLIC SECTOR AND ECONOMIC GROWTH
     Economists have always been interested in the growth of the
public sector. This interest is a reflection of their concern over
undesirable economic effects that can result from an excessive level of public expenditures. A number of recent studies raise the

strong suspicion that a large and growing public sector actually causes slower economic growth in Western advanced countries, even though these new studies differ in detail. In this section recent studies dealing with the relationships between the growing or unstable public sector and economic growth are reviewed in some detail without questioning the validity of each argument.

Smith

David Smith (1975) investigates the long-run effects of a permanently higher level of state consumption on the performance of a country with regard not only to economic growth but also to exports and inflation. In the discussion of the structural effects of increased public consumption, Smith argues that growing public consumption is more likely to hit investment than consumption, leading to deindustrialization, and gives three reasons to support his argument: (1) an increase in taxes to finance expenditure reduces saving; (2) monetary measures usually accompanied by expansionary fiscal policy push up the real rates of interest and reduce the rewards to investment; (3) taxation reduces the return on investment. Since this reduced capital formation is associated with a lower growth rate, Smith hypothesizes that an increase in the share of public expenditure in national income eventually leads to a drop in the rate of economic growth. With the data from 19 industrialized OECD member countries over the period 1961-1972, Smith presents the results of examining the above hypotheses by regression analysis (Table 7.8).

Equations (1) and (2) of Table 7.8 are concerned with explaining different growth rates in terms of investment ratios. The hypothesis that a larger public sector is associated with a lower investment ratio is confirmed by (3). Equations (4) through (7) directly relate the growth performance to the size of the state sec-

Table 7.8. Regression results on public consumption and economic growth

$GDP = -1.3559 + 0.2408I$		(1)
(0.89) (4.25)	$R^2 = 0.53$	
$PCGDP = 1.5290 + 0.2111I$		(2)
(1.00) (3.70)	$R^2 = 0.46$	
$I = 41.8911 - 0.9373X_1$		(3)
(8.42) (3.19)	$R^2 = 0.38$	
$GDP = 9.6437 - 0.2789X_1$		(4)
(6.42) (3.09)	$R^2 = 0.35$	
$GDP = 9.6658 - 0.1326X_2$		(5)
(4.97) (2.40)	$R^2 = 0.24$	
$PCGDP = 8.2585 - 0.2540X_1$		(6)
(5.84) (2.99)	$R^2 = 0.33$	
$PCGDP = 7.6979 - 0.1035X_2$		(7)
(4.01) (1.90)	$R^2 = 0.15$	

Source: D. Smith 1975, p. 27.
Note: GDP = growth rate in real GDP, 1961-1972; $PCGDP$ = growth rate in per capita real GDP; X_1 = ratio of public spending excluding transfer to national disposable income in 1972; X_2 = ratio of public spending, including transfer to national disposable income in 1972; I = proportion spent on gross domestic fixed capital formation averaged over 1961-1972.

tor; they assert that their conclusion--that government size is a
retarding factor in the "league of growth" performance of the econ-
omy--is confirmed. The implication of the result is that "a 1 percent rise in the share of the narrow definition of state consumption in NDI (national disposable income) produces roughly a drop of
0.2 in the percent growth rate" (D. Smith 1975, p. 28). Smith also
finds that transfer payments have far less impact on differences in
the growth rates than government spending for goods and services.
This fact is shown in the reduced estimated regression coefficients
in (5) and (7). One major problem in the empirical testing by
Smith is that he uses the end-year figure for public consumption.
More preferred and reasonable data should be an annual average for
the covering period, assuming all his theoretical arguments are
correct.

Bacon and Eltis

Robert Bacon and Walter Eltis (1975a, 1978) set out a new explanation of the decline of the British economy after World War II.
They show how a growing shift of Britain's resources after the
production of goods and services that can be marketed at home and
overseas to the provision of unmarketed public service (1) reduced
the rate of economic growth and weakened the balance of payments,
(2) reduced investment and Britain's ability to provide productive
jobs, and (3) accelerated inflation and occasioned the obstructive
trade union behavior from which Britain has suffered. Their central position is that "part of the economy produces a surplus that
made it possible for the remainder to function. If the surplus-
producing sector grows rapidly, the economy grows rapidly; if it
declines, the economy collapses" (Bacon and Eltis 1978, p. viii).
Bacon and Eltis follow Kaldor in believing that the growth of industry is of vital importance to the economy, but for markedly different reasons. They argue that the major problem during the last
decade has not been the lack of industrial productivity, which,
with a growth rate of approximately 4 percent per year has been
quite respectable, both in terms of previous historical experience
and by comparison with other industrial countries. They identify
the central problem as the fall by 14 percent in the number of people employed in industry over this period and suggest, "It is from
this fact that the disastrous course the British economy followed
in 1965-1975 stems, and this was the result of the real structural
maladjustment of the British economy that has occurred in these ten
years and is still occurring" (Bacon and Eltis 1978, p. 10).
Bacon and Eltis assume an economy with two sectors, for which
originally Jack Johnston (1975) set out a model of inflation. One,
the market sector, produces an output that is sold in the market.
The other, the nonmarket sector, adds to demand but does not add to
supply because goods are not sold in the market. Bacon and Eltis
start with a distinction between "productive" and "unproductive"
sectors, examine the implications of dividing the economy into an
industrial and a nonindustrial sector and into a tradable and a
nontradable sector, and finally adopt the distinction between market and nonmarket sectors, following Johnston. The market sector

is responsible for the production of everything that is privately
consumed--the economy's entire quantity of exports and all capital
investment. The market sector is financed from the proceeds of the
goods and services it sells. In contrast, the nonmarket sector, in
which free government services are provided, is not financed by
charging prices but rather by taxation or through government deficits. When the expanded public services are provided freely, the
principal test of their desirability is whether people will pay the
resulting taxes without demanding higher wages. Bacon and Eltis
cite the increased militance of British labor as a vivid example of
the hazards of an overblown public sector. Also, public sector employment could be expanded rapidly because extra jobs could be provided without an immediate need for extra capital.

In the view of Bacon and Eltis, Britain's crisis is very similar to that of the Old Regime in France to which F. Quesnay gave
full account, the only difference being that the surplus-producing
sector is the agricultural sector in Quesnay and the "market" sector in Bacon and Eltis. That is the reason Peter Jackson (1979, p.
130) labels Bacon and Eltis "Latter Day Physiocrats." The model
used by Bacon and Eltis to analyze the implications of growth and
inflation on a fall in the share of marketed output is an elaboration of the growth model classical economists use to argue that the
rate of growth depends on the proportion of an economy's activities
that are productive and the rate of surplus earned in the productive sector. Economists, classical or modern, differ about the
correct practical dividing line between the productive and unproductive sectors: R. Malthus maintains the position that only the
activities that produce physical and therefore investible output
are productive, whereas A. Smith came close to saying that all
profit-making activities are productive. The distinction between
productive and unproductive labor (sector) was nearly universally
abandoned by academic economists from the 1870s to the mid-1950s.
J. A. Schumpeter (1954, pp. 628-31) labels the distinction "mean-
ingless" and asserts that discussions of the distinction serve only
to "display the word-mindedness of economists and their inability
to tell a real problem from a spurious one." In the 1950s Marxist
economists revived theoretical interest in the distinction. Paul
Baran (1957, p. 32), for example, defines productive labor as "that
labor which creates the goods and services which would be required
in a rationally ordered society" (by which he means a socialist
economy). Although Bacon and Eltis (1978, p. 31) admit that "the
distinction between the market and non-market sectors of the economy is not the same as the distinction between the public and private sectors," they maintain that "all the civilized activities of
a modern society are wholly or largely non-marketed," implying that
the public sector belongs to the nonmarket sector in their distinction.

One of the key propositions in the Bacon and Eltis thesis is
represented by the basic identity:

$$i_m + b_m = e_m - c_u - i_u \eqno{(7.1)}$$

where i_m is the fraction of net market output invested in the market sector, b_m is the fraction that is surplus over the consumption of market sector workers, while c_u and i_u are the fractions consumed and used up as materials outside the market sector. To be more specific, the market sector produces output O_m, and C_m of this is consumed by the market sector workers. So the surplus in market sector is $E_m = O_m - C_m$. Of this surplus, the nonmarket sector workers consume C_u and the nonmarket sector uses up I_u in the form of investment and material uses. The market sector makes its own investment of I_m and the trade surplus of the marketed output is B_m. From the very definitions of each term, we have:

$$E_m = O_m - C_m = C_u + I_u + I_m + B_m \qquad (7.2)$$

Dividing through by O_m; defining $e_m = E_m/O_m = (O_m - C_m)/O_m$, $c_u = C_u/O_m$, $i_u = I_u/O_m$, $i_m = I_m/O_m$, and $b_m = B_m/O_m$; and finally rearranging the terms in the identity, we obtain (7.1) above.

The more than obvious conclusion from the above identity is that since the proportion of marketed output that can be reinvested and exported, $i_m + b_m$, is always equal to the rate of surplus of marketed output in the market sector e_m less the fractions of marketed output that are personally consumed and invested in the nonmarket sector, $c_u + i_u$, there must be a fall in $i_m + b_m$, and i_m can all too easily become insufficient for the steady growth of the economy when the government increases c_u and/or i_u for a given e_m, the proportion of marketed output that is surplus to the consumption of market-sector workers, or when the working class exercises its power to produce the unexpected result of the decrease in e_m. The market sector must produce output in excess of its own needs to provide for all the requirements of those in the market and nonmarket sectors. In modern societies that transfer resources from the market to the nonmarket sector, the nonmarket sector lives off the tax revenues provided by surpluses generated in the market sector. To repeat and to put in other words, Bacon and Eltis use the above identity to stress that devoting more labor to any one of the five activities means devoting less to one, some, or all of the others.

The mechanism by which a larger nonmarket sector share leads to slower growth and a balance of payments problem is to be found in shrinking profits (surpluses) and investment. The increased taxation required for a rising ratio of nonmarket output causes net-of-tax profits to fall. This leads to falling investment and thus to a lower rate of growth and balance of payment difficulties. In the words of Eltis (1979, p. 122):

> The principal condition which must be fulfilled if a continuous transfer of resources from the market to the nonmarket sector . . . is to be achieved is that the increase in taxation should be realized without damage to the underlying structure of production in the economy.

If the higher taxes resulting from higher government costs eat into

profits and savings in the market sector, the growth rate will fall
even if labor force and productivity growth remain favorable, because the rate of growth of the productive capacity falls as investment falls. In the overall scheme of Bacon and Eltis, slower
economic growth is not the only problem when the nonmarket sector
grows. If the share of output received by workers and salary earners in the market sector is reduced to provide the extra resources
the nonmarket government sector needs, and if workers do not acqui-
esce in reductions of their consumption, they will demand higher
wages, so wage inflation may accelerate. When workers and companies compete against each other for the same limited pool of resources, companies lose the struggle--particularly when unions are
powerful--with the result that profits and therefore investment are
squeezed again. The effort to check the accelerating inflation may
produce more unemployment.

In sum, the conceptual framework in the Bacon and Eltis formulation raises questions regarding (1) whether the market sector,
however defined, retains enough of its own product to sustain its
growth and (2) whether government policies, especially expenditure
and tax policies, are conducive to attitudes toward work, saving,
innovation, and productive investment. Though they voice important
questions, the argument they put forth is in no way complete and
convincing.

Theodore Geiger (1978) develops the Bacon and Eltis thesis on
an international level, descriptively rather than statistically, in
six European countries for the last 10 to 20 years. Although measures taken to improve welfare, which is the major source of growth
in the public sector, contribute to the increasing productiveness
of the economy by enhancing the skills, health, and morale of workers and by helping to sustain aggregate demand, the relationship
between welfare and efficiency, Geiger maintains, is essentially a
negative sum game because costs of increased welfare have to be met
by higher taxation or greater borrowing, both of which eventually
impair economic productiveness and efficiency. Therefore, in the
words of Geiger (1978, p. 13), "Too much or the wrong kinds of welfare, by undermining efficiency, lead in time to a reduction of
welfare as well."

In an appendix to Geiger's book, McMullen summarizes well the
nature of both the positive-sum and negative-sum relationships between taxes on the one hand and tax revenues and output levels on
the other and presents preliminary empirical findings on the negative-sum relationship. McMullen's conceptualization of the trade-
off between welfare and efficiency can best be presented by using
his own graph, reproduced in Figure 7.1. The vertical axis measures the output level and the horizontal axis measures tax rates as
a percentage of output. At zero or very low levels of taxation,
essential public services are not adequately provided because tax
revenues are not sufficient to finance them. Without essential
public services--such as justice, security, and defense--output is
very low. With increasing provision of essential public services,
concomitant with rising taxation, economic activity expands from 0

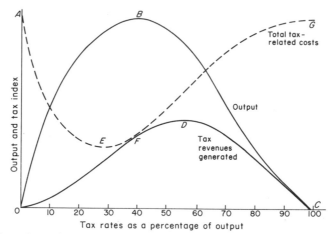

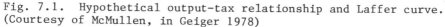

Fig. 7.1. Hypothetical output-tax relationship and Laffer curve.
(Courtesy of McMullen, in Geiger 1978)

up toward B. As tax rates increase to finance nonessential services and welfare needs, output levels begin to decline because
rising taxes reduce the efficiency. Thus the relationship between
output level and tax rates is represented by the curve OBC.

The curve OFDC shows the relationship between tax rates and
tax revenues generated, which is derived by multiplying output by
the tax rate. McMullen conjectures that tax revenues reach their
peak, such as D, at a higher tax rate than does the output level.
A measure of the total cost of the government's tax program to the
society in terms of output taxed away and output lost to inefficiency is represented by the curve AEFG. This is the difference
between the possible output peak and after tax income actually received. The total tax-related cost curve will take the shape
shown because the loss of output due to inefficiency at both very
low and high tax rates is overwhelming, and with adequate government provision of essential services within a range of tax rates,
efficiency improves dramatically and the total tax-related cost
falls sharply.

Given the framework as formulated by McMullen, society will
not choose two extreme points off the tax schedule, one identified
with anarchy at the low end and another with the confiscatory regime at the high end. Members of the society will disagree in
choosing the optimum point between two extremes, the choice depending upon how they benefit or lose from the increased tax and government expenditure. According to both Geiger and McMullen, in all
six countries of northwest Europe, except Germany, tax rates are
overshot, above the optimal rate such as B, and the symptoms of
overshooting are beginning to appear. Using pooled time-series and
cross-sectional data from five countries over the period 1965-1967,
McMullen also presents two regressions that show that increased
productivity (growth rate of output per work hour) is positively

correlated with investment as a proportion of GNP and negatively
correlated with high rates of inflation and high levels of government expenditures relative to GNP. More specifically, a 10 percent
increase in government expenditures, according to McMullen's statistical testing, is associated with an 11.9 percent fall in the
rate of productivity growth.

Instability Hypothesis: "Stop-Go" Policy and Economic Growth

An argument different from the ones we have discussed so far
has been made against one particular role of government in the
economy. Many economists and practitioners have argued that the
pace of economic growth, particularly in the United Kingdom, has
been greatly reduced by the continuous "stop-go" policies of government that have generated larger and more severe and erratic
fluctuations in output than normal economic forces would have produced. The proposition is that this artificially caused instability and unpredictability associated with it have hampered growth.
It is argued that greater stability would increase the average rate
of growth. Angus Maddison (1964, p. 49), a distinguished author on
the subject of long-run productivity growth, pointed out the retarded growth due to unsteadiness when he wrote: "The fact that
in the United Kingdom demand has continuously had to be interrupted by deflationary measures to right the balance of payments is
one of the major reasons why that country has grown more slowly
than the rest of Europe." It must be pointed out that Maddison
ascribes the better growth performance of OECD countries in the
postwar period than in the prewar period to the maintenance of
high and stable levels of demand.

There are two theses in the instability hypothesis: (1) poor
economic growth performance is caused by large and unpredictable
fluctuations in output and (2) these unstable cyclical movements
are generated by government stop-go policies. Only when these
theses are confirmed or justified can the instability hypothesis
hold true. Whether government stabilization policies destabilize
the economy or not is a heatedly debated question. Even though no
convincing empirical evidence has been put out yet, on the theoretical level the argument has been made that government-demand management policies generally destabilize rather than stabilize the
economy. Major factors often mentioned include our inexact knowledge of the relationship among the variables involved, decision
making subject to the pressures of interest groups, the well-known
lags in the actual operation of a policy, and conflict among policy
objectives. Suffice it to point out that though history never re-
peats itself in exactly the same way, much less fluctuation in the
postwar than prewar years has been achieved by government's stabilization efforts.

In what ways would one expect instability and large cyclical
variations in output to discourage growth? To Maddison (1964, p.
50), the source of evil lies in the decreased investment because of
uncertainty involved in investment decisions. "If government in-
tervenes in the economy erratically, then it is likely to lower in-

vestment incentives by increasing risk." Replete with uncertainties, firms may tend to adopt those investments with shorter pay-
off periods than would have been optimal. The main point here is
that some portion of the new investment that steadier growth would
have induced is not carried out and the reduction in investment
leads to slower economic growth than otherwise would have occurred.

According to Bacon and Eltis, the mechanism through which the
stop-go cycle hampers growth is the fall in the share of industrial
production going to industrial investment (Eltis 1969; Bacon and
Eltis 1975b). Faster growth cannot be achieved without a widening
of the industrial base of the economy and an increase in the ratio
of industrial production to the national product. In the stop-go
cycle, resources are shunted between industrial investment, nonindustrial investment, and the export surplus; if the nonindustrial
sector gains resources during cycles, which, according to Bacon and
Eltis, has been the case in the United Kingdom, the economy's production capacity shrinks because there will be less industrial investment. Deindustrialization resulting from government stop-go
policies is a major cause of growth retardation because increased
industrial investment would have raised the economy's capacity to
produce and added to industrial efficiency in future years.

In a study that attempts to put various forms of instability
experience of major industrial countries into an analytical framework to obtain some causal interpretations, Erik Lundberg (1968)
suggests an explanation for the link between economic growth and
fluctuations in demand that does not rest on the assumption that
investment causes growth. His main argument is that asymmetric behavior of wages during the stop-go cycle will lead to the cost-push
inflation, which in turn results in a fall in exports and therefore
in slow economic growth. During the upturn of a cycle, increasing
demand in the labor market raises wage rates and earnings. The
consequent increase of wage costs and prices is not compensated for
by developments during the downturn of the cycle. A low rise or a
decrease in productivity results in a larger rise in wage costs per
unit of product. While this increase in wages and prices does not
necessarily have a deflationary effect on home demand, it will lead
to a fall in exports. Assuming that the export-led growth hypothesis is a powerful explanation, the decrease in exports resulting
from the stop-go policy will discourage economic growth.

There are also some ad hoc explanations. It is argued that
the artificial instability caused by government stop-go policies
reduces confidence and liquidity and lowers the readiness to innovate and the efficiency of industrial firms and establishments.
Exactly in what way large cyclical variations in output or demand
exaggerated by government stop-go policies discourages growth is
not adequately explained in the argument. It is just assumed that
as confidence is destroyed and forward planning becomes difficult,
there will be less investment, with the result that economic growth
will be less.

To the author's knowledge, there have been only two attempts

to examine the empirical validity of the instability hypothesis:
one by Thomas Wilson (1966) and the other by A. Whiting (1976).
Both studies show evidence against the thesis that the continuous
stop-go policies of government have been one of the major constraints on growth through their destabilizing effect on demand and
output. The most difficult problem in the effort to test the instability hypothesis is how to find an appropriate measure of the
level of instability. Wilson employs range, standard deviation,
and a coefficient of variation of several variables such as GDP,
industrial production, and investment on an annual basis. Whiting
develops a sophisticated procedure and measures the level of instability in terms of the standard deviation of the percentage residuals from trend quarterly values of net output at constant
prices. Whiting's procedure provides a measure of the level of
fluctuation around a steadily growing output trend. According to
his comparison of the cyclical variations in manufacturing net output, the instability of United Kingdom manufacturing is the least
of all the seven countries examined for the period 1955-1973. Japan and Italy, with the fastest growth rates, show the largest percentage levels of instability.

Baumol
      Rising per unit costs in government activities are suggested
to account for the single most important component in the expanding
public sector. Empirical support for this argument has been examined in the previous section. One important explanation for cost
differences in public versus private sector activities was offered
by William Baumol (1967), who has suggested that the growth in government has occurred because of the relatively slower growth in
productivity in the public sector. Baumol divides the economy into
two sectors: one "technologically progressive" and the other reg-
istering only "sporadic increases in productivity." The latter includes services provided by government, education, the performing
arts, leisure time activities, and the like. The principal reason
why productivity in the government sector grows more slowly than
elsewhere is that many important government activities are highly
labor intensive.
      Our major concern here is not whether Baumol's nonprogressivi-
ty explanation or productivity lag hypothesis is right or wrong but
with the implication of his explanation on the growth performance
of the economy. One of the propositions Baumol derives from his
formal model of the unbalanced growth is that if for some reason
the less progressive public sector output is to be maintained at a
constant level or at a fixed ratio to the output of the technologically progressive private sector, then a rising proportion of national resources must be devoted to the less progressive sector
over time. In other words, balanced growth necessitates the transfer of resources from the progressive to the nonprogressive sector.
Baumol then moves on to show that a determination to retain a fixed
ratio between the outputs of the private and public sectors can act
as a drag on economic growth.

     An attempt to achieve balanced growth in a world of un-
balanced increases in productivity must lead to a declining
rate of growth of output per capita. In particular, if productivity in one sector remains constant, the rate of growth
of output per head will approach zero asymptotically [Baumol
and Oates 1975, p. 245].

What this proposition is suggesting is that as long as productivity
growth in the public sector does not match that in the private sector the growth of the economy will slow down; furthermore, the
growth of output per capita will come to a halt if productivity in
the public sector does not improve over time.

Defense Expenditure and Economic Growth

     The relationship between economic growth and one particular
category of government expenditures, defense spending, has been investigated in the literature, resulting in two opposing views.
Some authors, dealing with the economic implications of military
expenditure, have, above all, emphasized two disadvantages of a
large armaments budget: the allocation effect and the growth effect. The allocation argument shows how the absorption of public
expenditure in the military sphere leads to a shortage of funds
for pressing current requirements in other fields. The growth argument points out that some of the resources used for military purposes could have been made available for civilian investment or the
extension of the infrastructure, and these investment expenditures
would have led to a higher rate of economic growth.

     Some other authors have denied the negative effects of mili-
tary expenditure by pointing out that for no other purpose would it
have been politically possible to obtain such large government ap-
propriations. The alternative to military spending would therefore
not have been a better allocation, but more unemployment, and reduction of military research with its spillover effects would have
slowed down technologically induced growth.

     Marxist work on the economic role of military expenditures
starts from the premise that military expenditure has a necessary
role in the maintenance of the capitalist system and uses a Keynesian or underconsumptionist framework to argue that military expenditure is necessary to offset a tendency toward a stagnation
within capitalism (see Baran and Sweezy 1966).

     Empirical tests show mixed results on the relationship between
the growth of the economy and defense expenditures. Emile Benoit
(1973) shows that the evidence available for developed countries
from 1950 to 1965 is at least not inconsistent with the view that
defense expenditures slow down growth. His result shows that the
defense burdens are inversely related to the growth rate, but with
a strength too low to be viewed as significant at the 0.05 level.
In a large study of less developed countries, an opposite pattern
seems to appear. Benoit has found that in 44 less developed countries during the period 1950-1965, countries with a heavy defense
burden generally have the most rapid rate of growth, and those with

the lowest defense burdens tend to show the lowest growth rates.
The strong positive correlation between high defense burdens and
rapid growth rates is confirmed by a regression with $r = 0.55$ and t
$= 4.20$. A question arises about the direction of the interaction
between them. Benoit's (1973, p. 3) conclusion is that "the direct
interaction between growth and defense burdens seems to run primarily from defense burdens to growth rather than vice versa."

Albert Szymanski's (1973) testing of the Baran-Sweezy theory
of the role of military expenditure on economic stagnation using
the 18 wealthiest capitalist countries for the period 1950-1968 has
shown that nonmilitary spending plays a much more significant role
in advanced capitalist economies than does military spending, and
it has a more favorable effect than defense expenditures in increasing rates of growth.

In his study of economic consequences of military expenditure,
R. P. Smith (1977, 1980) investigates the relationships among share
of military expenditure, share of investment, unemployment rate,
and growth rate. He finds negative correlations between military
spending and growth and between investment and military expenditure, both statistically significant at the 95 percent level for
major advanced industrial countries. His results, which show a resource trade-off between share of output devoted to military expenditure M and investment I, allowing for the effect of growth G
and/or unemployment U, are:

$$I = 24.9 - 1.16M + 0.78G$$
$$(7.5) \quad (2.5) \quad\;\; (1.7) \qquad\qquad R^2 = 0.546$$

$$I = 28.04 - 1.303M + 0.419G - 0.642U$$
$$(35.6) \quad (11.3) \quad\;\; (5.0) \quad\;\; (6.2) \qquad R^2 = 0.517$$

Smith (1977, p. 76; 1980, pp. 31-32) concludes:

> The military expenditure incurred imposed a substantial cost,
> primarily in terms of lower accumulation and slow growth, and
> in many ways was a contradictory requirement of the system--
> undermining what it was intended to defend. . . . The balance
> of evidence . . . is that there is a negative association be-
> tween military expenditure and investment, and this result is
> robust whether the data are treated as time series, cross sec-
> tions, or pooled, and for a variety of assumptions about sto-
> chastic structure.

Denison's Conjectures

In a recent study investigating the "mystery" of how the adjusted growth rate of national income per person employed in the
United States fell from 2.6 percent a year in 1948-1973 to -0.6
percent in 1973-1976, a drop of 3.2 percentage points, Edward F.
Denison (1979), a well-known authority in the sources-of-growth accounting, examines the various ways in which the government may
have reduced output per unit of input. What is truly striking is

that Denison is left with a huge residual factor, which he labels
"advances in knowledge and not elsewhere classified." This residual factor accounts for over half (1.4 percent) of the 1948-1973
productivity growth (2.6 percent) in the United States. For 1973-
1976, the residual factor suddenly drops to -0.7, which is greater
in absolute value than the -0.6 rate of productivity growth that
occurred during these years.

Denison admits he simply does not know why the record suddenly turned so bad after 1973, and he calls it a mystery. However,
he examines 17 suggested causes of worsened productivity performance in the recent past and makes comments on specific suggestions
(Denison 1979, pp. 122-47). What is interesting from our point of
view is that about half of the suggested causes have something to
do with the government. Denison discusses them under the following headings: (1) diversion of input to comply with government
regulation (except pollution and safety), (2) government-imposed
paperwork, (3) regulation and taxation: diversion of executive attention, (4) government regulation: delay of new projects, (5)
regulation and taxation: misallocation of resources, (6) effects
of high tax rates on incentives and efficiency, and (7) capital
gains provisions of the Revenue Act of 1969.

These suggested causes are self-explanatory and popular among
practitioners and in the media. If it is indeed the case that
adapting to these changes in regulations and taxation by government
has caused inputs to be employed that make little contribution to
measured output (while such regulations may involve substantial
benefits not measured in GNP accounting), then measured productivity has suffered on this account. As Denison himself submits, one
important point against which we should guard in taking these seven
reasons as possible explanations for a productivity slowdown is
that all these factors will take effect gradually rather than cause
a sudden drop, if it is true that overregulation and overtaxation
are going to retard growth.

Denison lists ten other causes for reduced productivity: (1)
curtailment of expenditures on research and development, (2) decline in opportunity for major new advances, (3) decline of Yankee
ingenuity and deterioration of American technology, (4) increased
lag in the application of knowledge because of the aging of capital, (5) "people don't want to work any more," (6) impairment of
efficiency by inflation, (7) lessening of competitive pressure and
changes in the quality of management, (8) the rise in energy
prices, (9) the shift to services and other structural changes, and
(10) possible errors in the data.

To summarize, the arguments dealing with the undesirable economic impacts of the expanding public sector on economic growth
fall into several groups. First, an argument against the growing
government is made in terms of crowding out. It is maintained
that increased public consumption leads to decreased private investment. Several explanations have been offered for the causes of
the crowding out: rising interest rates resulting from expansionary fiscal policy and negative impacts on saving and investment be-

cause of rising taxes needed to finance higher spending. Second,
some economists believe that the public sector is inherently inefficient and unproductive and argue that once it is allowed to grow
beyond a certain level, overall productivity would suffer. Third,
too much government regulation of the private sector diverted productive resources to the unproductive use, and the extreme instability caused by the continuous stop-go policies of government hampers economic growth. Fourth, in contrast to most studies focusing
on fiscal effects on the capital input, some studies consider the
adverse effects of taxes on the labor input and their bearing on
the growth of output. These arguments will be critically examined
on both theoretical and empirical grounds in the following sections.

THE CROWDING-OUT CONTROVERSY

Theories and hypotheses discussed in the previous section are
concerned with explaining why growth of the public sector slows
down the growth of the economy. Explanations and theories we have
considered have already undergone some empirical testing, and all
of them deserve careful consideration as plausible hypotheses. Unfortunately, the evidence available is not sufficient to show the
validity of each argument. We can also raise numerous objections
to the value of the various arguments on theoretical grounds. We
will examine critically the main currents running through the arguments discussed before and try to put theories through empirical
examinations as much as available data will permit.

One main argument in many studies that raises the strong suspicion that a large and growing public sector actually causes
slower economic growth in industrialized countries is that government spending displaces a near-equal amount of private spending,
particularly private investment. This notion, known as "crowding
out," has been emphasized by those who warn against the growing
public sector in the "league of economic growth." Attention to
the crowding-out effects of government expenditures has been paid
at two different levels. At the policy level, where our present
interest lies, the crowding-out argument has been made to discuss
a deleterious effect of the growing public sector on the private
capital formation. At the academic or theoretical level, the
crowding-out controversy assumes prominence in the context of the
Keynesian-monetarist debate. The process of crowding out can be
explained either by the standard IS-LM framework or by the notion
of "ultrarationality." Using the IS-LM model, it has been argued
that increases in government spending drive up interest rates,
thereby discouraging private investment. The crowding out is reflected in the inability of fiscal policy actions to shift the IS
curve.

Economists such as R. J. Barro (1974), M. Feldstein (1975),
P. A. David and J. L. Scadding (1974), and L. A. Kochin (1974) have
analyzed some of the implications of ultrarationality in the relation between the private and public sectors. The notion of ultrarationality is based on the assumption that households regard the

corporate and government sectors as extensions of themselves--as instruments of their private interests. David and Scadding, for example, offered ultrarationality as an explanation for Denison's Law--the observed stability of the ratio of gross private saving to GNP in the United States. According to Denison (1958), gross private saving averaged 14.63 percent of GNP and never deviated more than one-half point from the average in the United States for the 1929-1956 period, excluding 1942-1947. This stability of the gross private saving ratio in the face of substantial variation in the government deficits implies, it is argued, the substitute relationship between private and public investments. Under the ultrarationality view, the expansionary impact of deficit financing is blunted either because households foresee the impact of a budget deficit on their own and their heirs' future taxes or because households treat deficits as public investment and view private and public investments as perfect substitutes.

The fact that the congestion (in modern parlance, crowding out) is due to the interdependence between the parameters of the planned spending (IS) function and the demand for money (LM) function was recognized by J. M. Keynes (1973, p. 222) 40 years ago. Keynes admitted the possibility of congestion (crowding out), but on a quite different ground. This is clear from his statement that "the investment market can become congested through shortage of cash. It can never become congested through shortage of saving. This is fundamental of my conclusions within this field." For a clear-cut discussion of Keynes's view of the crowding out and on recent arguments by monetarists, see Paul Davidson (1978).

Crowding out is not an all-or-nothing phenomenon. The signs and magnitude depend on the state of the economy and the nature of public expenditure. Complete crowding out will occur only if the demand for money is completely interest inelastic. As textbooks show, the effect of government expenditure depends crucially on the particular state of the economy. The occurrence of crowding out depends on the existence of real constraints in terms of lack of capacity or labor shortage to expand real output in the economy. Thus economists, such as monetarists, who espouse an expectations-augmented excess demand mechanism whereby the economy naturally tends toward full utilization of resources, naturally believe in crowding out in the long run. In a fully employed economy, the public sector competes with the private sector not only on the demand side of the market for final goods and services but also in factor markets and intermediate product markets for labor and other resources. Where production is below capacity, increased public spending can help bring the economy to its production possibility frontier without generating the crowding out. One important question we have to ask is whether the economy in most countries is working near full employment capacity. It is a little surprising that during the last ten years or so, when the output level in most industrial countries was far below their full capacity level, that the crowding-out debate gained particular prominence.

A functional analysis of government expenditures is needed to

determine the effect of the growing public sector on economic
growth. Government investment spending may be a substitute for, a
complement to, or independent of private investment spending. Similarly, government consumption spending may be a substitute for, a
complement to, or independent of private consumption spending. Unless there is a perfect substitution between private and public
spending, and unless we assume there is a noticeable difference in
productivity between the private and public sectors, the argument
that a larger public sector leads to a slower growing economy becomes weaker. A significant portion of public expenditure on goods
and services is used for an input in the production of goods and
services in the private sector. Government, for example, can improve skills and knowledge by education and research and give pub-
licity to the best-practice technology. A large portion of government investment spending induces private investment spending directly.

The empirical results on the crowding-out effect are mixed.
Studies by Leonall Anderson and Jerry Jordan (1968) and Michael
Keran (1969) produce results that lend support to the crowding-out
tenet. Gary Fromm and Lawrence Klein's (1973) simulation results
for a number of econometric models also indicate that crowding out
does occur in real terms over time. In contrast to these results
based on U.S. data, studies by M. J. Artis (1978) and P. Arestis
(1979) using British data report that no crowding-out effects occur
in the United Kingdom, or crowding out is negligible and, over the
longer haul, tends to be negative. The way that crowding out is
studied in these empirical works is usually through simulation results that show the implied "dynamic" expenditure and tax multipli-
ers.

EFFECTS OF HIGH TAXES ON INCENTIVES AND EFFICIENCY

One of the most common arguments that increased government
spending, as a share of economic aggregates, slows down the growth
rate of real output runs along the familiar line that the higher
taxes needed to finance the higher spending would weaken incentives
to work and to invest and would also absorb funds that otherwise
would have been saved and invested. More recently, increased government regulations are blamed for retarded growth of measured output.

Taxes and regulations have one of their major influences on
the economy through their impact on the supplies of capital and labor, which are two major sources of economic growth. When taxes
are levied, individuals may decide to alter their work, saving, and
investment patterns. Firms also make corresponding responses to
changed circumstances resulting from taxes and regulations. To the
extent that individuals and firms do respond, taxes and regulations
induce changes in the economy's potential output.

What happens to the economy's potential output and growth rate
as taxes and regulations change and increase? A large number of
studies, theoretical and empirical, have been conducted to ascer-

tain the effect of taxes on labor supply, saving, and investment. It is beyond our scope here to evaluate all of these studies, but following is a summary of some major results. For more detail, see Thurow (1971), Godfrey (1975), Brown and Jackson (1978), and Atkinson and Stiglitz (1980). A tax may have two kinds of effects on allocation decisions. An income effect arises if taxpayers alter their decision in response to the tax-induced reduction in disposable income. A substitution effect arises if taxpayers alter their decision in response to tax-induced changes in relative prices or in relative returns on alternative resource uses or in both. (Atkinson and Stiglitz [1980, p. 28] mention a third category they call "financial effect," which arises "where the same real activity can correspond to several different forms of payment, which are taxed at different rates. . . . The tax system may lead to . . . changes in the form of financial organization and the structure of transactions.") The answer to the question, What happens to the economy's output and growth? depends upon the relative strengths of the income effect of taxes leading to more work, saving, and investment in an effort to recoup the individual's standard of living and the substitution effects of taxes leading to less work, saving, and investment as a result of the lower net rate of return to work, saving, and investment. The answer cannot be determined theoretically, contrary to the currently popular ideology- and politics-inflicted argument that taxes have definitely negative and adverse impacts on work efforts, saving, and investment. More careful attention should be paid to empirical studies to determine the direction and the magnitude of tax impacts on major economic decisions under consideration.

Effect of Taxes on Work Effort

The modern theory of the work-leisure choice is based on the opposing substitution and income effects of a given wage rate or tax rate change. When the wage rate is reduced by an increase in tax rate, the reward for an additional unit of leisure is lowered, and for this reason the worker will tend to substitute leisure for work. At the same time, a lower wage rate due to a higher tax rate means a lower income from a given amount of labor, and with lower incomes, people normally will wish to have fewer units of leisure. A tax rate increase therefore normally induces a substitution effect unfavorable to work effort and an income effect favorable to it, the net outcome depending on the relative strengths of the two effects. As is well known, the work decision is a multidimensional one affected by many factors that are in turn influenced not only by taxes but also by a variety of other factors.

Empirical research on the effect of taxation on labor supplies relies mainly on three approaches: sample surveys, econometric studies, and income maintenance experiments. After conducting an intensive survey of empirical works available on the effects of taxes on work effort, Godfrey (1975, p. 126) concludes:

All three sets of empirical research therefore indicate that taxation does not have a large and significant effect on

the total supply of work effort, and that in particular the
net effect on the labor supply of male family heads is likely
to be very small. Moreover, there is some evidence that taxation has little influence on the choice of occupations.

Both theoretical conclusions and empirical results indicate that
the net effect of taxation on labor supply is not large enough to
be of great economic importance.

Impact of Taxes on Saving Decision

A second major effect of taxes concerns the saving and investment choices. The importance of the effects of tax policy on
saving and investment decisions in the economic growth context results from the belief that a crucial determinant of the long-run
growth of the economy is the saving of individuals and firms, providing funds for investment in new machines and new technology of
production. Since investment and saving decisions are made by two
different agents in the economy, both decisions need to be investigated to determine the impact of taxes. Government, individuals,
and business firms all save and invest. The following discussion
is based on the general assumption that individuals save and firms
invest, while the impact of saving and investment decisions by government is disregarded. Taxes on savings affect the potential supply of capital, while taxes on investment affect the demand for
capital. Heavy taxes on capital income embodied in the personal
income tax and directly in the corporate income tax reduce the net
rate of return to capital and saving.

The analysis of the effect of taxes on savings presupposses a
theory of what economic forces determine saving. As yet, no wholly
adequate theory exists that is consistent with observed facts. As
in the case of labor supply, the tax impact on savings depends upon
the income and substitution effects of taxes on interest income
from savings. An a priori argument about those effects is inconclusive because of offsetting income and substitution effects. It
is generally agreed that the magnitude of the relative price effect
from the taxation of interest income is likely to be small, perhaps
even insignificant as compared with the overall income effect. If
we neglect the relative price effect, the magnitude of the effect
of taxation on savings depends upon the marginal propensity to save
out of the income on which the tax falls. If this is the case, the
structure of the tax--progressivity and different tax rates on different sources of income--rather than the tax level becomes important in determining the impact on saving because the marginal propensity to save varies with the level of household income or
according to the sources of income. In most cases, however, the
response of saving to taxation has been inferred indirectly from
the interest elasticity of saving. If the relationship between the
volume of savings and net after-tax return is highly inelastic,
changes in the net return will have little adverse effect upon
saving, and vice versa.

Several studies have been made to estimate the interest elasticity of saving, but the differences in the results obtained are

substantial. A recent study by M. J. Boskin (1978) suggests that a
10 percent decrease in the after-tax interest rate may cause saving
to decrease by 4 percent. Some other studies indicate that saving
is not very responsive to changes in the interest rate. Studies by
C. Wright (1969) and A. S. Blinder (1975) show very low saving
elasticities. Even if Boskin's estimate represents the true state
of nature, reduction in saving from increased taxation will not be
large unless the effect of the tax is to reduce the net return on
savings substantially.

George Von Furstenberg and Burton Malkiel (1977, p. 837), after surveying the literature on the influence of government policies on capital formation, conclude on saving that "despite several
advances in econometric studies measuring the interest elasticity
of saving, considerable doubt remains whether the elasticity is
positive and significant and whether the efficiency gains will be
large from certain tax substitutions that have been proposed."

Impact of Taxes on Investment Decision

In addition to affecting the potential supply of capital goods
through their impact on savings, taxes can also affect the demand
for capital goods. The tax affects the capital formation in three
ways: through investment incentives, through changes in attitudes
toward risk taking, and through corporate saving and the availability of the supply of investable funds. (Taxes also have the macroeconomic effects of influencing the shape and position of the demand curve for capital goods. These effects are ignored in our
discussion.) It is often asserted that the corporate income tax
has serious disincentive effects on the decision to invest because
the taxation absorbs part of the return from investment and reduces
net posttax profits on investment. The corporate profit tax raises
the relative cost of capital, hence leads to less capital being employed for a given output. This negative effect depends crucially
on the assumption that the corporate income tax is not shifted and
that the marginal investment is financed out of equity rather than
debt capital. The shiftability of the corporate income tax depends
on the market structure of the output that new investment produces.
It can be shown that where investment is financed at the margin by
bond finance and true economic depreciation is allowed, the first-
order conditions for investment are unaffected by taxation, and the
cost of capital is unchanged. Under this limited condition the
corporate profit tax is neutral with respect to an investment decision.

The empirical study of the effects of taxation on a firm's behavior has been one of the most active areas of applied research in
economics. Considerable work has been conducted to investigate not
only the impact of taxation on investment but also the influence of
the corporate tax on company financial policy. The investment impacts of taxation have been studied mostly in terms of econometric
investment functions. While a number of recent works have substantially increased the empirical knowledge about investment behavior,
investigators have come to widely different conclusions about the

Table 7.9.   Extra investment
produced by 1 percent cut in
effective corporate income
tax rate in 1958 constant
prices

Author	$ billion
Jorgenson	0.4
Thurow	0.5
Okun	0.8
Brookings	0.0
Kuh	0.4
Klein	0.3
Eisner	0.0

Source: Thurow 1971, p. 33.

relative importance of various variables. All these studies on investment behavior discuss the impact of tax policy in terms of investment tax credit and/or special depreciation formulas, not in
terms of increased tax burden on investment. Table 7.9 presents a
good summary of the impact of a 1 percent reduction in the effective corporate income tax rate on the additional investment in the
United States for several investment functions considered by different authors.

Empirical results shown in the table indicate that investment
expenditures are relatively inelastic with respect to corporate income taxes. Assuming a symmetry of effect between tax cut and tax
increase and using the average value in Table 7.9 as a guide, each
1 percent increase in corporate income taxes leads to a 0.2 percent
decrease in investment. This low elasticity indicates that the impact of each 1 percent reduction in taxes is relatively small even
though the impact of a drastic change in corporate income taxes,
like its elimination or the sudden doubling of the tax rate, may be
substantial. The very fact that elasticities are low is because
other factors exert their influence more strongly than tax policy.
The most often mentioned factors include sales, profits, internal
cash flow, interest rate, and long-term debt capacity. These
forces may help neutralize the retarding effects on investment of a
corporate income tax.

The question of the effects of taxes on risk taking has been
debated extensively. The income tax reduces the return from risk
taking. But whether this increases or reduces the total amount of
risk undertaken is not easy to answer. As with any tax, there is
an income effect, which encourages persons or corporations to take
more risk in order to maintain their incomes, and a substitution
effect, which leads in the opposite direction. An early work by
E. D. Domar and R. A. Musgrave (1944) shows that proportional income taxes increase the willingness to undertake risky investment.
In a tax system where any loss from an unsuccessful investment can
be deducted against other income, the government tax system reduces
the private risk of any investment by sharing in any loss. With a
proportional income tax and full loss offset, the tax would reduce
yield and potential loss by the same amount. There is no incentive
to shift in the direction of less risk taking. However, there is
the income effect, which leads to more risk taking.

It turns out that this conclusion rests on some strong assump-

tions. Taxpayers must recognize the significance of the loss offset. M. J. Feldstein (1969) points out that the conclusion is valid only if (1) there is at least one truly riskless asset, (2) individuals become risk averse as their incomes rise, and (3) investors have a particular quadratic utility function such that the
standard deviation of the expected return serves as an adequate
measure of risk.

     Further works on the effects of taxation on risk taking based
on the theory of portfolio allocation show that, given that losses
can be set against taxation and interest paid on borrowed funds is
tax deductible, the critical parameters in determining whether or
not the proportional income tax increases risk taking are wealth
and the elasticity of demand for risky assets (see Atkinson and
Stiglitz 1980, pp. 97-127). A proportional wealth tax increases
(decreases) the proportion of the portfolio allocated to the risky
asset as the wealth elasticity of the demand for the risky asset is
less (greater) than unity. With respect to the income taxation effect on risk taking, the conclusion is that an income tax increases
(decreases) private risk taking if the wealth elasticity of demand
for the risky asset is negative (positive).

     Once it is seen that the magnitude of the wealth elasticity
of the demand for the risky asset is the critical element in drawing inferences about the effect of taxation on risk taking, an estimation of the elasticity is critical in giving the final word on
the relationship between tax and risk taking. Based on time series
evidence on the demand for money in the United States, K. J. Arrow
(1965) concludes that the wealth elasticity of demand for the risky
asset is positive but less than unity. In contrast, the cross-sectional studies, for example, by D. S. Projector and G. S. Weiss
(1966), suggest that the same elasticity is greater than unity (see
Atkinson and Stiglitz 1980, pp. 124-25). This evidence does not
lead us to a definite conclusion. Our discussion so far deals with
the portfolio choice between risky and safe assets. Though we do
not discuss it here, it must be mentioned that discussion of risk
taking is complete only when information on the linkage between
portfolio choice and real investment decisions of the economy becomes known. Much more remains to be investigated to make a conclusion.

     All other things being equal, the corporate income tax may be
expected to reduce the amount of corporate funds available for investment and reduce the ability to invest by draining off disposable income. This effect of the tax on the supply of funds may be
particularly important for new and growing enterprises. It is difficult for them to raise outside capital because they are not well
known and are regarded as particularly risky.

INEFFICIENCY AND LOW PRODUCTIVITY OF GOVERNMENT
     Wasteful spending, inefficiencies, and low productivity levels
are commonly cited as characteristics of government operations. A
popular view has been that the public sector is inherently ineffi-

cient because of the lack of a profit motive, the bureaucratic red
tape, political shenanigans, and so on. It is suggested that if
government adopted the kind of techniques resulting in cost saving
in business, all the advantage of business efficiency could be
achieved and there would be less taxation for any given level of
government output.

The relative efficiency of the public and private sectors has
been a subject for speculative disagreement. Though the conventional wisdom that the public sector is inefficient relative to the
private sector is not without merit, our position is that arguments
so far have been misplaced and involve some fallacies. No convincing evidence has yet been produced to justify the arguments.
First, efficiency is a many-sided concept, and statements about it
normally incorporate a personal value judgment that is often left
implicit. In general, the superiority in efficiency of the private
over the public sector is based on the assumption that efficiency
from the point of view of the private sector must imply economic
efficiency from the point of view of the society. Apart from efficiency in the use of resources for particular purposes, government
is also concerned with the broad aspects of efficiency that concern
the utilization of resources in general. Efficiency in the context
of public expenditure has a different connotation than in business.

Difficulty in measuring output of public services also contributes to the inefficiency argument of the public sector. Mancur
Olson (1973) points out that inefficiency on the part of government
is fundamental and in many cases incurable. His argument takes
four steps: (1) government produces a collective good or controls
an externality; (2) there is difficulty in getting consumers to reveal their preferences concerning a collective good or externality;
(3) the output of collective goods or controlling an externality
does not take the form of divisible physical units that can be
counted; (4) because of the inability to measure output, productive
efficiency cannot be measured and hence it cannot be achieved. It
is true that the lack of readily countable output of governments
that produce collective goods and the resulting lack of objective
bases for judging performance lead to complicated, cumbersome, and
expensive restrictions on public management. This source of government inefficiency is due primarily to the nature of goods and
services provided by the public sector, not to the inherent inability of the government to produce output efficiently. Since we cannot determine the volume or value of government output, we cannot
use conventional business enterprise measures to estimate or control the efficiency of government provisions of services without
major qualifications. An analogy between government and business
is misleading because output of the public sector is measured by
the use of inputs. Productivity growth in government is zero by
definition; output is measured by labor input (see Ardolini and
Hohenstein 1974; Searle and Waite 1980).

There is a close association between wastefulness in government and the view that goods and services produced publicly are of
a nonproductive nature. Such an interpretation is based on a rath-

er limited concept of what is productive and what is not. Many
types of public expenditures are basic intermediate outputs essential to the final output of private market goods and services, but
the nature of many such public goods precludes accurate measurement
of and changes in productivity.
        Francis Bator (1960, p. 103) warns against the comparative ef-
ficiency argument against the public sector based on a "double mis-
apprehension":

> For one, it involves a confusion of government spending with
> government production. About half of what is paid for by gov-
> ernment is produced by private, profit-guided producer. . . .
> But more important, the argument involves a play on the word
> "efficiency." It does no good to demonstrate that private
> producers produce their output with less waste than does the
> government its output if market cannot be counted on to induce
> private producers to provide the latter.

        While productivity growth in the public sector may lag behind
that in the private sector when properly measured, there are seg-
ments of the private sector, particularly the service industries,
that have productivity growth rates similar to that of government.
In a study of the U.S. economy, William Nordhaus (1973) finds that
shifts in the composition of output have accounted for over 90 percent of the slowdown in labor productivity that took place in the
United States between 1948 and 1971 but indicates that productivity
in agriculture, finance, insurance, real estate, and even durable
manufacturing was responsible along with government. The principal
reasons for the observed lag in productivity appear to be the same
for both the private service and public sectors. They include the
lower quality of the labor force, the slower rise and different
rates in capital per head, and different rates of technological
change and/or of economies of scale (see Fuchs 1968, 1969).
        When the techniques of efficiency and productivity measurement
are applicable for public production, comparative efficiency and
inefficiency of government production are both conceivable. Determination of relative efficiency becomes an empirical question. For
certain services the public sector might be more efficient than the
private sector. For example, William Pier et al. (1974) estimate
and compare production functions for a governmental and private
production of a service--garbage collection--in the medium- to
large-scale municipalities of Montana and establish the efficiency
of the public over the private sector.
        One also might argue that the criticisms of public sector ef-
ficiency are overdrawn. We have seen that the market system of the
private sector is by no means perfectly efficient; indeed, government's economic functions are an attempt to correct shortcomings of
the price system. The public sector may be subject to important
deficiencies in fulfilling its economic functions. But, as Otto
Eckstein (1973, p. 17) argues, "The relevant comparison is not between perfect markets and imperfect markets, nor between faulty

markets and all-knowing rational, benevolent governments, but between inevitably imperfect institutions." The concepts applied to
the theory of the market cannot be applied to a study of public
economy. In other words, the operation of the public economy cannot be analyzed in terms of supply, demand, and prices. Of course,
this does not mean that the public economy is completely extraneous
to the market.

AN EMPIRICAL TEST
     There is no convincing argument for or against the proposition
that the expanding public sector is detrimental to saving and investment, therefore to economic growth. Except for indirect or
casual studies of the effects of the rising government size on
saving, investment, and economic growth, there is little conclusive
evidence that government spending and taxes reduce saving and investment and work as a growth retardant. Following is an attempt
to investigate empirical relationships between the size of the public sector and saving and investment and that of the public sector
and economic growth using cross-sectional data from 18 industrial
countries and the 48 contiguous states. It must be mentioned in
passing that this test is based on simple regression, and results
presented are by no means complete. No effort is made to correct
statistical problems that might exist in the cross-sectional analysis, such as heteroscadasticity. However, given the availability
of data our test is comprehensive.
     Table 7.10 shows simple regression results of the relation be-
tween savings and various measures of the size of the public sector
for the sample of 18 industrialized countries. Equations (1) to
(6) are concerned with explaining different savings/GDP ratios in
terms of government consumption/GDP ratios. Government consumption
in (1) to (3) is measured in nominal terms, while in (4) to (6),
percentage of real gross domestic income devoted to public consumption is used as explanatory variables. These equations confirm the
negative relationship between savings and public consumption.
     The remaining 18 equations in Table 7.10 relate savings ratios
to different measures of tax revenues. When total tax revenue as a
percent of GNP is used as an independent variable in (7) to (10), a
positive rather than negative relationship is found between tax and
savings, though the relationship is not statistically significant
at all. In (10) to (12) a particular type of tax, a tax on personal income and corporate profit income, is singled out to examine
its effect on national savings. The results show the negative relation between savings and taxes on personal income and profits,
but the statistical relationship is not significant in all cases.
     The same relationships in (7) to (12) are repeated in (13) to
(18) using corresponding tax ratios now adjusted by each country's
level of per capita income relative to that of the United States.
If two countries impose the same tax rates on the same levels of
income, ceteris paribus, the ratio of tax to the national income
will be higher in the country whose per capita income is higher

Table 7.10. Regression results of the relation between saving and size of public sector

$S55 = 43.38 - 1.73GC55$	(1)
(4.67) (2.39) $R^2 = 0.26$	
$S65 = 38.49 - 0.95GC65$	(2)
(7.35) (2.57) $R^2 = 0.29$	
$S75 = 31.89 - 0.48GC75$	(3)
(6.92) (1.95) $R^2 = 0.19$	
$S60 = 39.79 - 1.16RPC60$	(4)
(5.51) (2.15) $R^2 = 0.22$	
$S65 = 41.47 - 1.20RPC65$	(5)
(8.11) (3.22) $R^2 = 0.39$	
$S75 = 38.93 - 1.06RPC75$	(6)
(9.50) (3.94) $R^2 = 0.49$	
$S55 = 19.97 + 0.19R55$	(7)
(6.20) (0.55) $R^2 = 0.02$	
$S65 = 23.76 + 0.14R65$	(8)
(13.03) (0.93) $R^2 = 0.05$	
$S75 = 22.43 + 0.02R75$	(9)
(6.08) (0.19) $R^2 = 0.00$	
$S65 = 25.76 - 0.05TIP65$	(10)
(8.52) (0.19) $R^2 = 0.00$	
$S70 = 31.27 - 0.38TIP70$	(11)
(8.23) (1.36) $R^2 = 0.10$	
$S75 = 24.70 - 0.11TIP75$	(12)
(7.33) (0.50) $R^2 = 0.02$	
$S65 = 27.45 - 5.02R65A$	(13)
(6.69) (0.56) $R^2 = 0.02$	
$S70 = 34.65 - 18.14R65A$	(14)
(6.15) (1.50) $R^2 = 0.12$	
$S75 = 30.34 - 15.21R75A$	(15)
(6.27) (1.53) $R^2 = 0.13$	
$S65 = 25.02 + 1.16TIP65A$	(16)
(7.08) (0.06) $R^2 = 0.00$	
$S70 = 31.67 - 30.46TIP70A$	(17)
(7.64) (1.33) $R^2 = 0.10$	
$S75 = 26.45 - 17.29TIP75A$	(18)
(7.94) (1.06) $R^2 = 0.07$	
$S65 = 18.09 + 5.09TR65$	(19)
(5.99) (2.45) $R^2 = 0.27$	
$S70 = 21.42 + 3.02TR70$	(20)
(4.40) (1.06) $R^2 = 0.07$	
$S75 = 18.62 + 2.24TR75$	(21)
(4.58) (1.14) $R^2 = 0.08$	
$S65 = 24.02 + 0.23SS65$	(22)
(14.95) (0.91) $R^2 = 0.05$	
$S70 = 24.92 + 0.24SS70$	(23)
(10.64) (0.76) $R^2 = 0.03$	
$S75 = 22.12 + 0.13SS75$	(24)
(10.94) (0.57) $R^2 = 0.02$	

Sources: Same as in Tables 4.3, 7.2, 7.3, 7.4, 7.6, and 7.7.

Note: $S55$, $S65$, $S70$, and $S75$ = ratios of saving to GDP in 1955, 1965, 1970, and 1975 respectively; $GC55$, $GC65$, and $GC75$ = government consumption as a percent of GDP in 1955, 1965, and 1975 respectively; $RPC60$, $RPC65$, and $RPC75$ = percentage of real gross domestic income devoted to public consumption in 1960, 1965, and 1975 respectively; $R55$, $R65$, and $R75$ = total tax revenue as a percent of GDP in 1955, 1965, and 1975 respectively; $TIP65$, $TIP70$, and $TIP75$ = taxes on personal income and corporate profits as a percent of GDP in 1965, 1970, and 1975 respectively; $R65A$, $R70A$, and $R75A$ = $R65$, $R70$, and $R75$, adjusted according to the level of relative per capita income; $TIP65A$, $TIP70A$, and $TIP75A$ = $TIP65$, $TIP70$, and $TIP75$, adjusted according to the level of relative per capita income; $TR65$, $TR70$, and $TR75$ = ratios of direct taxes to indirect taxes in 1965, 1970, and 1975 respectively; $SS65$, $SS70$, and $SS75$ = ratios of social security contribution to GDP in 1965, 1970, and 1975 respectively.

than in the other. Mutatis mutandis, the same tax ratio for two
countries implies that the country with a lower level of income is
imposing higher tax rates on given income levels and that the poor-
er country will show a lower tax ratio if two countries impose the
same tax rates. This point is discussed clearly by Vito Tanzi
(1969), though he pursues the matter for his own purpose in a different direction. The point is that the tax comparison should take
into account the level of development of a country. In our study
the adjustment of the influence of the relative income on tax burden is based on the per capita income calculated according to the
purchasing power parity, not to the official exchange rate. Regression results with these adjusted tax ratios show the negative
relation between total taxes and savings in (13) to (15) in contrast to the positive relationship between them in (7) to (9).

   Not only the level of taxation but also the structure of the
tax systems has a different impact on saving and investment. It
has been suggested that the relatively heavy reliance on direct
taxes on income and profits (including social security contributions) and the relatively light use of indirect taxes on goods and
services in some countries result in lower saving and investment
and that the slower rate of growth in those countries is the direct
consequence of their excessive reliance on direct taxation. Equations (19) to (21) try to shed some light on this argument. Our
independent variable measures the ratio of direct to indirect taxes
in benchmark years. If the argument suggested above is right, we
should expect negative signs in our regressions, but our test shows
the contrary results. Except for during the year 1965, the positive relationship between the saving ratio and the ratio of direct
to indirect taxes is not statistically significant.

   The regression results in (22) through (25) are worthy of our
attention, particularly in conjunction with results obtained in
other studies. In a 1974 econometric study, Feldstein (1974) finds
that social security has seriously depressed personal savings in
the United States. In replicating his work to see the implications
of alternative assumptions, Dean Leimer and Selig Lesnoy (1980)
discovered a programming error. Correcting for the error and simply replicating Feldstein's work, they produced results strikingly
different from his original findings. The new result by Leimer and
Lesnoy indicates a considerably smaller negative impact on saving
over the whole 1930-1974 period, and the effect is not statistically significant. More important and puzzling, Feldstein's model implies, according to Leimer and Lesnoy, that the impact of the social security system is to increase saving and inhibit consumption
in the United States for the postwar 1947-1974 period.

   Our result, based on cross-sectional data for 18 industrial
democracies, shows a positive association between national saving
and the social security contribution, though the association is not
statistically significant.

   In Table 7.11, regression results are reported for the same 18
advanced countries and show the relation between the investment ratio and various measures of government expenditures and tax reve-

Table 7.11. Regression results of the relation between investment and size of the public sector

$I55 = 25.69 - 0.44GC55$ (1)
  (2.71) (0.60) $R^2 = 0.02$
$I65 = 38.17 - 1.00GC65$ (2)
  (9.12) (3.39) $R^2 = 0.42$
$I75 = 29.67 - 0.32GC75$ (3)
  (5.87) (1.16) $R^2 = 0.08$
$I50R = 37.42 - 1.12RPC50$ (4)
  (7.79) (3.06) $R^2 = 0.37$
$I65R = 42.89 - 1.19RPC65$ (5)
  (11.50) (4.26) $R^2 = 0.53$
$I75R = 39.54 - 0.83RPC75$ (6)
  (6.11) (1.94) $R^2 = 0.19$
$I55 = 19.06 - 0.02R55$ (7)
  (4.78) (0.05) $R^2 = 0.00$
$I65 = 24.56 - 0.03R65$ (8)
  (12.84) (0.23) $R^2 = 0.00$
$I75 = 26.35 - 0.06R75$ (9)
  (7.05) (0.67) $R^2 = 0.03$
$I65 = 23.72 + 0.04TIP65$ (10)
  (8.90) (0.16) $R^2 = 0.00$
$I70 = 26.68 - 0.18TIP70$ (11)
  (9.11) (0.85) $R^2 = 0.04$
$I75 = 23.18 + 0.05TIP75$ (12)
  (6.67) (0.24) $R^2 = 0.00$
$I55 = 18.49 + 4.38R55A$ (13)
  (5.26) (0.25) $R^2 = 0.00$
$I65 = 24.44 - 1.57R65A$ (14)
  (13.85) (0.18) $R^2 = 0.00$
$I75 = 25.98 - 4.13R75A$ (15)
  (7.59) (0.63) $R^2 = 0.02$
$I65 = 21.57 + 15.84TIP65A$ (16)
  (7.09) (0.38) $R^2 = 0.04$
$I70 = 25.68 - 7.76TIP70A$ (17)
  (7.91) (0.43) $R^2 = 0.01$
$I75 = 22.34 + 8.31TIP75A$ (18)
  (6.36) (0.48) $R^2 = 0.01$
$I65 = 21.18 + 2.11TR65$ (19)
  (7.00) (1.02) $R^2 = 0.06$
$I70 = 22.94 + 0.85TR70$ (20)
  (6.12) (0.39) $R^2 = 0.01$
$I75 = 26.74 - 1.40TR75$ (21)
  (6.25) (0.68) $R^2 = 0.03$

Sources: Same as in Tables 4.2, 4.3, 7.2,
7.3, 7.4, 7.6, and 7.7.
Note: Same as in Table 7.10 except: $I55$,
$I65$, $I70$, and $I75$ = ratios of gross domestic investment to GDP in 1955, 1965, 1970, and 1975 respectively; $I50R$, $I65R$, and $I75R$ = percentage of
real gross domestic income devoted to domestic capital formation in 1950, 1965, and 1975 respectively.

nues. Overall results in Tables 7.10 and 7.11 are more or less
similar except that in Table 7.11--(7) to (9)--the investment ratio
is inversely related to the total tax revenue as a percent of GDP.
The evidence in Table 7.11 does not bear out the argument that excessive government spending or taxes reduce investment.
     Tables 7.12 and 7.13 provide more direct evidence on the rela-
tion between economic growth and the expanding public sector for
the sample 18 developed countries and the 48 contiguous states. In
Table 7.12, regression equations are reported for the 18-country
sample over the period 1950-1977, including three subperiods:

Table 7.12. Regression results of the relation between economic growth and size of the public
sector

$PY5060 = 6.09 - 0.22GC55$	(1)
$\quad$ (2.15) (1.01) $\qquad R^2 = 0.06$	
$PY6070 = 9.59 - 0.39GC65$	(2)
$\quad$ (4.52) (2.66) $\qquad R^2 = 0.31$	
$PY7077 = 2.91 - 0.03GC70$	(3)
$\quad$ (2.29) (0.40) $\qquad R^2 = 0.01$	
$PY5077 = 7.37 - 0.28GC65$	(4)
$\quad$ (3.96) (2.16) $\qquad R^2 = 0.23$	
$PY5060 = -0.84 + 0.32RPC50$	(5)
$\quad$ (0.33) (1.62) $\qquad R^2 = 0.14$	
$PY6070 = 4.69 - 0.05RPC60$	(6)
$\quad$ (1.93) (0.28) $\qquad R^2 = 0.01$	
$PY7077 = 2.58 - 0.01RPC70$	(7)
$\quad$ (1.78) (0.12) $\qquad R^2 = 0.00$	
$PY5077 = 5.33 - 0.14RPC65$	(8)
$\quad$ (2.45) (0.89) $\qquad R^2 = 0.05$	
$PY5060 = 2.12 + 0.14R55$	(9)
$\quad$ (2.62) (1.68) $\qquad R^2 = 0.15$	
$PY6070 = 3.95 + 0.06R65$	(10)
$\quad$ (5.16) (0.10) $\qquad R^2 = 0.00$	
$PY7077 = 1.48 + 0.03R70$	(11)
$\quad$ (1.63) (1.06) $\qquad R^2 = 0.07$	
$PY5077 = 2.91 + 0.05R65$	(12)
$\quad$ (4.70) (0.92) $\qquad R^2 = 0.05$	
$PY6577 = 4.75 - 0.12TIP70$	(13)
$\quad$ (5.49) (1.92) $\qquad R^2 = 0.19$	
$PY6577 = 3.50 - 0.13TCI70$	(14)
$\quad$ (4.31) (0.44) $\qquad R^2 = 0.01$	
$PY6577 = 4.01 - 0.38TP70$	(15)
$\quad$ (6.75) (1.61) $\qquad R^2 = 0.14$	
$PY6577 = 2.59 + 0.06TGS70$	(16)
$\quad$ (2.65) (0.62) $\qquad R^2 = 0.02$	
$PY6577 = 2.78 + 0.06SS70$	(17)
$\quad$ (4.97) (0.85) $\qquad R^2 = 0.04$	
$PY5060 = 1.49 + 11.83R55A$	(18)
$\quad$ (2.53) (3.67) $\qquad R^2 = 0.46$	
$PY6070 = 3.58 + 2.71R65A$	(19)
$\quad$ (5.07) (0.74) $\qquad R^2 = 0.03$	
$PY7077 = 1.41 + 2.12R70A$	(20)
$\quad$ (1.78) (1.33) $\qquad R^2 = 0.10$	
$PY5077 = 2.64 + 4.78R65A$	(21)
$\quad$ (4.80) (1.66) $\qquad R^2 = 0.15$	
$PY6577 = 3.30 - 0.81TIP65A$	(22)
$\quad$ (2.86) (0.12) $\qquad R^2 = 0.00$	
$PY6577 = 4.43 - 7.28TIP70A$	(23)
$\quad$ (4.46) (1.33) $\qquad R^2 = 0.10$	
$PY6070 = 3.62 + 0.28TR65$	(24)
$\quad$ (2.51) (0.28) $\qquad R^2 = 0.01$	
$PY7077 = 3.37 - 0.59TR70$	(25)
$\quad$ (3.34) (0.99) $\qquad R^2 = 0.06$	
$PY5077 = 3.13 + 0.19TR65$	(26)
$\quad$ (2.60) (0.24) $\qquad R^2 = 0.00$	

Sources: Same as in Tables 7.2, 7.3, 7.4,
7.6, and 7.7.

Note: Same as in Table 7.10 except: $PY5060$,
$PY6070$, $PY7077$, and $PY5077$ = growth rate of per
capita income during the periods 1950-1960, 1960-
1970, 1970-1977, and 1950-1977 respectively; $TCI70$
= ratio of tax on corporate income to GDP in 1970;
$TP70$ = ratio of tax on property to GDP in 1970;
$TGS70$ = ratio of tax on goods and services to GDP
in 1970; $SS70$ = ratio of social security contribution to GDP in 1970.

Table 7.13. Regression results of the relation between economic growth and size of the public sector for the 48 contiguous states

$TY5868 = 6.38 - 0.02R57$ (1)
(16.54) (0.81) $R^2 = 0.01$

$TY6878 = 9.24 + 0.01R67$ (2)
(32.64) (0.72) $R^2 = 0.01$

$TY5878 = 7.63 + 0.01R67$ (3)
(38.07) (0.79) $R^2 = 0.01$

$TY5878 = 7.57 - 0.01R$ (4)
(19.20) (0.48) $R^2 = 0.01$

$TY5868 = 7.00 - 0.07E57$ (5)
(6.62) (0.86) $R^2 = 0.02$

$TY6878 = 4.85 + 0.28E67$ (6)
(5.62) (5.35) $R^2 = 0.38$

$TY5878 = 6.26 + 0.09E67$ (7)
(8.39) (2.02) $R^2 = 0.08$

$TY5878 = 6.34 + 0.09E$ (8)
(6.32) (1.42) $R^2 = 0.04$

$TY5868 = 6.58 - 0.04E57A$ (9)
(5.32) (0.39) $R^2 = 0.00$

$TY6878 = 4.78 + 0.35E67A$ (10)
(4.00) (3.91) $R^2 = 0.25$

$TY5878 = 6.25 + 0.11E67A$ (11)
(6.58) (1.59) $R^2 = 0.05$

$TY5878 = 6.34 + 0.11EA$ (12)
(5.28) (1.18) $R^2 = 0.03$

$TY5878 = 8.73 - 0.93PE57$ (13)
(5.71) (1.73) $R^2 = 0.06$

$TY6878 = 3.60 + 1.52PE67$ (14)
(2.40) (3.88) $R^2 = 0.25$

$TY5878 = 6.31 + 0.38PE67$ (15)
(5.23) (1.20) $R^2 = 0.03$

$TY5878 = 5.19 + 0.66PE$ (16)
(3.57) (1.77) $R^2 = 0.06$

$TY6878 = 9.38 + 0.01FBPA$ (17)
(47.25) (0.15) $R^2 = 0.00$

$TY5878 = 7.75 + 0.01FBPA$ (18)
(55.25) (0.67) $R^2 = 0.01$

$TY6878 = 9.38 - 0.01FBPB$ (19)
(47.34) (0.44) $R^2 = 0.00$

$TY5878 = 7.75 + 0.01FBPB$ (20)
(55.05) (0.35) $R^2 = 0.00$

Sources: ACIR 1977; Bureau of the Census 1977, 1979.

Note: $TY5868$, $TY6878$, and $TY5878$ = growth rate of total income for the periods 1958-1968, 1968-1978, and 1958-1978 respectively; $R57$ and $R67$ = ratio of total tax revenue to total income in 1957 and 1967 respectively; R = average of tax revenue ratios in 1957, 1967, and 1977; $E57$ and $E67$ = ratio of total expenditure to total income in 1957 and 1967 respectively; E = average of total expenditure ratios in 1957, 1967, and 1977; $E57A$ and $E67A$ = total expenditure ratio excluding expenditures financed by federal government in 1957 and 1967 respectively; $EA = (E57A + E67A + E77A)/3$; $PE57$ and $PE67$ = public employment of state and local government as a percent of total population in 1957 and 1967 respectively; $PE = (PE57 + PE67 + PE77)/3$; $FBPA$ and $FBPB$ = measure of fiscal blood pressure using resident per capita income and representative tax method to estimate fiscal capacity respectively.

1950-1960, 1960-1970, and 1970-1977. A negative association is
found between economic growth and the share of public consumption,
whether measured in nominal or real terms, as shown in (1) to (8).

The rest of the equations in Table 7.12 show the relation between the growth of per capita income and different measures of tax
ratios. The results are not consistent. A very weak positive relation is found between the per capita income growth and the ratio
of total tax to GDP, whether the tax ratio is adjusted to account
for different levels of per capita income as shown in (18) to (21)
or not as reported in (9) to (12).

Equations (13) through (17) in Table 7.12 show the association
between the output growth and levels of different types of taxes:
taxes on income and profits, taxes on corporate profits only, taxes
on property, taxes on goods and services, and social security contributions. Taxes on the first three tax bases have a weak negative relation with economic growth, while there is a very weak positive association between economic growth and taxes on the last two
tax bases.

Economists have tried to link the rapid economic growth in
some countries to the fact that these countries rely heavily on indirect forms of taxation for their revenues. In the same vein, it
is maintained that the slower rate of growth of other countries may
be the direct consequence of their excessive reliance on direct
taxation. These arguments are not borne out by the evidence in the
case of developed economies of our sample, as shown in (24) to (26)
in Table 7.12.

Disparities in economic growth rates among various regions of
the United States have become sufficiently severe to attract serious attention. Exacerbating effects of federal taxing and spending
policies on regional growth were pointed out in the popular press.
One basic problem facing state and local governments is that their
jurisdictions do not straddle the entire national economy, and so
much of the economy is outside their sphere of control. Mobility
of resources is higher among regions within a country that cross
the national boundaries. Economic factors respond quite sensitive-
ly to policy decisions by state and local governments on taxation
and spending.

Our attempt to find any association between fiscal activities
of the national government and economic growth can be extended to
ascertain whether any definite pattern exists for the same association among states in the United States. Our sample of the 48 contiguous states provides more data points for statistical tests and
renders its sample points more homogeneous compared with the previous cross-sectional sample of 18 industrial countries. Table
7.13 reports regression results showing the relation between economic growth and various indicators of the public sector activities
among states. Growth rates of total income, the dependent variable, are calculated not only for the whole period 1958-1978 but
also for two subperiods: 1958-1968 and 1968-1978.

Equations (1) to (4) (Table 7.13) relate the growth perform-

ance to the ratio of tax revenue collected by state and local governments to personal income for states. Test results do not offer
any conclusions on the relationship between the growth of a state's
economy and its tax collection. The same conclusion can be drawn
with regard to the relationship between the growth of state income
and state and local expenditures, as shown in (5) through (12).
Total expenditures by state and local governments as a percent of
total income, regardless of the sources of financing, are used as
independent variables in (5) to (8), while state and local government expenditures financed by their own sources, excluding those
financed by the federal government, are employed as explanatory
variables in (9) to (12).

As we discussed earlier, the growth of government bureaucracy
in the United States and Canada is the result of growth in employment at lower levels of government. Federal government employment
as a percentage of the total labor force has remained stable for
the last 30 years, even declining slightly recently. Equations
(13) to (16) are concerned with explaining different growth rates
of a state's economy in terms of the size of bureaucracy--measured
by public employment in state and local governments--as a percentage of total population for a given state. No negative association
between the growth performance and the size of government bureaucracy is found from our tests.

In (1) through (4), a one-dimensional measure of tax revenue
(the ratio of total tax to total income) is used to measure fiscal
strains on state and local governments by economic activities. Despite its advantages in terms of simplicity and ease of calculation, the traditional one-dimensional measure has also a number of
weaknesses. Not only fiscal pressure at a given time but also fiscal trends over time should be included as a part of any estimate
of comparative fiscal position. The Advisory Commission on Intergovernmental Relations (ACIR) (1977) combines these two dimensions
into a single measure of "fiscal blood pressure" based on each
state's index numbers. The index of fiscal blood pressure uses as
the numerator the state's relative position in a given year and as
the denominator the state's relative change in pressure over a giv-
en period. Equations (17) to (20) use as explanatory variables two
measures of fiscal blood pressure put out by ACIR: *FBPA*, using
resident personal income, and *FBPB*, using the representative tax
method to estimate fiscal capacity. Regression results based on
these improved measures do not indicate an association between economic growth and fiscal pressure.

To summarize, though based on simple regressions, our results
using a variety of fiscal indicators and covering different periods
lead to the conclusion that no adverse relationship can be established between the expanding public sector and the growth performance of the economy, at least for the samples included in our empirical testing. Nor is the case for further expansion of public
sector established. Time-series study for each country remains to
be conducted to improve our understanding of the process involved.

CONCLUSIONS

The very question of whether or not modern economies have an excessive public sector has not yet been settled. Various writers have argued that there is a systematic bias leading to underexpansion or overexpansion of the public sector. A. C. Pigou, in his treatise, *Economics of Welfare,* argues that the market results in an undersupply of goods where marginal social benefits exceed the marginal private benefits. The basis of this argument is a familiar one--externality.

John K. Galbraith (1958, p. 261) holds that the political process leaves a deficiency in the provision for social goods because the consumer-voter is subject to intensive advertising pressure from the producers of private goods, without corresponding praise for the attraction of social goods, and because there are dependence effects associated with private economic activity such that new suppliers tend to generate their own demand. According to the Galbraithian "social imbalance" hypothesis, people would be better off if more of their income were taxed away and spent for them by the government. F. A. Hayek (1968) challenges the Galbraith argument on empirical grounds. He points out that some important publicly provided goods are subject to dependence effects, while not all private goods generate such an effect.

Anthony Downs (1960) obtains a similar conclusion as Galbraith. Extending the logic of his earlier published model of democratic political behavior (Downs 1957), he argues that democratic government budgets are not expanded enough in certain directions when vote-maximizing parties compete for the support of utility-maximizing voters. Since to Downs the correct benchmark budget is the one that would emerge if political parties and voters had perfect information, he argues that many benefits of government action will not be produced in a complex and interdependent democracy where parties must appeal to voters lacking perfect information. Citizens, in reaching their voting decisions, are more aware of taxes that reduce their purchasing power directly than of the potential and indirect benefits of government spending that are "remote" and "uncertain." Downs attempts to demonstrate that because the electorate is less than fully informed, these taxpayers invariably choose less than the optimum amount of government expenditure.

James Buchanan and Gordon Tullock (1962, Chap. 10) arrive at the position generally counter to that of Downs and Galbraith by employing a similar methodology as Downs. They consider the behavior of a representative government where decisions are made on the basis of less than unanimity. Their argument is based on the belief that the vote-trading processes that are inherent in majority rule cause more programs to be enacted than may be expected when each citizen is taxed according to the benefits he derives from the budgets. Beneficiaries of particular programs form conditions to secure passage of these programs financed at levels beyond the point where marginal benefits cover costs. By virtue of the fact that most taxes are levied on the whole taxing population, the beneficiary coalition bears less than the full cost of incremental additions of these programs. Since the winning coalition allows the individual voter to "reap benefits from collective action without bearing the full marginal social costs attributable to him" (Buchanan and Tullock 1962, p. 201), the political processes are predicted to produce too much of these types of services.

It is undoubtedly true that implicit vote trading on issues does exist. But it must also be admitted that information concerning the benefits and costs of government activity is costly. There is no a priori basis to conclude that budgets are either too small or too large, for this must be an empirical proposition. The results depend on the degree of "rational ignorance" prevalent among the electorate and the willingness of political parties to engage in logrolling.

Most of the discussions dealing with the impacts of a growing public sector on economic growth have been conducted along the neoclassical paradigm, emphasizing the close connection between saving and investment and economic growth. One of the major conclusions in the neoclassical economic growth theory, as we reviewed in Chapter 2, is that raising the rate of saving cannot affect the long-run or equilibrium rate of income growth. Efforts to break growth down into its components have typically attributed no more than 25 percent of growth in output to growth in capital. Given the neoclassical conclusion on the relationship between saving and economic growth and the empirical results from the source-of-growth accounting on the relative unimportance of capital in the growth process, the adverse effect of the growing public sector on economic growth via its detrimental impact on saving and investment cannot be overwhelming.

Because of the sharp decline in productivity growth and the deterioration of economic performance during recent years, capital formation and the government's role in it has moved to the forefront of national economic concern, although the issue of the appropriate size and role of the public and private sectors has been common to all mixed economies. Perhaps nowhere in economic theory does economics as ideology emerge dearer than in analyzing the proper role of government in economic activities. State activities are classified as consumption, and hence unproductive, and state intervention is invariably defined negatively.

Opponents of the expanding public sector view growing government expenditures and taxes with apprehension as part of an age-old struggle between people and government. They view the line between public and private spending as the dividing line between the areas of coercion and freedom. It can be safely said that the level of government spending is perhaps the most clear-cut battlefield between conservatives and liberals in many countries, particularly in the United States. Conservatives believe that the percentage of government spending in a national economic total is an inverse measure of the extent of freedom that exists in a country. As with many other controversies on economic issues, different value judgments and ideologies grossly distort the factual information in favor of one argument and against the other.

Examples of perverse effects of the expanding public sector and increasing regulations are available in the literature, yet no convincing evidence has been produced to indicate the adverse effects of big government on economic growth, saving behavior, the potential output, and the capital stock of the economy as a whole. Observations based on time-series data for each industrial country indicate that any connection between rising government expenditure and the retardation of growth is difficult to demonstrate because economies in almost all countries grew as rapidly in the 1950s as in the 1960s and in both decades more rapidly than in earlier decades, while the public sector had been growing throughout. Until new ground in the theory expounding the relation between the private and public sectors is broken and until the evidence upholding the theory is produced, there is only weak support for the claim that the retardation in economic growth and other economic problems facing most countries are due to the growing public sector.

The theory of the overall balance of production, according to John R. Hicks (1946, pp. 99–100), suffers from three main deficiencies, the second of which he defines as follows:

> It abstracts from the economic activity of the State; this is very important, but the State is a very incalculable economic unit, so that the extent to which its actions can be allowed for in economic theory is somewhat limited (this is, of course, a deficiency of economic theory as such, and as a whole).

We cannot do without nonmarket modes of allocation, while we can do without the market mode. Until we develop a better economic theory for the public sector, a full assessment of its economic effect, especially its impact on economic growth, will be hard to come by. Economies in industrial democracies are certainly ill, but perhaps not from the disease that has been diagnosed.

REFERENCES

Advisory Commission on Intergovernmental Relations (ACIR). 1977.
    Measuring the Fiscal Blood Pressure of the States--1964-1975.
    Washington, D.C.
Anderson, L. C., and J. L. Jordan. 1968. Monetary and fiscal action: A test of their relative importance in economic stabilization. *Fed. Reserve Bank St. Louis Rev.*, November:12-24.
Ardolini, C., and J. Hohenstein. 1974. Measuring productivity in the federal government. *Mon. Labor Rev.*, November:13-20.
Arestis, P. 1979. The "crowding-out" of private expenditure by fiscal actions: An empirical investigation. *Public Finance* 34(1):36-49.

Arrow, K. J. 1965. *Aspects of the Theory of Risk-Taking*. Helsinki: Yrjö Jahnssonin Säätio.

Artis, M. J. 1978. Fiscal policy and crowding out. In *Demand Management*, ed. Michael Posner. London: Heinemann Educational Books.

Atkinson, A. B., and J. E. Stiglitz. 1980. *Lectures on Public Economics*. New York: McGraw-Hill.

Bacon, R. W., and W. A. Eltis. 1975a. The implications for inflation, employment and growth of a fall in the share of output that is marketed. *Bull. Oxf. Univ. Inst. Econ. Stat.* 37:269-96.

————. 1975b. Stop-go and de-industrialization. *Natl. Westminster Bank Q. Rev.*, November:31-43.

————. 1978. *Britain's Economic Problem: Too Few Producers*, 2nd ed. London: St. Martin's.

————. 1979. The measurement of the growth of the non-market sector and its influence. *Econ. J.* 89:402-15.

Baran, P. 1957. *The Political Economy of Growth*. New York: Monthly Review Press.

Baran, P., and P. Sweezy. 1966. *Monopoly Capitalism*. New York: Monthly Review Press.

Barro, R. J. 1974. Are government bonds net wealth? *J. Polit. Econ.* 82:1095-1117.

Bator, F. M. 1960. *The Question of Government Spending*. New York: Harper and Brothers.

Baumol, W. J. 1967. Macroeconomics of unbalanced growth: The anatomy of urban crisis. *Am. Econ. Rev.* 57:415-26.

————. 1968. Macroeconomics of unbalanced growth: Comment. *Am. Econ. Rev.* 58:893-94.

————. 1972. Macroeconomics of unbalanced growth: Reply. *Am. Econ. Rev.* 62:150.

Baumol, W. J., and W. E. Oates. 1975. *The Theory of Environmental Policy*. Englewood Cliffs, N.J.: Prentice Hall.

Beck, M. 1976. The expanding public sector: Some contrary evidence. *Natl. Tax J.* 29:15-21.

————. 1979a. Estimating changes in real size of the public sector. *Econ. Let.* 2(3):245-49.

————. 1979b. Inflation, government spending, and real size of the public sector. *Atl. Econ. J.* 3:25-34.

————. 1979c. Public sector growth: A real perspective. *Public Finance* 34(3):313-43.

Bell, C. S. 1968. Macroeconomics of unbalanced growth: Comment. *Am. Econ. Rev.* 58:877-83.

Benoit, E. 1973. *Defense and Economic Growth in Developing Countries*. Boston: D. C. Heath.

Birch, J. W., and C. A. Cramer. 1968. Macroeconomics of unbalanced growth: Comment. *Am. Econ. Rev.* 58:893-96.

Bird, R. M. 1970. *The Growth of Government Spending in Canada*. Toronto: Canadian Tax Foundation.

Blackaby, F., ed. 1979. *De-Industrialization*. London: Heinemann Educational Books.

Blinder, A. S. 1975. Distributional effects of aggregate consumption function. *J. Polit. Econ.* 83:447-75.

Boskin, M. J. 1978. Taxation, saving and the rate of interest. *J. Polit. Econ.* 86:3-27.

Bradford, D. 1969. Balance on unbalanced growth. *Z. Nationalekon.* 24:291-304.

Bradford, D., R. Malt, and W. Oates. 1969. The rising cost of local public services: Some evidence and reflections. *Natl. Tax J.* 22:185-202.

Brown, C. V., and P. M. Jackson. 1978. *Public Sector Economics.* Oxford: Martin Robertson.

Buchanan, J. M., and G. Tullock. 1962. *The Calculus of Consent.* Ann Arbor: University of Michigan Press.

Bucovetsky, M. W., ed. 1979. *Studies in Public Employment and Compensation in Canada.* Montreal: Butterworth.

Bureau of the Census, U.S. Department of Commerce. 1977. *Historical Statistics on Governmental Finances and Employment,* vol. 6, no. 4. Washington, D.C.: USGPO.

————. 1979. *Census of Governments.* Washington, D.C.: USGPO.

Business Week. 1976. Government growth crowds out investment. October 18:138-45.

Clark, C. 1945. Public finance and changes in the value of money. *Econ. J.* 55:371-89.

————. 1970. *Taxmanship.* London: Institute for Economic Affairs.

David, P. A., and J. L. Scadding. 1974. Private saving: Ultra-rationality, aggregation and Denison's Law. *J. Polit. Econ.* 82:225-49.

Davidson, P. 1978. Why money matters: Lessons from a half-century of monetary theory. *J. Post-Keynesian Econ.* 1:46-70.

Denison, E. F. 1958. A note of private saving. *Rev. Econ. Stat.* 40:261-69.

————. 1979. *Accounting for Slower Economic Growth: The United States in the 1970s.* Washington, D.C.: Brookings Institution.

Domar, E. D., and R. A. Musgrave. 1944. Proportional income taxation and risk taking. *Q. J. Econ.* 58:388-422.

Downs, A. 1957. *An Economic Theory of Democracy.* New York: Harper & Row.

————. 1960. Why the government budget is too small in a democracy. *World Polit.* 21:541-62.

Drucker, P. F. 1969. The sickness of government. *Public Interest,* 5, Winter.

Eckstein, O. 1973. *Public Finance.* Englewood Cliffs, N.J.: Prentice-Hall.

Eltis, W. A. 1969. Is stop-go inevitable? *Natl. Westminster Bank Q. Rev.,* November:2-12.

————. 1979. How rapid public sector growth can undermine the growth of the national product. In *Slow Growth in Britain,* ed. W. Beckerman. Oxford: Clarendon.

Feldstein, M. J. 1969. The effects of taxation on risk taking. *J. Polit. Econ.* 77:755–64.

———. 1974. Social security, induced retirement and aggregate capital accumulation. *J. Polit. Econ.* 82:905–26.

———. 1975. Perceived wealth in bonds and social security: A comment. *J. Polit. Econ.* 83:331–36.

Foot, D. K. 1979. Political cycles, economic cycles, and the trend in public employment in Canada. In *Studies in Public Employment and Compensation in Canada,* ed. M. W. Bucovetsky. Montreal: Butterworth.

Friedman, M. 1962. *Capitalism and Freedom.* Chicago: University of Chicago Press.

———. 1976. The line we dare not cross: The fragility of freedom at 60 percent. *Encounter* 47:5–14.

Fromm, G., and L. R. Klein. 1973. A comparison of eleven econometric models of the United States. *Am. Econ. Rev.* 63:385–93.

Fuchs, V. R. 1968. *The Service Economy.* New York: National Bureau of Economic Research.

Fuchs, V. R., ed. 1969. *Production and Productivity in the Service Industry.* New York: Columbia University Press.

Galbraith, J. K. 1958. *The Affluent Society.* Boston: Houghton Mifflin.

Geiger, T. 1978. *Welfare and Efficiency: Their Interactions in Western Europe and Implications for International Economic Relations.* London: Macmillan.

Godfrey, L. 1975. *Theoretical and Empirical Aspects of the Effects of Taxations on the Supply of Labor.* Paris: OECD.

Hadjimatheou, G., and A. Skouras. 1979. Britain's economic problem: The growth of the nonmarket sector? *Econ. J.* 89:392–401.

Harrod, R. F. 1948. *Toward a Dynamic Economics.* London: Macmillan.

Hayek, F. A. 1968. The non-sequitur of the dependence effect. *South. Econ. J.* 27:346–48.

Hicks, J. R. 1946. *Value and Capital.* London: Oxford University Press.

Hymer, S., and S. Resnick. 1969. Interactions between the government and the private sector: An analysis of government expenditure policy and the reflection ratio. In *Economic Development and Cultural Change,* ed. I. G. Stewart. Edinburgh: Edinburgh University Press.

Jackson, P. M. 1979. Comparative public sector growth: A United Kingdom perspective. In *Studies in Public Employment and Compensation in Canada,* ed. M. W. Bucovetsky. Montreal: Butterworth.

Johnston, J. 1975. A macro-model of inflation. *Econ. J.* 85:287–308.

Keran, M. W. 1969. Monetary and fiscal influences on economic activity—the historical evidence. *Fed. Reserve Bank St. Louis Rev.,* November:5–24.

———. 1972. Macroeconomics of unbalanced growth: Comment. *Am. Econ. Rev.* 62:149.

Keynes, J. M. 1973. *The Collected Works,* vol. 14, p. 222. New York: St. Martin's.

Kochin, L. A. 1974. Are future taxes anticipated by consumers? *J. Money, Credit, Banking* 6:385–94.

Kravis, I., A. Heston, and R. Summers. 1978. *International Comparison of Real Product and Purchasing Power.* Baltimore: Johns Hopkins University Press.

Leimer, D. R., and S. D. Lesnoy. 1980. Social security and private saving. Paper presented at 93rd Annu. Meet. Am. Econ. Assoc., Denver, Colo., Sept. 4–7.

Lundberg, E. 1968. *Instability and Economic Growth.* New Haven: Yale University Press.

Lutz, J. R. 1969. Some economic effects of increasing public expenditure: An empirical study of selected developed countries. *Public Finance* 24(4):577–96.

Lynch, L. K., and E. L. Redman. 1968. Macroeconomics of unbalanced growth: Comment. *Am. Econ. Rev.* 58:884–85.

Maddison, A. 1964. *Economic Growth in the West—Comparative Experience in Europe and North America.* New York: Twentieth Century Fund.

McGrath, J. P. 1978. Public employment in the United States: A compilation of statistical trends. In *Studies in Taxation, Public Finance and Related Subjects,* vol. 2. Washington, D.C.: Fund for Public Policy-Research.

Nordhaus, W. D. 1973. The recent productivity slowdown. *Brooking Pap. Econ. Act.,* no. 3:493–545.

Nutter, G. W. 1978. *Growth of Government in the West.* Washington, D.C.: American Enterprise Institute.

Olson, M. J. 1973. Evaluating performance in the public sector. In *The Measurement of Economic and Social Performance,* ed. M. Moss. New York: National Bureau of Economic Research.

Organization for Economic Cooperation and Development (OECD). 1966. *National Accounts Statistics 1955-1964.* Paris: OECD.
———. 1967. *National Accounts Statistics 1956-1965.* Paris: OECD.
———. 1978. *National Accounts of OECD Countries, 1976,* vol. 2. Paris: OECD.
———. 1979. *Revenue Statistics of OECD Member Countries 1965-1978.* Paris: OECD.

Palomba, N. A. 1969. Stability and real economic growth: An international comparison. *Kyklos* 22(Fasc. 4):589–92.

Peacock, A. T., and J. Wiseman. 1968. Measuring the efficiency of government expenditure. In *Public Sector Economics,* ed. A. R. Prest. Manchester: Manchester University Press.

Pier, W. J., R. W. Vernon, and J. H. Wicks. 1974. An empirical comparison of government and private production efficiency. *Natl. Tax. J.* 27:653–56.

Projector, D. S., and G. S. Weiss. 1966. *Survey of Financial Characteristics of Consumers.* Washington, D.C.: Board of Governors of the Federal Reserve System.

Pryor, F. L. 1977. Some costs and benefits of market: An empirical study. *Q. J. Econ.* 91:81–102.

Rothschild, K. W.   1973.   Military expenditure, exports and growth. *Kyklos* 26(Fasc. 4):804–14.

Schumpeter, J. A.   1954.   *History of Economic Analysis*.   New York: Oxford University Press.

Searle, A. D., and C. A. Waite.   1980.   Current efforts to measure productivity in the public sector: How adequate for the national accounts?   In *New Developments in Productivity Measurement and Analysis*, ed. J. W. Kendrick and B. N. Vaccara. Chicago: University of Chicago Press.

Smith, D.   1975.   Public consumption and economic performance. *Natl. Westminster Bank Q. Rev.*, November:17–30.

Smith, R. P.   1977.   Military expenditure and capitalism.   *Cambridge J. Econ.* 1:61–76.

————.   1980.   Military expenditure and investment in OECD countries, 1954–1973.   *J. Comp. Econ.* 4:19–32.

Smith, V.   1975.   A note on Baumol's unbalanced growth model. *Public Finance* 30:127–30.

Spann, R. M.   1977.   The macroeconomics of unbalanced growth and the expanding public sector.   *J. Public Econ.* 8:397–404.

Summers, R., I. Kravis, and A. Heston.   1980.   International comparison of real product and its composition: 1950–1977.   *Rev. Income Wealth*, ser. 26:19–66.

Szymanski, A.   1973.   Military spending and economic stagnation. *Am. J. Sociol.* 79:1–14.

Tanzi, V.   1968.   Comparing international tax burdens: A suggested method.   *J. Polit. Econ.* 76:1078–84.

————.   1969.   *The Individual Income Tax and Economic Growth*. Baltimore: Johns Hopkins University Press.

Thurow, L. C.   1971.   *The Impact of Taxes on the American Economy*. New York: Praeger.

Von Furstenberg, G. M.   1980.   The effect of the changing size and composition of government purchases on potential output.   *Rev. Econ. Stat.* 42:74–80.

Von Furstenberg, G. M., and B. G. Malkiel.   1977.   The government and capital formation: A survey of recent issues.   *J. Econ. Lit.* 15:835–878.

Watson, W.   1978.   Bacon and Eltis on growth, government and welfare.   *J. Comp. Econ.* 2:43–56.

Whiting, A.   1976.   An international comparison of the instability of economic growth.   *Three Banks Rev.*, no. 109:26–46.

Whynes, D. K.   1979.   *The Economics of Third World Military Expenditures*.   Austin: University of Texas Press.

Wilson, T.   1966.   Instability and the rate of growth.   *Lloyds Bank Rev.*, no. 81:16–32.

Withers, G. A.   1980.   Unbalanced growth and the demand for performing arts: An econometric analysis.   *South. Econ. J.* 46: 735–42.

Worcester, D. A.   1968.   Macroeconomics of unbalanced growth: Comment.   *Am. Econ. Rev.* 58:886–93.

Wright, C.   1969.   Saving and the rates of interest.   In *The Taxation of Income from Capital*, ed. A. C. Harberger and M. J. Bailey.   Washington, D.C.:   Brookings Institution.

8

The Political Economy of
Comparative Economic Growth

As we have examined so far, the various models of economic
growth differ sharply in terms of the specification of the various
determinants of growth, but nearly all of them exhibit one important characteristic. The conditions of these models are almost invariably interpreted in a purely quantitative manner, without consideration of the possibility that quantitatively distinct patterns
of growth may reflect, or may be reflected by, qualitative changes
in the structural relations that underlie the growth process. What
this type of analysis fails to account for are the changes in economic institutions that are necessarily connected to, and implied
by, the extensive growth of the economy. The theory of economic
growth needs to go beyond the specification of the movement of economic magnitudes in order to establish the organic connections between economic growth and the development of the economic structure
as a whole.

Recently, Mancur Olson (1976) proposed a hypothesis on comparative economic growth. The essence of his theory stems from his
previous attempt to explain group conservatism by reference to rational economic behavior (Olson 1965). The overall structure of
Olson's theory of comparative economic growth goes as follows: he
first spells out a fundamental common feature of the common interest organizations that are the main economic agents in his model,
then suggests the ultimate patterns of organized interest groups,
and lastly discusses the impact that common-interest organizations
have on the rate of economic growth.

COMMON-INTEREST GROUPS: FUNDAMENTAL FEATURES
To understand the model of political economy of comparative
growth rates by Olson, it is necessary to understand the agents
that are essential to his model and the common feature that can be
derived from the behavior of those agents. The Olson model takes
account of a factor that other economists ignore: the associations

of firms or individuals that together have monopoly power or political influence or both. Among the obvious common-interest associations are labor unions, professional associations, farm organizations, trade associations, employers associations, lobbies, and
cartels. The informally or even tacitly collusive groups that are
not formally organized are less obvious but should be included.
This change in orientation is the simple result of a change in the
kind of question and in the perspective the theory is designed to
answer.

To understand these common-interest organizations and groups,
we must first define these associations and then have an adequate
model of their formation and functioning. What is an interest
group? Terminology used in the literature varies. Even a cursory
glance at the literature will reveal the following terms: political group, lobby, interest group, political interest group, special
interest group, organized group, voluntary association, pressure
group, cause group, sectional group, promotional group, attitude
group, protective group, institutional group, defensive group, ano-
mic group, associational group, exclusive group, partial group, and
the like. Terminology itself is not so important for our discussion. Demands are articulated by people acting individually and by
people working through groups. One major difficulty in defining
the common-interest group lies in distinguishing these activities
from one another. Since Arthur F. Bentley (1949), who developed
classical group theory, many writers in sociology and political
science have discussed the topic (see Olson 1965). Modern group
theorists' ideas of group behavior can be seen at a glance by looking at definitions of the interest group.

According to David Truman (1951, p. 37), "An interest group is
a shared-attitude group that makes certain claims upon other groups
in the society." Since Truman thought that most interest groups
are weak and divided in those circumstances in which they ask too
much from society--because of overlapping memberships among the
groups--he believed that interest groups attain the final equilibrium position of the social system and that this group equilibrium
tends to be just and desirable. S. E. Finer (1958, p. 237) defines
interest groups as "all groups or associations which seek to influence public policy in their own chosen direction, while declining
to accept direct responsibility for ruling the country."

A tradition of thought underlying these definitions holds that
collective decisions can be viewed as the result of the pressures
of all the interested groups and that policies determined in this
way are "just." The view has flourished in the United States, and
most traditional group theorists have maintained that whenever a
number of individuals share a common interest, they will act col-
lectively to further it.

Olson (1965, p. 127) put forward the most fundamental criticism of the traditional or orthodox group approach. He questioned
the whole rationale of group membership and argued that there are
fundamental inconsistencies in the thinking of the interest group
theorists. In his words, "The analytical pluralists, the 'group

theorists,' have built their theory around an inconsistency." The suggested inconsistency is that the group theorists "have assumed that, if a group had some reason or incentive to organize to further its interest, the rational individuals in that group would also have a reason or an incentive to support an organization working in their mutual interest." This logic is false, at least for large, latent groups with economic interests because "if the individuals in any large group are interested in their own welfare, they will *not* voluntarily make any sacrifices to help their group attain its political (public or collective) objectives (Olson 1965, p. 126).

To explain group membership, Olson (1965, p. 51) introduces the concept of "selective incentive." Thus an individual in a common-interest group will be stimulated to act in a group-oriented way "only through an incentive that operates, not indiscriminately, like the collective good, upon the group as a whole, but rather selectively toward the individuals in the group."

Though Olson's model and the hypotheses derived from it encompass some organizations and groups that many economic analyses ignore, the postulates underlying the behavior of common-interest organizations are those most commonly used in economic analysis. The basic model of group behavior used by Olson is one of Cournot behavior in the presence of a public good. In his model, each individual attempts to maximize his satisfaction, taking the behavior of others as given. A fundamental common feature of all interest groups and associations is that whatever else these groups do, each and every one provides some service to everyone in some group. In other words, each of the types of associations and combinations provides what the economist defines as a "public good": a good that goes to everyone in some group if it goes to anyone in that group.

More specifically, Olson (1976, p. 29) maintains that

> if a union wins high wages, the higher wages go to every worker in each relevant category; if a cartel raises the price of some good, every firm selling that good in the relevant market enjoys the higher price; if a farm organization or other lobbying group obtains legislation favorable to some group, everyone in that group benefits from it.

The reason why only coercion or other selective incentives can lead rational individuals in large common-interest groups to act in their common interest is that each individual gets only a miniscule share of the benefits of any action he takes in the group interest and will get the benefit of any amount of the public good that might somehow be provided by others whether he contributes or not. The external economy of individual action in the interest of a group that is too large for its members to bargain with one another ensures that voluntary action without selective incentives cannot lead to a level of provision of the service that is optimal for the group.

To summarize, it is difficult to organize and maintain interest groups, even if there are many latent groups of people with
similar interests. These difficulties stem from the fact that the
political and economic benefits provided by interest groups to
their members are public goods. Thus individuals are not interested in becoming or staying members since they have no reason to
sacrifice money and time to get the collective good that is either
provided in any case or the supply of which cannot be influenced by
them. As a consequence, Olson concludes that big latent groups can
only be organized if the interest groups in question provide private goods (besides indivisible public goods) or if they can en-
force the membership of the people in question.

ULTIMATE PATTERNS OF ORGANIZED INTEREST GROUPS
The logic of collective action has several implications for
the patterns of organization of interest groups in democratic society. One is that there is a different effectiveness in the organization of small and large groups. Olson (1965, p. 52) maintains
that "size is one of the determining factors in deciding whether or
not it is possible that voluntary, rational pursuit of individual
interest will bring forth group-oriented behavior. Small groups
will further their common interests better than large groups." Obviously, the difficulty of organizing a large group of scattered
interests lies in the fact that sufficiently large groups will not
be able to provide themselves with any of the public good whatever
unless there are selective incentives. Such groups as consumers,
taxpayers, the unemployed, and the poor are a good example in question. They certainly have important common interests and surely
would benefit substantially if there were effective mass organizations working on their behalf. As is evident from the logic of
collective behavior as well as from observation and experience,
consumers, taxpayers, the unemployed, or the poor have not found a
way of organizing their common interest on a systematic and massive
scale.
This different effectiveness of organization between small and
large group interests in Olson's theory makes a sharp contrast to
the traditional theory, which emphasizes the universality of participation in voluntary associations in modern societies and explains small groups and large associations in terms of the same
causes, like the "structural differentiation." Because in some
small groups each of the members, or at least one of them, finds
that personal gain from having the collective good exceeds the total cost of providing some amount of that collective good, certain
small groups can provide themselves with a collective good even
without relying on coercion or any positive inducements apart from
the collective good itself, as is true in the case of large groups.
The proposition that small groups are qualitatively different
from large ones does not imply that small common-interest associations will be organized easily and quickly as soon as the common
interests emerge, while the large and scattered interests will nev-

er be able to organize on a mass basis. Another implication of the
Olson logic of collective choice is that even those groups that can
be organized into effective voluntary associations usually will not
be organized until some time after the common interests emerge.

Historical experience confirms that it takes quite a bit of
time for groups with common interests to organize. It was not until 1851, or virtually a century after the start of the industrial
revolution, that the first true labor union (The Amalgamated Society of Engineers, in Britain) was formed. Although in the United
States there are many unions that go back to the second half of the
nineteenth century, the fastest growth of labor unions was during
the years between world wars I and II, long after the country had
achieved the industrialized condition most favorable to unions.
Some continental countries developed their most powerful unions
only after World War II, or have yet to develop them. Even though
farmers constituted a large part of the population and had significant common interests at the founding of the United States, it was
not until the organization of the Farm Bureau, just after World War
I, that there was any large and stable farm organization in the
United States. The slow accumulation of common-interest organization is not an accident, but a reflection of the inherent difficulty of organizing large groups to obtain public goods. Since bargaining, given the incentive to hold out for better terms, can take
a long while, even small groups will sometimes organize only slowly.

EFFECT OF COMMON-INTEREST GROUPS ON ECONOMIC GROWTH
The last part of Olson's theory of comparative growth concerns
the impact that common-interest organizations and informal collusive arrangement have on the rate of economic growth. The main
question is, "Will the accumulation of common-interest organizations deter or promote the growth of an economy?" Olson's answer,
based on his logic of collective action, depends on the comprehensiveness or the size of each group relative to the society of which
it is a part. To put the conclusion first, the accumulation of
narrowly based common-interest organizations will have a substantial adverse effect on the rate of growth of an economy, while
highly encompassing common-interest organizations, each of which
has a noticeable percentage of society's population of resources,
could increase social efficiency, take action in the interest of
society, and promote growth in the society. Since a great many
common-interest organizations are so small in relation to the economy as a whole, Olson concludes that the accumulation of most common-interest organizations will have an adverse effect on rates of
growth of national product.

We will discuss first the theoretical part upon which Olson's
main conclusion on the comparative economic growth is based and
then consider the various cases of experiences among countries and/
or among types of typical common-interest associations.

Why is the pursuit of the group interest by a small, narrowly

based common-interest organization detrimental to economic growth
and that by a comprehensive common-interest association conducive
to social efficiency, thereby promoting growth? Other things being
equal, the members of any common-interest group, regardless of the
comprehensiveness of the groups in the society, will be better off
if the economy in which they operate grows. If the people in the
rest of the society are better off, there will tend to be more demand for whatever the members of a common-interest group produce,
unless it is an inferior good. If the society in which a group operates is more productive, the odds are that its members will be
able to buy the goods they want on better terms. So, if it did not
cost anything, the typical common-interest group would opt for policies that would increase economic efficiency.

The pursuit of social efficiency at the expense of the group
interest involves a real cost to the members when the group is
small. Small groups are not like individuals in perfectly competitive markets, where individual self-interests promote both the private and common good. Through the elimination of some measures
(upon which the fate of a group in question depends) to promote social efficiency and economic growth, the members of the common-interest group (which accounts for a small portion of the society in
terms of its members or resources under its control) would normally
suffer a substantial loss, even if the total social gains from the
change were many times larger than the costs, since the members of
the common-interest group get only a negligible share of the gains
to the society at large, while they bear the full costs of the
change. Thus the narrowly based common-interest associations are
not likely to give a high priority to any measures that would benefit their members only to the extent that these members get a mi-
nute share of any increase they bring about in the size of the national pie.

The conclusion that common-interest groups have adverse effects on the rate of growth of the economy does not apply to those
groups that are highly encompassing. The reason is that in highly
comprehensive organizations a member can internalize most of the
external effects of action taken in the interest of the association. Common-interest organizations that are quite large in relation to the society will internalize much of the benefit of any action they take in the interest of society or much of the cost of
any action that reduces efficiency, raises prices, or slows growth
in the society.

Most of the common-interest organizations around us are not
highly encompassing ones. Labor unions, though their members run
into the tens or even hundreds of thousands, represent less than 1
percent of the work force. Though trade associations may represent
a number of substantial corporations, they do not account for more
than a miniscule share of a nation's capital stock. Other typical
common-interest organizations such as professional associations,
farm organizations, lobbies, and cartels, though they have sizable
resources under their control, do not have a noticeable percentage
of the society's population or resources.

While each inefficiency resulting from the pursuit of group

interests by the fragmented common-interest organization will bring
about only a one-time reduction in the absolute level of income
rather than a reduction in the rate of growth, the continuing accumulation of such inefficiencies over time, which Olson's logic of
collective action predicts, will lower the rate of growth in the
long run.

Before we examine a long list of growth-repressing, ineffi-
ciency-generating practices by the fragmented common-interest organization, we have to see whether, and why, interest groups are in
fact able to influence political decisions. The answer comes from
Peter Bernholz (1977), who shows that the platforms of political
parties whose aim is to win the election by catering to the wishes
of large groups of voters, whether they are organized or not, have
to follow the wishes of the interest groups favoring their members
to the disadvantage of unorganized parts of the population. In
studying the importance of interest groups with numerical examples,
Bernholz proves that under some conditions the influence of organized interest groups is greater than that of the same group of voters if they were unorganized. In Bernholz's (1977, p. 418) words,
"The power of parties and the government is supplanted by that of
the interest groups." The citation of Bernholz (1977, p. 12) from
his previous work (Bernholz 1969) that "the formation of interest
groups can imply additional political power for their members, if
they or their members enjoy market power or a quasi-monopoly of information in the fields of their activities" is quite pertinent to
our discussion.

Common-interest organizations reduce the rate of growth as
well as the level of income when they use their power to block some
of the technological advances or innovations. Advances in technology are one of the permissive sources of economic growth, but they
remain only as a potential. If technology is to be employed efficiently and widely, institutional adjustments must be made to effect the proper use of innovations generated by the advancing stock
of human knowledge. The ability of society to reap the benefits of
technological change depends on a variety of adjustment mechanisms
that transcend those directly connected with the process of technological change itself. These mechanisms, as well as those directly
related to the creation and utilization of new technology, determine the extent to which the range of economic choice is expanded
and thus the growth of the economy accelerated. If the mechanisms
do not work well, there will be serious social costs in terms of
elimination of expanded choice or reduced progress of society.

Among the most prominent of the adjustments required by technological advances are those involved in reallocating labor and
other resources to correspond to the changes in general equilibrium
and those involved in assuring that the growth in aggregate demand
matches the expansion of economic potential. A labor union often
has an incentive to try to repress each labor-saving innovation
that would reduce the demand for skilled workers. Unions become especially concerned when new techniques threaten the job security of
their members. The word "sabotage" was coined when laborers threw
their wooden shoes (sabots) into the works of the new machines

brought in by the Industrial Revolution to replace workers. Unions
in building trades have frequently restricted the use of spray
guns, fearing that workers will paint themselves out of jobs. Similarly, whenever a single firm develops an improved product or
method of production that its competitors could successfully copy
only after a substantial delay, the competitors will have an incentive to use their trade association or cartel to block or delay
the innovation. Moreover, when an industry is nationalized or regulated as a public utility, or for other reasons is subject to political dictations, and the pertinent common-interest organizations
have power to veto certain changes, innovations will take longer to
implement and the growth rate will be slowed.

The shifting of human and material resources is an essential
part of the mechanism by which society exploits the possibilities
opened by technological progress. Full exploitation of the benefits of technological advances requires also that those released
from superseded activities find productive work. If diesel engines
are to be produced, capital, labor, and materials must be mar-
shaled. If the men previously involved in producing steam engines
stand idle long, and the resources newly employed in the production
of diesel engines are drawn from high value alternatives, the net
value of the output generated by technological advance may even be
negative.

The choice of techniques and technological change are often
discussed as purely economic problems, but economists have not systematically taken account of the systems of political economy to
which their discussions refer. In almost all discussions, the
choice of techniques or the creation of new innovations is reduced
to a purely economic business under the assumption of a planned
economy with rather strictly defined characteristics. One contribution of Olson's political economy of comparative growth lies in
its pointing out that this type of conventional analysis cannot be
applied as it stands to an economy where there are many fragmented
common-interest organizations seeking their groups' interests at
the expense of the public interest. We have to take account of
economic and social organizations to see why certain techniques are
used and what consequences they have.

Even when there are no technological changes and innovations,
somewhere within the historically given structure, forces will be
pushing toward change and therefore toward a change in all parts of
the structure. Economic growth is almost always associated with
changes in the structure of the economy. Successful economic
growth therefore involves, inter alia, the maintenance of a high
degree of flexibility of resource use. Anything that obstructs a
transference of population and resources from the high productive
to the low productive sector(s) will hold back growth.

Even though the fact that an economy that finds it increasingly difficult to accommodate itself to these changes will necessarily encounter increasing difficulties in sustaining its growth was
recognized in the past, it was not dealt with systematically. For
example, Ingvar Svennilson (1954, p. 206) observes:

There is no doubt that, in the oldest and most advanced
industrial countries, transformation of the economy in accordance with the new trends in technology and demand meets with
strong resistance from the accumulated stock of capita, from
the traditional special skill of labor--in fact from the whole
organization of society. . . . On the other hand, resistance
is much weaker in a society which offers a virgin soil for the
development of manufacturing industries.

Svennilson's thesis presumes that the obstacles to resource mobility are increasing functions of an economy's maturity. This, exactly, is one of the propositions that Olson's theory of the common-interest group can predict. But Svennilson's thesis was just a
conjecture or an observation not based on a theory. Even if there
was considerable resource immobility in British industry, it is not
clear why these immobilities are greater than those in Japan.

Olson's theory of collective action applied to the common-interest associations provides reasons for the causes of immobility
and misallocation of resources--tariffs, fair trade laws, monopoly,
featherbedding, and tax loopholes. In each of these cases, a spe-
cial-interest group seeks to protect its economic advantage by limiting the movement of resources, which robs the nation of output.
Specific businesses and resource suppliers caught in declining industries have often sought, with government help, to impede the reallocation of resources essential to economic growth. Monopolies
in both product and resource markets have retarded the reallocation
of such resources. The principle of seniority seems to conflict
strongly with efficiency--the selection or retention of the most
able or productive worker for each job. The use of seniority to
govern layoffs and promotions has contributed to the secular decrease in the voluntary mobility of labor.

Other important restrictive practices in some unions are
featherbedding and a full crew rule. Featherbedding refers to any
rules imposed on employers merely for the purpose of keeping up the
demand for workers; a full crew rule specifies the minimum number
of workers to be employed for a given task. Unions involved in
featherbedding are narrowly organized along craft lines that are
characterized by noncompetitive operations. The specific labor
groups engaged in featherbedding do not allow employers to modify
job assignments of the workers. This implies that the elasticity
of substitution for specific groups in a firm is zero or close to
zero. Under this procedure, labor would be a semivariable cost.
Since the amount of redundant work to be performed by the firm is a
function of output, the featherbedding rule affects the height and
shape of the variable costs and, given the structure of the industry, reduces output.

One important way in which common-interest organizations reduce the rate of growth is by limiting entry into the industries
and occupations they control. One key feature of the market environment of firms for the determination of their behavior is the
ease with which new competitors can enter the industry. Expansion

of prosperous industries is a self-limiting process; as new firms
enter growing industries, economic profits are competed away.
Therefore, firms now established in these prosperous industries may
contrive monopolistic restrictions upon the entry of new firms in
an effort to preserve economic profits for themselves. Of course,
the monopolistic practices by the firms already in the industry are
not the only barrier. An entry barrier can also be created by factors such as huge capital requirements and product differentiation,
partly natural and partly created through advertising.

The control of labor supply is often considered to be a source
of union power. The most effective type of control is control over
the number of people who can be trained for an occupation or profession. By limiting the number trained, the organization can protect or raise the earnings of its members. There is strong evidence that the American Medical Association has had such power.
The closed shop, which requires employers to hire only union members, is a type of entry-limiting practice. In licensed occupations such as plumbers, electricians, and barbers, the unions sometimes nominate members of the licensing boards. If such boards
deny licenses to qualified workers, they can help raise the wages
of license holders.

Olson's theory predicts that a society with greater barriers
to entry not only will have a lower absolute level of income but
also will grow less rapidly than an otherwise identical society
with lesser barriers to entry.

The list of examples of restrictive efficiency-reducing practices by the fragmented common-interest groups can be extended beyond the cases we have discussed so far—innovation slowing, entry
limiting, and reallocation resisting. One such extended example is
tariffs or quotas. While nations as a whole usually gain from
free international trade, particular industries and groups of resource suppliers can be hurt. For example, specialization and
trade adversely affect the American coffee and Brazilian steel industries. It is easy to see, with Olson's theory, why such groups
seek to preserve or improve their economic positions by persuading
the government to impose tariffs or quotas to protect them from
the deleterious effects of free trade. If such a group goes out
for free trade or some other measure to increase economic efficiency, its members will bear the full cost of the campaign but
only a miniscule share of the benefits, since they are, by stipu-
lation, a miniscule part of the economy. Similarly, even if the
total social gains from the removal of all tax loopholes or the
elimination of subsidies or a cartel were many times larger than
the costs, the trade association or professional organization does
not favor the change, since its members suffer a substantial loss
from the change and get only a negligible share of the gains to the
society at large.

Robert J. Lieber (1974) analyzes the influence of interest
groups in the formation of British policy toward successive European unity developments in the years from 1956 to 1967. Even
though Lieber's main objective was (by testing two hypotheses:

group politics and functionalists) to show that due to the effective politicization of the European issue the power of sectional
pressure groups over Britain's European policy-making declined
over successive periods (1950-1960, negotiations for a Free Trade
Area and then a European Free Trade Association; 1961-1963, the
Macmillan government attempt at Common Market entry; 1966-1967,
the Wilson government renewal of the Common Market entry), his
study makes a very good case of how interest groups pursue their
own interests at the expense of public interest. Three of the most
important groups treated in Lieber's paper are the Confederation of
British Industry (CBI), National Farmer's Union (NFU), and Trade
Union Congress (TUC). As expected, throughout the initial period,
all three groups were hostile to the idea of outright Common Market
membership, fearing that this would constitute a first step toward
complete integration and development of a central authority that
would overrule national governments on important economic matters,
thus eliminating the privileges they were enjoying.
      Lieber (1974, p. 33), based on logic similar to Olson's, ob-
serves:

      Basically, pressure groups influence policy formation
      whenever the criteria for judgement are based more upon the
      foreseeable balance of economic gain and loss than upon broad-
      er conceptions of national interest or political benefit. As
      a result, policy initiatives which threaten identifiable costs
      to significant interests, even though these may represent a
      minority of the sector involved, are likely to be opposed.
      Comprehensive groups such as CBI and NFU will tailor their po-
      sition so as not to outrage important sectors of their member-
      ship; and in a setting which remains nonpoliticized, political
      parties will play little role in the policy process. The re-
      sult, therefore, is likely to be that profound new ventures
      such as those involving European unity cannot be made so long
      as pressure groups provide the main constituency for policy
      makers.

The decline in opposing pressures by the major groups was caused by
the effective politicization of the European unity as a matter of
major national importance rather than as a relatively specialized
or economic question.
      Albert Rees (1962, pp. 194-95), who is a leading expert in la-
bor unions, arrived at the conclusion that unions have an adverse
effect on growth, when he wrote:

      If the union is viewed solely in terms of its effect on
      the economy, it must in my opinion be considered an obstacle
      to the optimum performance of our economic system. It alters
      the wage structure in a way that impedes the growth of employ-
      ment in sectors of the economy where productivity and income
      are naturally high and that leaves too much labor in low-in-
      come sectors of the economy like southern agriculture and the

least skilled service trades. It benefits most of those workers who would in any case be relatively well off, and while
some of this gain may be at the expense of the owners of capital, most of it must be at the expense of consumers and the
low-paid workers. Unions interfere blatantly with the use of
the most productive techniques in some industries, and the effect is probably not offset by the stimulus to higher productivity furnished by some other unions.

     In our discussion so far, monopolistic practices by the com-
mon-interest associations have not been listed as one of the costs
to society. Common-interest organizations and collusions do exercise monopoly power and maximize profits when they equate marginal
revenue rather than price to marginal cost. We do not intend,
here, to review the extensive literature on monopoly theory, which
may be roughly classified into three categories: the so-called
antitrust literature, which generally criticizes monopoly from the
standpoint of the competitive model; that concerned with the secular trends operating in a highly developed capitalist system; and
the theory of imperfect or monopolistic competition, essentially
an outgrowth of the competitive model. But it is useful to discuss
the main outline to see the magnitude of losses from the divergence
between the marginal cost and price.
     The result of the monopolization is that consumers have to
contract their consumption of the product; resources that would
have been used in that industry go elsewhere to produce other products less wanted by consumers. The neoclassical method for measuring the welfare loss from monopoly was employed in 1959 by A. C.
Harberger (1954, 1959) and has been developed by many others (see
Kamerschen 1966; Schwartzman 1966; Bergson 1973; Worcester 1973;
Carson 1975; Cowling and Mueller 1978).
     The numerical estimates of the welfare costs have been undra-
matic, as is seen from the apparently small size of the deadweight
loss triangle. Harberger estimates that the deadweight welfare
loss from monopoly in the manufacturing sector was equal to 0.1
percent of GNP at most. There have been some important modern
counterattacks on the Harberger analysis, the most notable being
those of David Kamerschen, Gordon Tullock, R. A. Posner, and Keith
Cowling and Dennis Mueller.
     Kamerschen (1966) followed essentially the Harberger method-
ology but assumed an elasticity of demand consistent with monopoly
pricing behavior at the industry level and obtained welfare loss as
high as 6 percent.
     Tullock (1967) contended that the Harberger measure of the so-
cial costs of monopoly is biased downward. This is mainly because
resources are wasted in the competitive bidding for the monopoly
"prize." Not only are resources invested in lobbying for the monopoly power but opponents spend money trying politically to prevent the success of the protectionists. Tullock (1967, pp. 228,
232) continues, "These expenditures, which may simply offset each
other to some extent, are purely wasteful from the standpoint of
society as a whole; they are spent not in increasing wealth, but in

an attempt to transfer or resist transfer of wealth." The current
neoclassical analysis of the deadweight loss is conducted in an institutional vacuum; individuals pursue their self-interest within
given rules that are costlessly imposed. "The total cost of monopoly should be measured in terms of the efforts to get a monopoly by
the unsuccessful as well as by the successful."

More important, Posner (1975) argued that monopoly pricing
would be more successful in industries where regulatory agencies
limited entry and price competition. His estimate of the social
costs of monopoly in regulated industries was around 1.7 percent of
GNP, much higher than the result by Harberger. Though the problem
of identifying and measuring the welfare loss of monopoly is difficult, the losses can be substantial when entry is blocked or where
interest groups can, through their link with the government, make
private and social cost diverge to some degree.

Leveling several objections against the Harberger-type approach, Cowling and Mueller (1978) obtain estimates significantly
greater than those of previous studies. (Their four criticisms are
constant price elasticity of demand in all industries, constant degree of monopoly, aggregation bias based on the use of industry
profit rates, and abstraction of the social costs in the acquisition of monopoly positions.) Using the data at the firm level,
they obtain estimates ranging between 4 and 13 percent of the gross
corporate product for the United States during 1963-1964. The aggregate estimates of welfare loss for the United Kingdom range between 3.9 and 7.2 percent of the gross corporate product for the
1968-1969 period. Even using the same method that Harberger adopted produces a higher welfare loss, ranging 0.4 to 7 percent for the
United States and 0.2 to 3 percent for the United Kingdom.

We have discussed in some detail a variety of examples of how
some types of common-interest groups can make their members better
off by reducing economic efficiency. From Olson's logic of collective action and from the cases examined above, one can reach a conclusion that most common-interest organizations will have an adverse effect on rates of growth of national output. Therefore, it
follows that a society with more powerful common-interest groups
will not only have a lower absolute level of income but will also
grow less rapidly than an otherwise identical society with weaker
common-interest associations.

While a great many common-interest organizations, which are so
small in relation to the economy as a whole, pursue their own group
interest detrimental to the performance of the overall economy, the
common-interest organizations that are sufficiently encompassing
will internalize much of the costs of inefficient policies and have
an incentive to give great weight to economic growth and to the interests of society as a whole. Olson (1976, p. 39) took the case
to the logical extreme and said that "the national government itself encompasses everyone in a society; this means that . . . the
national government itself, when not influenced by lobbying groups,
has an incentive to promote efficiency and growth."

Examples of the highly encompassing organizations and their
productivity-promoting behavior are found in the experiences of

some European countries. In Sweden the main common-interest organizations are unusually encompassing. Walter Galenson (1961, pp.
73-74), who is a well-known expert in this field, described Sweden
as the "organizational society par excellence" in the Western
world. The main trade union federations--the Confederation of
Swedish Trade Union (LO), the Central Organization of Salaried Employees (TCO), and the Swedish Professional Association (SACU)--to-
gether represent the highest percentage of workers in any market-
oriented economy. The employers, in turn, are represented by the
Swedish Employers Association (SAF), whose main aim is to safeguard
the interests of the employers in questions concerning their relations with employees.

Evidence of the extreme centralization and coordination of
Swedish labor policy is to be seen in the structure and functions
of the national Labor Market Board, which is composed of two members of the SAF, two from the LO, one from the TCO, one representative each from agriculture and female workers, and three representatives of government. The board has broad responsibilities in labor planning and policy. Collective bargaining is forced to remain
socially oriented as well as oriented to the special interests of
each side of the bargaining process. Strikes, though not illegal,
are little used because Swedish unions realize that in the long
run, worker incomes depend on increased productivity and strikes
are incompatible with that goal. Sweden has the highest percent of
unionized work force but the lowest strike level. The rate of unionization ranges from about 88 percent of all workers in Sweden to
about 74 percent in Finland, 72 percent in Denmark, 50 percent in
Italy, 40 percent in Germany and the Netherlands, 35 percent in
Japan and Canada, 25 percent in the United States, and 22 percent
in France (see *OECD Observer* 1978). As Olson's model predicts, the
Swedish system advocates various growth-increasing policies, combining micro and macro interests.

Though the degree of unionization is not high (about 38 percent), trade unions in the Netherlands are quite encompassing:
three major national trade union federations represent 80 percent
of all organized workers. Collective bargaining between employers
and employees is more apt to be bargaining between the interested
parties through their representatives on the Social and Economic
Council, which consists of members from labor, business, and government represented equally. The constant involvement of the Dutch
union in national policy decisions has created a "remarkable system
of bargaining," as Galenson (1961, p. 33) has called it. An observation by John Windmuller (1969, p. 383) that "macro-economic considerations have always been uppermost in the economic policies of
the unions, especially at federation levels," well characterizes
the Dutch industrial relations.

The spirit of the encompassing trade unions in the Nordic
countries and the Netherlands makes a sharply contrasting case with
the prevailing spirit of the American and British union movement,
often summed up in the descriptive phrase "business unionism,"
which means that the union is primarily engaged in advancing the

interests of its members through seeking improvements in their own
wages, hours, and working conditions and is only secondarily concerned with pursuing socially efficient policies.

OPERATIONAL HYPOTHESES

We can now summarize the argument by Olson and put it in operational hypotheses to be tested later. From the public-good nature
of the services provided to members of the interest group, several
propositions can be derived for the pattern of organization of interest groups in a democratic society and for the relationship between formations and functions of common interest groups and economic growth.

Olson's model of comparative rates of economic growth is based
on the economist's theory of public goods, which shows that the
gradual accumulation of common-interest organizations is not a historical accident but rather is inherent in the logic of the formation of organized groups. This logic of collective action implies
that the largest and most scattered interests will presumably never
be able to organize on a mass basis, and even those interest groups
that can be organized into effective voluntary associations are not
usually so organized until some time after the common interests
emerge. This characteristic of organization and formation is stated in hypotheses I and II.

Hypothesis I. Some groups in democratic societies will not be
effectively organized to promote their common interests, even when
gains to the group as a whole from such organization would far exceed the costs, no matter how long a period is available to promote
a common-interest organization.

Hypothesis II. Common-interest organizations accumulate gradually in societies with continued freedom of organization.

According to Guy Caire (1977, pp. 13-14), "Freedom of associations entails, in particular, the rights for workers and employers,
without distinction whatsoever, to establish and to join organizations of their own choosing without previous authorizations; . . .
there can be freedom of association without a number of civil lib-
erties."

The expected functional relationship between the common-interest associations and economic growth is stated in hypotheses III
and IV.

Hypothesis III. Common-interest organizations and informally
coordinated collusive groups that do not control a sizable share of
a society's resources will have an adverse net effect on the rate
of economic growth.

Hypothesis IV. Highly encompassing organizations will have
policies that are less restrictive of growth than common-interest
organizations or collusions that control only a negligible proportion of resources in a society.

Having identified the formation pattern of common-interest groups and their effects on growth, we can advance some derivative hypotheses. Those that concern us most in the study of comparative rates of growth are II and III. If hypotheses II and III are correct, we would expect the following hypothesis to be supported:

Hypothesis V. The longer the period in which a country or a region has had a modern industrial pattern of common interests, and, at the same time, democratic freedom of organization without upheaval or invasion, the greater the extent to which the growth rate will be slowed by organized interests.

Specifically:

Hypothesis V-a. There exists a positive association between the power of common-interest organizations and the length of time interest groups have been in existence.
Hypothesis V-b. Both the length of time interest groups have been in existence and the strength of the power they have should have a negative relationship with the economic growth of the community.

OBSERVATIONS OF OLSON'S THEORY
AGAINST COUNTRY AND REGIONAL EXPERIENCES OF THE UNITED STATES
Although detailed statistical tests of the hypotheses put forward in the previous section are to be presented in the following chapter, it would be worthwhile to examine the relevance of the theory against the experiences of some countries and of regions in the United States.
From hypothesis V, it follows that countries whose common-interest organizations have been emasculated or abolished by totalitarian governments and foreign occupation should tend to grow relatively quickly after a free and stable legal order is established. This helps explain why the defeated, war-torn countries--Germany, Japan, and Italy--saw the unexpected high rates of growth. In these countries, totalitarian governments were followed by allied occupiers who were determined to promote institutional change and ensure that institutional life would start almost anew after World War II.
Nazi control of Germany had done away with independent unions, as well as all other dissenting groups, while the occupation of Germany by the Allies emasculated cartels and organizations with right-wing backgrounds. When common-interest organizations were established in Germany after World War II, it appears that they were, for the most part, highly encompassing. The DGB (Deutsche Gewerkschafts Bund) is the dominant national trade union federation, and it represents most of the organized workers. The employers' associations are very highly organized, strong, and centralized. The codetermination by employees and employers in the management of industrial activities forces both sides to remain socially oriented.

Prior to World War II, government policy in Japan was hospitable to cartels and to the growth of the Zaibatsu. The American occupation introduced an antimonopoly law designed to foster competition and also thereby, in conjunction with several other major measures, to promote the democratization of Japan. The Allied powers dissolved the Zaibatsu into separate units and purged leaders of it and other organizations. This had a salutory effect: the purge put enterprising young men in the saddle. The assertion that the Japanese economy has been highly competitive accords ill with the common view of Japan as a country where the state exerts great influence over the economy and where economic power is concentrated. According to Eugene Rotwein's (1976) calculation, the proportion of the Japanese national income originating from "high market concentration" was 16 percent in 1956, while the corresponding figure in 1970 was 18.6 percent. This small shift in market concentration over a long period of time implies that effective collusive arrangements are not present now. Eleanor Hadley (1970), who has done extensive work on the internal structure of the "big three"--Mitsui, Mitsubishi, and Sumimoto--has shown in considerable detail that these groups are substantially less unified than the Zaibatsu of the prewar period. The keenness of competition in Japanese industry is also shown by the ineffectiveness of cartels and price-fixing bodies. The different fortunes of the British and Japanese steel industries, for example, are not wholly unconnected with the contrasting price policies in the two countries. These conditions have favored rapid structural changes in response to altered markets, for a readiness to discard old industries and to turn to new ventures is necessary to keep up a high pace of economic growth. The Japanese government, on the whole and except for agriculture, has been faithful to this principle.

The ethnic and religious homogeneity of Japanese society contributed to the establishment of common-interest organizations having a relatively encompassing character. Thus the absence of any very dense accumulation of powerful fragmented common-interest organizations proves to be a valid and powerful explanation for the unprecedented record of the Japanese economic growth. G. C. Allen (1974), a well-known student of Japanese economic growth, points out the same underlying causes of remarkable growth when he writes, "The expansionist economy . . . is not simply the product of the successful application of the technical devices of economic management. It has derived its nourishment from the nation's social and political institutions and the attitude they foster."

Though France suffered less institutional destruction from totalitarianism and occupation during World War II than the defeated Axis powers, nonetheless it has not maintained an environment where many common-interest organizations could accumulate. French political experience since the defeat in 1940 contains a series of shocks and crises that have inescapably involved the whole nation, calling into question accepted assumptions and disturbing established habits. The experience of the German occupation, the resistance movement, the liberation, and other types of instability that might have produced such inclement climate for investment have hindered the development of common-interest organizations and collusions.

French experience shows that political stability, as such, is not necessary for growth to take place in investment and production. As Olson's model predicts, the fact that France has maintained an environment where many common-interest organizations would not effectively accumulate explains why it has had relatively good postwar growth performance and has achieved levels of income broadly comparable with other advanced countries, despite the fact that the investment climate has often been so precarious.

Tom Kemp (1962) also attributed the more rapid rates of growth achieved by the French economy since World War II to the weakening of the structural impediments inherited from the past. After investigation of the factors responsible for self-sustaining growth in France since 1945, compared with an alternate of rapid growth and relative stagnation, Jean Francois Hennart (1982) came up with the same conclusion when he said, "The main source of economic growth has not been an increase in the quantity of factors of production, but a better utilization of existing resources. The postwar expansion can thus be attributed for a large part to the realization of potentialities which previously had been neglected."

It is well known that economic growth in the United Kingdom has been decidedly slower than that of other developed countries since World War II, though no consensus about the cause has emerged. The logic of the argument in Olson's theory predicts exactly this. Great Britain has been the most stable country of all major nations, enjoying democratic freedom of organization the longest. There has been no invasion, no dictatorship, and no political upheaval in this century. The longest history of immunity from invasion and disruption, along with the fact that it has the longest history of industrial revolution, implies that it will suffer most from growth-repressing organizations and combinations. Britain has well-known powerful trade unions and less famous but strong interest groups such as a farmer's association and professional associations. Many of the powerful common-interest organizations in the United Kingdom are narrow rather than encompassing. From Olson's point of view, it follows logically that the United Kingdom, which has had the longest history of democratic freedom of organization, should have a lower rate of growth than other developed industrial countries.

Some pointed out that the root of the British industrial decline lay in the unsuccessful necessary adjustments delayed by vested interests and institutions (see Jewkes 1951). When Olson's theory proves to be correct and valid, a statement like, "For whatever reason, the pressures for achieving high levels of efficiency seem less in Britain" (Pratten 1972, p. 191), becomes quite self-explanatory.

In addition to Great Britain, the United States is surely one of the countries that has enjoyed political stability and security against invasion. Since achieving independence, the United States

has never been occupied by a foreign power. It has also been industrialized for longer than various other countries, thus maintaining the atmosphere where common-interest organizations develop.
Common-interest associations are usually narrow and less encompassing in relation to the economy as a whole than those in other
countries. The United States is also known for the conspicuous
lobbying by its pressure groups. In view of Olson's theory, it
logically follows that the United States is second to Britain in
slowness of the growth rate because it is second to Britain in the
length of time it has had freedom of organization and immunity from
foreign occupation.

One fascinating point of Olson's theory of comparative rates
of economic growth is that it can predict not only the overall
growth performance of the U.S. economy in relation to other democratic industrial countries but also regional variations in growth
rates. The duration of stable freedom of organization in the
United States varies among the regions. Whereas some parts of the
country have enjoyed stable freedom of organization for nearly 200
years, other parts were settled and organized into states only at
the turn of the century. One part of the United States, the South,
has by no means enjoyed political stability and universal democratic freedom of organization very long. The Confederate States
were defeated and devastated in the Civil War. For the states that
belonged to the Confederacy, the period of freedom of organization
and political stability is far shorter, not only because of the in-
terruption of stability by the Civil War but also because of carpetbagging and the century of restrictions on black political participation that followed the war.

Since Olson's model predicts that the longer an area has had
stable freedom of organization the more growth-retarding organizations it will accumulate, those states that belonged to the Confederacy or were settled recently should grow faster than those whose
stability and freedom of organization were not limited by the Civil
War and racial repression. Olson's theory provides a possible explanation of why the South and the Southwest are growing fast,
while the Northeast and Midwest are lagging behind.

CONCLUSIONS

The central idea in Olson's theory--advanced to cover a hypothesis explaining the phenomena of different rates of economic
growth among countries or regions in a country--is that a democratic society has an inherent tendency to develop growth-retarding
institutions or elements (common-interest groups) if it enjoys
long-term peace, stability, and freedom to form associations. The
overall rate of growth slows down as a result of the continuing accumulation of economic inefficiencies, which, in turn, develop as a
result of the efforts by common-interest organizations to make
their members better off. The underlying concept is "the logic of
collective action," using the theory of public goods.

Economists have worked a lot on the proximate causes of eco-

nomic growth and know the growth process much better now than before. But we are less secure when we try to go backward along the
causal chain toward more fundamental explanations. Olson's theory
of economic growth is one of the contributions that may have advanced our understanding of the growth process. Students of economic growth know from the beginning that political, social, and
economic forces are interacting to determine the dynamic process of
capitalistic society. But it can be fairly said that such interactions were considered as obscure and were not explicitly integrated
into any modern analysis of economic growth. Olson's theory touches the fundamental causes of different growth performance, incorporating various ad hoc explanations or "amateur sociology" (Solow
1970) such as the special industriousness of population, attitudes
of one social class or another, lack of entrepreneurial drive, rigidities in the class system, and style of education.

Interest groups have played a more powerful role in recent
decades. This is inevitable once it is largely agreed by all parties that governments should collect and spend over a third of the
national income; tremendous pressures are bound to be brought to
bear to influence the distributions of the burden and benefits of
public spending on this scale. Fiscal decisions are a means by
which group interests are expressed. Various groups maintain lobbies to exert these pressures and to advocate the particular interests they represent. Olson's theory points out flaws in the democratic process by which individual preferences are translated into
group social decisions, especially in the overall performance of
the economy in the long run.

The frame of analysis by Olson could be enlarged to accommodate inflation and perhaps employment as well. The public-good rational choice paradigm provides an elegant and parsimonious way of
cutting into a vastly complicated domain. One reservation is that
the paradigm itself does not help to solve the problem identified.

REFERENCES

Allen, G. C. 1974. Why Japan's economy has prospered. *Lloyds
    Bank Rev.*, January:29-41.
Bentley, A. F. 1949. *The Process of Government*. Evanston, Ill.:
    Principia. (First published in 1908.)
Bergson, A. 1973. On monopoly welfare loss. *Am. Econ. Rev.* 63:
    853-70.
Bernholz, P. 1969. Einige Bermerkungen zur Theorie des Einglusses
    der Verbänd auf die politische Willensbildung in der Democra-
    tie. *Kyklos* 22:276-88.
————. 1977. Dominant interest groups and powerless parties.
    Kyklos 30:411-23.
Caire, G. 1977. *Freedom of Association and Economic Development*.
    Geneva: International Labor Office.
Carson, R. 1975. On monopoly welfare losses: Comment. *Am. Econ.
    Rev.* 65:1008-14.

Castles, F. G. 1969. Business and government: A typology of pressure group activity. *Polit. Stud.* 17:160–76.

Chamberlin, J. R. 1976. A diagrammatic exposition of the logic of collection action. *Public Choice* 26:59–74.

Cowling, K., and D. C. Mueller. 1978. The social cost of monopoly power. *Econ. J.* 88:727–48.

Finer, S. E. 1958. In *Interest Groups on Four Countries*. Pittsburgh: University of Pittsburgh Press.

Galenson, W. 1961. *Trade Union Democracy in Western Europe*. Berkeley: University of California Press.

Hadley, E. M. 1970. *Antitrust in Japan*. Princeton, N.J.: Princeton University Press.

Harberger, A. C. 1954. Monopoly and resource allocation. *Am. Econ. Rev.* 44:77–87.

————. 1959. Using the resources at hand more efficiently. *Am. Econ. Rev.* 49:136–46.

Hennart, J. F. 1981. The political economy of comparative growth rates: The case of France. In *The Political Growth of Economy*, ed. D. C. Mueller. New Haven: Yale University Press.

Hibbs, D. A., Jr. 1976. Industrial conflicts in advanced industrial societies. *Am. Polit. Sci. Rev.* 70:1033–58.

Jewkes, J. 1951. The growth of world industry. *Oxf. Econ. Pap.*, n.s. 3:10–11.

Kamerschen, D. R. 1966. An estimation of the welfare losses from monopoly in the American economy. *West. Econ. J.* 4:221–36.

Kemp, T. 1962. Structural factors in the retardation of French economic growth. *Kyklos* 15(Fasc. 2):325–52.

Kimber, R., and J. J. Richardson, eds. 1974. *Pressure Groups in Britain: A Reader*. London: Dent.

Lieber, R. J. 1974. Interest groups and political integration: British entry into Europe. In *Pressure Groups in Britain: A Reader*, ed. Richard Kimber and J. J. Richardson. London: Dent.

Mueller, D. C., ed. 1982. *The Political Economy of Growth*. New Haven: Yale University Press.

Murrell, P. 1982. The comparative structure of the growth of West Germany and British manufacturing industries. In *The Political Economy of Growth*, ed. D. C. Mueller. New Haven: Yale University Press.

OECD Observer. 1978. Collective bargaining and government policy. *OECD Observer*, no. 94:4.

Olson, M. L. 1965. *The Logic of Collective Action*. Cambridge: Harvard University Press.

————. 1976. The political economy of comparative growth rates. In *U.S. Economic Growth from 1976 to 1986: Prospects, Problems, and Patterns*, vol. 2: *The Factors and Processes Shaping Long-Run Economic Growth*. Joint Economic Committee, 94th Cong., 2nd sess. Washington, D.C.: U.S. Government Printing Office.

————. 1982. *The Rise and Decline of Nations*. New Haven: Yale University Press.

Posner, R. A.   1975.   The social cost of monopoly and regulation. *J. Polit. Econ.* 83:807-27.

Pratten, C. F.   1972.   The reasons for the slow economic progress of the British economy. *Oxf. Econ. Pap.* 24:181-96.

Rees, A.   1962.   *The Economics of Trade Union.*   Chicago: University of Chicago Press.

———.   1963.   The effects of unions on resource allocation. *J. Law Econ.* 6:69-78.

Rotwein, E.   1976.   Economic concentration and monopoly in Japan: A second view. *J. Asian Stud.* 36:57-78.

Schwartzman, D.   1966.   The burden of monopoly. *J. Polit. Econ.* 68:627-30.

Solow, R. M.   1970.   Science and ideology in economics. *Public Interest* 21:102.

Sturmthal, A.   1960.   Unions and economic development. *Econ. Dev. Cult. Change* 8:199-205.

Svennilson, I.   1954.   *Growth and Stagnation in the European Economy.*   Geneva: United Nations Economic Commission for Europe.

Truman, D.   1951.   *The Governmental Process.*   New York: Alfred Knopf.

Tullock, G.   1967.   The welfare costs of tariffs, monopoly and theft. *West. Econ. J.* 5:226-32.

Windmuller, J. P.   1969.   *Labor Relations in the Netherlands.*   Ithaca: Cornell University Press.

Worcester, D. A., Jr.   1973.   New estimates of the welfare loss to monopoly: U.S. 1956-1960. *South. Econ. J.* 40:234-46.

2
Empirical Testing
with Cross-National Data

Our main concern in this and the next chapter is with the empirical testing of the negative relationship between economic growth and institutional arthritis (or sclerosis) implied by Olson's theory, using various measures of the dependent and explanatory variables. One major problem in our testing of Olson's rather grand theory is that the power of common-interest associations or the degree of institutional sclerosis resulting from the accumulation of group interests in a country is difficult to measure, and relevant data, even proxies, are not readily available. We will deal with the problem in two different ways. One approach is to construct a measure of institutional sclerosis that the accumulation of common-interest groups might breed, based on the assumption that the degree of institutional arthritis is proportional to the length of time during which each country has had democratic freedom of organization without upheaval or invasion. In our second approach we start with a methodological discussion of how to measure the power of an individual or group, then move to an alternative test of cross-country growth performance based on several indicators.

PRELIMINARY DISCUSSION
   The dependent variable for our cross-country analysis is easy to identify and measure. Our natural choice for the growth measure is the growth rates of GDP, which have been employed to test various hypotheses in all previous chapters. Unlike the dependent variable, the explanatory variables in Olson's theory are somewhat hard to measure, and the data are not readily available. We will begin with rough proxies and then move to more refined measures.
   One important variable in Olson's theory is the power of common-interest associations in a country or the strength of institutional sclerosis resulting from the accumulation of group interests. This power or strength is rather difficult to measure. Since, other things being equal, the longer the period a country

has enjoyed political stability and freedom of organization, the greater the extent to which common-interest groups build up power or cause institutional sclerosis age of a nation is, as a first proxy, employed to measure the power of common-interest groups or institutional sclerosis.

Given the importance of studying institutional development, especially in political science, it is curious (if not dismaying) that so little work has been done in measuring the age of modern political entities. One effort to provide an indicator of institutional age was made by Cyril Black (1966). He classifies countries according to the dates of the consolidation of modernizing leaderships. The consolidation is marked by three characteristics: (1) the assertion of the determination to modernize, (2) an effective and decisive break with the institutions of an agrarian way of life, and (3) the creation of a national state with an effective government and a reasonably stable consensus on political means and ends by inhabitants.

In the absence of better data, it is postulated that the earliest development of common-interest associations concurs with such consolidation. Since the longer the period a country has enjoyed the freedom of organization without disruption, the stronger the power of common-interest groups in the country, the length of time since the beginning of the consolidation is taken as a first proxy to measure the power of common-interest groups. Refinements of this proxy have been made in the next section to derive a more germane index.

In the first test, computing a simple linear regression by the method of least squares, with the growth rates of GDP across 18 countries for 1950-1978 as the dependent variables and the length of time since the consolidation of modernizing leadership (CML) as the independent variables, we obtain the following equations:

$$TY5078 = 6.190 - 0.013CML$$
$$(6.82) \quad (2.13) \qquad R^2 = 0.22$$

$$PY5078 = 5.230 - 0.013CML$$
$$(5.55) \quad (2.04) \qquad R^2 = 0.21$$

where $TY5078$ and $PY5078$ are growth rates of total GDP and per capita GDP respectively and the numbers in parentheses are the values of the t-statistic for the coefficients estimated.

The regression results show that the coefficients of determination R^2 and statistical significance of the estimated coefficient are not impressive, but the signs of the calculated coefficients are in the expected direction. Because Japan is recognized by several economists as an exceptional case, which fits various hypotheses at the same time, we follow them in excluding Japan. When Japan is excluded from the sample, the two equations above become:

$$TY5078 = 5.009 - 0.006CML$$
$$(8.44) \quad (1.60) \qquad R^2 = 0.15$$

$$PY5078 = 4.129 - 0.007CML$$
$$(5.73) \quad (1.41) \qquad R^2 = 0.12$$

While the force of the negative relationship between economic growth and the length of time a country has had institutional stability remains true, the relationship is not significant in terms of R^2 and t-ratios. These poor results are mainly because of the poor proxy measure of our independent variable.

One important aspect our proxy (the duration of institutional stability) does not account for is the disruptions that have occurred to reduce the strength and power of the common-interest associations since they began to accumulate. One simple way of dealing with these disruptions is to use a dummy variable. When we assign a dummy to all countries that have undergone social disruptions, such as upheaval, invasion, or occupation, we obtain the following results:

With Japan included:

$$TY5078 = 5.472 - 0.012CML + 1.034DUMMY$$
$$(6.01) \quad (2.12) \qquad (1.98) \qquad R^2 = 0.38$$

$$PY5078 = 4.314 - 0.011CML + 1.319DUMMY$$
$$(4.90) \quad (2.13) \qquad (2.61) \qquad R^2 = 0.46$$

With Japan excluded:

$$TY5078 = 4.614 - 0.006CML + 0.696DUMMY$$
$$(8.27) \quad (1.75) \qquad (2.22) \qquad R^2 = 0.37$$

$$PY5078 = 3.552 - 0.006CML + 1.019DUMMY$$
$$(5.73) \quad (1.66) \qquad (2.93) \qquad R^2 = 0.45$$

This gives a much improved fit and a significant coefficient for the dummy variable at the 95 percent confidence level or more.

CONSTRUCTION OF AN INDEX OF INSTITUTIONAL SCLEROSIS

One of the main conclusions of Olson's theory is that common-interest groups have adverse effects on economic growth except when they are highly encompassing. To test this conclusion, we need to measure the power of common-interest associations or the degree of institutional sclerosis resulting from the accumulation of powerful interest groups. The major problem is that it is hard to measure this power or the degree, and the data that might be used to measure them are not available for all types of common-interest associations.

Since common-interest organizations accumulate gradually in societies with continued freedom of organization, there exists a positive association between the power of common-interest organizations or the degree of institutional sclerosis and the length of time interest groups have been in existence. However, the measure-

ment of institutional sclerosis by the mere length of time interest
groups have been in existence does not allow for a decrease in the
power of interest groups or the reduction in the institutional
sclerosis resulting from the control of a society by a totalitarian
government, an occupation by foreign forces, or a social upheaval,
all of which deter the accumulation of common-interest groups or
abolish the vested interests enjoyed by these groups.

In the preceding section we put a dummy variable in our regression to account for disruptions of various kinds, and we obtained relatively good and improved results. One major problem
with this technique is that the degree and duration of major disruptions have not been taken into account. In the following, we
construct an index that makes due allowance not only for disruptions, per se, but also for their degree and duration. The construction of the index is based on the idea that institutional
sclerosis accumulates along a logistic curve unless disruptions develop, in which case accumulation is deterred or, in part, destroyed.

The choice of the logistic curve for the accumulation function
is somewhat arbitrary. But there are some good reasons why institutional sclerosis follows a path akin to the logistic. A common-
interest organization can be seen as an organism. Any change in
the organization can be viewed as an inevitable growth and decay
process intrinsic to the organism. The development of the organism
usually follows an S-shaped growth path. Within a given cycle, or
over the lifetime, the growth rate of an organism is not constant
in time. At first the organism grows slowly, but the rate of
growth reaches a maximum. After that point is passed, the rate of
growth becomes progressively slower, finally tapering off. There
are several S-shaped functions. The cumulative normal distribution
density curve and the logistic curve are used most widely for this
purpose. As there is almost no difference between the two, the logistic was chosen because it is simpler to fit and easier to interpret. The logistic curve is not applied as often in economic studies as in other social science studies such as the theory of social
change and population growth analysis. In economics, the logistic
curve was used by S. Kuznets (1930) in his study of the long-term
growth of industry and by Zvi Griliches (1957) in his investigation
of how technological change is generated and propagated.

Now, the basic idea behind the construction of the index is
portrayed in the three figures, A, B, and C of Figure 9.1. They
represent the typical cases. In each figure the vertical axis
measures the degree of institutional sclerosis, while the horizontal axis denotes chronological (historical) time. Our objective is
to measure the degree of institutional sclerosis at a historical
point in time X, say as of 1950. The country represented by Figure
A has enjoyed political stability, and common-interest groups in
the country have accumulated power since they were given the freedom to organize. As of time X, the country reaches institutional
sclerosis to the degree of AX.

Common-interest organizations in the country in Figure B began

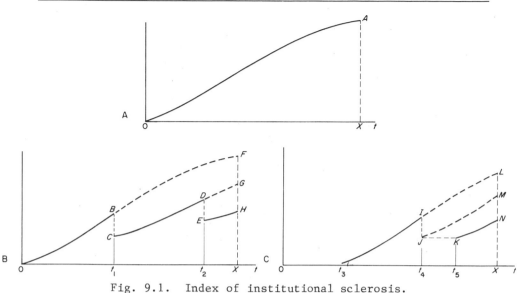

Fig. 9.1.   Index of institutional sclerosis.

to accumulate at the same time as those in Figure A.   However, two major disruptions, at times t_1 and t_2, destroyed parts of the accumulated power of the growth-retarding forces, the degree of destruction at each time being indicated by BC and DE respectively. Without these two upheavals (invasions or occupations) the country in Figure B should have had institutional sclerosis as measured by the distance FX.   If the country had undergone only one disruption, at time t_1, it would have accumulated growth-retarding power up to XG.   The second disruption at time t_2 leads the country to reach institutional sclerosis to the degree of XH instead of XG, given the first disruption at time t_1.

The country depicted in Figure C was a late starter or a newly-settled country.   Accumulation of common-interest associations began at time t_3.   One major disruption occurred in this country at time t_4.   Unlike the disruptions in Figure B, which were instantaneous in nature and produced a once-and-for-all reduction in the power of common-interest groups, the disruption in Figure C lasted over the period t_4-t_5.   As of time X, the country reached institutional sclerosis up to the level XN.   Were it not for the continuation of the supression of growth-retarding activities of the common-interest organizations during the period t_4-t_5, the country would have maintained an XM level of institutional sclerosis.

In summary, Figures A, B, and C depict the evolution of institutional sclerosis resulting from the accumulation of common-interest groups in societies that experienced different historical developments.   It is not claimed that the figures cover all possible interesting cases, but it is believed that they describe the cases most relevant to our purpose.   It should be noted that the deriva-

tion of a numerical index of institutional sclerosis requires the
following data: (1) the time common-interest groups in each country began to accumulate; (2) what the major disruptions were, when
they occurred, and how long they lasted; (3) how strong each disruption was; and (4) a formula for the logistic curve along which
the accumulation follows.

As a first step toward the construction of an index of institutional sclerosis, we need to choose a beginning year. Nations
differ in their degrees of institutionalization, civil order, political stability, extent of freedom allowed, and levels of organization. So finding such a year for every country in our sample demands a detailed examination of the history of each country; complete agreement on any year that is chosen by various experts in
the field may not be possible. A group of political scientists engaged in the study of modernization and political development among
nations has produced some interesting series, as shown in Table
9.1. Four indicators of institutional age are presented: beginning year of consideration of modernizing leadership, beginning
year of economic and social transformation, year of the first con-
stitution, and beginning year of takeoff. Years for the takeoff
(the last column) are not available for all countries in our sample. Given that only a limited number of series are available, and
an ideal series is not within our grasp, our best judgment is to
take the consolidation of modernizing leadership as a proxy for the
onset of common-interest group accumulation. This consolidation is
a dividing line between preindustrial feudal and industrial modern
environments.

Our index construction demands a rather detailed examination
of major disruptions in each country that might have deterred or
destroyed the accumulation of common-interest groups. We emphasize
only those events that have had strong influence on the augmenta-

Table 9.1. Alternative years for onset of institutional sclerosis

Country	Beginning year of consolidation of modernizing leadership	Beginning year of economic and social transformation	Year of first constitution	Beginning year of takeoff
Australia	1801	1901	1900	1901
Austria	1848	1918	1920	n.a.
Belgium	1795	1848	1831	1833
Canada	1791	1867	1867	1896
Denmark	1807	1866	1849	n.a.
Finland	1863	1919	1919	n.a.
France	1789	1848	1791	1830
Germany	1803	1871	1848	1848
Ireland	1870	1922	1922	n.a.
Italy	1805	1871	1848	1895
Japan	1868	1945	1889	1885
Netherlands	1795	1848	1795	n.a.
New Zealand	1826	1907	1852	n.a.
Norway	1809	1905	1814	n.a.
Sweden	1809	1905	1720	1868
Switzerland	1798	1848	1898	n.a.
United Kingdom	1649	1832	1688	1783
United States	1776	1865	1787	1843

Sources: Cols. 1, 2—Black 1966, pp. 90-91; Col. 3—Rustow 1967, p.
230; Col. 4—Rostow 1960, p. 38, 1978, pp. 373-465.

Table 9.2. Major disruptions

Australia	None
Austria	Occupation during 1938-1955
Belgium	Occupation during WW I, WW II
Canada	None
Denmark	Occupation during WW II
Finland	None
France	Revolutions in 1789-1814, 1830, 1848-1852; authoritarian government during 1852-1860; occupation during WW II
Germany	Defeat during WW I, totalitarian government during 1933-1945, defeat and occupation during 1943-1949
Ireland	None
Italy	Totalitarian government since 1922, defeat during WW II
Japan	Totalitarian government and defeat during WW II; occupation during 1945-1952
Netherlands	Occupation during WW II
New Zealand	None
Norway	Occupation during WW II
Sweden	None
Switzerland	None
United Kingdom	None
United States	Civil War during 1861-1865, large portions settled after 1865

Sources: Russell et al. 1968; Langer 1972.

tion or retrogression of the power accumulated by common-interest associations since the consolidation of modernizing leadership. The major disruptions chosen for inclusion involve occupation by foreign forces, indigenous totalitarian government control, defeat during major wars, and revolutions. According to this definition, the major disruptions relevant to our purpose are listed in Table 9.2.

Under our assumption that institutional sclerosis develops along a logistic curve, we need to formulate an equation for the curve. In a most general form, this can be specified as

$$Y = K/(1 + Ae^{-bt}) \tag{9.1}$$

where K, A, and b are parameters that will determine the shape of the curve and t is the variable. Under this general form, Y will take an asymptotic maximum value of K, and Y is equal to $K/(1 + A)$ when $t = 0$, as shown in Figure 9.2.

A particular form of the logistic curve is chosen for our purpose:

$$I = 200/(1 + e^{-bt}) - 100 \tag{9.2}$$

The shape of the logistic curve under this formulation is shown in Figure 9.3. The derivation of (9.2) is as follows: By adding a new term, the curve is shifted to start at the origin.

$$Y = K/(1 + Ae^{-bt}) - K/(1 + A) \tag{9.3}$$

Setting A equal to 1 for simplicity and K equal to 200 so that the

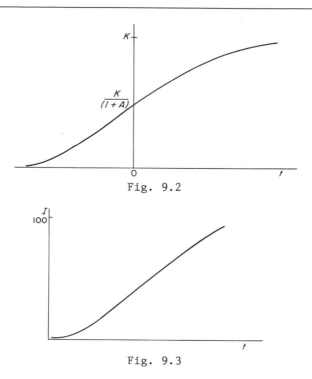

Fig. 9.2

Fig. 9.3

maximum value of Y becomes 100, we have (9.2). Our index of institutional sclerosis I will have an asymptotic value of 100 and start
at the origin. The slope of the curve depends on the parameter b
and still has to be determined. We have chosen a value of b such
that the country having the longest history of accumulation of common-interest organizations, the United Kingdom in our case, reaches
the institutional sclerosis level of about 90 as of 1950. This assumption gives us a value of b equal to 0.01. For the United Kingdom, the beginning year of the consolidation of modernizing leadership is 1649. So the period during which common-interest groups
built themselves is t = 1950 - 1649 = 301. Solving the equation,
90 = 200/(1 + e^{-301b} - 100, we obtain a value of b equal to 0.01.
So institutional sclerosis develops along the curve

$$I = 200/(1 + e^{-0.01t}) - 100 \qquad\qquad (9.4)$$

Using for t in (9.4) the period from the consolidation of modernizing leadership shown in the first column of Table 9.1, to
1950, which is the beginning year of our growth rate sample period,
we obtain the value of our index, as shown in the first column of
Table 9.3. This value indicates the degree of institutional sclerosis each country might have reached if there had been no disruptions after the consolidation. Adjustments for the disruptions a
number of countries experienced have not been made. Based on this

unadjusted index, the United Kingdom, the United States, Belgium, and Canada are the top four countries in our index, while Japan, Ireland, Finland, and Austria are the bottom four in the accumulation of institutional sclerosis.

The last step in constructing our index involves making adjustments for the major disruptions listed in Table 9.2. Since different people will put different weights on different events and arbitrary elements cannot entirely be eliminated, we try to apply a simple rule: that the degree of each disruption is proportional to the duration of that disruption. Once we obtain an average degree of accumulation per unit of time (year), multiplication of the average by the length of any particular disruption provides the total degree of adjustment for the disruption in question. An average degree of accumulation has been calculated in two ways. The first is to apply the average degree of accumulation per unit of time for the United Kingdom (our reference country) to the rest of our sample countries. The second is to calculate an average degree of accumulation per year for each country, which is obtained by dividing the unadjusted index, shown in the first column of Table 9.3, by the total number of years without disruption since consolidation, shown in the second column. Using symbols and simple mathematics, the procedure applied to obtain the total degree of adjustment for disruptions can be put as follows. Suppose there are two countries: A, which has not been subjected to any disruption from time t_0 to t_n, and B, which has undergone one disruption over the period t_2 to t_3. Country B is also a late starter, and its common-interest groups began to accumulate power at time t_1. When we choose F for the curve along which accumulation of institutional sclerosis follows, average degree of accumulation $D_A = [F(t_n) - F(t_0)]/(t_n - t_0)$ for country A, and $D_B = [F(t_2) - F(t_1) + F(t_n) - F(t_3)]/(t_2 - t_1 + t_n - t_3)$. The total degree of adjustment for the disruption

Table 9.3.   Index of institutional sclerosis

Country	Unadjusted index of institutional sclerosis	Sum of years without disruption since consolidation	Sum of years with disruption since consolidation	Adjustment for disruption Using U.K. weights	Adjustment for disruption Using country's own weight	Adjusted index of institutional sclerosis A	Adjusted index of institutional sclerosis B
Australia	62.36	149	0	0.00	0.00	62.36	62.36
Austria	41.48	90	12	3.59	5.53	37.89	35.95
Belgium	65.72	145	10	2.99	4.53	62.73	61.19
Canada	65.26	159	0	0.00	0.00	65.26	65.26
Denmark	59.77	138	5	1.49	2.17	58.27	57.60
Finland	40.26	87	0	0.00	0.00	40.26	40.26
France	54.10	118	23	6.88	10.54	47.22	43.56
Germany	56.01	124	22	6.58	9.34	49.43	46.07
Ireland	37.34	80	0	0.00	0.00	37.34	37.34
Italy	54.27	117	23	6.88	10.67	47.39	43.60
Japan	32.17	68	24	7.18	11.35	24.99	20.82
Netherlands	63.59	150	5	1.50	2.18	63.89	63.21
New Zealand	54.29	124	0	0.00	0.00	54.29	54.29
Norway	59.11	136	5	1.49	2.17	57.61	56.94
Sweden	59.90	141	0	0.00	0.00	59.90	59.90
Switzerland	63.21	112	0	0.00	0.00	63.24	63.24
United Kingdom	36.08	301	0	0.00	0.00	90.08	90.08
United States	78.86	170	5	1.50	2.32	77.36	76.54

of country B during t_2 to t_3 is $D_A(t_3 - t_2)$ with reference to country A, and $D_B(t_3 - t_2)$ with its own reference. The average degree of adjustment using U.K. data is 0.2993 per unit year. The corresponding figures for the other countries range from 0.4104 for Canada to 0.4731 for Japan. Our index of institutional sclerosis after adjustment for major disruptions is shown in the last two columns of Table 9.3. The adjusted index A is based on adjustments using an average degree of accumulation for the United Kingdom, while index B makes allowance for the disruptions using each country's own average degree of accumulation. The results indicate that, due to a long history of industrialization, political stability, and democratic freedom of organization without much disruption, the United Kingdom, the United States, Canada, and Switzerland are the four countries whose institutional sclerosis is most severe. The adjusted index of institutional sclerosis is lowest in countries like Japan, Ireland, Austria, and Finland.

TESTING WITH AN INDEX OF INSTITUTIONAL SCLEROSIS

Recall that a preliminary testing of Olson's theory was implemented using, as a rough proxy, the mere length of time since the consolidation of modernizing leadership. In the preceding section we developed an index that measures the institutional sclerosis resulting from the accumulation of common-interest organizations. It is believed that, given the assumptions used in the conceptualization and estimation, the index obtained is quite close to that implied in the very general, broad theory of comparative growth of Olson and is pertinent to the testing of this theory.

Since Olson's theory predicts a negative relationship between economic growth and the institutional sclerosis accumulated by growth-retarding organizations, those countries having the most sclerotic institutions ought (ceteris paribus) to have the lowest rates of economic growth. The results showing the relationship between our two measures of the dependent variable--the growth rates of total and per capita income--and our two measures of institutional sclerosis as the independent variables--index A and index B --are shown in Table 9.4, with t-values in parentheses. To check

Table 9.4. Test results with index of institutional
            sclerosis

A. Growth rates of total income as dependent variable

All countries: $N = 18$

$$TY5078 = 7.526 - 0.057 \text{ Index } A \qquad (1)$$
$$(8.25) \quad (3.60) \qquad\qquad R^2 = 0.45$$
$$TY5078 = 7.443 - 0.057 \text{ Index } B \qquad (2)$$
$$(9.13) \quad (3.84) \qquad\qquad R^2 = 0.49$$

Excluding Japan: $N = 17$

$$TY5078 = 5.775 - 0.029 \text{ Index } A \qquad (3)$$
$$(8.11) \quad (2.41) \qquad\qquad R^2 = 0.28$$
$$TY5078 = 5.806 - 0.030 \text{ Index } B \qquad (4)$$
$$(8.89) \quad (2.69) \qquad\qquad R^2 = 0.33$$

Source: Same as for index of institutional sclerosis.

Table 9.4. *(continued)*

Countries with no major disruptions: $N = 8$
$$TY5078 = 4.686 - 0.016 \text{ Index } A \qquad (5)$$
$$ (4.35) \quad (0.92) \qquad R^2 = 0.12$$
$$TY5078 = 4.686 - 0.016 \text{ Index } B \qquad (6)$$
$$ (4.36) \quad (0.92) \qquad R^2 = 0.12$$

Countries with some major disruptions: $N = 10$
$$TY5078 = 9.350 - 0.085 \text{ Index } A \qquad (7)$$
$$ (9.27) \quad (4.60) \qquad R^2 = 0.73$$
$$TY5078 = 8.887 - 0.080 \text{ Index } B \qquad (8)$$
$$ (9.96) \quad (4.71) \qquad R^2 = 0.73$$

Largest countries: $N = 9$
$$TY5078 = 9.586 - 0.081 \text{ Index } A \qquad (9)$$
$$ (12.02) \quad (6.26) \qquad R^2 = 0.85$$
$$TY5078 = 9.034 - 0.074 \text{ Index } B \qquad (10)$$
$$ (11.81) \quad (5.84) \qquad R^2 = 0.83$$

Smallest countries: $N = 9$
$$TY5078 = 4.941 - 0.020 \text{ Index } A \qquad (11)$$
$$ (4.77) \quad (1.02) \qquad R^2 = 0.13$$
$$TY5078 = 5.049 - 0.022 \text{ Index } B \qquad (12)$$
$$ (5.06) \quad (1.17) \qquad R^2 = 0.16$$

B. Growth rates of per capita income as dependent variable

All countries: $N = 18$
$$PY5078 = 6.936 - 0.064 \text{ Index } A \qquad (13)$$
$$ (7.97) \quad (4.21) \qquad R^2 = 0.53$$
$$PY5078 = 6.841 - 0.0633 \text{ Index } B \qquad (14)$$
$$ (8.94) \quad (4.68) \qquad R^2 = 0.59$$

Excluding Japan: $N = 17$
$$PY5078 = 5.486 - 0.041 \text{ Index } A \qquad (15)$$
$$ (6.96) \quad (3.03) \qquad R^2 = 0.38$$
$$PY5078 = 5.514 - 0.042 \text{ Index } B \qquad (16)$$
$$ (7.74) \quad (3.41) \qquad R^2 = 0.44$$

Countries with no major disruptions: $N = 8$
$$PY5078 = 3.868 - 0.021 \text{ Index } A \qquad (17)$$
$$ (4.04) \quad (1.36) \qquad R^2 = 0.24$$
$$PY5078 = 3.868 - 0.021 \text{ Index } B \qquad (18)$$
$$ (4.04) \quad (1.36) \qquad R^2 = 0.24$$

Countries with some major disruptions: $N = 10$
$$PY5078 = 8.764 - 0.090 \text{ Index } A \qquad (19)$$
$$ (12.31) \quad (6.88) \qquad R^2 = 0.86$$
$$PY5078 = 8.356 - 0.084 \text{ Index } B \qquad (20)$$
$$ (13.01) \quad (6.95) \qquad R^2 = 0.86$$

Largest countries: $N = 9$
$$PY5078 = 8.373 - 0.084 \text{ Index } A \qquad (21)$$
$$ (9.54) \quad (5.63) \qquad R^2 = 0.82$$
$$PY5078 = 7.892 - 0.075 \text{ Index } B \qquad (22)$$
$$ (10.14) \quad (5.77) \qquad R^2 = 0.83$$

Smallest countries: $N = 9$
$$PY5078 = 5.141 - 0.038 \text{ Index } A \qquad (23)$$
$$ (3.31) \quad (1.30) \qquad R^2 = 0.20$$
$$PY5078 = 5.297 - 0.041 \text{ Index } B \qquad (24)$$
$$ (3.56) \quad (1.47) \qquad R^2 = 0.24$$

the robustness of the model with respect to the sample countries
included, some different combinations of countries were tried. The
overall results of this cross-sectional study of advanced industrial countries seem to support Olson's theory of the political economy of comparative growth quite well. Our measures of the independent variable appear to explain about half of the variation in
growth rates among the 18 countries even at the 1 percent significance level. While countries that experienced disruption of one
sort or another and countries that are large in terms of population
produce surprisingly good results, counterpart countries exhibit
relatively poor results, which might be due to the influence exerted by factors associated with other theories. The contrasting results between countries with and without disruptions may be ascribed to the fact that the encompassingness of common-interest
groups in a given country has not been adequately accounted for in
our construction of an institutional sclerosis index.

TESTING WITH SOURCES-OF-GROWTH DATA
        One might argue that Olson's model does not take into consid-
eration several major factors that might have had strong effects on
economic growth. According to this argument, Olson's theory is
supposed to explain best variations in growth rates not occasioned
by direct increases in the various resources used in the production
of output. In the following, we attempt to see what statistical
light can be thrown on this issue by using the sources-of-growth
data produced by Edward Denison (1967), Dorothy Walters (1970), and
William Chung (see Denison and Chung 1976). Unfortunately, the use
of these data reduces our sample from 18 to 11 countries and includes mostly the period 1956-1962. Since, except for Canada, Japan, and the United States, data on the sources of growth are
available only for the distant past, we turn for help to two recent
productivity studies. L. R. Christensen et al. (1980) provide an
international comparison of postwar patterns of economic growth for
the United States and eight of its major trading partners, including one developing country, Korea. Their study covers the period
from 1947 to 1973 for the United States and as much of this period
as is feasible for each of the eight remaining countries. In a report prepared for the Council on International Economic Policy,
John Stein and Allen Lee (1977) develop and assemble indices of
output, labor input, and capital stock for the years 1963-1974.
Again, following several economists who recognize Japan as an exceptional case or an outlier, we present regression results with
and without Japan in our sample. Also, in each of the following
tables are two sets of equations, one with growth rates of the dependent variables calculated from the total quantity of each category and the other from the per-employee quantity of each category
of the dependent variable in question.
        Table 9.5 summarizes the results of our simple regression
equations of growth rates of national income, total and per employee, using two alternative measures of institutional sclerosis, in-

Table 9.5. Test results with national income data
A. Total income as dependent variable

All countries: $N = 11$

$$GROWTH = 9.4029 - 0.0845 \text{ Index } A \qquad (1)$$
$$(9.70) \quad (5.30) \qquad R^2 = 0.76$$
$$GROWTH = 8.9185 - 0.0786 \text{ Index } B \qquad (2)$$
$$(10.30) \quad (5.40) \qquad R^2 = 0.76$$

Excluding Japan: $N = 10$

$$GROWTH = 8.4597 - 0.703 \text{ Index } A \qquad (3)$$
$$(6.37) \quad (3.45) \qquad R^2 = 0.58$$
$$GROWTH = 8.0602 - 0.0654 \text{ Index } B \qquad (4)$$
$$(6.84) \quad (3.35) \qquad R^2 = 0.60$$

B. Income per employee as dependent variable

All countries: $N = 11$

$$GROWPE = 8.6633 - 0.0895 \text{ Index } A \qquad (5)$$
$$(6.51) \quad (4.08) \qquad R^2 = 0.65$$
$$GROWPE = 8.2456 - 0.0849 \text{ Index } B \qquad (6)$$
$$(7.19) \quad (4.40) \qquad R^2 = 0.68$$

Excluding Japan: $N = 10$

$$GROWPE = 8.6306 - 0.0889 \text{ Index } A \qquad (7)$$
$$(4.44) \quad (2.89) \qquad R^2 = 0.51$$
$$GROWPE = 8.2834 - 0.0855 \text{ Index } B \qquad (8)$$
$$(4.97) \quad (3.18) \qquad R^2 = 0.56$$

Sources: Denison 1967; Walters 1970; Denison and Chung 1976.
Note: $GROWTH$ = growth rate of total national income; $GROWPE$ = growth rate of national income per employee.

dex A and index B. The results are impressive. All of the estimated regression coefficients turn out to be statistically significant at the 5 percent significance level or less. The coefficients
of multiple determination also indicate that the regressions provide a quite close fit to the data when we recall that these data
are cross-sectional and our sample includes only 10 or 11 countries. The results in Table 9.5 indicate that our model is not
sensitive to the inclusion or exclusion of Japan.

Table 9.6 is concerned with explaining growth rates of factor
productivity in terms of our alternative indices. The results are
extremely impressive in terms of t-values and R^2s.

The importance of technological change to economic growth,
whether embodied or disembodied, is commonly accepted. Empirical
studies, however, have nominated many candidates to explain the
"residual" in economic growth. Early empirical work often assigned
the residual to technical change by default (Solow 1957). Later,
as data and estimating procedure improved, other explanations were
offered such as education, improved resource allocation, advances
in knowledge, and economies of scale. It seems clear, from the
work of Denison and others, that factor inputs (which include education) account for only about half of the growth rates, while the
remainder are distributed as residuals among the variables mentioned above, as discussed in Chapter 2.

The above discussion is not intended to describe or characterize the residual part of the sources of growth but to indicate that
they varied across nations and over time. Despite several theoret-

Table 9.6. Test results with total factor productivity data
A. Total factor productivity as dependent variable

All countries: $N = 11$
$RESIDU$ = 5.8742 − 0.0558 Index A (1)
       (12.27)   (7.08) $R^2 = 0.85$
$RESIDU$ = 5.5872 − 0.0524 Index B (2)
       (14.26)   (7.96) $R^2 = 0.88$

Excluding Japan: $N = 10$
$RESIDU$ = 5.9933 − 0.0575 Index A (3)
        (8.61)   (5.23) $R^2 = 0.77$
$RESIDU$ = 5.7132 − 0.0544 Index B (4)
       (10.09)   (5.96) $R^2 = 0.82$

B. Total factor productivity per employee as dependent variable

All countries: $N = 11$
$RESIPE$ = 6.6487 − 0.0690 Index A (5)
        (6.04)   (3.82) $R^2 = 0.62$
$RESIPE$ = 6.3364 − 0.0657 Index B (6)
        (6.67)   (4.11) $R^2 = 0.65$

Excluding Japan: $N = 10$
$RESIPE$ = 7.1706 − 0.0767 Index A (7)
        (4.54)   (3.08) $R^2 = 0.54$
$RESIPE$ = 6.8624 − 0.0737 Index B (8)
        (5.08)   (3.38) $R^2 = 0.59$

Sources: Same as in Table 9.5.
Note: $RESIDU$ = growth rate of total factor productivity;
$RESIPE$ = growth rate of total factor productivity per employee.

ical attempts to explain the residual in terms of technical change, no empirical tests have been applied to this "ignorance of our knowledge." Since Olson's model implies that institutional sclerosis is a retardant of growth disproportionately through its effect on the residual factor, an attempt is made to find out the causal link between the residual and our measures of institutional sclerosis, the results of which are shown in Table 9.7. The regression results show that both independent measures appear to explain more than 70 percent of the variations in the growth rates of the total residual and about 50 percent of the variations when growth rates of the residual per employee are taken as the dependent variable. As with the test of other categories of sources of growth, our test results with residual data remain significant whether or not Japan is included in our sample.

Since most of the available data on sources of growth are for the 1950s and early 1960s, we need to extend our empirical tests to data covering more recent years. Therefore, we subject our hypothesis to data on growth rates in output and factor productivity reported in two recent studies by Stein and Lee (SL) and Christensen, Cummings, and Jorgenson (CCJ). Unfortunately, the data estimated are not as large as might be desirable and cover only ten countries in SL and nine (the United States and its eight major trading partners) in CCJ. Looking at our regression results with the data reported in Table 9.8, we see that the relationships are strongly in line with the expectations of Olson's hypothesis. The variations in growth rates in output, labor productivity, and total factor

Table 9.7. Test results with residual data

A. Total residual as dependent variable

    All countries: $N = 11$

$$OTHER = 3.4634 - 0.0295 \text{ Index } A \qquad\qquad (1)$$
$$(9.39) \quad (4.86) \qquad\qquad R^2 = 0.72$$
$$OTHER = 3.3174 - 0.0278 \text{ Index } B \qquad\qquad (2)$$
$$(10.51) \quad (5.23) \qquad\qquad R^2 = 0.75$$

    Excluding Japan: $N = 10$

$$OTHER = 3.7989 - 0.0345 \text{ Index } A \qquad\qquad (3)$$
$$(7.46) \quad (4.29) \qquad\qquad R^2 = 0.70$$
$$OTHER = 3.6319 - 0.0326 \text{ Index } B \qquad\qquad (4)$$
$$(8.47) \quad (4.71) \qquad\qquad R^2 = 0.74$$

B. Residual per employee as dependent variable

    All countries: $N = 11$

$$OTHEPE = 3.1599 - 0.0292 \text{ Index } A \qquad\qquad (5)$$
$$(6.03) \quad (3.39) \qquad\qquad R^2 = 0.56$$
$$OTHEPE = 3.0172 - 0.0276 \text{ Index } B \qquad\qquad (6)$$
$$(6.54) \quad (3.55) \qquad\qquad R^2 = 0.58$$

    Excluding Japan: $N = 10$

$$OTHEPE = 3.0868 - 0.0281 \text{ Index } A \qquad\qquad (7)$$
$$(4.04) \quad (2.33) \qquad\qquad R^2 = 0.40$$
$$OTHEPE = 2.9684 - 0.0268 \text{ Index } B \qquad\qquad (8)$$
$$(4.43) \quad (2.48) \qquad\qquad R^2 = 0.44$$

Sources: Same as in Table 9.5.
Note: *OTHER* = growth rate of total residual; *OTHEPE*
= growth rate of residual per employee.

Table 9.8. Test results with data from Stein and Lee and
    Christensen, Cummings, and Jorgenson

A. Stein and Lee: $N = 10$

    Growth in output

$$SLOP = 12.0112 - 0.1166 \text{ Index } A \qquad\qquad (1)$$
$$(6.14) \quad (3.64) \qquad\qquad R^2 = 0.62$$
$$SLOP = 11.2121 - 0.1064 \text{ Index } B \qquad\qquad (2)$$
$$(6.19) \quad (3.50) \qquad\qquad R^2 = 0.61$$

    Growth in labor productivity

$$SLOPPE = 11.5809 - 0.1249 \text{ Index } A \qquad\qquad (3)$$
$$(6.15) \quad (4.05) \qquad\qquad R^2 = 0.67$$
$$SLOPPE = 10.8191 - 0.1157 \text{ Index } B \qquad\qquad (4)$$
$$(6.35) \quad (4.06) \qquad\qquad R^2 = 0.67$$

B. Christensen, Cummings, and Jorgenson: $N = 8$

    Growth in gross private domestic product

$$CCJAA = 9.9797 - 0.0752 \text{ Index } A \qquad\qquad (5)$$
$$(7.15) \quad (3.30) \qquad\qquad R^2 = 0.64$$
$$CCJAA = 9.4748 - 0.0690 \text{ Index } B \qquad\qquad (6)$$
$$(7.39) \quad (3.22) \qquad\qquad R^2 = 0.63$$

    Growth in total factor productivity

$$CCJBB = 10.7249 - 0.0863 \text{ Index } A \qquad\qquad (7)$$
$$(6.45) \quad (3.18) \qquad\qquad R^2 = 0.63$$
$$CCJBB = 10.1251 - 0.0788 \text{ Index } B \qquad\qquad (8)$$
$$(6.59) \quad (3.07) \qquad\qquad R^2 = 0.61$$

Sources: Stein and Lee 1977; Christensen et al. 1980.
Note: *SLOP* = growth rate of total output; *SLOPPE*
= growth rate of labor productivity; *CCJAA* = growth rate of
gross private domestic product; *CCJBB* = growth rate of total
factor productivity.

productivity reported in the two studies are fairly well explained by our measures of institutional sclerosis. Though not reported in the table, the sample excluding Japan still produces a statistically significant result, with reasonably high explanatory power.

The above results indicate the explanatory power and generality of Olson's theory in the study of cross-national data. The model is clearly satisfactory when judged in terms of the usual criterion of overall goodness of fit as well as the signs and significance of the estimated regression coefficients. It is also satisfactory when judged in terms of data sensitivity.

MEASUREMENT OF POWER AND EMPIRICAL TESTING BASED ON INDICATORS

This section deals primarily with two questions not considered explicitly so far. We start with a methodological discussion of how to measure the power of an individual or group and then move to an alternative test of cross-country growth performance based on several indicators. The aim is to illustrate how to improve our statistical test when more relevant data are available rather than to maintain that the results obtained below provide a necessary empirical support to Olson's theory.

It is not easy to measure the power of a particular common-interest group, not to mention the power of all common-interest groups as a whole in the country, because the diversity of interests and objectives makes it difficult to analyze its behavior in a simple manner. The differences in historical development of common-interest groups are so pronounced across countries that generalization from one country to another is still more difficult.

Most people have an intuitive notion of what the word "power" means. But a statement of the concept of power has not been formulated rigorously enough to be of use for our own analysis and in the systematic study of other important social phenomena. In the following, a methodological issue of how to measure power has been touched upon briefly. It should be noted that any formal definition of power that seems to catch the central, intuitively understood meaning of the word is not easy to apply in concrete research problems. Operational definitions modeled on the formal one vary from one case to another.

Several authors in the theory of bargaining games have discussed the measurement of power. For our purpose, we shall rely on the main ideas postulated by R. A. Dahl (1957) and John C. Harsanyi (1962). Dahl has suggested five dimensions--base, means, scope, amount, and extension--along which power can be measured. Harsanyi adds two more--the cost and strength of power. Roughly, these can be divided into three categories: the sources of power, the means of power, and the results of power. The sources of power cover both the base of power and the opportunity costs bargaining partners have to bear. The means of power relate to the set of actions by which one party utilizes its resources to influence the other's behavior. The results of power comprise the set of specific actions one side can get the other to perform by using its means of

power and the amount of power, i.e., the net increase in the probability of one's opponents actually performing some specific action
X by using the means of power against it.

Of these three main ways, it would, for our purpose, be beg-
ging the question to attempt to measure power of common-interest
groups by its results. Without controlled experiments, it is not
possible to know what would have been achieved without common-interest groups, particularly what growth performance each country
would have achieved without growth-retarding behavior by these
groups. We may then consider either the sources or the means of
power.

The chief difficulty with using the sources of power is that
these dimensions constitute only a potential source of actual influence. The union, for example, is free to use or not to use its
available resources for any specific purpose. The union also has
the discretionary power to incur the opportunity cost of bargaining. The sources of power provide us only with measures of power
in what Harsanyi calls a schedule sense. Power is in a point sense
when it is defined in terms of the specific values of power variables; power is in a schedule sense when it is specified by mathematical functions that connect the costs of power with other dimensions of power. We can only specify the values of the various dimensions of power at any point in time if we know how much resources an interest group is prepared to sacrifice to achieve a
given end.

All we can observe in the real world is actual exerted influence. It is probably for this reason that much attention has been
focused on militant behavior as the means of power by some interest
groups. Union militancy, based on industrial disputes, for example, has been examined in relation to the business cycle and cost-
push inflation. Assuming that we can successfully identify and
measure observable correlates of the militancy concept and that we
have established some theoretical link between sources of power and
the putative results of power, then, other things being equal, variations in the proxies for interest group militancy will correspond
to variations in the degree to which a given potential group influence is actually being exerted.

Our discussion of how to measure the power of a common-interest group leads us to conclude that, assuming relevant data is
readily available, our effort to measure the power should be directed in terms of the sources and the means of power. The sources
of power are resources such as economic assets and popular prestige
that an interest group can use to achieve given ends. The means of
power imply those specific actions such as promises and threats a
group can actually use to pursue its own interests.

So far, our discussion has been concerned with the measurement
of the power of a particular interest group, whether it be a labor
union, a farm organization, an employers' association, or a professional group. What we mostly need in our examination of Olson's
political economy of comparative economic growth is a measure of
the social power of all common-interest groups in the country.

Since available data are quite limited and the problem of how to aggregate the power of all interest groups has not yet been solved, measurement of social power does not seem possible at the moment. Given these problems, what one can do is to use indicators to see what statistical light can be thrown on the issues. It cannot be emphasized too strongly that the following discussion is merely a statistical exploration of the possibilities of constructing a measure of power of all common-interest groups in the country. Statistical results obtained below are qualified accordingly.

     Two methods of analyzing data are employed. Faced with the task of constructing a summary of a statistical measure of the power of interest groups, it would seem sensible to begin by using a simple method. Among the least demanding statistics are measures of association using rank, and we might rank all the countries in our sample for each indicator. Countries are then given scores ranging from 1 to 18 for each indicator. If we aggregate these scores over the indicators, we obtain an overall ranking score for every country. Though the rank sum method is a useful starting place, and index construction places few demands on the accuracy of the data, this approach has two disadvantages. First, the overall rank score takes no account of the value of any indicator, merely the rankings. Even if, from a purely statistical point of view, the ranking method ignores much of the information present in the data, ranking might be a better representation than the value of the variable for a given indicator. Second, the indicators are given equal weight in the determination of the index.

     The second method is to subject data to factor or principal components analysis. Essentially, this is a method of finding that linear combination, or weighted average, of the variables that explains the largest proportion of their variance. This combination, or the first component, consists of the number of each observation calculated to capture as much of the variation in the individual indicators as possible. Second- and higher-order principal components can be chosen to minimize the residual variance after all previous principal components have played their part; they are constructed so as to be orthogonal to each other. Thus the contribution any one component makes to explaining the overall variance is independent of the contribution of any other. The extent to which the first principal component is a useful index number depends on the proportion of the overall variance it accounts for and the weights implicit in the calculation.

     Statistics on five indicators were collected for 18 countries in our sample (Table 9.9). The indicators are: (1) degree of urbanization (Russett et al. 1964, pp. 49–85), (2) percentage of economically active male population engaged in professional and technical occupations (Taylor and Hudson 1972, pp. 335–37), (3) percentage of labor force employed in nonagriculture (Russett et al. 1964, pp. 177–79), (4) workers involved in strikes (per strike or relative to labor force) (International Labor Office, selected years), and (5) work days lost in strikes (per strike or relative to labor force) (International Labor Office, selected years).

     The choice of indicators was dictated largely by the availa-

Table 9.9. Factor analysis of five indicators

	Unrotated loadings		Rotated loadings	
	Factor 1	Factor 2	Factor 1	Factor 2
URBAN	0.66	0.39	0.77	-0.01
MPEPTO	0.69	0.45	0.82	0.03
NAGREM .	0.81	0.25	0.32	-0.20
WIS	-0.54	0.72	-0.10	0.90
WIL	-0.47	0.79	-0.01	0.92

	Sorted rotated loadings		
	Factor 1	Factor 2	Communality
URBAN	0.82	0.00	0.59
MPEPTO	0.32	0.00	0.67
NAGREM	0.77	0.00	0.72
WIS	0.00	0.92	0.81
WIL	0.00	0.90	0.85

Note: URBAN = degree of urbanization; MPEPTO = percentage of
economically active male population engaged in professional and
technical occupations; NAGREM = percentage of labor force employed
in nonagriculture; WIS = workers involved in strikes; WIL = work
days lost in strikes.

bility of data and the requirement that they should be "backyard"
variables for institutional sclerosis in their own right or that
they constitute the sources of power or means of power of at least
one common-interest group in the country. There are few statistics
for both groups. The degree of urbanization and the percentage of
labor force employed in nonagriculture represent the first group,
while the other three variables of the five mentioned above represent the second group. Industrialization and urbanization proceed
hand in hand, and both expedite the development of common-interest
groups. For example, unions are likely to be strongest in heavily
urbanized regions. The inclusion of the percentage of the economically active male population engaged in professional and technical
occupations is open to objection. However, a naive assumption is
that the larger the number of professionals and technicians relative to population, the larger the influence they can exert. The
two indicators relating to strikes represent the means of power,
though these strike statistics themselves may not be comparable
across countries.

In our first simple test, all the countries are ranked for
each indicator and the scores are aggregated over the indicators to
obtain an overall ranking score (ORS) for every country. A score
of 1 is given to that country having the highest point for each indicator. Each indicator is positively correlated to institutional
sclerosis. Thus all regression coefficients we will obtain should
be positive. The value of the ORS and its rank are presented in
Table 9.10. When we take this ORS as our independent variable and
growth rates of total income (TY5878) or per capita income (PY5878)
as our dependent variable, we obtain the following regression results:

$$TY5878 = 3.181 + 0.025 ORS$$
$$(3.20) \quad (1.24) \qquad R^2 = 0.09$$

$$PY5878 = 1.379 + 0.043 ORS$$
$$(1.48) \quad (2.28) \qquad R^2 = 0.25$$

Table 9.10.   Rank scores and first principal component

Country	Overall ranking scores		First principal component	
	Value	Rank	Value	Rank
Australia	22	2.5	1.106	3
Austria	63	16.0	-0.598	12
Belgium	49	6.0	-0.262	10
Canada	31	4.0	1.051	4
Denmark	55	13.0	-0.244	9
Finland	54	12.0	-1.362	17
France	50	7.5	-0.625	13
Germany	51	9.5	0.383	8
Ireland	60	15.0	-1.390	18
Italy	50	7.5	-1.204	16
Japan	59	14.0	-0.915	15
Netherlands	52	11.0	0.462	6
New Zealand	34	5.0	0.995	5
Norway	64	17.0	-0.683	14
Sweden	51	9.5	0.384	7
Switzerland	71	18.0	-0.403	11
United Kingdom	22	2.5	1.398	2
United States	17	1.0	1.907	1

In the above test, both the dependent and independent variables are
cardinal measures in nature.

An interesting alternative is to have ranking scores for both
the dependent and independent variables. Running a simple regression using rank order of growth rates of total income (RT) or per
capita income (RP) as the dependent variable and average rank
scores (ARS) as the independent variable yields:

$$RT = 4.503 + 0.520ARS$$
$$(1.12) \quad (1.30) \qquad R^2 = 0.10$$

$$RP = -0.738 + 1.077ARS$$
$$(0.23) \quad (3.28) \qquad R^2 = 0.40$$

It is worth remarking that the scores, overall, do correspond in a
rough way to what one might expect. A nonparametric analysis of
the association between growth rates and the ORS shows Spearman
correlation coefficients of 0.77 and 0.33 for total income and per
capita income respectively. The corresponding significance levels
are 1 and 9 percent.

As mentioned before, an appropriate statistical tool for constructing indices to be used as new variables in later analysis is
factor analysis, the purpose of which is to represent each variable
as a linear combination of several underlying factors. The coefficients that relate the observed variables to the common factor, referred to as factor loadings, play the same role in factor analysis
as do regression coefficients in correlation analysis. Since the
squared factor loadings represent the relative contribution of each
factor to the total standardized variance of a variable, the sum
for each variable of its squared loadings, known as communality,
indicates the extent to which the common factors account for the
total unit variance of the variable. One of the important points
in factor analysis is that the signs of factor loading should agree
with a priori expectations. All of these points for the case under

consideration are provided in Table 9.9. We have 18 observations
on five variables, and we ask the question, "Is it possible to find
a proxy variable that captures a significant proportion of the variance of these variables?" Principal components analysis finds
that linear combination of the five variables accounts for the
highest proportion of the overall variance. This is done by mini-
mizing the sum of the squares of the discrepancies between the actual values of the variables and the approximate values implied by
the proxy variable. This combination is called the first principal
component.

The values of the first principal component, based on the five
indicators, are given in Table 9.10. Since the first principal
component has been normalized, above average values are positive
and below average negative. We are now in a position to use this
first principal component in our parametric and nonparametric statistical analysis. Calculation of rank correlation coefficients
for the association between economic growth and the first principal
component yields the coefficient values of 0.10 and 0.59 for the
growth rates of total income and per capita income respectively.
The statistical significance of the association between growth
rates of total income and the first principal component is very
weak (42 percent), while that between growth rates of per capita
income and the first principal component is strong (0.5 percent).

When a simple linear regression is used with growth rates--
$TY5078$ and $PY5078$ as the dependent variables and the first principal components (FPC) based on five indicators--we obtain:

$$TY5078 = 4.114 - 0.252FPC$$
$$(22.94) \quad (1.37) \qquad R^2 = 0.11$$

$$PY5078 = 3.190 - 0.587FPC$$
$$(18.51) \quad (3.32) \qquad R^2 = 0.42$$

The results, though not impressive, do agree with our a priori expectations.

In the analysis above, we have used two index numbers for each
country, an FPC, and an ORS. One interesting and good test of the
robustness of our results is to compare these two indices. The FPC
and the ORS may be compared by ranking the countries by the two index numbers and seeing if the rankings are similar. An inspection
of Table 9.10 reveals a close similarity in the orderings. A more
rigorous test of the degree of similarity is provided by calculat-
ing Spearman's rank correlation coefficient. The rankings given by
the two methods produce a correlation coefficient of 0.40, which is
significantly different from zero at the 5 percent level. The fact
that the same broad picture is painted by both methods is reassur-
ing.

In summary: First, it is difficult to construct an acceptable
index number that reflects the power of common-interest groups in
the society. In this connection, our problems are methodological
and empirical. A methodological discussion of how to measure the

power of a group and how to aggregate it over groups has not been
completed, and operational equivalents of the formal definition do
not come easily. Moreover, available data are very scant. Second,
despite this, our two index numbers, the overall ranking scores and
the first principal component (although constructed in very different ways) agree quite closely on the ranking of the countires in
the sample, each explaining a large proportion of the variations in
the growth rates across countries. However, it would be misleading
to claim that the above results provide strong empirical support to
Olson's theory and that the tests employed are in any sense the
most preferred ones. All are intended to be suggestive and to provide an illustration.

REFERENCES

Allen, G. C. 1974. Why Japan's economy has prospered. *Lloyds
    Bank Rev.*, January:29–41.
Black, C. E. 1966. *The Dynamics of Modernization: A Study in
    Comparative History*. New York: Harper & Row.
Christensen, L. R., D. Cummings, and D. W. Jorgenson. 1980. Eco-
    nomic growth, 1947–1973: An international comparison. In
    New Developments in Productivity Measurement and Analysis, ed.
    J. W. Kendrick and B. N. Vaccara. Chicago: University of
    Chicago Press.
Dahl, R. A. 1957. A concept of power. *Behav. Sci.* 2:201–15.
Denison, E. F. 1967. *Why Growth Rates Differ*. Washington, D.C.:
    Brookings Institution.
————. 1974. *Accounting for United States Economic Growth 1929–
    1969*. Washington, D.C.: Brookings Institution.
Denison, E. F., and W. K. Chung. 1976. *How Japan's Economy Grew
    So Fast*. Washington, D.C.: Brookings Institution.
Griliches, Z. 1957. Hybrid corn: An exploration in the economics
    of technological change. *Econometrica* 25:501–22.
Harsanyi, J. C. 1962. Measurement of social power, opportunity
    cost, and the theory of two-person bargaining games. *Behav.
    Sci.* 7:67–80.
International Labor Office. Selected years. *Yearbook of Labor
    Statistics*. Geneva, Ill.
Kendrick, J. W. 1973. *Postwar Productivity Trends in the United
    States, 1948–1969*. New York: National Bureau of Economic Re-
    search.
Kuznets, S. 1930. *Secular Movements in Production and Prices*.
    Boston: Houghton Mifflin.
Langer, W., ed. 1972. *An Encyclopedia of World History*. Boston:
    Houghton Mifflin.
Rostow, W. W. 1960. *The Stages of Economic Growth: Non-Communist
    Manifesto*. London: Cambridge University Press.
————. 1978. *The World Economy: History and Prospect*. Austin:
    University of Texas Press.

Russel, B. M., J. D. Singer, and M. Small. 1968. National political units in the twentieth century: A standardized list. *Am. Polit. Sci. Rev.* 62:932-51.

Russett, B. M., H. R. Alker, Jr., K. W. Deutsch, and H. D. Lasswell. 1964. *World Handbook of Political and Social Indicators*. New Haven: Yale University Press.

Rustow, D. A. 1967. *A World of Nations: Problems of Political Modernization*. Washington, D.C.: Brookings Institution.

Solow, R. M. 1957. Technical progress and productivity change. *Rev. Econ. Stat.* 39:310-20.

Stein, J., and A. Lee. 1977. *Productivity Growth in Industrial Countries at the Sectoral Level 1963-1974*. Santa Monica: Rand Corporation.

Taylor, C. L., and M. C. Hudson. 1972. *World Handbook of Political and Social Indicators*. New Haven: Yale University Press.

Walters, D. 1970. *Canadian Growth Revisited, 1950-1967*. Staff Study 28,. Economic Council of Canada. Ottawa: Queen's Printer.

10
Empirical Testing
with U.S. Regional Data

The very fact that the United States is a large and diverse
federation of separate states with often very different histories
and policies allows a disaggregated test of various hypotheses.
This is very fortunate indeed, for the 48 contiguous states offer
many more data points than can be obtained from aggregate data on
the developed industrial countries. One strong point of Olson's
theory of the political economy of comparative economic growth is
that it can predict not only the overall growth performance of the
U.S. economy in relation to other advanced democracies but also regional variations in growth rates in the United States. It would
be beneficial to do some research into the question of how well Olson's argument fits the different regions of the United States.

Unlike the dependent variable, the growth rates of income received by labor and proprietors (used throughout our testing), the
ideal data required for the underlying conditions that determine
the length of time and power of common-interest groups in the U.S.
regions are not readily available, as in the cross-country case.
The length of time a state has had political stability and freedom
of organization is not easy to measure. For the states that had
not been members of the Confederacy, the period during which common-interest organizations could accumulate in stable conditions is
measured approximately by the number of years since statehood was
achieved. For the states that were defeated in the Civil War, the
period of freedom of organization and political stability is far
shorter. This is so not only because the South's stability was interrupted by the Civil War but also because carpetbagging and a
century of restrictions on black political participation followed
the war. It was not until the civil rights and voting rights legislation of the mid-1960s that black Southerners could participate
fully in integrated organizational and political life. Organizations of workers or farmers could not be complete or comprehensive
unless they were racially integrated, and such organizations could
not operate--at least on the same basis as in other parts of the

country--before the passage of the civil rights and voting acts of 1964 and 1965.

We will suppose that 1965 is the best single year to use for the onset of democratic freedom of organization in the South; but in recognition of the fact that some kinds of common-interest organizations could have been formed earlier, we will also consider earlier dates. In particular, on the arbitrary but prominent assumption that there was half as much opportunity to form common-interest organizations in the Confederate states between 1865 and 1965 as after, the midpoint in that interval, 1915, will also be used. Also, the earliest conceivably appropriate year, 1865, will be used, though that is surely much too early. The length of time a state could have accumulated common-interest organizations will be measured by the years since its date of statehood, unless it was a Confederate state, in which event, 1965, 1915, and 1865 will alternately be taken as the years when the clock began to run in the South.

Any arguments about the length of time the South has had the freedom of organization can be bypassed by treating defeat in the Civil War as a dummy variable and combining it with other appropriate explanatory variables. Since both duration of democratic stability and length of time a state has had a modern urban pattern of interests help determine the extent to which an area has common-interest organizations capable of retarding its current rate of growth, the percentage of urbanization in 1880 (which is the earliest date for which data are available across states on a comparable basis) is employed as an indicator of the length of time to be combined with a dummy variable for defeat in the Civil War.

As in the case of intercountry analysis, no data on common-interest organizations by state are available except for labor unions. From a material point of view, looking at union membership alone, interpreting the degree of unionization as a proxy measure for membership in common-interest organizations is not unreasonable and is less tenacious in the examination of U.S. regional economic growth. Accordingly, union membership as a percentage of employees in nonagricultural establishments is taken as a proxy measure for membership in common-interest groups in the following empirical tests of our hypotheses against the U.S. state data.

The political stability of the Deep South was profoundly interrupted by the Civil War and its very extended aftermath, and full freedom of organization and political participation was effectively denied to racially integrated and black groups in that region until the federal civil rights and voting rights acts of 1964 and 1965. If Olson's model is correct, the former Confederate states should have growth rates more akin to those of the newer western states than to the older northeastern states, now that there has been a definitive and presumably stable answer to the question of whether the South can have significantly different racial policies than the rest of the nation, and the disproportionate black out-migration to the North has ceased or reversed itself. So, taking the years since 1964-1965, we must ask if the formerly

Confederate states have a higher average growth rate than the other
states, or at least the comparably old ones. They definitely do
according to our measures of economic growth. The exponential
growth rate from 1958 to 1978 for the ex-Confederate states is 8.47
percent for total income and 7.77 percent for per capita income,
whereas the corresponding figures are 7.53 and 6.87 percent for the
37 states that were not in the Confederacy.

We need to test the hypothesis that the mean values of growth
rates for the Confederate and non-Confederate states are different
because the samples have been drawn from two different populations
against the null hypothesis that there is no difference in growth
rates between two groups, which might be the result of the fluctuations involved in drawing the random sample from a single population. Assuming that variations in growth rates are normally distributed, we can calculate the probability that these two samples
are from different populations. It was found that the difference
in growth rates on this basis was statistically significant. To
guard against any possibility that any outlying states or spurious
cardinality accounted for this result, a nonparametric test (the
Mann-Whitney U-test) was used, and by this test, also, the difference in average growth rates between the South and the rest of the
United States was statistically significant. These results hold
true whether the growth of total or per capita income is at issue.

The finding that there is a statistically significant difference in growth rates of income between the Confederate and non-Confederate states obviously argues in favor of Olson's model of comparative growth rate and should also help to allay any fears that
regression results during years since statehood for the non-Confederate states were the result of any frontier settlement that might
have taken place recently.

Since our model predicts that the longer an area has had stable freedom of organization the more growth-retarding organizations
it will accumulate, those states that have been settled and politically organized the longest ought (other things being equal) to
have the lowest rates of growth, unless their stability and freedom
of organization were limited by the Civil War and racial repression. Thus, if we exclude the states that were once members of the
Confederacy, a simple regression between years since statehood and
rates of growth should provide a very simple preliminary test of
our model. The results are as follows:

$$TY5878 = 8.659 - 0.009 STAHOD$$
$$(19.18) \quad (2.64) \qquad R^2 = 0.16$$

where $TY5878$ is rate of growth of total income of labor and proprietors during 1958-78 and $STAHOD$ is years from statehood to 1965.

Within a country in which there are no barriers to the migration of workers, migration should eventually make real per capita
income much the same in all parts of the country, so the regressions use measures of total rather than per capita income as dependent variables. When the corresponding measures of growth of

per capita income by state ($PY5878$) are used, there is still a negative and statistically significant relationship:

$$PY5878 = 7.959 - 0.009STAHOD$$
$$(29.69) \quad (4.28) \qquad R^2 = 0.34$$

It is also conceivable that the duration of statehood and political stability should not be conceived of as a cardinal variable and that nonparametric tests focusing only on rank orders should be used instead to guard against the possibility that the result might be an artifact of outlying states or spurious intervals. The nonparametric tests run on the same variables equally support the hypothesis in Olson's model.

DETERMINANTS OF GROWTH

Since parametric and nonparametric tests provide the same results for the 37 non-Confederate states, and since examination of growth data shows that Confederate and non-Confederate states are two samples from different populations, we can now reasonably consider the data on all the 48 states together and estimate the equations by least-squares regression techniques.

The results of estimating linear regression equations for the economic growth rate and various measures of the explanatory variables are shown in Table 10.1, with t-values in parentheses. The overall results of this cross-sectional study among the contiguous states seem to support our hypothesis quite strongly. All the regressions using year of statehood for the non-Confederate states as the date at which the accumulation of common-interest groups could begin and any year after the end of the Civil War (specifically 1865 for $STACIV1$, 1915 for $STACIV2$, and 1965 for $STACIV3$) as the date at which the ex-Confederate states came to have stable freedom of organization are providing a statistically significant explanation of the variation in the growth rates by state--(1) to (3) and (9) to (11) in Table 10.1. If the passage of the civil rights and voting rights acts by 1965 is taken to mark the onset of universal freedom of organization and stability, the years-of-freedom-organization variable ($STACIV3$) explains one-third to one-half of the variance in growth rates--(3) and (11).

Since organizations that could most directly constrain modern urban and industrial life have had more time to develop in states that have been urbanized longer, the level of urbanization in 1880 ($UR1880$) was also used as an independent variable. This variable is significant and of the correct negative sign--(4) and (12). In combination with a dummy variable for defeat in the Civil War, the urbanization in 1880 explains a fair amount of variance--(5) and (13). When the duration of freedom of organization and urbanization variables are combined, the contribution by these two together in explanatory power of the equations does not increase much from the level to which each alone contributes, or one of the two variables becomes insignificant. This insignificant increment in R^2 or

Table 10.1. Determinants of growth

A. Total income

$$LPI = 9.050 - 1.966 \; STACIV1 \tag{1}$$
$$(3.45) \qquad\qquad R^2 = 0.21$$

$$LPI = 8.871 - 1.878 \; STACIV2 \tag{2}$$
$$(4.35) \qquad\qquad R^2 = 0.29$$

$$LPI = 8.518 - 1.443 \; STACIV3 \tag{3}$$
$$(4.41) \qquad\qquad R^2 = 0.30$$

$$LPI = 8.207 - 0.021 \; UR1880 \tag{4}$$
$$(2.85) \qquad\qquad R^2 = 0.15$$

$$LPI = 7.904 + 0.688 \; CIVWAR - 0.014 \; UR1880 \tag{5}$$
$$(2.11) \qquad\qquad (1.85) \qquad R^2 = 0.23$$

$$LPI = 8.937 - 1.521 \; STACIV1 - 0.008 \; UR1880 \tag{6}$$
$$(1.98) \qquad\qquad (0.87) \qquad R^2 = 0.22$$

$$LPI = 8.527 - 1.374 \; STACIV3 - 0.012 \; UR1880 \tag{7}$$
$$(3.07) \qquad\qquad (0.24) \qquad R^2 = 0.30$$

$$LPI = 8.621 + 1.202 \; CIVWAR - 0.009 \; STAHOD \tag{8}$$
$$(4.03) \qquad\qquad (2.92) \qquad R^2 = 0.30$$

B. Per capita income

$$PCLPI = 8.333 - 1.892 \; STACIV1 \tag{9}$$
$$(5.14) \qquad\qquad R^2 = 0.37$$

$$PCLPI = 8.160 - 1.805 \; STACIV2 \tag{10}$$
$$(7.01) \qquad\qquad R^2 = 0.52$$

$$PCLPI = 7.820 - 1.387 \; STACIV3 \tag{11}$$
$$(7.14) \qquad\qquad R^2 = 0.53$$

$$PCLPI = 7.628 - 0.025 \; UR1880 \tag{12}$$
$$(5.65) \qquad\qquad R^2 = 0.41$$

$$PCLPI = 7.382 + 0.559 \; CIVWAR - 0.019 \; UR1880 \tag{13}$$
$$(2.98) \qquad\qquad (4.39) \qquad R^2 = 0.51$$

$$PCLPI = 8.107 - 0.998 \; STACIV1 - 0.016 \; UR1880 \tag{14}$$
$$(2.18) \qquad\qquad (2.92) \qquad R^2 = 0.47$$

$$PCLPI = 7.867 - 1.028 \; STACIV3 - 0.011 \; UR1880 \tag{15}$$
$$(4.06) \qquad\qquad (2.11) \qquad R^2 = 0.57$$

$$PCLPI = 7.884 + 1.144 \; CIVWAR - 0.008 \; STAHOD \tag{16}$$
$$(6.38) \qquad\qquad (4.50) \qquad R^2 = 0.51$$

Sources:_ Growth rates of income--Bureau of Economic Analysis 1979 (these data have income by state of employment rather than residence, which is better for our purpose); Civil War, length of time--Parish 1975; Council of State Governors 1976; Urbanization--Bureau of the Census 1976a.

Note: LPI = exponential rate of growth of income of labor and proprietors, 1965-1976; PCLPI = exponential rate of growth of per capita labor and proprietors' income, 1965-1976; CIVWAR = dummy variable 1 for defeated (Confederate) states and 0 for non-Confederate states; YEAR = for Confederate, 100, for non-Confederate, length of time since statehood; YEAR2 = for Confederate, 50, for non-Confederate, length of time since statehood; YEAR3 = for Confederate, 0, for non-Confederate, length of time since statehood; STACIV1 = YEAR/178; STACIV2 = YEAR2/ 178; STACIV3 = YEAR3/178; 178 = 1965 - 1787 (earliest year of statehood); STAHOD = years since statehood; UR1880 = percentages of people who resided in cities in 1880.

significant reduction in *t*-statistics is because of the multicollinearity between two explanatory variables.

FORMATION OF A COMMON-INTEREST ORGANIZATION

Olson's model predicts that common-interest organizations should be more powerful in places that have had stable freedom of organization. This prediction should be examined by an appropriate test. Unfortunately, the only common-interest groups on which we have found membership statistics across states are labor unions.

Table 10.2. Growth of common-interest organizations (unionization as dependent variable)

$UNON64 = 12.107 + 18.478 \; STACIV1$ (1)
           (3.06) $R^2 = 0.17$

$UNON64 = 12.178 + 20.347 \; STACIV2$ (2)
           (4.63) $R^2 = 0.32$

$UNON64 = 15.441 + 16.689 \; STACIV3$ (3)
           (5.19) $R^2 = 0.37$

$UNON74 = 10.073 + 17.679 \; STACIV1$ (4)
           (3.44) $R^2 = 0.20$

$UNON74 = 10.897 + 18.205 \; STACIV2$ (5)
           (4.84) $R^2 = 0.34$

$UNON74 = 14.044 + 14.505 \; STACIV3$ (6)
           (5.19) $R^2 = 0.37$

$UNON64 = 18.536 + 0.262 \; UR1880$ (7)
           (3.64) $R^2 = 0.22$

$UNON70 = 18.842 + 0.212 \; UR1880$ (8)
           (3.25) $R^2 = 0.19$

$UNON74 = 16.586 + 0.234 \; UR1880$ (9)
           (3.79) $R^2 = 0.24$

$UNON64 = 22.924 - 9.74 \; CIVWAR + 0.167 \; UR1880$ (10)
           (3.28)   (2.34) $R^2 = 0.38$

$UNON70 = 22.478 - 8.307 \; CIVWAR + 0.134 \; UR1880$ (11)
           (2.94)   (2.02) $R^2 = 0.32$

$UNON74 = 19.922 - 7.584 \; CIVWAR + 0.162 \; UR1880$ (12)
           (2.82)   (2.57) $R^2 = 0.35$

Sources: Same as in Table 10.1; Bureau of Labor Statistics 1967, 1971; Bureau of the Census 1976b.

Note: *UNON64, UNON70, UNON74* = union memberships as a percentage of employees in nonagricultural establishments in 1964, 1970, and 1974; other variables, same as in Table 10.1.

Even though Olson's model is based on all types of groups pursuing common interests for each group (including labor unions), it is not unreasonable to employ labor union membership as a proxy measure for the membership in and strength of all common-interest organizations. There should be a positive relationship between the degree of unionization and the duration of political stability and freedom of organization a state has enjoyed.

From the results shown in Table 10.2, it is immediately clear that labor union membership is greatest in the states that have had stable freedom of organization--(1) to (6). Equations (7) to (9) show that urbanization in 1880 is also a satisfactory and significant predicator of union membership in the period from 1964 to the present. The dummy variable, defeat in the Civil War, is also a significantly important variable in explaining the variation in the unionization among states--(10) to (12).

EFFECTS OF COMMON-INTEREST GROUPS ON ECONOMIC GROWTH

As the previous results would lead one to expect, there is also a statistically significant negative relationship between union membership and the rates of economic growth. This result, as presented in Table 10.3, holds for both total and per capita measures of income.

Thus there is not only statistically significant evidence of the connection between the duration of stable freedom of organization and growth rates predicted by our model, but also (at least as far as labor unions are concerned) distinct and statistically sig-

Table 10.3. Common-interest organization membership and economic
growth
A. Total labor and proprietors' income as dependent variable

LPI = 8.651 - 0.037 $UNON64$ (1)
        (2.83) R^2 = 0.15
LPI = 8.651 - 0.038 $UNON70$ (2)
        (2.57) R^2 = 0.13
LPI = 8.139 + 0.647 $CIVWAR$ - 0.022 $UNON64$ (3)
        (1.79)   (1.45) R^2 = 0.21

B. Per capita labor and proprietors' income as dependent variable

$PCLPI$ = 7.957 - 0.036 $UNON64$ (4)
          (4.10) R^2 = 0.27
$PCLPI$ = 7.955 - 0.037 $UNON70$ (5)
          (3.66) R^2 = 0.23
$PCLPI$ = 7.472 + 0.612 $CIVWAR$ - 0.022 $UNON64$ (6)
          (2.63)   (2.22) R^2 = 0.37

Sources: Same as in Tables 10.1 and 10.2.
Note: Variables are the same as in Tables 10.1 and 10.2.

nificant evidence that the process the model predicts is going on,
i.e., that the accumulation of common-interest organizations is occurring, and that common-interest organizations do, on balance,
have the hypothesized negative effect on economic growth.

John W. Kendrick (1973), in his study of total factor productivity in the manufacturing industry, examines the effect of unionization on productivity. (Similar results using recent data are
discussed in Kendrick and Grossman 1980, Chapter 6.) He did not
specify the impact of unionization on total factor productivity a
priori; he let the data determine the net effect of unionization on
productivity. Kendrick's regressions with 21 manufacturing industry groups seem to support one of Olson's hypotheses from a different perspective. His regression results are:

$$\dot{Pty} = 3.179 + 0.305O - 0.035U$$
$$\qquad\quad (4.475)\quad (2.810) \qquad\qquad\qquad R^2 = 0.773$$

$$\dot{Pty} = 0.568 + 0.407Ed - 0.037U$$
$$\qquad\quad (2.364)\quad (2.319) \qquad\qquad\qquad R^2 = 0.593$$

$$\dot{Pty} = 1.084 + 0.254Ed + 0.046R\&D + 0.0002H - 0.037U$$
$$\qquad\quad (1.102)\quad (0.554)\quad (0.976)\quad (2.156)\quad R^2 = 0.633$$

where $\dot{Pty}$ is the average annual percentage change 1948-1966 in total factor productivity, O is the average annual percentage rate of
change in output over the same period, U is the percentage of employees of the industries belonging to the union in 1958, Ed is the
average education of employees, $R\&D$ is the ratio of research and
development outlays to sales, and H is average hours worked.

The unionization variable is statistically significant in all
the above regressions, and the relationship with productivity
growth is negative. The negative influence of the degree of unionization tells us that the influence of labor unions with regard
to the rate of innovation and changes in economic efficiency has
apparently outweighed possible positive influences.

TESTING WITH INDUSTRY DATA AND SMSA DATA
    A few objections can be made to the empirical testing of Ol-
son's theory of comparative growth rates using U.S. state data as
to the proper proxies and possible intervening forces. An effort
is made in this section to exclude a bias that might have produced
results in favor of Olson's model. One recurrent objection to our
results discussed above is that we cannot distinguish between
growth-retarding or promoting forces in line with Olson's theory
and other intervening forces that have impact on growth.
    It may be that southern states are growing fast because they
have vast room to grow, while the economic growth in northeastern
states is slow because no more room is left for further growth. Or
it may be that those states that happen to have some fast-growing
industries will exhibit a higher growth rate than those with slow-
growing or declining industries through forward and backward linkage effects. To put both points another way, the states with
"frontiers" are growing fast since they are still in the process of
being settled, creating disequilibria for unusual rates of growth
of total, if not per capita, income. In the following, we discuss
regression results using industry and Standard Metropolital Statistical Area (SMSA) data.
    One can argue that we obtain satisfactory results in the pre-
ceding sections that are consistent with Olson's theory, not because forces behind his model exert their influences, but because
independent factors having nothing to do with Olson's theory work
in his favor. One particular argument in this connection is that
the southern states have grown fast primarily because they have new
or fast-growing industries, such as construction associated with
the "flight to the Sunbelt," contrary to the Olson claim that the
states that were once members of the Confederacy grow fast because
their stability and freedom of organization were limited by the
Civil War and racial repression.
    To guard against the above argument that the fast growth in
the southern states is associated with the rapid expansion of a
group of industries, disaggregated industry data are employed to
test the Olson theory. Growth rates of total income were calculated for ten major industries (1-digit) with a subclassification
(2-digits) for manufacturing. (Three 2-digit manufacturing industries whose income data are not available in more than 25 states
were excluded from our analysis. They are textile mill products,
leather and leather products, and ordinance.) The same five proxies (*STACIV*1, *STACIV*2, *STACIV*3, *UR*1880, and *UNON*64) used previously are alternatively employed as our independent variable in our
simple regression. The results are summarized in Table 10.4.
    The results using industry data are quite consistent with Ol-
son's hypothesis, the only contrary case being agricultural services, forestry, and fisheries, where our five proxies produce
"wrong" regression coefficients. This result is not significant
since factors other than the forces behind Olson's hypothesis are
more important as determinants of income growth rates in these industries. Unionization in 1964 also produces a wrong sign in both
petroleum and coal products and transportation equipment. However,

Table 10.4. Regression results of Olson's theory using industry data

Industry	Number of observations	STACIV1 t	STACIV1 R²	STACIV2 t	STACIV2 R²	STACIV3 t	STACIV3 R²	UR1880 t	UR1880 R²	UNON64 t	UNON64 R²
1. Farm	48	0.66	.01	0.97	.02	1.07	.02	0.89	.02	0.43	.00
2. Agricultural services, forestry, and fisheries	48	1.13*	.03	1.07*	.03	0.94*	.02	1.81*	.06	2.17*	.09
3. Mining	48	1.59	.05	2.00	.08	2.06	.08	2.21	.10	1.00	.02
4. Construction	48	6.59	.49	6.62	.49	5.60	.41	5.91	.43	4.37	.29
5. Manufacturing	48	7.32	.54	7.17	.53	5.93	.43	6.30	.46	5.36	.38
Food and kindred products	47	5.55	.41	6.85	.51	6.56	.49	5.93	.44	3.88	.25
Apparel and other textile products	38	7.14	.59	6.04	.50	4.93	.40	3.47	.25	3.07	.21
Paper and allied products	39	3.35	.23	3.03	.20	2.63	.16	3.29	.23	2.81	.18
Printing and publishing	46	6.94	.52	6.76	.51	5.56	.42	6.04	.45	4.96	.36
Chemical and allied products	43	3.56	.24	3.21	.20	2.69	.15	1.62	.06	3.75	.26
Petroleum and coal products	30	1.35	.06	1.42	.07	1.36	.06	1.42	.07	0.28*	.00
Rubber and plastic products	40	4.63	.36	6.03	.49	6.08	.49	4.12	.31	2.61	.16
Lumber and wood products	39	3.33	.23	3.04	.20	2.57	.15	2.56	.15	0.60	.01
Furniture and fixtures	40	3.91	.29	3.59	.26	3.08	.20	3.09	.20	2.96	.19
Primary metal industries	43	4.85	.36	6.04	.47	5.96	.46	4.19	.30	3.81	.26
Fabricated metal products	48	4.90	.34	5.24	.37	4.75	.33	4.04	.26	4.52	.31
Machinery	47	6.87	.51	6.00	.44	4.79	.34	4.72	.33	4.74	.33
Electric and electronic equipment	41	2.18	.11	2.87	.17	3.02	.19	1.40	.05	2.78	.16
Transportation equipment	37	1.73	.08	1.36	.05	1.03	.03	1.33	.05	0.07*	.00
Motor vehicles and equipment	36	3.66	.28	2.83	.19	2.13	.12	1.68	.08	2.34	.14
Stone, clay, and glass products	48	5.85	.43	5.60	.41	4.71	.33	3.90	.25	5.09	.36
Instruments and related products	29	3.29	.29	2.31	.16	1.69	.10	0.92	.03	0.50	.01
Miscellaneous	46	3.94	.37	4.81	.34	3.59	.23	3.36	.20	2.83	.15
6. Transportation and public utilities	48	4.17	.27	6.30	.46	6.96	.51	3.80	.24	5.56	.42
7. Wholesale trade	48	4.12	.27	4.17	.27	3.71	.23	5.28	.38	4.76	.33
8. Retail trade	48	3.94	.25	5.24	.37	5.41	.39	3.55	.22	4.41	.30
9. Finance, insurance, and real estate	48	1.77	.06	3.41	.20	4.24	.28	2.17	.09	4.44	.30
10. Services	48	1.38	.04	2.44	.16	2.42	.11	1.36	.04	3.11	.17

Sources: Same as in Tables 10.1 and 10.2.
Note: All regression coefficients have correct signs except for those with an asterisk. Variables are the same as in Tables 10.1 and 10.2.

none of these wrong coefficients is statistically significant.

Other than the insignificant exceptions noted above, our regression results clearly indicate that the significant statistical results for Olson's hypothesis using the state aggregate data obtained in the previous sections are not due to the spurious factor, the incidental rapid growth of a group of booming industries in fast-growing states. If a rapid expansion of a few industries in the state is a main determinant of the overall growth rate of income, data with slow-growing or declining industries should not produce results consistent with Olson's theory. Since this is not the case, as shown in Table 10.4, we can conclude that the growing industry bias that might have produced results in favor of Olson's model is absent.

While some argue that the southern states are growing fast because some rapidly expanding industries lead the growth, others argue that economic growth in the northern states is slow because no more room is left for further growth. The northern states are growing slowly because they are already "crowded." Income data from SMSAs are employed to guard against this crowding bias in testing Olson's model using U.S. state data. The reason why the crowding bias will be removed or at least reduced by using SMSA data rather than the aggregate state data is that employment of SMSAs renders data points more homogeneous. An example will illustrate this point more clearly. Let us take two symbolic SMSAs: Atlanta, Georgia, and Pittsburgh, Pennsylvania. Of course, the degree of crowding is greater in Pennsylvania than in Georgia. We expect, however, that the difference in the degree of crowding is smaller between Atlanta and Pittsburgh than between the two states in which the cities are located. Therefore, testing with SMSA data will reduce crowding bias and make ceteris paribus assumptions much stronger.

Simple linear regressions are computed using growth rates of total and per capita incomes across 83 large SMSAs for 1960-1973 as the dependent variable and alternative measures for Olson's model as the independent variable. Number of SMSAs and the period are arbitrarily chosen. The availability of data in a convenient form dominates our choice. But since, for example, regressions based on 71 SMSAs, excluding those 12 that are larger in population than the largest SMSA in the south (Houston), show the consistency of the results with Olson's model, an increase in data points will not affect, to any great extent, the discussion. The regression results, shown in Table 10.5, seem to support Olson's hypothesis. To comment briefly, the R^2s are not uncharacteristically low for cross sections, all coefficients have correct signs, and the associations are significant in terms of t-values.

Comparison of the results obtained with SMSAs in Table 10.5 with those using the U.S. states in Table 10.1 indicates that other factors such as crowding or frontier, though existent, are not strong enough to invalidate Olson's theory. This conclusion is based on the fact that the estimated coefficients are highly statistically significant in the cases using both state and SMSA data,

Table 10.5.   Regression results of Olson's theory using SMSA
data

| | Growth rates | | | |
| | Total income as dependent variable | | Per capita income as dependent variable | |
	t	R^2	t	R^2
A. For overall (central city plus suburb) SMSA:				
STCIV1	5.64	0.28	2.64	0.08
STCIV2	5.97	0.31	4.01	0.17
STCIV3	5.60	0.28	4.47	0.20
STAHOD	4.09		0.14	
		0.30		0.21
CIVWAR	4.43		4.60	
B. For central city in SMSA excluding suburb:				
STCIV1	4.97	0.23	2.92	0.10
STCIV2	6.14	0.32	5.23	0.25
STCIV3	6.22	0.32	6.23	0.33
STAHOD	2.63		0.70	
		0.30		0.40
CIVWAR	5.37		7.15	

Sources: Same as in Tables 10.1 and 10.2; Advisory Commission on Intergovernmental Relations 1977.
Note: Variables are the same as in Table 10.1.

and the explanatory power of the variation in the growth rates is slightly higher in the former case than in the latter.

It is also conceivable that crowding in older SMSAs might be different in their working against growth from that in new SMSAs. To account for this possibility, regressions employing growth rates of income from the central cities in SMSAs (excluding suburbs) as the dependent variable and three variations of institutional stability as the independent variable were run.   The results are shown in part B of Table 10.5.   The exercise reinforces Olson's argument further, because comparison of the results obtained with only central city data with those employing the overall SMSA data shows that the explanatory power and statistical significance are higher with only central city data in SMSAs than with the overall SMSA data, contrary to our expectation that SMSAs in the South grow faster because of lack of crowding.

Our tests of Olson's theory using data from the 48 contiguous states show that there is not only statistically significant evidence of the connection between the duration of stable freedom of organizations and growth rates, as postulated by Olson's hypothesis, but also distinct and statistically discernible evidence that accumulation of common-interest organizations is occurring, and that common-interest groups do, on balance, have the hypothesized negative influence on economic growth.   Every properly specified test based on alternative measures of the independent and dependent variables produces results that are favorably consistent with Olson's theory.

REFERENCES

Advisory Commission on Intergovernmental Relations.   1977.   *Trends in Metropolitan America*.   Washington, D.C.:   USGPO.

Bureau of the Census, U.S. Department of Commerce. 1976a. *Historical Statistics of the United States--Colonial Times to 1970*. Washington, D.C.: USGPO.

————. 1976b. *Statistical Abstract of the United States*. Washington, D.C.: USGPO.

Bureau of Economic Analysis, U.S. Department of Commerce. 1979. Computer printout on regional income.

Bureau of Labor Statistics, U.S. Department of Labor. 1967. *Directory of National Unions and Employee Associations*. Washington, D.C.: USGPO.

————. 1971. *Directory of National Unions and Employee Associations*. Washington, D.C.: USGPO.

Council of State Governors. 1976. *The Book of the States, 1976-1977*, vol. 21. Lexington, Kentucky.

Judge, C. S. 1979. *The Book of American Rankings*. New York: Facts on File.

Kendrick, J. W. 1973. *Postwar Productivity Trends in the United States 1948-1969*. New York: National Bureau of Economic Research.

Kendrick, J. W., and E. S. Grossman. 1980. *Productivity in the United States*. Baltimore: Johns Hopkins University Press.

Parish, P. J. 1975. *The American Civil War*. New York: Holmes and Meier.

Sigelman, L., and R. E. Smith. 1980. Consumer legislation in the American states: An attempt at explanation. *Soc. Sci. Q.* 61: 58-70.

Troy, L. 1965. Trade union membership, 1897-1962. *Rev. Econ. Stat.* 47:93-113.

Index